Globalizing India

India's recent economic transformation has fascinated scholars, global leaders, and interested observers alike. In 1990, India was a closed economy and a hesitant and isolated economic power. By 2016, India has rapidly risen on the global economic stage; foreign trade now drives more than half of the economy and Indian multinationals pursue global alliances. Focusing on second-generation reforms of the late 1990s, Aseema Sinha explores what facilitated global integration in a self-reliant country predisposed to nationalist ideas. The author argues that globalization has affected trade policy as well as India's trade capacities and private sector reform. India should no longer be viewed solely through a national lens; globalization is closely linked to the ambitions of a rising India. The study uses fieldwork undertaken in Geneva, New Delhi, Ahmedabad, Mumbai, and Washington, DC, interviews with business and trade officials, as well as a close analysis of the textile and pharmaceutical industries and a wide range of documentary and firm-level evidence to let diverse actors speak in their own voices.

ASEEMA SINHA is an associate professor in the Department of Government at Claremont McKenna College, California. She holds the Wagener Chair of South Asian Politics and is a George R. Roberts Fellow.

Business and Public Policy

Series Editor
ASEEM PRAKASH, University of Washington

Series Board
Vinod K. Aggarwal, University of California, Berkeley
Tanja A. Börzel, Freie Universität Berlin
David Coen, University College London
Peter Gourevitch, University of California, San Diego
Neil Gunningham, The Australian National University
Witold J. Henisz, University of Pennsylvania
Adrienne Héritier, European University Institute
Chung-in Moon, Yonsei University
Sarah A. Soule, Stanford University
David Vogel, University of California, Berkeley

This series aims to play a pioneering role in shaping the emerging field of business and public policy. *Business and Public Policy* focuses on two central questions. First, how does public policy influence business strategy, operations, organization, and governance and with what consequences for both business and society? Second, how do businesses themselves influence policy institutions, policy processes, and other policy actors and with what outcomes?

Globalizing India

How Global Rules and Markets Are Shaping
India's Rise to Power

Aseema Sinha

Claremont McKenna College, California

CAMBRIDGE
UNIVERSITY PRESS

CAMBRIDGE
UNIVERSITY PRESS

University Printing House, Cambridge CB2 8BS, United Kingdom

Cambridge University Press is part of the University of Cambridge.

It furthers the University's mission by disseminating knowledge in the pursuit of education, learning and research at the highest international levels of excellence.

www.cambridge.org
Information on this title: www.cambridge.org/9781107137233

© Aseema Sinha 2016

First published 2016

Printed in the United Kingdom by Clays, St Ives plc.

A catalogue record for this publication is available from the British Library

Library of Congress Cataloguing in Publication data
Sinha, Aseema, 1966–
Globalizing India : how global rules and markets are shaping India's rise to power / Aseema Sinha.
New York : Cambridge University Press, 2016. | Series: Business and public policy
LCCN 2016002044 | ISBN 9781107137233 (hardback)
LCSH: India – Economic conditions – 21st century. | India – Economic policy – 21st century. | India – Commerce. | Globalization – India.
LCC HC435.3 .S576 2016 | DDC 382.0954–dc23
LC record available at http://lccn.loc.gov/2016002044

ISBN 978-1-107-13723-3 Hardback
ISBN 978-1-316-50241-9 Paperback

For
Brian

Contents

Figures

Tables

Preface and acknowledgments

This book charts the emergence of India onto the international economic stage. In the 1990s, Indian policymakers, politicians, and private sector actors were wary of opening their borders to trade flows. By 2016, trade constituted almost half of India's GDP, and India had become an integral part of the world order. Today, Indian policymakers negotiate strongly at the global level, and Indian companies have moved into new markets and formed global alliances. Yet, India's economic rise at the global level was not inevitable. The process by which India is transforming is the focus of this book. I explore the economic rise of India through the actions of domestic state and private actors, who have changed what they want and how they mobilize in a very short span of time. Underlying this global emergence is a quieter revolution represented by changing trade capacities and private sector reform and transformation. The transformations described in this book have spread across larger arenas of the Indian economy, resulting in Indian consent and appetite for globalization. Scholars have to document this changed reality even if they are ambivalent about the effects of India's ongoing reform trajectory, as I am.

Was the rise of India made possible by changing economic conditions and global opportunities? Did globalization represent a new set of market incentives and price signals? While market opportunities have played a role, this transformation is also authored by the *trading state*, which pursues a strategy of global engagement in very different ways from the *dirigiste state* (1960s) or the *reforming state* (1991). The Indian state, now, pursues, *tradecraft*, introducing new trade policies, negotiating in trade forums in more capable ways, creating new interests, and partnering with globally oriented Indian firms. This transformation has also shifted domestic trade politics, creating export-oriented firms and sectors within India's political economy. *New interests favoring global engagement were created* within India's public and private sectors. *Woodwork reformers* sought to create spaces for trade reform within a sticky domestic political economy. New perception of opportunities presented by globalization led to a realignment of interests among globalization's opponents. Sectors and groups that lost as a result of these developments found it more difficult to mobilize against globalization, as the balance of power shifted toward a more globally open trade agenda. A broader coalition supports India's engagement with the world, and diverse sections of the population support a more proactive stance overseas.

These developments are better understood with an open-economy framework that brings together both international and domestic factors to understand the sources of India's rapid economic rise. In this book, I formulate and describe such an integrated open-economy framework called the Global Design-in-Motion framework. Simply put, India can no longer be viewed through a purely national lens. Globalization is closely linked to the nationalist ambitions of a rising India. Indian actors, institutions, and policies are deeply embedded within global forces through international markets, organizations, and the flows of people and ideas. This finding not only challenges our notion of an India that is internally driven but should also change the way we think of globalization.

I began work on this project in the early 2000s when globalization was a buzzword used to describe almost everything around us. At that time, the hype around India's rise had not yet begun, and doubt about how globalization would affect India was a common theme. This book opens up the blackbox of globalization. The subjects of this book are not only firms and markets but also organizations such as the World Trade Organization (WTO) that span the globe, creating new forms of regulation and governance structures. I find that rules matter for the performance of global markets. The rules and practices articulated by the WTO have become essential to functioning global markets. They have nudged, coerced, and catalyzed change in even the most recalcitrant of countries such as India. The WTO regime – rules as well as practices – has seeped into countries despite domestic resistance. Simultaneously, India, the world's most populous democracy, is becoming a globally integrated economy, even as its internal state capacity to manage global trade is increasing.

This transformation suggests an agency to shape its national agenda in the world. Yet, by now, India is also deeply embedded in global markets and institutions, even as its domestic institutions both resist and modify such interactions. I suggest that the manner in which India came to be embedded in national institutions and policies in global contexts shaped the ability of Indian actors to implement new domestic agendas as well as seek global status. The effects of globalization on domestic policy cannot be treated as exceptions; they are formative influences on Indian business, trade, politics, and policy. Globalization, understood both as markets and rules of the game, has begun to shape India in powerful ways; it is not just a set of constraints on Indian growth and ambitions.

This book undertakes an ambitious task to map preferences and interests of private actors as they engage with global forces. It holds that the distribution of interests in the domestic political economy can no longer be treated as exogenous but that it shifts in interaction with domestic and global changes. Interests are elusive and difficult to observe under normal circumstances. But interests in motion may offer an unanticipated analytical advantage, as we are able to observe the shifting of preferences. The emergence of the WTO, a rule, setting body, in 1995 provides the larger exogenous context – an almost quasi-experimental windfall – against which I can hope to observe changes in interests and capabilities of state and private sector actors.

Academic projects take many years to complete. The length of completion time has its compensations, as I found many friends, colleagues, and institutions along the way. Numerous individuals and organizations were partners in this endeavor. This book took shape when I was a faculty member at the University of Wisconsin–Madison (2000–2011) and where I received tenure. I received numerous grants from the university and support from its Department of Political Science. A year-long senior fellowship from the American Institute of Indian Studies (AIIS) was crucial for the extensive empirical research on this project. I visited New Delhi (India), Ahmedabad (India), Mumbai (India), Geneva (Switzerland), and Washington, DC (United States) to collect primary research materials for the book. I was also a Fellow at the Woodrow Wilson Center in DC, which allowed me to complete core empirical sections and conduct interviews in DC. In 2011, I joined the Government Department at Claremont McKenna College (CMC). The working and research environment at CMC has been conducive to the completion of this project. I have found great colleagues and friends in this small but generous community.

I especially thank all my interviewees in India (New Delhi, Bombay, and Ahmedabad), Switzerland (Geneva), and the United States (Washington, DC). They gave me information, their time, and a lot of data. They shall remain anonymous, but without them this project would not be as real and comprehensive as I hope it is.

I thank the participants of various conference contexts where the ideas of this book were presented. Initial ideas were presented at the Woodrow Wilson Center for Scholars (DC). I also presented parts of the book at the South Asia program at Cornell University, the India-China Institute at New School University, McGill University (Canada), Georgetown University, Harvard Business School, University of Washington, Seattle, Research seminar at the Keck Center for International and Strategic Studies at Claremont McKenna College, Center for South

Asia (UW–Madison), Comparative Politics Workshop at UW–Madison, University of Berkeley, State Capacity Conference, Annual Conference on South Asia at UW-Madison, and various annual meetings of the political science association (APSA).

Discussions about this book with many friends and colleagues have made it a pleasure to write. V. Narayana Rao has read many versions of this book and has been a valuable commentator and reader. Dr. Sanjaya Baru gave me invaluable feedback and help with data collection. Conversations with Ed Freidman are always a pleasure. Surupa Gupta and I collected the data for this at the same time, which meant that I had a friend and comrade-in-arms. We shared many data sources.

It is a pleasure to thank Lucy Rhymer, editor at Cambridge University Press, for her professionalism in shepherding this book through the review process. I could not have asked for better reviewers. The comments by the two anonymous reviewers helped to make the theoretical argument stronger and also addressed crucial issues of generalizability. The reviewers read it carefully, understood the import of the arguments, but were also willing to criticize in a constructive manner. Their feedback has made this a much better book. I also thank Ian McIver and Karthik Orukaimani and his team for a smooth copy-editing process. Therese Parent did a thorough index speedily and carefully.

Comments from many colleagues and friends were extremely valuable. T. V. Paul read the whole manuscript and gave me very helpful feedback. John Echeverri-Gent has offered generous advice on many parts of the manuscript. Comments from and conversations with Vinod Aggarwal, Hilary Appel, Bill Ascher, Leslie Armijo, Rakesh Besant, Pradeep Chhibber, Mark Copelovitch, Errol D'Souza, Brian Dunham, Anthony D'Costa, Sagarika Dutt, Sumit Ganguly, Scott Gehlbach, Ron Herring, Yoi Herrera, Anil Jacob, Miles Kahler, Peter Katzenstein, Steve Lobell, Jon Pevehouse, Melanie Manion, Akshay Mangla, Lisa Martin, Andrew Mertha, Rahul Mukerji, Minxin Pei, Dann Naseemullah, Ambassador Kishan Rana, Susan Sell, Ken Shalden, Emily Sellers, Heidi Swarts, Aili Tripp, Ashutosh Varshney, Kristin Vekasi, and Jim Vreeland were indispensable in helping me revise. I thank Brian Dunham for proofreading and editing help and for making the tables and figures user friendly.

Simanti Lahiri, Adam Auerbach, Kristin Vekasi, Nayantara Mukherjee, Peter Nasuti, Eunsook Jung, Ning Leng, and Tricia Olsen were my graduate students at UW–Madison. They taught me much more than they know.

I received excellent research help from many students over the years: Himanshu Jha, Jenanne Vaccaro, Lauren Thomas, Meina Cai, Ilia Murtazashvili, Christine Wilkes, Brandon Lamson, Ning Leng, Maria

Kamenetsky, Bridget Moran, Kristin Vekasi, Dalton Lin, Koffi Yves, Nayantara Mukherjee, Lauren D'Souza, and Padma Gollapudi. I especially thank Ning Leng, Meina Cai, and Maria Kamenetsky for the data coding. Maria helped me pack my voluminous research materials as part of the transcontinental move, which was very valuable. Jen Vaccaro helped me crosscheck all my references in the last stages of the book in a capable and efficient way. Christine Wilkes helped with the editing of the final manuscript in gracious and efficient ways. The contribution of all these students to the book project was indispensable.

Tricia Olsen started as my graduate student, but she became a co-author and friend. Together we wrote an article on India and Brazil, which germinated at the interstices of this book. I thank her for many conversations and for sharing ideas about this project.

My friendships with V. Narayana Rao and Sanjaya Baru, which I found as the book traveled with me, will be treasured always. David Good became a good friend in DC. I also value my friendships with Heidi Swarts, Christina Rivers, and Sarah McKibben; we started our scholarly journeys at Cornell University and were then spread apart as we found jobs in different places. Heidi has been a warm and supportive friend, with an empathy and generosity of spirit that is rare to find.

My mother and my sister have been a source of support if only to say: "How long have you been working on this so-called book?!" My brother's home was a refuge when I was in Delhi collecting data for the book. His home and my mother's support were the invisible threads that bound my life together while on field work.

This book has spanned many changes and transitions in my life. It began in Madison but carried me to locations around the world. I finished the book in Claremont, California. As I grew with this project, I found a unique partner. The book did not start with him but it will be finished with me alongside him. He is really glad for the book to be completed and I am still amazed by his presence in my life! This book is gratefully dedicated to him – my trusted friend and companion. He makes life worth living.

Note on currency translation

USD approximations are simplified and only intended to give the reader a sense of scale – the history is much more complicated. Currency fluctuations make the conversion from rupees into dollars more complex. Therefore, I have used an approximation of Rs. 20 per USD for transactions in and before 1990 (when the rupee exchange rate was government dictated at an artificial rate) and Rs. 50 per USD for transactions from 1991 onward (postliberalization), which is a reasonable average – accurate within 20 percent over most of this time period.

Abbreviations

ADB	Asian Development Bank
AEPC	Apparel Export Promotion Council
ANDA	Abbreviated New Drug Application
APE	Apparel Parks for Exports
API	Active Pharmaceutical Ingredient
APSA	American Political Science Association
ARV Drugs	Antiretroviral Drugs
ASEAN	Association of Southeast Asian Nations
ASSOCHAM	Associated Chambers of Commerce and Industry of India
ATC	Agreement on Textiles and Clothing
ATMI	American Textile Manufacturers Institute
BICP	Bureau of Industrial Costs and Prices
BIS	Bureau of Indian Standards
BJP	Bharatiya Janata Party
BRICS	Brazil, Russia, India, China, and South Africa
BRS	Bristol-Myers Squibb
BS	Business Standard
Bt cotton	*Bacillus thuringiensis* cotton
CAD	Computer-Aided Design
CAM	Computer-Aided Manufacturing
CENVAT	Central Value-Added Tax
CEO	Chief Executive Officer
CIF	Cost, Insurance, and Freight
CII	Confederation of Indian Industry
CITI	Confederation of Indian Textile Industry
CLCS	Credit-Linked Capital Subsidy
CMA	Center for Management in Agriculture
CMAI	Clothing Manufacturers' Association of India
CMC	Claremont McKenna College
CMIE	Centre for Monitoring the Indian Economy
COTAAP	Cotton and Allied Products

CRS	Contract Reservation System
CSIR	Council of Scientific and Industrial Research
DC	District of Columbia
DCM	Delhi Cloth Mills
DG	Deputy Governor
DGAD	Directorate General of Anti-dumping and Allied Duties
DPCO	Drug Pricing Control Order
DRL	Doral Financial Corporation
DRL	Dr. Reddy's Laboratories
DSB	Dispute Settlement Body
EC	European Community
EEC	European Economic Community
EOUs	Export-Oriented Units
EPCG	Export Promotion Capital Goods
ERP	Enterprise Resource Planning
ESCAP	Economic Social Commission for Asia and the Pacific
EU	European Union
EWA	Enterprise-Wide Applications
EXIM	Export-Import Bank of India
FAITMA	Federation of All India Textile Manufacturers Association
FDI	Foreign Direct Investment
FERA	Foreign Exchange Regulation Act
FIASWI	Federation of Indian Art Silk Weaving Industry
FICCI	Federation of Indian Chambers of Commerce and Industry
FIPS	Federal Information Processing Standards
FITEI	Federation of Indian Textile Engineering Industry
FMCGs	Fast-Moving Consumer Goods
FRG	Federal Republic of Germany
G-20	Group of 20
G-22	Group of 22
GATS	General Agreement on Trade in Services
GATT	General Agreement on Tariffs and Trade
GDM	Global Design-in-Motion (Framework)
GDP	Gross Domestic Product
GDR	Global Depository Receipt
GEA	Garment Exporters Association
GFTAM	Global Fund to Fight AIDS, Tuberculosis, and Malaria
GHCL	Gujarat Heavy Chemicals Limited

GM	General Manager
GMP	Good Manufacturing Practices
GOI	Government of India
GOTS	Global Organic Textile Standard
GRD	Global Rules and Design
GSK	GlaxoSmithKline
GSP	Generalized System of Preferences
HIV-AIDS	Human Immunodeficiency Virus–Acquired Immuno deficiency Syndrome
IBEF	India Brand Equity Foundation
IBRD	International Bank for Reconstruction and Development
ICMF	Indian Cotton Mills Federation
ICRIER	International Council of International Economic Relations
IDMA	Indian Drug Manufacturers Association
IDPL	India Drug and Pharmaceutical Limited
IIFT	Indian Institute of Foreign Trade
ILO	International Labor Organization
IMF	International Monetary Fund
IO	International Organizations
IPO	Initial Public Offering
IPRs	Intellectual Property Rights
IR	International Relations
ISA	Indian Spinners Association
ISO	International Organization for Standardization
IT	Information Technology
ITA	Information Technology Agreement
IWMF	Indian Woolen Mills Federation
JCT	Jagatjit Cotton Textile Mills Limited
KSA	Kurt Salmon Associates Technopak
LDC	Least Developing Countries
LNJ	L.N. Jhunjhunwala Bhilwara Group
LTA	Long-Term Agreement
M&A	Mergers and Acquisitions
MAPE	Maximum Allowable Post-Manufacturing Expense
MEA	Ministry of External Affairs
MEE	Manufacturers-Exporter's Entitlement
MERCOSUR	Mercado Común del Sur ("Southern Common Market")
MFA	Multifibre Agreement
MFN	Most Favored Nation

MIDS	Madras Institute of Developmental Studies
MNCs	Multinational Corporations
MOC	Ministry of Commerce
MOF	Ministry of Finance
MTL	Mortared Textiles Limited
NAFTA	North American Free Trade Agreement
NAMA	Nonagricultural Market Access
NASSCOM	National Association of Software and Service Companies
NCAER	National Council of Applied Economic Research
NCUTE	Nodal Center for Upgradation of Textile Education
NEMAI	Narrow Elastic Manufacturers Association of India
NGOs	Nongovernmental Organizations
NIEL	Nahar Industrial Enterprises Limited
NITMA	Northern India Textile Mills Association
NQE	Nonquota Exporter Entitlement
NTC	National Textile Corporation
OECD	Organization for Economic Cooperation and Development
OPPI	Organization of Pharmaceutical Producers
PCPs	Pentachlorophenols
PDEXCIL	Powerloom Development and Export Promotion Council
PEE	Powerloom Exporter Entitlement
PHDCCI	Punjab, Haryana, and Delhi Chamber of Commerce and Industry
PM	Prime Minister
PMO	Prime Minister's Office
PPE	Past Performance Entitlement
PR	Public Relations
PSE	Public Sector Entitlement
PTI	Press Trust of India
QR	Quantitative Restrictions
R&D	Research and Development
RGE	Ready Goods Entitlement
RIS	Research and Information System for Developing Countries
RMG	Ready-Made Garments
SAARC	South Asian Association for Regional Cooperation
SACC	Science Advisory Committee to the Cabinet
SEZs	Special Economic Zones
SICA	South India Cotton Association

SITP	Scheme for Integrated Textile Parks
SRTEPC	Synthetic and Rayon Textiles Export Promotion Council
SSI	Small-Scale Industries
SVP	Senior Vice President
SWG	Sectoral Working Groups
TA	Textile Association of India
TCID	Textile Centre Infrastructure Development
TCIDs	Textile Centre Infrastructure Development Scheme
TEA	Tirupur Exporters Association
TEXPROCIL	Textile Export Promotion Council
TLO	Transnational Legal Order
TMC	Technology Mission on Cotton
TPD	Trade Policy Division
TRIM	Trade-Related Investment Measures
TRIPS	Trade-Related Aspects of Intellectual Property Rights
TTF	Taiwan Textile Federation
TUFS	Technology Upgradation Fund Scheme
UAE	United Arab Emirates
UK	United Kingdom
UN	United Nations
UNCTAD	United Nations Conference on Trade and Development
US	United States
USD	United States Dollars
USFDA	United States Food and Drug Administration
USITC	United States International Trade Commission
USSR	Union of Soviet Socialist Republics
USTR	United States Trade Representative
UW	University of Wisconsin
VERs	Voluntary Export Restraints
VFC	Vanity Fair Corporation
VGP	Virtus Global Partners
VP	Vice President
WHO	World Health Organization
WHO-GMP	World Health Organization–Good Medical Practices
WIPO	World Intellectual Property Organization
WTO	World Trade Organization

1 How global rules and markets are shaping India's rise to power

"Self Reliance Means Trade, Not Aid"   Manmohan Singh[1]

That India marches to its own tune in world politics "is a familiar platitude that happens to be true."[2] For much of its history, India has acted as a "reclusive porcupine," slow-footed, defensive, and prickly in its interactions with the global world.[3] It has shown a remarkable ability to resist global pressures and integration imperatives.[4] Many scholars and policymakers would concur with Joseph M. Grieco, who said: "India possesses [in the 1970s] one of the world's most restrictive, cumbersome, and 'assertive' regimes regulating foreign direct investments" (Grieco 1984, 16). Consequently, India's export share of world trade declined from 2.42 percent in 1948 to 0.41 percent in 1979; this was at a time when the newly industrializing countries in East Asia (Japan and South Korea, for example) were increasing their world market penetration (Wolf 1982, 18). As late as 1991, India's commerce minister, the Harvard-trained Dr. Subramanian Swamy, said: "India does not need GATT [the General Agreement on Trade and Tariffs, a global trade agreement] because of its large size."[5] By 1991, India's share of world trade was dismally low, a mere 0.51 percent (Gangopadhyay 1998, 46). This insular attitude was mirrored in a self-driven industrialization drive, "export pessimism"

---

[1] Manmohan Singh, India's prime minister from 2004 to 2014, in an interview with PBS (USA), 2001, accessed December 11, 2015, http://tinyurl.com/zt98dk4.

[2] In his famous book, *Social Origins of Dictatorship and Democracy*, Barrington Moore started the chapter on India with the following words: "That India lives in two worlds is a familiar platitude that happens to be true" (Moore 1966, 314).

[3] This metaphor is from Mohan (2003, 260).

[4] This is a widely held view: Nayar and Paul (2003, 10), for example, note that India has been less integrated in the global system than one would expect given its size and potential capabilities: "India remains less integrated in the international order than most other major actors of similar power capabilities at comparable stages of their development. ... India's own policies and strategic choices, especially in the economic arena, have been part of the reason for it lack of integration" (2003, 10). Scholars who hold this view are Nayar (2001), Srinivasan (2000, 2002), Lal (1999), and Panagariya (2004).

[5] "India Took Firm Stance: Swamy," *Indian Express*, December 11, 1990; "Swamy: Make No Trade Concessions," *Hindustan Times*, July 28, 1991.

1

(Bhagwati and Srinivasan 1984), and suspicion of global alliances. India's embrace of economic reforms and global integration occurred much later, starting only in the 1990s, by which time other countries – China, Chile, Brazil, and Mexico, for example – had already implemented numerous reforms (Draper, Alves, and Sally 2009). This delay continues to haunt the trajectory of India's reforms, manifesting in a weakness of the Indian currency and a lack of foreign investment as well as key weaknesses in infrastructural development.[6]

Despite this delayed start and intermittent crises, many Indian actors have embraced globalization and transformed India into a more open economy and an active participant in global alliances, all in a remarkably short span of time. In 2005 Manmohan Singh, India's prime minister, declared: "Being an open democratic polity and an open economy empowers India."[7] Analogously, an Indian official in India's foreign ministry said to me: "In the earlier era India was a free rider; now it is a negotiator."[8] The Bharatiya Janata Party's (BJP) leader and the then prime minister, Atal Bihari Vajpayee, likened India's success in information technology (IT) to the new temples of modern India[9]: "I see a happy confluence of Saraswati, Lakshmi and Shakti. The new economy is driven by knowledge. It is a producer of wealth and prosperity. ... However going beyond being a miracle of the mind and the market, information technology is also a source of great strength for our nation."[10] The India of 2016 is a different world from that of 1990. Indra Nooyi, CEO of PepsiCo, recently said: "The country I go back to is not the same country I left. It is somehow the same and yet changed beyond all recognition."[11]

---

[6] James Crabtree, "'Hot Money' Stays Sticky in India as Rupee Crisis Looks Over," *Financial Times*, September 17, 2013, www.ft.com/intl/cms/s/0/7fc7bbf2–1f92–11e3–8 861–00144feab7de.html#axzz2kpwEkhkh.

[7] Manmohan Singh, "Open Democracy and Open Economy," *India Abroad*, vol. VI, no. 12, August 26, 2005, p. 8, North America edition. Interestingly, Manmohan Singh's view of the global system was much more pessimistic a few years earlier. In an interview in 2001, he viewed the global trading system as imposing restrictions on India. He said: "It [globalization] offers opportunities, but problem areas remain. ... For example, we are part of the world trading system. There are opportunities, but also the introduction of a large number of extraneous elements into Uruguay [the 1986–1994 Uruguay Round]. For example, the TRIPS [the International Property Council of the WTO] legislation has created burdens in terms of the prices of essential drugs. The TRIPS legislation is a negative [agreement for India]" (interview, February 6, 2001, available at www.pbs.org/ wgbh/commandingheights/shared/minitextlo/int_manmohansingh.html#5).

[8] Interview with author, Washington, DC, September 1, 2005.

[9] A parallel to Nehru's, India's first prime minister, statement that dams were the temples of modern India.

[10] "IT Parks Are the New Temples of Modern India, Says Vajpayee," *Rediff*, January 19, 2001, www.rediff.com/money/2001/jan/19pm.htm.

[11] Indra Nooyi, "Interview," *India Abroad*, vol. XXXVII, no. 38, June 20, 2008, p. 1.

This change in orientation had a definite impact on the extent of India's external integration. After declining and stagnating for decades, India's share of world trade started to climb after 1993 and then accelerated after 2004.[12] In 2014, India's share of world merchandise trade stood at 2.6 percent, rising fivefold from a low of 0.51 percent in 1991.[13] By 2014, its share of world commercial services trade rose to 4.1 percent from a nonexistent level in the 1990s.[14] In comparative terms this may sound miniscule, but it is a very rapid change in a short amount of time. By 2013, foreign trade in goods and services constituted more than half of GDP (53.2 percent), a remarkable trend for an erstwhile insular economy like India.[15] Strikingly, in 2012, 2013, and 2014 India's trade to GDP ratio was higher than China's.[16]

India has also seen a whole range of changes in its trade regime, encompassing institutions, interests, and strategies, pointing to a deeper impact that reaches beyond tariffs or trade policies.[17] The whole architecture of India's trading state has been radically reformed, enhancing India's capacity to deal with outside forces and organizations (Sinha 2007). India negotiates strongly at the global level, as is evident in a number of recent negotiating successes.[18] Kohli suggested that a new state–capital alliance forges India's reform agenda (2007). India's firms have restructured and globalized, seeking new markets, alliances, and technology outside its borders (D'Costa 2012; Naseemullah 2016; Parthasarathi and Joseph 2004; Ramamurti and Singh 2009; Saez and Chang 2009; Sauvant and Pradhan 2010).[19] Some Indian firms have

---

[12] As late as 2000 India's world market share was merely 0.7 percent (Srinivasan and Tendulkar 2003, 102).

[13] Calculated by author from WTO (International Trade Statistics 2015).

[14] WTO (International Trade Statistics 2015).

[15] World Bank (2013). In 2014, trade as a share of GDP was 49.6 percent as a result of the global slowdown (World Bank 2015).

[16] China's trade to GDP ratio was 51.8 percent for 2012 and 50.2 percent for 2013, while India's was 54.7 percent (2012) and 53.2 percent (2013). I thank John Echeverri-Gent for alerting me to this interesting fact. This is on account of a severe contraction in China's trade sector after 2008. In 2014, China's trade as a share of GDP was 41.5 percent, while India's was 49.6 percent.

[17] Interestingly, economists have found that the impact of trade liberalization on profit margins of firms works through such behavioral mechanisms as research and development expenditure, focus on exports, and other strategic variables rather than through pure price effects (Kambhampati and Parikh 2007).

[18] In July 2014, India's trade officials negotiated for protecting India's food stocks by delaying India's acceptance of the Trade Facilitation Agreement at the WTO. This is one of the few cases of a cross-linkage across agreements made by a developing country and an example of the dexterity with which India has learned to pursue its interests in global trade negotiations.

[19] Also see Chapters 4, 6, and 7 of this book for evidence about Indian firms' global activities.

become multinationals, seeking global presence in both developing and developed markets (Sauvant and Pradhan 2010). As a result, a stronger India seeks global integration but on its own terms.

India's recent global integration and trade openness forms the first puzzle addressed in this book. This puzzle generates a research question: *How did India turn toward the global world in such a short span of time?* While many scholars and public commentators have observed India's changing interaction with the outside world,[20] we still don't know enough about the deeper sources for this surprising shift.[21] This puzzle urges us to revisit the conventional ways in which India is viewed in comparative politics and comparative political economy.

Comparatively, India's rapid global integration is anomalous, given its delayed start and late entry into the global system. Most studies of India have rested on the assumption that the Indian model of capitalist development is organized within its national borders, thereby suggesting that the national economy should be the unit of analysis.[22] Most of the scholarship on India's economic reforms, including my previous work, adopts such a domestic-oriented lens (Bardhan 1984, 2010; Corbridge and Harriss 2003; Jenkins 1999; Kale 2014; Kohli 2012; Mukherji 2014; Nooruddin 2011; Ruparelia et al. 2011; Sinha 2005a).[23] In contrast, this book places India's developmental trajectory within a broader global context, urging the need to go beyond "methodological nationalism"[24] and pay attention to how global factors *jointly interact* with powerful domestic imperatives within India. Globalization has erased the usual distinctions between the domestic and the global levels; therefore the interplay of domestic and international factors is foregrounded in this book.[25] I offer a *Global Design-in-Motion* (GDM) framework that starts with diverse domestic actors, interests, and institutions but finds that international markets and rules have disrupted the coalition of interests that supported an inward-oriented policy and pushed them toward a more globally proactive trade and economic agenda.[26] In international

---

[20] Nayar (1999), Purfield and Schiff (2006), Winters and Yusuf (2007), Panagariya (2008), Nayar and Paul (2003), Jaffrelot (2009), Mahbubani (2008), Subramanian (2008), Baru (2006), and Friedman (2005).

[21] For a few exceptions, see Alamgir (2009) and Mukherji (2014).

[22] Three exceptions are Kapur (2010), Ye (2014), and Alamgir (2009). Naseemullah (2016) adopts a firm-level analysis that also examines local and global strategies of firms.

[23] Some early studies of the 1991 reforms did emphasize the role of external constraints, but the global level was seen as pressure or a constraint in these studies.

[24] Callaghan (2010).

[25] For an important work in this genre, see Garrett and Lange (1996).

[26] See Lake (2009) for a discussion on open-economy politics framework, which focuses on domestic interests but in an open framework. The Global Design-in-Motion framework I propose offers a dynamic element and greater role for interdependence to change domestic interests and coalitions (see Chapter 2).

relations this is referred to as "outside-in" or second-image reversed analysis (Gourvetich 1978).

Once old vested interests were disrupted, new reform actors, whom I call *woodwork reformers*, seemingly emerged out of the woodwork, slowly in the late 1990s but more surely after 2000s. This group of reformers consisted of bureaucrats, technocrats, diverse business actors, exporters, revamped business associations, diasporic intellectuals, and key political actors.[27] These woodwork reformers together with the trading state saw the opportunity to craft a distinct Indian response to external changes. Indian firms initiated diverse global alliances and became supporters of freer trade as well as diverse protections at home. State actors became more proactive, seeking new markets as well as challenging the dominance of United States and European Union in global trade negotiations.

These findings have strong implications for our analysis of India's political economy. The distribution of domestic interests was not exogenous or static but changed in this period, giving sustainability to India's reforms. Counterintuitively, though, the strength of Indian firms overseas is not the cause but an effect of state policies and global forces. Yet, global forces are not uniform or autonomous, nor are they deterministic. They shape and are shaped by states that negotiate the terms of global engagement. The interactions between India and global forces (supply chains, markets, and global rules of the game) are reciprocal, dynamic, and strategic. Indian actors, policies, and institutions have been changed by the interaction with external forces, and they, in turn, reshape the global trading order, creating an endogenous dynamic that contributed to greater trade integration of India's economy.

To understand India's interactions with the outside world, we must analyze globalization. In common parlance, globalization is equated with global markets, global prices, and supply chains. Many treat it as an undifferentiated exogenous context for the actions of domestic actors. In most open-economy politics arguments as well as scholarship on India, the global level is treated as "a blackbox that generates problems which unitary states then solve through traditional means of negotiation" (Farrell and Newman 2014). In marked contrast, Kapur suggests that studies of globalization expand their attention to migration and how the transfer of people across borders affects Indian policies and interests (2010). In a parallel vein, this book argues that a global trading

---

[27] The idea of *woodwork reformers* has not been used in political economy analysis. I draw this concept from an analogous one used to analyze the emergence of the women's movement in the United States. Jo Freeman (1975) first used this idea to refer to feminists who were placed inside institutions and were somewhat invisible yet effective in mobilizing for the women's cause in the 1960s in the United States.

order – comprising global *agreements* such as the Agreement on Trade Related Intellectual Property Rights (TRIPS), *rules* articulated by international organizations like the World Trade Organization (WTO) (such as nondiscrimination or Most Favored Nation status), and *features* such as ministerial meetings and country trade policy review – is as important as global markets. In fact, the movement of goods, services, and people – globalization – is undergirded by new rules, governance structures, and constraining standards, both voluntary and involuntary.[28] These are the invisible *threads* that hold the economic and social transactions of globalization together, and their effect must be analyzed separately and independently of global markets. This view is the new emerging consensus in the field of global political economy. As Goldstein and Steinberg note, "International trade transactions are among the most regulated activities in the world. Indeed, the history of international trade since the seventeenth century cannot be understood without accounting for the changing ways by which public authority has interacted with, and influenced, private transactions" (Goldstein and Steinberg 2009, 211).

In 1995, a new global trading order, represented by the World Trade Organization (WTO), became a focus of debate for both the defenders of free trade and its opponents. Economists and globalizers saw in it a bulwark against rising protectionist sentiments. Peasants in poor developing countries, as well as affluent activists in the Western world, railed against its power to change lives and livelihoods, a power that reached even to remote corners of the globe. Both sides claim that it has remarkable power to shape national policy as well as change trade patterns and production profiles of countries. Yet, the WTO, compared to the World Bank and International Monetary Fund (IMF), is a small body, with scant resources.[29] Paradoxically, its power to extract compliance has risen precisely when it has become *less* controlled by hegemonic powers such as the European Union and the United States. Compared to GATT, the WTO has presided over remarkable trade liberalization, somewhat at odds with assumptions of domestic distributive politics, its organizational strength, and its budget.

 This raises a second puzzle: *How do international organizations and agreements unleash changes in state behavior without substantial coercive and*

---

[28] The WTO is more than an organization as it encompasses new procedures, rules, and legal processes. This book uses the name, the WTO, in this more expansive sense to include agreements, rules, standards, and practices.

[29] The WTO's secretariat has 668 staff members compared to 6,800 of the World Bank (IBRD) and 2,400 of the IMF. Even the Asian Development Bank (ADB), a regional organization, has a staff of 2,400 (professional staff plus support staff). Similarly, the WTO's budget is Swiss Franc 189 million compared to 1,375 million USD of the World Bank and 845 million USD of the IMF (Yearbook of International Organizations 2012–2013).

enforcement capacity?[30] Strong nationalist countries, such as India, China, Brazil, and other emerging powers, pose a special challenge to theories of international effects, as they have strong domestic responses to international rules. Are such international organizations able to transform trade politics in such self-reliant countries? *If so, what are the mechanisms through which international organizations shape and affect domestic political economy?* These two puzzling developments – global integration of India and the emergent power of global regimes, such as the WTO, to reorient state priorities and create new interests – are positioned together in this book. Resolving these twin puzzles is crucial to understanding why and how international institutions matter and in outlining the interaction between domestic and global levels in India. Building on a significant corpus of international relations and comparative politics literature, this book offers a conceptual and empirical framework with which to analyze multiple dimensions of globalization (markets and supply chains but also rules of the game) and the responses by domestic actors within specific countries such as India.

1.1 The puzzle: trade reform and institutional change in India

The interaction of domestic and international politics is the central theme of this book. The specific empirical puzzle, however, is India's recent and surprising global integration. An Indian Rip van Winkle who went to sleep in late 1980s or early 1990s and woke up in the 2000s would have been astonished by the huge change in a short amount of time. The India of 2016 is a different world from that of 1990 in terms of both trade policy and multilateral global engagement. India views the world very differently today, but even more so, the world regards India in very different ways.[31]

Until recently, India, an autarkic yet democratic country, was weakly internationalized. India's trade policy was inward looking and characterized by "export pessimism" (Bhagwati and Srinivasan 1984; Narayana 2001). This tendency toward export pessimism was strengthened by its long-established democratic institutions, which encouraged strong interest groups to resist trade liberalization. These tendencies were mirrored in India's multilateral policies. Although an original member of GATT, India successfully resisted any trade liberalization for decades. Through much of its history, India's trade policy was defensive and reclusive, seeking to avoid the impact of GATT on its domestic industry and

---

[30] The power of weak international institutions is emphasized by Dai (2007).
[31] Friedman (2005) and Prestowitz (2005).

trade policy (Narlikar 2006). About 65 percent of all imports and 90 percent of manufacturing imports were subject to nontariff barriers in 1990. While the import-weighted average tariff was 87 percent and the unweighted average tariff was 128 percent, the highest tariff rate was 355 percent, one of the highest in the world (Dijck and Rao 1994; Panagariya 2004; Srinivasan 2000, 33–34).[32] Between 1989 and 1994, 99 percent of India's trade with the outside world was subject to very high nontariff barriers, which only declined to 93.8 percent between 1995 and 1998.[33] Quantitative restrictions, combined with high tariffs, meant that Indian borders for the inflow of goods and services were effectively closed. At the same time, tariff revenue constituted a large part of government revenue.[34] India exported a small basket of primary and low value-added products: agriculture goods, cotton cloth and jute products, minerals such as coal, mica, and manganese, and gems and jewellery.

Trade liberalization began in the mid-1980s, but the progress was nonlinear – slowly moving forward but then sliding backwards. An opening appeared in the mid-1980s when Rajiv Gandhi, then prime minister, took a tentative step toward the West. After some reversals, domestic liberalization was formally initiated in 1991 when Manmohan Singh, then finance minister, was forced to take an IMF loan. He used this as a reason to initiate regulatory reforms at both external and domestic levels.[35] India reduced its peak applied tariff rate, which was 355 percent in 1990, to about 87 percent; average tariff rates went to 40 percent in 2000; and by 2007 they were 12 percent, reduced to 7.2 percent by 2014.[36] In the 1990s, only 6 percent of Indian tariff lines were bound,

[32] As late as 1985, the mean tariff for intermediate goods was 146 percent and for capital goods 107 percent. Import quotas protected Indian industry through a plethora of licensing mechanisms. In April 1990, there were 153 capital goods on the restricted import list and 927 items of raw materials and consumer goods under the restricted and limited permissible list (Goswami 1998, 127).

[33] Parikh (2007, 11).

[34] Tariff revenue as a proportion of imports went up from 20 percent in 1980–1981 to 44 percent in 1989–1990 (World Bank 2013).

[35] As noted by a scholar of the 1991 reforms, "Most fundamental corporate sector reforms of the last five years occurred in the first two" (1991–1992) (Goswami 1998, 115). In June 1991, two sharp devaluations (July 1 and 3, 1991) "brought an overvalued exchange rate in line." This was followed by a "dismantling of the industrial licensing regime," de-reservation of some public sector monopolies, liberalization of the Foreign Exchange Regulation (FERA) Act to encourage FDI and portfolio investment, reduction of import quotas, and a fall in the peak tariff rate from over 300 percent to 50 percent in 1994–1995, liberalization of capital markets, banking sector reforms, and encouragement for FDI (Goswami 1998, 115).

[36] See Sharan and Mukherji (2001, 28). Also see the 2005 budget speech of Indian Finance Minister P. Chidambaram, Speech, *Indian Budget*, February 28, 2005, http://indiabud get.nic.in/ub2005–06/bs/speecha.htm.

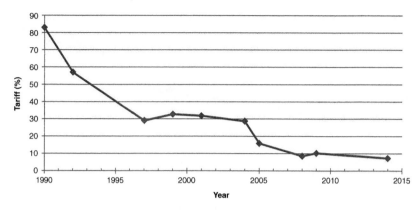

Figure 1.1 India's average tariff rates over time
WTO (2013).

allowing India to raise tariffs across the majority of products when needed.
While an average tariff of 7.2 percent still compares unfavorably with
those of India's Southeast and East Asian neighbors, the movement,
over a span of a decade, was significant – a decline of 95 percent.[37]
Despite significant trade liberalization in the early 1990s, policy reversed
its course – moving toward higher tariff rates in the mid-1990s.[38] India's
import-weighted average tariff rate rose to 32 percent in 1999–2000.[39]
Moreover, the effective rate of protection remained high during the 1990s,
even after significant liberalization had been initiated in 1991 (Banga and
Das 2012; Das 2003; Gang and Pandey 1998). Figure 1.1 shows this
reversal in tariff rates in the mid-1990s. The trade policy process retained
its insular, ineffective character in the 1990s, and India was on the verge of
being ignored and isolated in global trade negotiations.[40] Trade reform
was not followed by institutional reform in the early to mid-1990s, ensuring a lack of sustained trade reform and unsuccessful negotiation
outcomes.

Between 1980 and 1995, India possessed a large market but low levels of
economic interdependence, an isolationist ideology that balked at US pressure, and strong pressure groups within a highly fragmented political

[37] In this context, see editorial, "Open or Closed: The Case Against India is Over-Stated,"
Financial Express, March 16, 2004, p. 6.
[38] Montek Ahluwalia's (an architect of the reforms of 1991) comments about the 1990s
confirm this pattern of reversal in trade policies in the mid-1990s (Ahluwalia 2006).
[39] In 1990–1991 it was 87 percent. In 1994–1995 it declined from 33 to percent 27.2 but
again rose to percent 29.7 in 1998–1999 and to 38.5 percent in 2001–2002 (WTO 2013).
[40] Sen (2003), Narayan (2005), and author's interview with Indian trade negotiators.

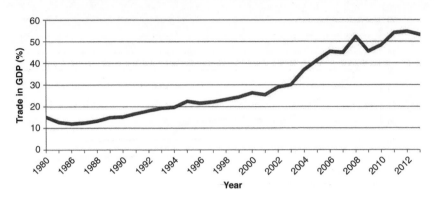

Figure 1.2 Trade in goods and services as percentage of GDP
World Bank (2013).

process.[41] Consequently, India's trade strategy seemed unlikely to respond
to the constraints and opportunities presented by global markets and
regimes.[42] This may explain why the 1985 reforms were reversed by 1989
and the 1991 reforms faced a reversal and increasing tariffs between 1995
and 1998.

Yet, the late 1990s saw the beginning of a number of changes in India's
trade strategies that resulted in genuine trade liberalization. Quantitative
restrictions were abolished on April 1, 2001, after India lost a WTO case
that forced it to dismantle its system of quotas and quantitative restrictions. Average tariffs declined from 24 percent in 2001 to 7 percent in
2009 (Banga and Das 2011). Recently, India's exports of goods and
services have grown faster than world exports; India's share in world
export of goods and services, which had declined from 2 percent to 0.5
percent by the mid-1980s, rose back to 2.31 percent by 2013 (Panagariya
2004, 13; WTO 2015).[43] In 1999, its trade (exports plus imports) ratio to
GDP was a mere 24.4 percent, up from a low of 12.7 percent in 1985 (see
Figure 1.2). This rose to 52.3 percent by 2008 (World Bank, WDI 2014)
and 53.2 percent by 2013 (World Bank, WDI 2014). By 2015, India had

[41] Most of India's industries were in import-competing sectors and lobbied extensively to
protect high tariff walls. India continued to have coalition governments with multiple
veto points and interests in the 1990s.
[42] David Lake characterizes American trade strategy in a similar way (Lake 1988, 3). The
similarities between the United States between 1887 and 1939 and India between 1991
and 2016 are striking.
[43] India's share of world trade in commodities has risen significantly – from a low of 0.5
percent in 1983 to 0.8 percent in 2004 to 2.6 percent in 2014 (WTO 2015).

bound 74.4 percent of tariff lines.[44] Its applied simple average tariff rate came down to 6.2 percent by 2013.[45] India began exporting many manufactured and value-added goods such as engineering goods, refined petroleum, textile and garments, electronic goods, marine products, and chemical and pharmaceutical products. Starting in the early 2000s, trade has become a driver of change within India, catalyzed by WTO effects and Indian responses. It is important to note that the real change in India's trade to GDP ratio has taken place only in the 2000s, specifically after 2002–2003.

Even more interestingly, India's behavior in multilateral forums became more participative and assertive. India formed the core of the G-20 group at Cancun; this led then Commerce Minister Arun Jaitley to claim: "The various meetings of the G-22 were held in India's hotel room."[46] India was invited to be part of the five interested parties (FIPS), which included Australia, Brazil, the European Union, India, and the United States, excluding Japan. Again in July 2005, India, as chair of the G-20 group, played a crucial mediating role between the United States and the European Union[47] – a rare phenomenon and inconceivable in the GATT years.[48] In 2006, India, Brazil, the European Union, and the United States came to an agreement about the Doha Round. In 2014, a bilateral meeting between India and the United States on the Agreement of Agriculture allowed the Bali Package decisions to move forward. Thus, India was no longer the passive receiver of international rules (rule-taker) but had begun to shape both negotiations and the institutional culture of the WTO (rule-maker).

Many scholars have noted a definite change in India's negotiating positions, as well as a change in its willingness to concede and bargain (Chanda and Sasidaran 2007; Karmakar 2007; Kumar 1993; Sinha 2007). Some see this as India's co-optation into the hegemonic international system, but it also reflects the fact that India is no longer a passive recipient of international changes and is seeking a more engaged role at the global level. Aggarwal and Mukherji (2008, 219) note that India's trade policy "shifted from a regional focus on SAARC ... and a multilateral focus on the WTO. ... India is now involved in a large array of accords and is actively negotiating multilateral and bilateral accords."

---

[44] World Trade Organization, Trade Profiles, www.stat.wto.org/CountryProfile/WSDBC ountryPFView.aspx?Language=E&Country=IN, accessed November 26, 2015.
[45] World Trade Organization, Trade and Tariff Indicators, www.wto.org/english/res_e/sta tis_e/statis_maps_e.htm, accessed November 26, 2015.
[46] "Cancun Travails," *Financial Express*, October 3, 2003.
[47] "Hopes Rise for Deal in Farm Trade Talks," *Financial Times*, July 13, 2005, p. 7.
[48] See Narlikar (2010, 2013) for India's role in new alliances at the WTO.

Overall, India has achieved good negotiation outcomes across many areas such as agriculture, services, and bilateral trade negotiations. Why and how did this transformation happen?

1.2   The argument

The story of India's rise is a story of domestic change and initiative, but not under conditions of its own making, to paraphrase Karl Marx's famous dictum.[49] The circumstances that shape domestic interests and institutions derive their power as much from structural changes within India as from external sources. Future opportunities in anticipation of the future shape of global markets have begun to drive Indian economic and political actors. This account differs from the implicit story of "India's turn,"[50] which seems an explanation only rooted in internal expansion and growth of the economy.[51] This view would suggest that internal growth unleashed in the 1990s induced external integration – a "growth-inducing globalization" story.

This book provides a more balanced account, one that brings in the role of global factors in interaction with domestic factors, rather than viewing India's actions as self-driven or autonomous. This account of transformation in India suggests that global markets (cross-border economic activity) and global trade regimes (international organizations, laws, rules as well as processes) catalyzed a change in domestic interests and preferences as well as a change in domestic policies and strategies for global integration. I specifically focus on identifying sources and pathways of India's changing global ambitions and improving capacity to negotiate. I take the idea found in Kohli (2007) to the next level, examining the *sources* of the state–capital alliance that took shape, in my argument, in the late 1990s rather than the 1980s. It is worth exploring the ways in which business and state came closer in the 2000s and crafted a new global strategy in keeping with India's rise. In doing so, the book marries a historical institutionalist understanding of diversity of interests and

[49] In *The Eighteenth Brumaire of Louis Bonaparte,* Marx wrote: "Men make their own history, but they do not make it as they please; they do not make it under self-selected circumstances, but under circumstances existing already, given and transmitted from the past" (1852, 2).

[50] The term is from Subramanian (2008).

[51] In 1985, some limited and short-lived liberalization started, which was followed by a more comprehensive and systematic liberalization in 1991. These policy reforms unleashed a higher growth rate (4–5 percent between 1991 and 1995 and 6 percent from 1995 to 2003, and it accelerated to 9 percent between 2003 and 2007) (Government of India, Economic Survey, various years). Liberalization of industrial and trade policies in the early 1990s increased the competitiveness of much of India's industry and service sectors, sparking robust growth in output and consumer demand.

institutions with an open-economy framework that unites a second-image reversed analysis (Gourevitch 1978) with a systematic focus on how domestic interests *shift and change in the crucible of domestic change and global design-in-motion*. While most of the international relations scholarship and studies of comparative politics focus on cross-sectional variation, I focus on variation over time, where the rigid domestic institutions and interests shift over time, challenging the path-dependence assumption common in much of the historical institutional arguments.

1.2.1   Empirical findings

While the events of both 1985 and 1991 were crucial (in different ways) in starting the reform process, India's external integration truly began in the late 1990s, after which trade became a driver of economic change. The policy and structural changes under way in India since 1985 and 1991 were important, even necessary, for globalization of the Indian economy, but they were not sufficient. Domestic Liberalization happened in 1991, in a piecemeal, "reform by stealth" manner (Jenkins 1999) and then reversed in the mid-1990s, similar to the reforms of the mid-1980s. For example, Indian policymakers successfully resisted intense bilateral pressure from the United States to comply with the global patent regime in the mid-1990s. Trade reform or external liberalization also suffered a setback in the mid-1990s when protective tariffs were raised in response to domestic pressures. Around 1995–1997, scholars would have been correct to write the story of the second attempt at "half-hearted liberalization"[52] in India. Yet, in the late 1990s, the trajectory changed to a more sustained open economy. This time (late 1990s) a deeper and more comprehensive external integration started, when trade reform spread across different sectors of the economy. The WTO and its practices played a major role in pushing India to the next stage of deeper global engagement, which was *not* predicted by the first stage of economic reforms. How did this deeper integration happen despite domestic opposition and constraints? This book focuses on the global mechanisms and domestic political economy dynamics that drove this second, deeper integration in India.

While it is easy to attribute powerful agency to India's actions at the global level, the real story is more complex. Despite policy change in 1991, domestic interests continued to resist openness through the 1990s. Reform in the external sector continued to lag behind through much of the 1990s. "Mass politics and elite politics"[53] slowed changes

---

[52] Harriss (1987).   [53] The distinction is from Varshney (1999).

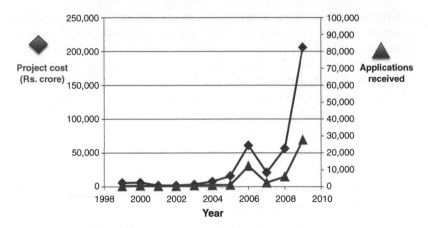

Figure 1.3 Investment plans of the textile industry
Author's calculations from Technology Upgradation Scheme data
available at the Ministry of Textiles (2013)

and delayed globalization in the early to mid-1990s. Large-scale industry
continued to lobby the government for retaining or increasing tariff walls
rather than opening them, even at late stages of the game.[54]

Industry changed its market strategies and collective action but after –
and in response to – the changes unleashed by the WTO. As an illustration, I briefly outline the investment plans of textile companies as revealed
through the number of applications for technological upgradation assistance received by the government. Figure 1.3 reveals that the textile
industry reoriented its investment and modernization plans significantly
but only around 2005 and 2006 after the abolition of the Multifibre
Arrangement (MFA), despite the fact that the abolition of the MFA
had been planned since 1995. Until as late as the mid-1990s, India's
policymakers, especially in the Commerce Ministry, were resistant to any
trade policy and tariff changes; they adopted mostly defensive postures to
protect local interest groups. The low level of openness in India in the
1990s, combined with the increase in import competition and the onset of
some external liberalization initiated in 1991, indicated that state
responses would be defensive and change incrementally (Nooruddin
and Simmons 2009). This was exactly what happened between 1991
and 1997, but this argument cannot explain the radical changes in India
after 1998–1999. Domestic factors alone no longer explain government
responses.

[54] "India Inc. Wants Custom Tariff Levels to Stay," *Business Line*, January 9, 2002.

1.2.2   Changes in state capacity and a new tradecraft

This book presents a complex, mediated argument about the interactive effect of global and domestic factors in steering trade reform within India. External effects related to the WTO regime as well as global markets were crucial levers that nudged change within India. India lost two major cases at the WTO – one on TRIPS and the second related to quantitative restrictions in 1998 – after which resisting the WTO regime became very difficult. The policy process surrounding trade, which continued to be insular and closed until the late 1990s, changed almost overnight. Combined with a reduction of tariffs, abolition of quantitative restrictions, and reduction of custom duties, India's trade policy regime changed radically in the late 1990s (after 1998).

Both policies and procedures changed (see Chapter 3). New channels of business–state consultation and feedback were created after 1999–2000 to discuss trade policy. Rather than a few bureaucrats making decisions, the trade policymaking process became much broader, involving many more governmental officials, but just as important, the process began to involve nonstate actors in a more formal and regular manner. Consultations with the so-called stakeholders were initiated, new committees were formed, and new channels were created for seeking expert advice at both the crucial policymaking and the implementation stages. The government appointed reform-minded ministers who were seen to resist protectionist pressures from both outside and within the party as well as enjoying the protection of the prime minister.[55] Reformist woodwork politicians emerged with reformist bureaucrats, disrupting the old nexus of vested interests. These woodwork reformers created new policy and institutional openings, arguing for the need to respond to the threat posed by the WTO rulings and arguing for recognition of a global world that India could no longer avoid. New institutions, new coalitions, and new collaborations were forged to evolve India's trade policy. Research entered into the policy process more frontally than before, as did new political and business actors and legal experts. The distributional political economy of India's trade was transformed in the process, as new winners and reform coalitions were created, while segments, regions, and industrial sectors that lost sought to delay trade liberalization but were less effective. Specific features of the global trade regime created implementation and transaction costs but also information revelation about the shape of new, future markets. Even as global markets were held at bay temporarily in the 1990s, businesses

[55] Arun Shourie and Arun Jaitley, India's commerce ministers in the BJP government, were considered reformers.

began to perceive the possibilities and the necessity of new opportunities in global supply chains, markets, and alliances.

All these changes had a definite impact on the skill set of Indian negotiators as well as institutions that supported trade ministers (Sinha 2007). Until the late 1990s, Indian negotiators received rigid instructions from New Delhi, and their stance in multilateral forms, while very competent and principled, remained quite negative.[56] After 1998, India's negotiating capacity increased dramatically. The state created new institutions (Tariff Commission and Patent Administration), streamlined existing institutions to protect Indian industry (Anti-dumping Administration), and radically transformed the role of expertise and information in the policy process. Also, the larger political support for external openness radically changed: societal opposition to trade integration was transformed into engagement that sought to shape the nature of trade openness rather than challenge it entirely. New global interests were created, and many economic groups realigned their interests within India. Many of the losing sectors were told to adjust or go out of business. The government faced much less domestic criticism of its trade policies and positions than it did in the early and mid-1990s. What is remarkable is the notable *change over time in policies, policy process, and institutional capacity* despite India's low level of global integration.

The state was transformed in the process of global change and domestic reform. Yet, I do not imply that the state was intrinsically capable. Left to its own devices, the old political economy nexus would have never created reform coalitions or a strategy of tradecraft; that was the crucial missing element in earlier years. State capacities were augmented despite strong opposition and delays as a result of India's engagement with global rules, norms, and enforcing process. New openings within the state allowed woodwork reformers to create a new consensus around globalization. The state also "developed mechanisms of resistance against future trespasses on its sovereignty."[57] This view challenges the conventional idea that global effects create new market incentives or price signals. This book suggests that global levers may also encompass institutional change and insertion of diverse forms of expertise within the domestic state creating new capabilities for economic actors.

1.2.3   Global levers and causal mechanisms

Three global pillars have shaped and changed India's own calculus and interests as well as the institutional capability of dealing with the outside

[56] S. Narayan (2009, 179), a prominent government official at that time, confirms this view.
[57] I thank an anonymous reviewer for this formulation of my argument.

world: (a) geopolitics, (b) global markets, and (c) a global organization, the WTO. Together they generated microcausal mechanisms such as *transaction costs, sovereignty costs, private costs, legal framing, and nonmarket mechanisms such as public information about new markets and new threats.* This analysis of causal mechanisms differs from the existing discussions of conditionality or coercion in suggesting that legally framed sovereignty costs were more difficult for states such as India to resist. Sovereignty costs worked with other elements of the global system to create public information about the opportunities presented by global markets, creating an impetus for private sector adaptation and reorienting of business strategies toward global reach.

First, at the highest level of abstraction, the *changing global security structure* (or balance of power), represented by the decline of the former Soviet Union and emergence of the United States as the sole power, as well as the rise of China, changed the external environment for India, creating new *sovereignty costs*.[58] These changes necessitated a pro-US shift in India's overall global orientation and a wariness of China.[59] This also drove the reforms of 1991 when domestic fiscal crisis, combined with a changing global order, created initial conditions for a paradigmatic change in economic policy. Geopolitical shifts had a direct albeit unanticipated economic effect: bilateral trade relationships with the former Soviet Union ended, forcing the private sector to look for alternative markets.[60] Economic threats generated by larger external changes were more important than price signals in creating new *private costs* for business actors. Exchange rate liberalization in the early 1990s played a facilitative role in these shifts (Gangopadhyay 1998, 50). These system-level shifts at the geopolitical level were the initial necessary conditions that were crucial for Indian policymakers to initiate change internally. Interestingly, security concerns and economic threats posed by China reinforced each other (after 2000) as China began exporting cheap goods to India.

Such systemic shifts in the global order, combined with the *pull factors of global markets* and the *push factor of institutions* (such as the WTO), drove trade liberalization deeper in India. I show, through an analysis of textile and pharmaceutical sectors, that global markets – the movement of goods, services, and people – created new opportunities, as well as new threats, which mobilized private sector actors as well as state actors, who

---

[58] For a theoretical treatment of balance of power theory and the changes brought about by the rise of the United States, see Paul (2005).

[59] See Paul (2007) for these arguments.

[60] In 1980 the Soviet Union was India's main trading partner, accounting for 16 percent of India's exports. By 1995 this had declined to 3.69 percent. The data are from IMF, *Direction of Trade Statistics*, 2006, cited in Aggarwal and Mukherji (2008).

were forced to design new policies and institutions to deal with such external changes. Global institutions and negotiations provided an arena for concentrated *information discovery and transmission,* which was not possible in decentralized global markets. Observers of India's rise expect that the private sector in India would favor openness without providing any direct evidence of their preferences. I seek to assess private sector preferences directly and arrive at a curious finding that the private sector was more of an enforcer of bargains struck by state officials and did not argue for proactive change. Internationalization of Indian firms was neither inevitable nor automatic but a product of firms' responses to changing global conditions and the domestic support that nudged them toward global strategies. Nonmarket mechanisms played a major role in this transformation of interests, preferences, and firm strategies.

The third pillar of influence thus consists of global regimes and institutions that generated some of these nonmarket effects and pushed against the country's boundaries of policy autonomy; they also created onerous *transaction and implementation costs* that catalyzed new internal responses and capacities. Chapter 2 elaborates on the triangular theoretical framework that generates ideas about new concepts and causal mechanisms generated by global rules of the game.

The enhancement of such capacity is not a generalized phenomenon, though. It has been most evident only in India's trade-making apparatus, where, I argue, the sovereignty and transaction costs associated with global regimes have been felt directly. The loss of the two important cases – one related to intellectual property and the other related to quantitative restrictions – was crucial. The impact of global rules is as powerful on the private sector. The WTO rules and framework yield concentrated and centralized information, which is even more valuable than market-mediated information and price signals. The WTO rules also spurred new forms of collective action among the private sector players, mobilizing export-oriented firms and subsectors. While India's engagement with the outside world has changed, global forces have also changed Indian actors and institutions so that the usual distinctions between domestic and global have become less clear.

1.2.4   Woodwork reformers: domestic agents and responses

The process of external integration unfolded through four distinct movements within the domestic political economy. First, the creation of enhanced state capacity to negotiate at the global level was a direct result of the transaction costs imposed by the WTO and its legal rulings. Second, global changes disrupted vested interests and distributional coalitions that had prevented change and supported protectionism for the   past five decades. And third, new winners and incipient reformers emerged from the woodwork within both the state and the private sector. Moreover, new exporting interests created new forces, such as revamped business associations, and reorganized the nature of collective action across many sectors. Fourth, the new losers were unable to mobilize the state, although they were able to delay trade liberalization to some extent.

I contend that external forces condition Indian policymakers, in both visible and invisible ways, and the private sector acts to defend their interests. Paradoxically, global forces have emboldened internal state capacity and private technical capabilities, which can lead to an effective defense of India's interest in global arenas. Global changes incite actors in the domestic polity to alter the regulatory framework, thereby changing the incentives and opportunities faced by downstream actors. Thus, more coherent and strong actions by Indian policy and private actors at the global level, as suggested by realist frameworks, *are the consequence not the cause* of global integration.

Domestic actors are not passive players; rather, they shape the nature of domestic responses. Clearly, the structural changes in the 1980s – such as the green revolution, the rise of a consuming and linked middle class, and industrial change in key sectors such as information technology – prepared the ground for the opening up that started in the early 1990s. The IMF loan of 1991 and Manmohan Singh's policy shift were also crucial necessary preconditions. Yet, global factors nudged India toward a deeper integration in the 2000s. Through the 1990s, key state, public, and private sector interests continued to resist further globalization. Intriguingly, through this process of resistance and compliance, Indian interests began to shift and move in perceptible and subtle ways. Woodwork reformers learned to deploy external threats and opportunities in ways that strengthened national capacity and responses while simultaneously creating indigenous political support for global integration. Thus, my story does not negate the role of internally driven compulsions but instead suggests the need to see the actions of Indian elites in a more open-economy framework, where the sources and nature of changes underway in India are traced and analyzed more systematically. The study of countries like India teaches us that in a global world, elites and domestic actors cannot and do not act unilaterally but seek to carve out as much autonomy as possible while complying with their global commitments. This book, then, puts forward the claim that the tension between resistance to global pressures (state autonomy) and integration (compliance) is misleading. I suggest that India's attempts to increase its power may better be characterized as the desire to use its commitment space (after compliance/convergence) to extract as much autonomy and to deploy the flexibility provisions in global agreements.[61]

1.2.5   Creating interests and realigning interests for global reach: analysis of pharmaceutical and textile sectors

This book focuses in an intensive way on two important sectors (pharmaceutical and textiles and garments) and proposes the need for careful studies of diverse sectors in a dynamic open-economy framework where the causal mechanisms that shape domestic change are explored explicitly and the interaction of domestic and global factors is foregrounded.[62] I analyze the diversity of actors within the two sectors and how they were affected by and responded to the changing dynamic of global and domestic policy changes. Chapters 4, 5, and 6 demonstrate that globalization has very similar consequences for different types of sectors.[63] This analysis should have implications for many other industries as India's commitments at the WTO also shaped corporate strategies across a wide variety of sectors such as pharmaceuticals, textiles and garments, automobiles, hardware and electronics, software, and telecommunications and services. While some sectors were affected directly through specific agreements, such as the intellectual property rights agreement, almost all sectors were affected by the mandated and bound decline in tariff rates negotiated as part of the NonMarket Access Negotiations (NAMA).

Both sectors, one capital and knowledge intensive (pharmaceutical) and the other labor intensive (textiles and garments), were affected by international agreements, such as the Trade Related Intellectual Property Rights Agreement (TRIPS) and the Multifibre Agreement (MFA). Both sectors are domestically important. While the pharmaceutical industry was the poster child of state autonomy during the *dirigiste* period, textile and garment firms employ around 35 million people and have a large domestic weight. Despite their different structures, both were forced to adjust to a fast-changing global environment and did so in similar ways. Technological upgrading and global strategies became necessary in both sectors. New firms across India's industrial economy became global players, modernizing and growing beyond India's borders. Changing global and local alignments with the emerging strength of export-oriented sectors and encompassing business associations are the

---

[61] One direct example is Article 3(d) in the Indian Patent Act of 2005 that "represents an 'innovative' exploitation of TRIPS flexibilities by India to further national interest" (Basheer 2007, 3). See Olsen and Sinha (2013) for an elaboration of this argument.

[62] For recent analysis of economic changes across India's sectors, see Hsueh (2012) and D'Costa (2009).

[63] Tarrow (2010) recovers the value of most-difference design.

common dynamic across both industries. Even in a knowledge-driven industry like the pharmaceutical sector, partnership with the state became necessary in bringing business and states closer together.

This study's paired comparison deploys a lesser-used comparative method in political science, John S. Mill's most-different systems design, which uses the differences in characterization of the cases to get at the similar mechanisms of the phenomenon — globalization – under study (Tarrow 2010). This approach enables us to see the common imperatives and varied responses of actors within very different industrial organizations (more on that later in this chapter). In one case (textiles and garments), new winners were created and mobilization of interests became possible, while in the pharmaceutical sector realigning of the domestic industry toward patents and branded generics was the modal pattern. There were losers within each industry (powerlooms, handlooms, cotton, and small-scale sector), but they were no longer able to shape regulation and trade policy.

[margin note: Mill design]

Some subtle differences are also apparent in terms of the changing role of the state across the two sectors. In the case of the pharmaceutical industry, the state supported the private sector during the heyday of the *dirigiste* economic policy in the form of a process patent regime. At the same time, the state's role for important segments of the textile sector was much more negative during the *dirigiste* period. During the globalization era, the role of the state reversed in the two sectors. After 1995, the role of the state in nudging and facilitating change within the declining and stagnant textiles sector was much more crucial than in the pharmaceutical sector, where earlier state support (process patent regime) had already created a stronger industry. Legal changes in the form of a TRIPS-compliant internal policy regime was necessary in the pharmaceutical story, whereas the policies, state action, and disruption of the nexus of interests were prerequisites for textile upgradation. In the case of textiles, the state tied its own hands by committing itself to domestic policy changes, which created a much more credible signal to the private textile sector to adjust. Here, one must not underestimate the more active role of a *new developmental state*[64] in identifying new export markets for textiles and garments, providing loans for technological upgradation in the globally relevant subsectors, and providing some support for the losing subsectors such as handlooms (see Chapter 5 for details). As a result, in 2013, India became the world's largest textile exporter, beating competitors like Italy, Germany, and Bangladesh. The chairman of the business association representing exporters, Virendra Uppal, admitted that the role of the

[64] Trubek et al. (2013), Riain (2004), and Stubbs (2011).

state was crucial: "Government policy of diversification of market and product base helped us and we ventured into the newer markets, which paid huge dividends."[65] Thus, while organizations and actors within the two sectors were faced with the common dilemmas and imperatives generated by global markets and new rules of the game, the role of the state was indispensable in ensuring the continued survival and successful upgradation of the textile sector. The pharmaceutical sector in 1995 had a decade to adjust given the transition time dictated by the global agreement (1995–2005) and therefore needed the state less, although crucial state decisions also played a facilitative role.

How generalizable is this story of positive state support for global adjustment across diverse sectors? I suggest not that the state's role is always facilitative, but when faced with external global constraints, it may nudge some industrial sectors to adjust and change the incentives. The domestic responsiveness of the industrial sector is also a crucial variable that interacts with external opportunities and constraints. The level of sovereignty demands and costs arising out of compliance pressures at the global level play a crucial role in ensuring a concentrated sense of threats, mobilizing both state and private actors in turn. In those industrial sectors and segments where that concentrated threat is absent, domestic change may be slower, nonexistent, or driven by domestic imperatives. Paradoxically, the weakness of the business interests within the textile sector created conditions for a directive role for the state to urge technological adaptation faced with the abolition of the global quota regime. The changing supply chains do play a role in nudging change even without global rules, but that process may be slower or more hesitant. In sectors unaffected by direct WTO compliance pressures, the nature of change may also take different forms, with more protective strategies dominating free-trade strategies.

Some subsectors did not gain as much from a positive state development. Some segments, such as handlooms and powerlooms, lost the state support they had earlier gained and had to learn how to deal with the new domestic and global environment on their own. Similarly, the hardware and electronics sector, faced with a much stronger software sector, did not get policy attention, even though the potential of the hardware sector was significant. While the Information Technology Agreement (ITA) of the WTO did initiate some mobilization on behalf of the hardware sector, it was not followed with a multipronged approach that proved crucial in

---

[65] PTI, "India World Second Largest Textile Exporter: UN Comtrade," *Economic Times*, June 2, 2014, http://articles.economictimes.indiatimes.com/2014–06–02/news/502728 49_1_textiles-exports-india-calender-year.

the textile and garments sector. The framework outlined in this book can help us assess the precise levers of change (or the lack of change) in these other sectors even though this study is limited to two sectors.[66] We can no longer ignore the interplay of global and domestic factors in shaping industrial adjustment in India and other emerging powers.

1.3   Measuring interests, preferences, and policy change

We need more studies of how specific countries implement globalization. Frieden and Martin note in a review of the literature (2002, 144): "However, empirical work at the international level [on international institutions] differs in that much of it has focused on broad concepts such as cooperation, or stability. While useful, this focus has sometimes distracted from in-depth attention to specific issue areas and particular institutions" and, I would add, specific countries. This book responds to their call. They further note:

The potential for future research seems particularly promising as we explore the functioning of specific economic institutions in much more detail and compare institutionalized interaction to interaction without the structuring effects of institutions. Doing so will, in part, require a turn away from broad synthesizing concepts to a focus *on more concrete variation in state behavior such as patterns of trade and investment flows and specific policy decisions* [Frieden and Martin 2002, 144–145, emphasis added].

Interestingly, in a similar vein, interests and preferences are also difficult to measure and are rarely the focus of scholarship. Most economists argue that we can only observe "revealed preferences" and not real interests. Assessing and measuring changes in interests – a dynamic variable – may be easier to observe but more difficult to attribute to its causes. Both of these concerns – a study of compliance and a study of shifting interests – require long-term firm-level data rather than cross-sectional or cross-national data. I also suggest that the creation of a new exogenous body, the WTO, provides an ideal backdrop against which we can see and measure changing interests and preferences.

---

[66] For example, the telecommunication sector can also be analyzed using the framework outlined in this book. There is some evidence to suggest that global factors such as the GATS agreement as well as concerns about India's reform reputation combined with a "steering state" (Jacobs 2010), shaped policy and institutional change in the telecom sector. Anil Jacobs's (2010) excellent dissertation documents these changes.

1.3.1   Case selection, methodology, and data sources

How would one design such a study? I argue that cross-national studies of global effects are methodologically insufficient. Such studies measure single-year snapshots but do not highlight the dynamic nature of compliance, which, by its very nature, unfolds over time. A longitudinal study of one country, over time, is therefore more appropriate, as it expands our notion of compliance and measures effects in a more detailed yet comprehensive manner.

I do utilize variation across GATT versus WTO and across very different sectors – pharmaceutical and textiles – to assess variable cross-sectoral effects, but I am also sensitive to change over time. A number of variations are the focus of this book. I focus on variation in state behavior across the GATT and WTO and across agreements within the WTO (TRIPS vs. ATC). I analyze intended effects (reducing trade protection, for example) as well as unintended effects on domestic trade politics (for example, increased effectiveness in anti-dumping actions and capacity to launch dispute cases). Changes in the industry interests across two important sectors (textiles and pharmaceuticals) within India also form the main focus of this book. Both these sectors were affected by exogenous changes at the global level at the same time (in 2005). Variation across time (1980s vs. 1990s; 1991–1998 vs. 1998–2014) in one country (India) is exploited to analyze the mechanisms and levers of change.

The two sectors chosen for study were affected by *exogenous changes in the global trade regime* at the same time in 2005. A pharmaceutical industry is a research- and capital-intensive sector, while the textile industry is labor intensive, allowing an exploration of different political dynamics and constraints. This allows me to flesh out an argument about variation in institutional effects across sectors and, most crucially, across time. Institutional evolution and change in India's trade policy regime is striking for a number of reasons, and I both trace the changing biography of a specific policy arena (trade) over time and explore the differences across sectors and across different international institutions. This methodology is most appropriate to study the mechanisms through which global forces shape domestic patterns and structures, allowing us to address *how, rather than whether*, global linkages affect countries like India. This is also in line with the most-different design (Tarrow 2010). Table 1.1 outlines the research design and cases.

Relatedly, aggregating data is not as fruitful as documenting diverse business histories that are better able to get at the motivations of businesses as they respond to the changing domestic and global environment. Such business histories are especially useful when preferences and the

Table 1.1 *Study design and cases*

GATT to WTO	India
1948–1995: GATT	1. State policy and state structures
	2. Textile industry
	3. Pharmaceutical industry
1995–2016: WTO	4. State policy and structures
	5. Textile industry after MFA abolition
	6. Pharmaceutical industry after TRIPS

larger political environment are in transition, and firm behavior measures (like prices) do not accurately represent how businesspeople make decisions and how their decision calculus changes. Also, actors may misrepresent their interests publicly. Confidential interviews and careful cross-checking may be in order. These issues required that I collect my own data.

1.3.2   Interviews

Data were collected for this project at numerous sites: New Delhi (India), Geneva (Switzerland), Ahmedabad (India), Mumbai (India), and Washington, DC (USA). I collected unpublished archival documents from various business associations, conducted archival research, and conducted 131 interviews. In early November 2002, I visited Geneva to gather information on the role of the WTO and India's negotiating strategies. There I interviewed most members of the Indian mission and other WTO officials. I also interviewed key officials of Brazil's mission in Geneva. In India (from August 2003 to July 2004), I conducted interviews with policymakers in the trade ministry, business associations, and CEOs of firms. In Washington, DC, I interviewed policymakers at the office of the US Trade Representative (USTR), the US–India Business Council, and the officials of the Confederation of Indian Industry (CII), an Indian business association with an office in DC and active in the WTO negotiations. In India, I conducted interviews with retired and current officials of the government and members and officials of many sectoral and national associations (CII, FICCI, ASSOCHAM, OPPI, and IDMA, among others). The Appendix to this book lists the interview names and affiliations.

1.3.3   Newspaper database

Longitudinal analysis demands specific and time-sensitive data. The analysis relies, for historical record, on daily newspaper clippings from twenty-five to thirty newspapers from 1990 onward until 2011 for specific themes.[67] I deploy this unusual source of data for documenting the emergent policy regime in the pharmaceutical and textile sectors (Chapters 4 and 5). This rich database also reveals firm-specific and time-sensitive clues about the how the private sector responded to the policy regime in the specific sector as well as the global changes (Chapter 7). Statements and views of firms are documented. A definite advantage of these data is that they reveal information about how firm owners think, including their views on policy and global changes apart from information about their business strategies. This database also allows me to distinguish between the role played by global markets vs. WTO rules and nonmarket mechanisms on firms' strategies.

How were these data collected? First, I collected newspaper stories on pharmaceutical and textile policies from twenty-five to thirty newspapers on a day-to-day basis, covering the period 1990–2011. For the period after 2000, in addition to the print editions, I also accessed the web-based versions of the same newspapers. I collected newspaper stories on intellectual property rights and textile agreements of the WTO for the same period. I supplemented this collection with a painstaking search of the Factiva newspaper database, which covers newspapers from India.[68] This massive database of daily newspaper articles from many different newspapers allowed me to carefully document pharmaceutical companies' statements and their strategies and activities (revealed preferences). For example, the news clippings yielded systematic and historically accurate information on the rise and development of business associations in India, information that cannot be found in any other database. I coded this large material to capture changes within the textiles, intellectual property rights, and pharmaceutical sectors. From these files I constructed databases on "Activities on GATT/WTO Issues," "US–India Negotiations," "Policy and Institutional Events Database, 1990–2011," "Statements by Associations," "Protest Activity on GATT and WTO," "Business Strategies and Events," and the changing "Positions of Experts and Other Actors." For example, the database "Policy and Institutional Events Database, 1990–2011" itself generated close to 800–1,000 data points for each year (approximately a total of 10,000 data entries), which were then analyzed and carefully coded. These databases were quantified to generate an aggregate measure of business strategies and policies. I use

[67] *The Hindu, The Economic Times, Business Standard, Financial Express, Business Line, Indian Express, The Asian Age, The Hindustan Times, The Telegraph, The Independent, and Business and Political Observer,* among many others.
[68] Other researchers have also used Factiva to document the changing strategies of pharmaceutical firms. See Kedron and Bagchi-Sen (2011).

this to measure, analyze, and quantify the types of strategies pursued by firms and also to analyze the context and the mechanisms that lead to those strategies. Since this information was quite rich, I was able to assess and cross-check information revealed through interviews.[69]

This collection allowed me to assess the historical evolution of India's trade policy and its relationship with global trade institutions. This access to journalistic stories provided the background information for more fine-tuned interview questions. While reliance on newspapers can pose some problems, the use of 25–30 *different* newspapers on the *same topic* allowed me to cross-check information and get a more accurate sense of the information reported therein. It also allows a more detailed narrative of multilateral institutions than possible with only either newspapers or interviews. Newspapers were relied upon to report activities, events, statements, and factual developments; no use was made of the opinions expressed by reporters. Speculations were ignored. Editorial comments were not used unless written by eminent public officials who might reveal some aspects of the business–politics relationship in their official capacity. Furthermore, some of the salient pieces of information were confirmed in interviews.

1.3.4 Primary sources

I also relied on a number of primary sources. I gathered internal, confidential memoranda and internal policy documents issued by business associations and individual companies to assess directly the changing interests around patents. I supplemented this with interviews with key actors within the textile and pharmaceutical sector, where confidentiality was assured, enabling more honest interviews. For an analysis of policy debates and policy change, I relied on original government and parliamentary reports that documented testimony by private sector and other government actors. In fact, many committees set up by the government and parliamentary committees record the views of many interested public and private sector actors. This treasure trove of primary documents has rarely been analyzed before, and the documents paint a comprehensive picture of the changing policy environment and changing balance of interests.[70] I collected and used annual reports of various sectoral and

---

[69] Other studies that rely on newspaper reporting of business strategies are, Madanmohan and Krishnan (2003), who focus on a few firms and do not use the newspaper data systematically.

[70] A few of the documents that I use are: Rajya Sabha (Parliamentary Standing Committee on Commerce), "Third Report, Draft of Dunkel Proposals," 1993–1994; Rajya Sabha (Standing Committee on Petroleum and Chemicals), "Proposed Drug Policy," 1994–1995. Also see Jacob (2010), who also relies on similar documents for his analysis.

national associations, annual reports of research institutions, such as the Research and Information System for Developing Countries (RIS) and Indian Council of Research on International Economic Relations (ICRIER), and unpublished memoranda submitted by various business actors and organizations. I collected a voluminous set of annual reports of many government departments, such as the Ministry of Commerce and Industry, the Department of Industrial Policy and Promotion, the Ministry of Textiles, and the Department of Intellectual Property. This allowed me to build a longitudinal analysis of policies and institutions. I made use of many other publications of the Ministry of Commerce – for example, the WTO Newsletter, WTO Watch, and Communiqué. This book analyzes and integrates a massive collection of parliamentary documents and reports, which revealed the intricate process of policy-making. I used Lok Sabha debates, parliamentary committee reports, and questions and answers submitted to the parliament. Other sources of data included press releases, annual reports of the CII and FICCI (Federation of Chambers of Commerce and Industry), and submissions and pamphlets and brochures released by NGOs, parties, and businesses. Such a detailed and rich collection of primary documents ensures that the conclusions are based on original documentary evidence and therefore more reliable.

1.4   Organization of the book

Global institutions can constrain and enable behavior, change preferences and interests, and affect relative power balances. Global forces also enable new interests to congeal, new rules of the game to emerge, and new capacities to develop. Consequently, global institutions and markets become objects of choice for actors affected by them. Strategic internationalism and a new tradecraft are the *joint products* of global mechanisms and domestic priorities allowing a new reform coalition to craft a globally active agenda and strategy. Chapters 3 to 7 show that the international organization that deals with international trade – the WTO – shaped the two building blocks of policy and institutional change in India: preferences (or interests) of domestic actors and domestic institutions. Ideas held by domestic negotiators and industry actors were slower to change and continue to lag behind. Yet, the interaction among the transformed elements has created a radically different regime of trade politics in a country that had traditionally resisted change. Chapter 2 lays out the theoretical parameters of the book, outlining the plausible explanations and a synthetic analytical framework, Global Design-in-Motion, to understand the puzzles introduced in Chapter 1. I outline the logic of relational causal mechanisms such as transaction costs, sovereignty costs, legal framing, and nonmarket mechanisms such as public information, learning, and threats both in general terms and viewed from the perspective of domestic states.

In Chapter 3, extending the idea that wars make states, I argue that a country's participation in a rule-bound global trading system reforms states, changes the direction of their trade policy, and shapes domestic institutional development. The story of changing state capacities raises the question of changing interests and preferences. How do international trade institutions – GATT and WTO – shape the nature and extent of distributional conflict in India and collective action within industries and sectors? I trace the story of changing interests in Chapters 4, 5, and 6 with a detailed analysis of India's pharmaceutical and textile sectors. Chapter 4 focuses on policy and industry change in the pharmaceutical sector. The story of India's textile sector is a narrative of unexpected change, of global preeminence followed by decline, but replaced by a significant revival in the late 1990s and 2000s. Chapter 5 explicates the process of policy change in this important sector – textiles and garments. Some state agents used India's commitment to the MFA abolition in 2005 as a means of encouraging domestic businesses to transform their decades-old ways of doing business, tying their hands in favor of reform. In order to do so, they fought many vested interests within the state and within the private sector. Chapter 6 traces the story of changing interests and skills among India's textile and garment industry. I provide direct evidence of the evolution of business preferences to analyze changes among India's private sector. Are the phenomenal changes documented in this book the result of market and competitive forces? Chapter 7 addresses this question. Three nonmarket mechanisms – public information about future markets and global standards, threats from competitors, and learning through joint ventures and new alliances – proved crucial for the private sector. Even in the world of decentralized markets and private action, interdependent action and learning from competitors and collaborators play a crucial role. Threats are powerful within the world of rational businesspeople in mobilizing and upgrading capacity. The conclusion outlines how global trade and international organizations have affected India. I outline the implications of this book's arguments for our understanding of globalization, the nature of the evolving development state in India, and the multiple and unexpected transformations across the private sector.

2   A theory of causal mechanisms and Global Design-in-Motion

States operate in an open, interdependent system where national policies are shaped by global interactions and flows. Equally significantly, globalization of commodities, people, and services is undergirded by global rules, laws, organizations, and mechanisms of global compliance. Yet, we do not know enough about *how global trade rules of the game get translated and modified* in diverse countries. While many ideas offer theoretical expectations about compliance and cooperation, rigorous empirical analysis of how globalization is embedded in specific countries lags behind such theoretical development.[1] This book builds a new theoretical framework, the *Global Design-in-Motion (GDM) Framework*, and conducts an original empirical analysis of how global markets and global order-design shape Indian trade politics. This focus resonates with an argument "against compliance"[2] and shifts attention to how global rules are interpreted by governments and shape and transform Indian institutions and preferences in turn. In order to understand this complex transformation within India and other large emerging countries, the triangular framework proposes a set of *relational causal mechanisms* that interact across domestic and global jurisdictions and might explain the long chain of implementing globalization within countries.

This book also offers a new perspective on India's ongoing transformations. I argue that India's trajectory of globalization can only be understood by relocating (or displacing) India from a predominantly national context to a more open, global framework where national politics and international regimes are not treated as dichotomous. Faced with a severe fiscal crisis, the Indian government liberalized its economy in 1991 in order to qualify for an IMF loan. Yet, between 1993 and 2000, trade liberalization slowed, and the government raised tariffs again.[3] Despite

---

[1] See Ruggie (1983) for the idea of embedded liberalism. Also see Ruggie (1993).

[2] Martin (2013) urges the need to examine the impact of international institutions on state policy and behavior rather than the legally narrow concept of compliance. For classic writings on compliance, see Simmons (1998, 2000).

[3] The weighted average tariff decreased from 87 percent in 1990–1991 to 24.6 percent in 1996–1997 before it gradually increased to 38.5 percent in 2001–2002 (World Bank 2013).

30

the radical changes of 1991, a definite reversal in India's trade orientation was evident from 1993 to 2000 as the country returned to protectionist policies. India's global strategies were hesitant and inward oriented during the 1990s.[4]

The year 2000 saw another paradigmatic shift, bringing India closer to global markets. This time, a more open economic paradigm was sustained throughout the 2000s. By 2013, foreign trade in goods and services had increased beyond expectations, constituting 53.2 percent of India's GDP (World Bank 2013). The 1999-2000 reforms represent a turning point in India's ongoing reform trajectory; they transformed India into a more open, global economy. Simultaneously, India became a rising power and, in 2015-2016, the fastest growing economy in the world. Why did India pursue comprehensive trade liberalization after 2000, opening up its markets, passing TRIPS-compliant legislation, and nudging its industries toward global reach and modernization, whereas previously, between 1993 and 2000, Indian reforms moved at a slower pace?

Scholarly literature on India predicts stasis (Chibber 2003; Herring 1999; Kruger 1974) or a gradual but steady pace of reform (Ahluwalia 1995, 2002, 2006; Jenkins 1999). Analogously, while historical institutionalism has taught us much about the mechanisms that underpin institutional inertia – path dependence, for example – we don't know enough about the mechanisms that lead to institutional change within countries. Recent literature on India's reforms focusing on changes over time argues exclusively about the influence of domestic politics. For some scholars, state elites undertook reform by stealth (Jenkins 1999) or moved in a pro-business direction (Kohli 2007), while others emphasize the role of technocratic ideas in changing policy (Mukherji 2014; Shastri 1997). This book proposes that a focus on domestic politics must be enhanced with an analysis of the effect of international political economy – both rules and markets – on *altering* a country's constellation of interests, institutions, and capacities for trade liberalization. This perspective examines the *sources of India's rise and stronger activism* in world affairs rather than assume it as given.

This book also offers a new way to incorporate international variables in our analysis of India's ongoing reform trajectory. The existing arguments about India conceptualize the international level in a distinct way, as pressure or coercion. The enabling effect of international-level variables

[4] Many observers confirm this insular character of the Indian economy even after the reforms of 1991. See Sanjaya Baru's interview on YouTube, where he notes this reversal in the 1990s, www.youtube.com/watch?v=ffhCBG28QFA. Montek Ahluwalia, one of the architects of the reforms of 1991, also reflects on the slowness of trade liberalization in the 1990s (Ahluwalia 2006).

on states (Weiss 2003, 2005), or in creating new interests and in changing the domestic balance of power, needs to be attended to in our understanding of the globalization trajectory of India. *Transaction and sovereignty costs* unleashed by global organizations may lead to institutional reform and augmentation of capacities that allow the Indian trading state to craft a new global strategy. Global forces not only constrain Indian actors and policies but also encourage *information discovery about opportunities* created by globalization. In the process, globalization transforms state–society relations, and policymakers are motivated to cooperate with business to reorient India's path to globalization. The international changes, together with cooperative relations between state and business, endogenously transform the interests of inward-oriented policymakers, politicians, and private sector actors accustomed to a closed economy.[5] Woodwork reformers emerge silently.

These arguments are reinforced by a new theoretical framework, which will be elaborated in this chapter. This framework moves away from "compartmentalized examinations of causal mechanisms such as regulatory capacity and sequencing in individual jurisdictions into *relational concepts* interacting across them" (Farrell and Newman 2014, 333). I define new concepts in service of a theory of causal mechanisms and argue that they are superior to notions of compliance, diffusion, complementarity, or two-level interactions commonly found in analyses of domestic–international interactions. This theory is most similar to the idea of interdependence, which suggests the need to focus on causal mechanisms across levels of analysis (Farrell and Newman 2014). It also resonates with an emerging literature on India's international political economy.[6] My framework has some affinity with the translational legal order (TLO) framework but is much more general and comprehensive than the TLO framework, which applies mostly to legal order and its effects.[7] In contrast, I develop a more inclusive theory that seeks to understand institutional change across diverse dimensions in a nationalist country over time. I contend that this theory can also be applied to other countries.

I start by outlining basic elements of a triangular theoretical framework, Global Design-in-Motion, in Section 2.1. Section 2.2 articulates a theory of causal mechanisms that may explain an unexpected and definite shift in domestic preferences and strategies toward global integration. I also build a set of propositions for empirically evaluating the impact of international

---

[5] I thank an anonymous reviewer for this formulation.

[6] Kapur (2010), Alamgir (2009), Ye (2014), this book, and Sengupta (2009) represent an emerging subfield of international political economy of India.

[7] The TLO framework is articulated in Halliday and Shaffer (2015).

organizations. In Section 2.3, I compare the basic concepts of this model with other similar concepts such as complementarity, transnational legal order, and two-level games, as well as plausible alternative explanations generated from theories of domestic politics.

2.1   A triangular framework to understand global–national interactions

This chapter builds an ambitious triangular theoretical framework, a Global Design-in-Motion, to explain the interaction of global organizations, like the WTO, with nationalist and self-reliant countries such as India. This framework has three components. First, I open up the black box of international organizations and analyze how global institutions actually work. I pay specific attention to the institutional design of GATT and WTO in a comparative frame. This leads me to posit how the internal institutional architecture of the global organization concerned with trade – the WTO – generates distinct mechanisms that form the core of the theory developed in this chapter and empirically analyzed in the rest of this book.[8] These mechanisms are (i) *transaction and implementation costs*, (ii) *sovereignty costs and private costs that are* (iii) *legally embodied (legal framing), and* (iv) *nonmarket rules, which may contribute to public information discovery about future markets and global regulations.*

Simultaneously, it is important to understand the effect of global causal mechanisms from the perspective of domestic actors who are faced with the task of implementing them in diverse contexts. While these mechanisms arise as a result of institutional features of the international order in question (in this case the global trading institution, the WTO), the effect of these catalytic mechanisms is to alter domestic actors' preferences, ideas, and institutions, mediating global strategies and internal debates on globalization. This framework thus pays specific attention to how these mechanisms are interpreted and transformed by states and nonstate actors within countries.

Globalization's agents include not only state actors but also the private sector, which shifted its preferences and strategies as it dealt with the new constraints of a rule-bound global order. Importantly, new actors, such as

[8] This resonates with the "institutional design" literature in international relations. These arguments urge attention to how institutions are designed rather than whether international institutions matter (Abbott and Snidal 1998; Downs and Rocke 1995; Krasner 1983; Koremenos, Lipson, and Snidal 2001; Koremenos 2005; Botcheva and Martin 2001; Martin 1999). For a focus on the role of institutions in American domestic politics, see Bailey, Goldstein, and Weingast (1997).

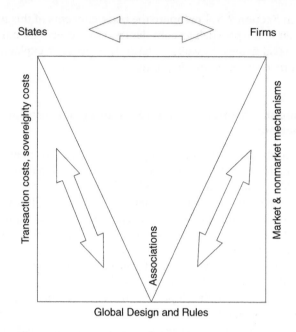

Figure 2.1 A triangular framework

legal or economic experts, as well as new business associations, have become more important to this story. So the *second element* of this framework is its *triangular nature* as it seeks to explain the effect of global order and markets, states, and diverse nonstate actors such as the private sector and experts and the relationship between them (see Figure 2.1). Contrary to conventional wisdom that a rule-based environment is giving way to a market-mediated one, I find *that globalization rests on the interplay between market and nonmarket mechanisms, such as price signals (market mediated), global standards and threats, public information, and learning (nonmarket mediated).* Chapter 7 shows how business strategies change as a result of public information about future markets, threats from competitors, and coercive mechanisms such as global standards and learning through cooperative means (global alliances and joint ventures, for example).

Importantly, global forces have not only led businesses to come closer to their national governments but also have transformed the nature of business representation in a more encompassing direction and facilitated greater public–private coordination. Paradoxically, new developmental state actors mediate the relationship between states, firms, and new global demands. Any study of globalization must understand these evolving changes through the lens of a triangular framework where the role of mediation between global forces and domestic agents and between states, expertise, and private sector has become more, not less, important. This triangular interactive process offers new insight into the literature on new developmental states (O'Riain 2004; Santos 2012; Trubek et al. 2013) as well as challenges the idea that globalization requires a withdrawal of the state.[9] So the revival of state capacity and the creation of new state capacities in shaping and mediating a country's response to global markets and regulations are an untold story that emerges in the pages of this book. This confirms the intuition that global rules, while causally significant, are *in motion*, being transformed by state-level interpretations and adaptations.

A *third* element of this framework is, then, its interactive, dynamic movement of change (through cooperative means as well as tensions and disputes) over time. The implementation or negotiation of global laws, rules, and commitments (Global Rules and Design – GRD) can no longer be understood without examining how the institutional design of international organizations is shaped, modified, and adapted in practice by states and actors within states. Thus, the global set of organizations must be analyzed in motion, giving rise to a unified framework: Global Design-in-Motion (GDM).

2.2   Causal mechanisms of impact

This section examines how the institutional design of global regimes looks if perceived from the perspective of states facing compliance and implementation. It draws upon diverse streams of literature – transaction cost theory, institutional design of international organizations, and business strategies literature – to analyze the workings of distinct mechanisms that play a large role in determining how states comply with and private sector players adjust to global rules of the game. Four mechanisms of impact, viewed from the perspective of domestic politics, emerge as crucial: *transaction costs, sovereignty and private costs, legal framing, information revelation, and transmission*. Nonmarket mechanisms are as crucial as market mechanisms. This chapter defines these mechanisms and outlines

---

[9] The classic developmental-state literature argued for state intervention to initiate industrialization in contexts where supply of capital was weak (Rosenstein-Rodan 1943). Another strand hoped to understand the emergence of miracle economies such as Japan, Taiwan, and South Korea by outlining the role of developmental states in pursing growth (Johnson 1982; Wade 2003) and creating nascent industrial sectors (Amsden 1989).

Table 2.1 *Diverse effects on states and private sector*

State Behavior	Private Sector Behavior
Sovereignty Costs Empirical Case: State Capacity Change (Chapter 3) **Legal Framing** Empirical Case: Patent Reform (Chapter 4) **Transaction Costs** Empirical Case: State Capacity Change (Chapter 3) **Pre-Commitment: Tying of One's Hands** Empirical Case: Textile Policies (Chapter 5)	**Market-Mediated Pressure** (Chapters 4, 6, and 7) • Prices • Market Competition • New Export Markets **Public Information about Future Markets and Regulations** (Chapter 7) • Conveyed through WTO Negotiations • Compliance with Standards • New Rules • Anti-Dumping Procedures **Threats from Trade Rivals (e.g., China)** (Chapters 4 and 7) • Market Threats Arising from Geopolitical Changes and Shifting Markets (Fall of FSU)

their logic and possible effects. Table 2.1 summarizes the theory of causal mechanisms elaborated in this chapter. The rest of this book shows how these mechanisms work in India's domestic context across sectors and over time.

2.2.1   High transaction costs and their effects

If one has to go beyond compliance and analyze the long-term effects of global organizations on state behavior, the varied costs of implementing and embedding global rules of the game in domestic contexts – transaction and implementing costs – must be analyzed. What are transaction costs? Building on the insights of neoinstitutional theory, I propose that we think of global regimes or global rules as incomplete contracts. An incomplete contract is one where one can never specify or anticipate every contingency or possibility, creating transaction costs (Hart 1995). Transactions costs can be of different types, including *information costs, contracting costs, agency costs, and enforcement costs.*[10]

[10] Coase (1937, 1960) defined transaction costs as the costs of using the price mechanism. For Williamson (1996, 1985, 1975), transaction costs arise as a result of frequency of transactions, uncertainty, bounded rationality, and maladaptation costs. Others define transaction costs as the costs of establishing and maintaining property rights (Allen 1991; Barzel 1997) or the resources expended to complete a mutually beneficial exchange (Dahlman 1980). Most economists define transaction costs to include identification, contracting, and enforcement costs, including the costs of identifying partners of an

Transaction costs may also be defined as the varied costs of implementing global agreements and commitments. They may arise out of a lack of information about preferences of target actors, or complexity of compliance commitments, and the technical nature of the agreements.

The dominant consensus in international relations is that international institutions facilitate compliance by *reducing* transaction costs and creating a more consistent and coherent legal environment (Goldstein 1998, 137; Keohane 1984; Martin 1992, 56–57). Yet, while global organizations reduce negotiating costs for state-to-state cooperation and for hegemons within the institution (Martin 1992, 55–58), their impact on domestic states might be the reverse, an effective *increase in transaction and implementation costs.* I posit that the WTO demands an onerous implementation regime and higher transaction costs in domestic contexts, thereby disturbing assumptions of unconditional, joint positive-sum impacts (Sinha 2007). In addition, specific features of the organization under study, such as "nestedness," adds to the complexity of global rules: a number of agreements within the WTO nest within each other and are interlinked to each other.[11] For example, during the Uruguay Round deliberations, TRIPS (Intellectual Property Rights) and MFA (Textile Agreement) negotiations were directly linked to each other. The principle of "single undertaking" further obligates each country to *all* the agreements, and the dispute-settlement procedure adds legal complexity to the process.[12] Domestic states, especially developing ones, are burdened with technical, financial, informational, and coordination costs necessary for compliance with most of the agreements, especially in such policy domains as intellectual property rights (TRIPS) and environmental agreements (e.g., Montreal Protocol). Chapter 3 offers a detailed analysis of how the complex nested structure of the WTO rules and practices creates onerous transaction and implementation costs for states like India.

2.2.2   *Effect of transaction costs on domestic actors*

It is important to clarify the logic of this causal mechanism from the perspective of domestic actors and explore how they travel across borders

[11] exchange, costs of writing an acceptable contract, and costs of enforcing agreed-upon bargains.

[11] Aggarwal (1998) suggests that nesting of specific agreements within the broader framework of principles helps to ensure a high degree of conformity and institutional strength of that international organization. Others who emphasize the importance of linkage within global trade rules are Croome (1995), Paemen and Bensch (1995), and Davis (2004).

[12] The Marrakesh statement stated: "The Representatives *agree* that the WTO agreement shall be open for acceptance as a *whole*, by signature or otherwise" (WTO 2002, 2). Also, Article II states: "the agreements and associated legal instruments included in Annexes 1, 2, and 3 . . . are integral parts of the agreement, binding on all members" (WTO 2002, 4).

and levels. These transaction and implementation costs of global regimes may create paradoxical or unintended effects on domestic actors and how they view global commitments. Counterintuitively, the WTO catalyzes state capacity even if its apparent goal is to free markets and spur trade among nations. However, the indirect and direct effects of the WTO agreements support the development of market-oriented reforms. Yet the WTO also indirectly shapes how states pursue economic reforms along a new developmental state model. Rather than the state weakening in light of market forces, the state has strengthened itself through diffusing expertise and working with private professionals and economic stake-holders. This dual movement – of embedding freer markets and unleashing stronger state capacity – is a paradox highlighted by this book. This paradox helps us understand why countries like India act strongly in global arenas as predicted but not fully explained by realist arguments.[13]

Why do these effects happen? For state actors, these higher transaction costs imply two somewhat different logics: (1) a *functional* logic and (2) a more political, *strategic* logic. Initially, governments don't know or have imperfect information about the functional requirements of compliance. The complexity and technical nature of WTO rules and agreements create a number of related effects. Compliance demands more information about the interests and preferences of groups and the potential costs of compliance. State officials don't know what their interests should be and seek greater consultations with societal groups and knowledge communities to figure out their interests. In response, interaction with knowledge communities and policy-expert linkages may be activated even in countries where no such previous tradition of consultation exists (India, for example) or where no resources exist (Bangladesh, for example). In addition, the technical character of the agreements demands research input and technical expertise. Interestingly, interactions with the WTO's dispute-settlement process may stimulate legalization within the domestic state (Shaffer, Nedumpara, and Sinha 2015; Shaffer 2013). Thus, a *functional* imperative is unleashed that can lead to an enhancement and reorganization of institutions to seek information about preferences as well as technical knowledge (which may be legal, economic, or sectoral specific) about compliance requirements. This, partly, stimulates

---

[13] Realism argues that states maximize their power in international affairs with an eye toward security and power. Nayar and Paul (2003) offer a realist account of India's search for "major power status." Yet, the predictions of the realist framework are not easy to assess. In 2010, India represented 8 percent of global power, measured in terms of hard power measures such as GDP, military expenditure, and technological developments, which is not very high (Kumar 2011). This book shows that India's rising power may be the result of domestic changes that need to be accounted for in any understanding of rising powers.

the significant institutional reform underway in many countries. Rules of the game of the WTO thus shape state choices but, strikingly, stimulate significant policy reform, changes within the state, and Changes in its relationship with different research communities. While the form and nature of such forums differ across countries, in keeping with domestic patterns and historical traditions, state actors explicitly justify the creation of these forums in terms of information needs related to their international commitments.

Equally important, as member states learn how the global regime works, they also begin to perceive a strategic advantage of *high* transaction costs as they begin to anticipate the effects of these costs. Thus they find that in subsequent international negotiations, domestic administrative reform allows them to defend and articulate their national interests better, leading to stronger negotiation and strategic capacity.[14] High transaction costs, therefore, enjoin a political, strategic logic apart from a functional one. Overall, I contend that the unintended effect of high transaction costs is to stimulate domestic state reform and institutional change in countries that are able to meet the financial cost of such enhancement.[15]

2.2.3   Sovereignty costs (on states) and private costs (on private sector)

In an incomplete contract framework, power or authority relations usually play little role. Yet, as Hart notes briefly (1995, 2–4), the incomplete character of a contract should make authority relations among the contracting parties key to completion and implementation of the contract. Hart hints that because many possibilities cannot be predicted *ex ante*, the one who has power matters in the *ex post* implementation of a contract or an agreement. He, however, does not elaborate on this intuition, and this idea was ignored by the neoinstitutional turn in political science. Analogously, from a realist perspective in international relations, the one who has power to enforce compliance of international agreements matters. Boundaries of sovereignty and power thus become important. *I define sovereignty costs as the extent of changes demanded by global rules in national laws and regulations, which may be defended by specific sanctions and punishment in case of noncompliance.*[16] In other words, *sovereignty costs are*

---

[14] This is, again, consistent with the realist framework.

[15] In countries without such state and research capacity, NGOs may provide technical and expert input, enhancing the expert communities in society. For example, in Bangladesh, a poor and least developing country, an NGO, the Center for Policy Dialogue, created a research department and began providing policy and research help to the government on WTO-related matters in the late 1990s.

[16] Sovereignty costs may refer to a loss of decision-making authority, displacement of the locus of authority to a level beyond a country's borders, or outcomes not preferred by the

constraints on the autonomy of a nation-state. Sovereignty costs are similar to the notion of "conditionality" used in the literature on international organizations and connotes the idea that global decisions are defended by international law and not imposed by a single power. They are, therefore, more legitimate. Dispute-settlement procedures are therefore crucial. Conditionality, in contrast, refers to a blanket element of external pressure. Analogously, *private costs are regulations, standards, or threats that affect private businesses and may change their market and nonmarket decisions.* Their effect is analyzed separately later in this chapter and also empirically assessed in Chapter 7.

International organizations vary widely in how much change in national laws they demand or expect. GATT, the General Agreement on Trade and Tariffs, was an agreement among contracting nation-states, while WTO, the World Trade Organization, is an organization with equal legal and institutional standing to the World Bank and the IMF.[17] While the legacies of GATT's origins and history do shape the WTO, the differences in organizational structure, rules of the game, and informal norms far outweigh similarities. The WTO has more power than the GATT or the World Bank or the IMF. The WTO's long arm into domestic sovereignty differentiates it from GATT and even the World Bank and the IMF. The principle of "single undertaking" further obligates each country to all the agreements. As one large developing country's trade minister said, "GATT disciplines have been concerned mainly with commercial policy instruments and have left the contracting parties free to design their domestic economic policies. The infinite complexity of the exercise of the last four years [Uruguay Round: 1990–1994] has been due to the fact that there has been *relentless and vigorous attempts to move the negotiations upstream into the realm of domestic economic policymaking.*"[18] This movement into domestic policy space was a result of two transformations in the scope of global trade negotiations: the *extension* of global trade rules from commodities to services and intellectual property and the *mandatory* nature of commitments made in the Uruguay Round. Trade rules affect not only traditional goods but

---

population of a sovereign state. See Abbott and Snidal (2000a, 436–437) for a definition of sovereignty costs.

[17] GATT was signed in 1947; the WTO came into being on January 1, 1995 as the outcome of the Uruguay Round of trade negotiations. Finlayson, Zacher, and Krasner (1983, 274) note: "The GATT, however, was never intended to be the basis of postwar international trade order and was not even conceived of as an international organization." Also see Dam (1970), Jackson (1969), and Krasner (1983) for similar conclusions.

[18] Statement of Dr. Subramanian Swamy, union minister of commerce, law and justice, speaking to the Plenary Ministerial Session of the Uruguay Round in 1994.

also new intangible goods, services, and knowledge and information goods. This meant that the Uruguay Round and the resulting WTO reached out to other organizations – WIPO (World Intellectual Property Organization) and ILO (International Labour Organization) – and took over authority and jurisdiction over their policy domains. Yet, counterintuitively, this makes the negotiating dynamic between the international regime and domestic actors even more salient and unpredictable as domestic actors face *higher* domestic trade-offs in implementing its rules and commitments. High *sovereignty costs* may, under some conditions, catalyze stronger domestic responses than is necessary with lower sovereignty costs.

Combined with its encompassing character, the WTO is unique in its monitoring, enforcement, and sanctioning capacity. Rather than coercion, the WTO uses nondiscretionary rules, legal jurisdiction, and norm diffusion to achieve compliance; this has been referred to as "legal framing" (Davis 2004). Key instruments aid the organization to achieve these goals: contractual obligations, regular and frequent ministerial-level meetings,[19] trade policy monitoring,[20] an elaborate and effective dispute-settlement mechanism,[21] training, and, if all else fails, multilaterally authorized trade sanctions. These instruments ensure greater compliance with WTO agreements because governments and interest groups are able to delay but not deny domestic legal, policy, and institutional changes. Even in closed and resistant economies, trade liberalization and global integration proceed more expeditiously than under GATT or bilateral pressure or under the aegis of the World Bank and the IMF. As an illustration, the Trade Policy Review Mechanism ensures that WTO members adhere to rules, disciplines, and commitments made under the WTO agreements. While the purpose is transparency, and not enforcement, it has the effect of ensuring compliance. Thus, both directly and indirectly, WTO imposes high sovereignty costs on states and actors within states. Global organizations like the WTO are trade organizations and therefore affect the private sector's global reach and strategies, a form of sovereignty cost for private firms. How may we think about the effect of global rules of the game on global markets and private actors?

---

[19] Under GATT, high-level meetings were few and far between; the WTO regulations mandate meetings to be held every two years with additional meetings – what are called mini-ministerial meetings – in the interim. This regularity of ministerial-level meetings gives WTO deliberations a salience rare among international organizations.
[20] WTO (2002), Annex 3, pp. 380–382.   [21] WTO (2002), Annex 2, pp. 354–379.

2.2.4   *Private costs and regulation: coercion and constraining effect on markets and firms*

Globalization of markets rests upon global rules of the game. WTO, for example, helps countries and companies trade with each other by ensuring nondiscrimination among trade partners and by regulating protectionist policies that hinder exchange across borders. Global rules, it is believed, support the development of market-based exchange between companies and states across borders and remove barriers to trade. In keeping with this conventional belief, scholarship largely focuses on what may be called "contract-enforcement institutions"[22] – market mediated – that help the workings of global markets and contracts. Yet, global trade and flows also require institutions that constrain and coerce private actors to follow global standards in service of global public goods, such as the environment or banning child labor, or market goods, such as protecting geographic indications or preventing dumping. Such global rules and standards reach across borders and affect traders and businesses seeking to export their goods, who must comply with these standards as a precondition for exporting or setting up new production facilities across the world. Such standards, as well as anti-dumping regulations, are constraining institutions that affect more and more businesses and private actors. Other constraining rules (ISO standards, for example) aid in the formation of new markets by ensuring transparent signaling of quality to traders across borders. These coercive and constraining institutions serve to concentrate threats for businesses, conveying an urgent sense of new regulatory demands not conveyed by price signals. Such constraints may also create the infrastructure of markets (rules of the game) and protection of global public goods (such as protection of child labor or environmental protections). We can no longer understand globalization of markets or global business strategies without paying attention to what I call the coercive and constraining effect of global rules. The co-evolution of markets and non-market-constraining institutions in the field of global trade must be analyzed much more carefully than before. This resonates well with the literature on "private regulation of the global economy" (Buthe and Mattli 2011). As Buthe and Mattli note about standards in the realm of financial markets, "Financial reporting standards specify how to calculate assets, liabilities, profits and losses – and which particular types of transactions and events to disclose – in a firm's financial statements to create accurate and easily comparable measures of its financial position. The importance of these standards runs much deeper. Through

---

the incentives they create, financial reporting standards shape research and development, executive compensation and corporate governance, they affect all sectors of the economy and are central to the stability of a country's financial system" (Buthe and Mattli 2011, 1). In Chapter 7, I demonstrate the effect of such nonmarket mechanisms – economic threats and sanctions – in creating new markets and new regulatory rules for businesses and traders.

2.2.5   Legal framing

While the WTO trade regime constrains a nation's sovereignty, it does so through the rule of law, which is of common knowledge to all concerned. International institutions vary in their extent of legalization that allows a rule-and-law-bound adjudication of disputes and third-party enforcement (Abbott et al. 2000b). GATT/WTO regimes, as an illustration, are more legalistic than the World Bank or the IMF in that they allow a quasi-judicial procedure and dispute-settlement mechanisms that are formal and independent.[23] GATT established a quasi-judicial process of settling disputes between parties in which a panel of three neutral diplomats hears formal legal arguments.[24] The 1989 reforms of the GATT and the establishment of WTO in 1995 certainly increased compliance and ensured policy changes even without enforcement power (Busch and Reinhardt 2002; Davis 2004; Hudec 1993), apart from changing the nature of the debate and shaping the arguments of the trade disputes.[25] Yet, Goldstein and Martin (2001) caution that legal agreements may also have domestic costs, when domestic groups hurt by the agreements oppose the implementation of the agreement. According to them, legal agreements are more rigid, and this lack of flexibility can raise the stakes of compliance under the right domestic circumstance.

It is clear that the legal structure of international agreements interacts with domestic structures and traditions. This raises a question of mechanism of influence: what are the possible ways in which legalization works in

---

[23] The World Bank has developed formalized procedures for environmental impact assessment, treatment of indigenous people, and project evaluation, which are then incorporated in loan documents and become legally binding on loan recipients and are enforced by the World Bank's inspection panel. Yet this procedure, while legalistic, does not require dispute settlement or third-party enforcement. As Abbott et al. note, the World Bank is characterized by low levels of obligation and precision and high levels of delegation to national governments rather than to a neutral or an independent body (2000b, 22).

[24] See Jackson (1969) for legal history of GATT and Jackson (2000) for a more up-to-date analysis of WTO.

[25] Burley and Mattli's (1993) analysis of the European Court of Justice shows how the court proceedings affect what countries can argue and the outcomes of the negotiations.

a domestic context? Information, transparency, and legitimacy might be the causal mechanisms through which legal framing changes states, reformers, and domestic opposition toward compliance. Legal processes may reveal a lot of information about the nature of markets or a rival's preferences, forcing actors to think about their own interests. Moreover, the process of defending one's position against challenges – transparency – also clarifies interests and reduces uncertainty about winners and losers.

Legal injunctions create certain patterned domestic effects; reputation costs prevent cheating and noncompliance. Legal agreements raise the cost of noncompliance; even the most intransigent country has to think twice about flouting legal decisions and compliance pressures. Bilateral sanctions and pressures enable domestic actors to mobilize domestic protests against complying. It is much harder to do so with multilateral legal agreements and judgments. India, for example, has very rarely bowed to US pressure yet has complied with the WTO dispute-settlement rulings without any murmur or domestic protest. As one senior negotiator said, "India's domestic traditions are extremely self-reliant and it has always resisted international pressure, but at the same time, it wants to be seen as a responsible actor in international affairs. Denying or refusing to comply with a legal international obligation would go against how India sees itself in the international context."[26] Legal agreements also enhance the credibility of compliance and allow domestic actors to credibly tie their hands against domestic opposition. Thus, their power for domestic persuasion is high as a result of their reciprocal and credible character. The "legitimacy conferred by legal framing persuades leaders and their domestic audience" that compliance may be necessary (Davis 2004, 53).

However, the nature of domestic politics is likely to determine the importance given to legal pressures and the specific ways in which different mechanisms – information, reputation, and persuasion – work in some contexts but not in others. Thus, an empirical analysis of how the legal structure of international agreements is received in specific countries may be useful to confirm (or disconfirm) as well as elaborate on the working of different mechanisms. An analysis of India's domestic responses to bilateral pressure (US pressure on TRIPS, for example) versus the WTO provides an interesting test of some of the competing arguments and allows me to flesh out the working of how legal framing works in a country that has traditionally resisted any external pressure (see Chapters 3 and 4). Table 2.2 summarizes these expectations.

[26] Author's interview with a senior negotiator, August 30, 2005, Washington, DC.

Table 2.2 *Design of global trade institutions and their effects on domestic states*

Institutional Rules	GATT	Effect on Domestic Variables	WTO	Effect on Domestic Variables
Sovereignty Costs and Private Costs	**Low**	**Minimal**	**High**	**Extensive and varied**
(1) Scope of issues	Limited	No impact on the policy process	Expansive	Increased interaction and coordination within the state and with societal actors
(2) Membership	Limited	Being outside the system is not as consequential	Large and growing	Compliance pressures increase; even strongly nationalist countries are willing to comply; private sector is forced to comply
(3) Compliance	Voluntary	Low policy volumes and low visibility to the trade policy process	Mandatory	Increase in policy and institutional output intensity
(4) Monitoring	No	No institutional innovation	Yes	Institutional innovation and creation
(5) Strong threats	Minimal	Limited	High and concentrated	Mobilization of countermeasures such as anti-dumping, technological upgradation
Legal framing	**Medium**	**Minimal**	**High**	**Enhancement of legal capacity**
Dispute-settlement System	Somewhat but no court-like system	Not much legalization observed in countries	Strongly legalistic	Legal expertise included; learning over time; decline of opposition

Table 2.2 (*cont.*)

Institutional Rules	GATT	Effect on Domestic Variables	WTO	Effect on Domestic Variables
Transaction costs	**Low**	**No institutional development**	**High**	**Internal state "reform"**
(1) Complexity	Simple	No formalization and institutionalization needed	Complex	Need for institutionalized process and coordination
(2) Nested agreements	None	No need for inter-agency interactions	Many such agreements	Coordination across state agencies
(3) Technical	Somewhat	No experts involved	Highly technical	Research networks activated; economic, legal capacity building

2.2.6   Testing the role of transaction costs, sovereignty costs, and legal framing

How can we test some of these conclusions? Did the process of WTO implementation change the trade policy process and the domestic institutional structure and capacity in India, a country known for its insular policy process (Hurrell and Narlikar 2006; Narayan 2005; Sen 2003; Wade 1985)? How may we test the intuitions generated by an analysis of transaction costs and sovereignty costs? This proposition can be easily tested as this nestedness was enhanced with the formation of the WTO regime in the 1995. In contrast, the GATT was a one-dimensional body, without a high degree of complex nestedness. I document the change in state capacity (measured in terms of new institutions, involvement of expertise, and funding) from the GATT to the WTO regime in India (see Chapter 3). I seek evidence about Propositions 1 and 2 for India in Chapter 3.

Proposition 1: Some international institutions can increase transaction costs for states, stimulating significant enhancement of technical and expert capacity within the domestic state.
Proposition 1a: This enhancement of cognitive and technical capacity increases negotiating capacity.
Proposition 2: Repeated interactions and the demonstration of actions by other states in a multilateral environment can lead to learning and enhancement of capacity by emulation. The specific negotiation structure of the WTO system,

where delegates meet together in various councils and meetings, can enhance this process of learning.

A natural corollary emerges as salient. An international regime can *reinforce or reduce* intrastate bureaucratic politics shaped by the logic of appropriateness of its rules and domestic fit.[27] Some global institutions seek direct functional interactions and fit with functional departments within domestic states. In such cases (for example, IMF–Ministry of Finance, Montreal Protocol–Ministry of Environment, and WHO–Ministry of Health), individual departments may become stronger and develop direct links with the relevant international organization. For example, the ministries of finance or the treasury departments in diverse countries are strengthened as a result of implementing IMF programs and adjustment schedules. Even more interestingly, various state officials in that ministry may come to adopt ideas and policy preferences akin to the global regime in question. For example, the Ministry of Finance officials in India are much more pro-liberalization than similarly placed officials in other ministries. Such linkages also allow that ministry to pursue its independent interest in isolation from other departments. Thus, the Ministry of Finance in India pursues its own agenda favoring liberalization. They use the WTO's requirements to urge and force compliance from other departments within the government.[28]

How would an international regime with such interlinked rules of the game affect internal intrastate interactions? First, a regime's specific procedures and processes may enhance the need to bargain, coordinate, and build consensus across departments. Such is the case with negotiations under the various WTO rounds. Second, the relative domestic power of the relevant department will shape but may also be affected by the negotiation imperatives. In many countries, one department or ministry gains in power and prestige as a result of the demands of coordination and overlapping agreements. Simultaneously, formal and informal mechanisms of consultation across bureaucratic departments are created or activated in response to, and in anticipation of, WTO rounds and negotiations. For example, in Brazil, the Ministry of External Affairs became more important in trade negotiations as a result of the preexisting power of the ministry but also because negotiation in the Doha Round required the evolution of consistent and comprehensive positions across trade, agriculture, and foreign and other line ministries. Similarly, in

---

[27] See March and Olsen (1998) for elaboration of two logics: the logic of appropriateness and the logic of consequences.

[28] In Chapter 3, I outline how, in 1997, the Ministry of Finance undermined the Ministry of Commerce's position in a dispute with WTO over quantitative restrictions.

India, the Ministry of Commerce was designated the "nodal ministry" for WTO bargaining and negotiations, displacing both the Ministry of External Affairs and the Ministry of Finance. Simultaneously, the Ministry of Commerce sought to consult with numerous ministries while evolving its negotiation strategies enhancing the process of decision making by bargaining and compromise. Thus, the specific structure of the international governance regime may unleash intrabureaucratic politics in a distinct way. And the tasks associated with participating in and complying with international institutions can shape the *relative power* and prestige of some domestic state actors, magnifying bureaucratic politics.

In this analysis, though, we cannot assume away the regime type or the extent of fragmented structure. Thus, in a presidential system, the power of the president vis-à-vis the Congress, or that of the United States Trade Representative (USTR) vis-à-vis the Department of Commerce, may increase. Also, global rules and structures may either *reinforce or weaken* the veto points and enhance interdepartmental bargaining; conflict and compromise catalyze changes in the shape of intrastate bureaucratic politics. In a parliamentary system, one would expect an increase in the power of the relevant ministry, despite a collective responsibility ethos in a cabinet system. Simultaneously, the WTO's complex nestedness also demands greater coordination across state agencies than ever before. Thus, the formal and informal mechanisms of interagency interaction are likely to be activated in both presidential and parliamentary systems.

Proposition 3: The state agency responsible for trade policy is likely to see an increase in its power. New agencies may be created to give greater autonomy and expertise to negotiators. The nested structure of the international institution, and the extent to which it demands cross-issue interactions, will demand greater coordination across state agencies within the state.

As outlined by the GDM [Global Design-in-Motion] framework, the effects of global rules of the game on private actors are even more salient and interesting. What mechanisms of influence affect private parties and actors?

2.2.7   Effect of global nonmarket mechanisms on the private sector

So what are the plausible effects of international institutions on domestic cleavages and private sector actors? Competing theories – factor of production or sector specific – predict alternative hypotheses. In *Commerce and Coalitions*, Rogowski (1989), building and extending the Stopler-Samuelson approach, stressed that international price movements affect the owners of factors of production and thus mobilize broad class groupings such as labor, managers, and farmers. In contrast, another body of research argued that more specific cleavages, those around specific industry sectors (Frieden 1991b; Lipson and Krasner 1983; Gourevitch 1986; McGillivray 2004) or firms (Milner 1988), may be more relevant. While an extensive body of research has attempted to assess these competing accounts, a relevant question is how international institutions organized to regulate international trade – GATT or WTO – affect mobilization on factorial or sectoral lines. I suggest that in addition to tendencies created by the structural map of a relevant economy, the global regime may shape the organization of political alignments.[29] Thus, societal interest groups and emerging alignments may *mirror* the rules of the game of the global regime. GATT was essentially an agreement to reduce tariffs across sectoral lines and should therefore encourage mobilization along tariff lines or industry-specific cleavages. WTO, with its attempt to bring together a number of issue areas into one agreement, TRIPS, for example – should encourage some coalition building across the diverse sectors under TRIPS. Similarly, the GATS (services) agreement should encourage the mobilization of all service industries.

Yet, simultaneously, collective action conflict *within sectors* could change. The WTO, by enhancing export markets for some groups at the cost of others, could create divisions within the previously unified sectors. Thus, for example, India's pharmaceutical industry was, until recently, organized according to ownership, with one association representing indigenous firms (IDMA) and another representing foreign MNCs (OPPI). Yet, the TRIPS agreement created fissures within the Indian sector, with the externally oriented Indian sector seeking a separate organization and lobbying initiatives. Thus, the pharmaceutical sector in India became more fragmented with the onset of WTO through the creation of new exporting interests (see Chapter 4). Thus, the structure of international rules will have a direct impact on the type of cleavages and political mobilization around those cleavages. Within industry groups, new fissures (cleavages), coalitions, and interest groups may be created and empowered as a result of new global opportunities. Trade regimes affect trade movements more than decentralized price signals. Thus, two plausible propositions worth examining might be

---

[29] See Young and Levy (1999, 26), who suggest that "regimes affect behavior by creating new constituencies or shifting the balance among factions, or subgroups vying for influence within individual states or other actors." Farrell and Newman also observe that it is important to assess "how interdependence transforms the distribution of domestic interests and the institutions of the system's units" (2014, 333).

Proposition 4: International trade agreements stimulate sectoral mobilization rather than class mobilization.
Proposition 5: Some agreements may create new exporting and global elements within the domestic industry, catalyzing differentiation within sectoral groups.

It is to be expected that internationalization may embolden the tradable sector[30] in the domestic political economy. Yet, we don't know enough about the aggregation of that emergent power into policy. Thus, the impact of international institutions requires a specific fine-grained analysis that looks not only at the economic power of domestic actors but also at how the relevant international institution may affect the possibilities for political influence and political access of different economic actors.

Proposition 6: Global trade regime could increase the power of the export-oriented, tradable sector of the economy and make the views and arguments of organized and transnational actors more visible and powerful in the policy process. In this way, WTO compliance may also disrupt earlier patterns of interest mobilization within the domestic sector.

I also show that global institutions can become an object of strategic choice by domestic actors. In doing so, the interaction of global and national levels changes the *collective action* inside a country, giving birth to new coalitions that come closer to the state (Chapters 5 and 6). Table 2.3 summarizes these conclusion and effects. Kohli (2007) argues that the Indian state became pro-business without telling us why. I show that the deeper sources for this change stem from a combination of global and domestic changes that happened in the late 1990s and 2000s. In many contexts, new business associations became more powerful, gained access to the state, and lobbied in more encompassing ways (textile and pharmaceutical). In turn, the private sector demanded both greater support from the state and trade liberalization and mobilized differently vis-à-vis the national state and global agreements. These varied effects work through market-mediated routes but also through nonmarket mechanisms of public information discovery and transmission. In the next section, I explore the role of information discovery, especially about future markets.

2.2.8   The role of public information within global markets

Private sector preferences change in reaction to global changes; very few industry actors were in favor of global integration before it happened. Firms and private industry have very short-term interests and do not always know

---

[30] A tradable sector refers to a segment of an industry where exports or imports constitute a significant portion of its production profile.

Table 2.3 *Global trade institutions and their effects on the private sector*

Mechanisms	GATT	Effect on Domestic Variables	WTO	Effect on Domestic Variables
Collective action effects	**Moderate effects**	**Fragmentation of collective action**	**Changes the logic of collective action**	**Significant**
Creation of winners and new interest groups	Minimal	Moderate	Significant	Export-oriented sectors created across many sectors
Mobilization	Interest group defined by tariffs and quotas	Divided mobilization	Enhanced with greater threats	Strong and in a encompassing direction
Differentiation within sectors	Minimal	Low	High	Strong
Business representation	Narrow and specialized or "distributional coalitions" (Olson 1982)[a]	Particularistic and narrow	Widespread and "encompassing"[a]	Movement away from distributional coalitions to encompassing ones
Public information	**Medium**	**No institutional development**	**High**	**Strong**
Extent of Information revealed	Limited	Negligible	High	Strong
Information about new markets and opportunities	Negotiations limited to commodities	Some	New topics like IP, services, etc.	Varied and high
Increased knowledge about threats and competitors	Some but many developing countries had exceptions and escape clauses	Limited	Medium	Strong

[a] Olson (1982) proposed the concept of narrow, "distributional" associations *vs.* encompassing associations to articulate the idea that a business organization must reflect the interests of all or most of its members rather than the narrow segment or faction. He also argues that an encompassing business association must reflect sectoral diversity and represent a wide variety of groups from the larger society.

what they want or what is in their material interest, even assuming full knowledge of the various market possibilities. The short-time horizon of their strategic contexts arises both because they operate for profit and because they lack the information necessary for long-term planning and anticipating future market trends. Another problem is more serious: industry actors are unable to foresee how the changing market and regulatory conditions affect their interests. This accounts for the fact that many industry actors were unaware of the changes unleashed by the Uruguay Round in the mid-1980s.[31] Globalization produces important dilemmas in an already difficult environment by creating the need to keep track of developments outside of the border – a capability many businesses may lack. Second, and more important, the usual source of information for businesses are markets and price signals, which give some clues about market trends and how to change their inventories. Yet, these price signals are decentralized and fragmented and not able to discover future market trends. Therefore, many business actors rely on meetings and networks, market research, conferences, and exhibitions as well as trade journals to acquire information about technological developments, market trends, and competition. Interestingly, contacts and interactions with government serve a similar purpose, and many such interactions are as much about "defining preferences as they are about influencing the stances defended by negotiators" (Woll 2008, xii).

Interestingly, I found that the WTO deliberations and meetings, as well as the consultation process with private sector initiated by the government of India in 1999, served an important purpose in revealing information about future markets and future global rules (such as global standards and sanctions) that would shape the nature of competition in the following ten to fifteen years. In doing so, the industry actors were made aware of their preferences in a future world. Many firms realized that they needed to enhance their monitoring and compliance mechanisms to ensure consistency with global norms. The WTO structure – regular ministerial meetings, ongoing council meetings in Geneva, trade monitoring, and review meetings – embodied a concentrated and centralized arena of information production, revelation, and transmission to government actors and indirectly to the business actors, which were forced to think about new market strategies as well as ways of influencing the emerging rules of the game. Crucially, most of this information about the future markets was concentrated and organized by the WTO's secretariat and the respective governments. In my argument, this structure carried new and different sorts of information in a very centralized and concentrated ways and created new

---

[31] Numerous interviews with industry actors and government officials confirmed this fact.

interests and powerful incentives for firms to reorient their business plans. Preferences were created and revealed in the process of negotiating and learning about the global rules of the game. The impact of an international organization, like the WTO, on private interests reveals the role of learning and unveiling new information about future markets as well as global sanctions and threats through discussions and debates during the WTO negotiating process. Global market prices are blunt instruments for information gathering. Firms rely on non-market-mediated mechanisms – what I call rule-mediated mechanisms – to make decisions about technology upgrades or increasing capacity. This information is conveyed through government channels and WTO-mediated disputes rather than prices. Public information emerges as more salient than market-mediated price information during such periods of crises or transition in the global economy. Table 2.3 outlines how information discovery and transmission worked across GATT versus WTO.

Proposition 7: Global organizations create new markets. Negotiations and discussions within global bodies can lead to information discovery about future markets and new regulations that may constrain markets and private actors. The role of public information is vital in ensuring private sector participation in newly emerging global markets.

2.3   Global Design-in-Motion framework – its alternatives

We need more research on the *mechanisms* through which international regimes shape domestic policy as well as the interests and politics around trade. International relations (IR) scholars mostly focus on broad variables, such as global cooperation or the level of trade across nations. They tend to lack empirically rigorous studies of the precise links between global trade interdependence and a state's changing level of economic openness (Frieden and Martin 2002). This section outlines alternative explanations drawn from comparative politics and international relations literatures.

2.3.1   Domestic politics arguments: pressure-group trade politics

Research on trade policy focuses on "pressure-group politics" (Kindleberger 1951) and how "the expansion of trade affects domestic cleavages" (Rogowski 1989).[32] The main divide has been between so-called factorial (referring to factors of production like land, labor, and

---

[32] Schattschneider (1935) was an early proponent of this view, and this approach has spawned an immense literature. I cite a few selective works: Rogowski (1989), Frieden (1991a, 1991b), Milner (1988), Gilligan (1997), Grossman and Helpman (2001), and (Milner 2002).

capital) versus sectoral theories of preferences. Factorial theories rely on the Stopler-Samuelson theorem (1941), which shows that when factors of production, such as labor and capital, can move freely among sectors, a change from free trade to protection will raise the income of factors that are relatively scarce in a country and lower the income of relatively abundant factors. Thus, scarce factors will support protection, whereas abundant ones will oppose it. Rogowski (1989) builds the Stopler-Samuelson theorem into an innovative argument claiming that changing exposure to trade sets off either increasing class conflict or urban rural conflict according to the factor distributions of different countries (labor-intensive vs capital-intensive countries, for example). In contrast, sectoral and firm-based theories of trade preferences follow from the Ricardo-Viner model of trade, also called the "specific-factors model", in which, because at least one factor is immobile, all factors attached to import-competing sectors lose from trade liberalization, while those in export-oriented sectors gain. Conflict over trade policy thus pits labor, capital, and landowners in sectors besieged by imports against those who export their production.

Scholarship on India seems to agree with class-based models of mobilization. Achin Vanaik suggest that the agrarian bourgeoisie in India has been replaced by "big capital, Indian and Foreign, [which] is increasingly powerful" (2011, 15). Vanaik further notes that "urban-based Indian capital and export-oriented sections of the agrarian bourgeoisie now see no alternative to working with and alongside foreign capital by going in for mergers and joint ventures, subcontracting arrangements, or directly competing against foreign capital in the belief that expanding market will enable it to secure its own market shares" (Vanaik 2011, 232–233). As Corbridge et al. suggest, "as these capitalists have become more mobile and transnationalised, India and its ruling elites have been brought closer to the US" (2011, 15). Chatterjee argues that the balance of class equilibrium analyzed by Bardhan has been replaced by an ascendance in the power of the capitalist class (Chatterjee 2011). Despite the plausibility of these theoretical expectations, no direct evidence about the preference of these mobile capitalists and their strategies toward the global economy is presented by the existing accounts. We are provided no information on this class's preferences and views regarding globalization in Chatterjee's account. Should this emerging powerful class pursue nationalist policies or support an open economy? Interests, economic power, and preferences, by themselves, cannot change trade policy; we need a theory of how these interests gain political access and influence in a changing context (Milner 1988). The transition from cleavages and interests to outcomes and influence needs some unpacking and specification. Rogowski also does not offer a detailed account of how powerful classes gain power and affect policy change in the domestic context. The Indian scholarship fails to address or even raise questions such as Why did the Indian capitalist class adopt mergers and joint ventures despite low-level capabilities and skills? What were the sources of these shifts in preferences?

This book addresses these questions directly, providing new evidence on the rise of a global capitalist class from India. My argument does not deny the importance of domestic interests and their preferences about openness but argues that material interests in favor of trade or protectionism are simply not enough. To have an effect, interests need catalysts, mobilizing entrepreneurs, organizations, and information. International institutions and their specific rules of the game can serve as an important catalyst and signal for both private sector and state actors. International price signals, while important, are often lost and fragmented. Given these dynamics, international institutions may serve to convey market signals in a concentrated and speedy manner and to stimulate domestic mobilization. It may be safe to posit, given the power of vested interest groups in the domestic political economy, that in the absence of specific international institutions, they would have slowed external integration. Thus, the effect of changes in international prices, a variable of interest to the Frieden and Rogowski framework (1996), is mediated by the specific rules of the game governing international trade. What are the mechanisms of this impact? I outline the effect of three important global mechanisms on societal interests: perception of threats and regulatory constraints (private costs), public information about new markets and new opportunities, and through the nesting of interests, an impact on coalition building or fragmentation of alliances (see Table 2.3).

2.3.2   Domestic politics arguments: institutions

Explanations that stress domestic cleavages or interest groups may not be wrong but often are *insufficient* to explain how interests are mobilized, gain power, and are aggregated. Domestic institutions mediate the mobilization and interests and cleavages. Legislatures, for example, are more sensitive to large numbers of losers, rendering their demands harder to resist.[33] Analogously, delegating the control of trade policy into the hands of the executive has coincided with greater liberalization in the United States as well as many developing countries.[34] Electoral rules of the game

---

[33] Many have argued that protectionist policies in the United States can be explained by the fact that the US Congress controlled trade policy exclusively before 1934 (Baldwin 1976; Destler 1995; Goldstein 1993).

[34] The Reciprocal Trade Act of 1934 did so for the United States. Also see Haggard and Webb (1994) for the importance of delegating trade policies to those agencies that are

also shape the aggregation of interests. Rogowski (1987) argued that countries with large electoral districts and proportional representation (PR) systems insulate policymakers from protectionist pressures.[35] Other institutional explanations look to the structure of the government and the party systems, that is, the extent of partisan conflict. Lohmann and O'Halloran (1994) and O'Halloran (1994) argue that in a divided government – when one party controls the legislature and the other controls the executive branch – protectionism is likely to be higher.[36] Thus, "political systems with weak executives, and fragmented party systems, divided government and decentralized political structures [respond] poorly to crises" (Haggard and Kaufman 1995, 378) and find it difficult to initiate economic reforms, including trade liberalization. While most of the institutional literature sees fragmented systems to be negative for reform programs, Jenkins (1999) and Nooruddin (2011) argue the opposite. Jenkins offers a powerful explanation for the reforms of 1991, arguing that when national elites faced obstruction or delay, reforms could continue due to the India's federal institutions, which "[have] been an important ingredient in helping to make India's economic reform programmed politically sustainable – that is, in reducing the pressure on political decision-makers in the central government to abandon reform" (Jenkins 1999, 127–128). This happened by creating multiple sources of reform and reducing the power of resisting groups to block programs (Jenkins 1999, 128–143; 2003). Domestic institutional explanations thus provide a very important piece of the puzzle by showing us how societal interests succeed or fail in getting what they want (Bailey, Goldstein, and Weinagst 1997). In this way, institutional explanations serve as intermediate variables, translating preferences into actual outcomes. Different institutions do so differently, leading to variation in policies (Verdier 1994).

Explanations that stress the domestic balance of interest groups or domestic institutions are not wrong but cannot explain the extent, and timing, of the change witnessed in India in the 1990s. In terms of domestic institutions, India's constitution gives trade policymaking authority to the executive and the cabinet; this structure has *not* undergone a massive change for the period under consideration (1990s). Trade policy is still considered to be the domain of bureaucracy and the political executive. Yet, with the onset of weak, minority, and coalition governments in the

insulated from "routine bureaucratic processes, from legislative and interest group pressures and even from executive pressure" (1994, 13).

[35] Although Busch and Mansfield (1995) find that the opposite is the case: that is, larger districts and a PR system (that is, insulation) lead to more protection. Also see Rogowski (1999).

[36] Also see Milner and Rosendorf (1996) and Milner (1997).

1990s, one should expect a *rise* in protectionist sentiment and a turn inward. India in the 1990s seems to fit the description of Haggard and Kaufman of a situation where policy change should *not* happen (Haggard and Kaufman 1995, 378). In 1991, India was ruled by a minority government that depended on opposition parties for support, indeed for survival. Since 1996, three elections produced hung parliaments and coalitions. Clearly, the institutionalist explanation does not explain the direction (toward openness), nature (greater trade liberalization), and timing of trade policy changes evident in late 1990s India.

on 1990s example

2.3.3   *International organizations literature*

The literature on international organizations (IOs) contributes the most to the concerns of this book by outlining varied theoretical claims about how global institutions coerce, constrain, and change state behavior defined as compliance,[37] as well as how they transform preferences, interests, and relative power balances.[38] Recent scholarship analyzes how global institutions persuade and socialize,[39] facilitate legal changes,[40] and catalyze new capacities.[41] Many others suggest that developing countries are affected differently by international organizations and face adverse situations in implementing agreements.[42] Despite this extensive literature, we don't know enough about how specific countries implement agreements or how global rules change state behavior going beyond legal compliance. This IO literature focuses on specific mechanisms but less so on specific countries or changes in a country over time. This book highlights important mechanisms through which global trade integration and institutions shaped the domestic politics of trade in India but also how new alliances and groups become joint participants in support of a pro-export trade policy and a very different domestic political economy. The Global Design-in-Motion framework resonates with recent literature in international relations and the study of global institutions. In this

---

[37] Some of these mechanisms are uncertainty, flexibility, and durability of agreements. See Pevehouse (2002), Hafner-Burton (2009), Mansfield and Pevehouse (2008), and Koremenos (2005).

[38] Goldstein (1998).

[39] Johnston (2001), Kelley (2004), Acharya (2004), Greenhill (2010).

[40] Steinberg (2002), Zangl (2008), Goldstein et al.

[41] Sinha (2007); Shaffer, Sanchez, and Rosenberg (2008); Chayes and Chayes (1995); Kim (2008); Shaffer (2005).

[42] Busch and Reinhardt (2002); Shaffer (2003, 2005, 2006, 2009); and Kim (2008). Also see Barnett and Finnemore, who highlight the pathological effects of international organizations (1999).

section, I compare the concepts and mechanisms of this framework with similar ideas such as two-level games, complementarity, and translational legal order.

2.3.4   Two-level games framework

An analysis of domestic–international interactions must acknowledge the basic game theory concept that actors sit at different tables and are engaged in two-level games (Putnam 1988; Schelling 1981; Tsebelis 1990). Putnam argues that the final terms each negotiator agrees to must not only be acceptable to his international counterpart but also must fall within his domestic win set, represented by domestic support and domestic coalitions. Despite a claim to focus on *both* international and domestic levels simultaneously, for Putnam, domestic politics determines "the degree to which the strategies of international negotiators are successful in shifting their boundaries" (Schoppa 1997, 29).[43] This book takes these criticisms seriously and explores the interaction of India and the WTO both at the international and the domestic levels. I argue that in the two-level framework, the domestic win set is static and does not change over time. International negotiations reflect the changed domestic balance of forces, but the analysis does not offer clues about how the win set (or balance of forces) may change over time, which should be reflected in different negotiating strategies.

The literature on trade offers some clues. We know that international economic movements have serious domestic impacts on domestic cleavages of a country (Frieden 1999; Rogowski 1999). But we don't know enough about the impact of international organizations on trade policy and the logic of trade reform in a country.[44] For example, Frieden and Martin (2002) note that existing empirical work on international economic institutions is limited and that the "scope for careful empirical work" that takes the insights of institutionalism and applies them to specific international institutions is "enormous" (2002, 143).[45] The

---

[43] See, for a similar critique of Putnam, Evans (1993, 416) and Drezner (2003, 4–6).

[44] Important books on international organizations include Bates on the International Coffee Organization (1997), Vreeland on the IMF (2003), Moravcsik (1998) and Pollack on the EU (2003), Devesh Kapur et al. (1997) on the World Bank, and Pevehouse (2002) on regional organizations. Yet most of these studies examine the impact of IOs on international outcomes and do not look at how institutions impact domestic politics in specific countries. Pevehouse (2002) looks at how IOs achieve democratization, but the focus is on the cross-national processes of democratization.

[45] Similarly, Milner notes that "more dynamic models of how international trade and domestic politics interact are an important area of research. They may tell us a good deal about what affects trade policy choices. For example, will global liberalization process bring increasing pressure for more openness and more democracy? Or will it

trade-policy literature privileges the role of interest groups shaped by international forces, while the international institutions literature looks at the impact of international organizations on international cooperation, democratization, and human rights compliance, apart from other such global concepts. A second-image tradition in international relations analyses the structural context of global factors but does not pay enough attention to the *institutional* context of global changes. Thus, the two concerns – domestic trade politics and international organizations – have not been brought together.[46] Clearly, we need analytical case studies of how international economic institutions affect domestic trade politics in a wide variety of countries. Do international organizations merely enhance the impact of economic flows? Or may their impact run in unintended or unexpected directions? Even more important, how do we understand significant variation in institutional effects across time, across institutions, and across countries? This book addresses these gaps in the conventional literature. While there has been some criticism of the largely domestically driven framework found in the two-level game literature or the "open-economy politics" arguments (Farrell and Newman 2014; Oatley 2011), fewer studies examine *both the international and domestic levels* simultaneously.

2.3.5   Institutional complementarity

Buthe and Mattli (2011) post that domestic institutions are extremely important to our understanding of transnational standards and compliance with such standards, but these must be complementary with international standards. In their view, the theory of complementarity posits: "When one international organization is the clear focal point for setting global rules, the ability of firms and others to influence the specific outcome of private rule-making is a function of the fit between these stakeholders' domestic institutions and the international organization – as well as their technical expertise and economic resources" (Buthe and Mattli 2011, 43). What does complementarity do? They argue that "domestic institutions that are more complementary with a particular international institution confer on stakeholders with access to such domestic institution a strategic advantage by amplifying their voices in the international standardization process" (Buthe and Mattli 2011, 49). They isolate two

---

undermine itself and breed demands for closure and backlash against the governments and international institutions which support openness?" (2002, 457).

[46] A few exceptions are Moore (2002), who analyses China, and Goldstein (1993) and Lake (1988), who studied the United States. Katznelson and Shefter (2002) adopt a "second-image reversed" analysis to ask how war and trade have shaped American political development.

interesting distinctions where fit with the international level is relevant: hierarchical political systems and fragmented institutions. Their argument is that the fit between the character of domestic institutions (hierarchical or fragmented) with the relevant international regimes will shape whether international standards are adopted. However, they never define or specify complementarity, and using their definitions proves difficult. Is India hierarchical or fragmented? Are Indian institutions consistent with the WTO institutional structure? It is not very clear how we would assess such assumptions. Their argument also does not say much about change over time, which is a crucial weakness of their work. In my argument, Indian domestic institutions were enabled to comply with WTO rules and obligations over time, despite a lack of complementarity with international levels. Thus, their framework does not account for hybrid regimes such as India, where both hierarchy and fragmentation may exist and where change, despite a lack of complementarity, has been possible.

2.3.6   Transnational legal order

More recently, Halliday and Shaffer (2015) in an edited volume propose the concept of transnational legal order. They also aim to examine the transnational context of law making as well as how national and local actors embed the transnational legal norms in divergent contexts. Additionally, they look at how transnational legal ordering affects state change (Shaffer, Nedumpara, and Sinha 2015). They rely on empirical work done by a groups of collaborators to assess the empirical scope of their concept. This concept is similar to the Global Design-in-Motion framework that I develop here, but the scope of the concept of TLO is more specific as it focuses on legal ordering. While I agree with their overall approach, my framework is more ambitious in examining how different elements of the global architecture, including but going beyond its legal structure, affects states. I also posit that it is important to distinguish between legal norms and institutions – like the dispute-settlement procedures and their rulings. The legal institutional structure has greater effect as it binds and restricts a state's sovereignty directly. Thus, the concept of TLO is at once too specific and narrow but also does not differentiate among different mechanisms that may be driving the result in different countries. For example, the legal institutional mechanisms of sovereignty costs explain India's compliance despite delays. We don't know which specific mechanism drives change in Bangladesh, where, given its "least developing country" (LDC) status, legal norms or diffusion may explain its compliance better. Thus, the concept of TLO is a great addition to the literature but does not offer a discriminating theory of what elements of the TLO have what effect.

2.4   Conclusion

This chapter builds a theory about how global institutions affect countries. This framework synthesizes a second-image reversed (Gourevitch 1978) argument plus an "open-economy politics framework" (Lake 2009), combining an outside-in argument with attention to domestic actors and their preferences.[47] This generates a new triangular framework, Global Design-in-Motion. What distinguishes this framework is that it takes the microfoundations of domestic interests and ideas within India seriously but also focuses on how the global context transforms the domestic structure and creates a coalition with new ideas, preferences, and capacities with respect to the international economy. As David Lake acknowledged, the open-economy politics arguments need a more dynamic framework, where the "feedback effects of decisions taken at the international level on the constellation of interests and institutions within societies" are added to a purely domestic frame of reference.[48] This book develops such a dynamic framework, exploring both sides of the causal circle and combining an outside-in and inside-out explanation. Analysis that traces the consequences of global forces on domestic politics needs to move into the second generation of research wherein *both* the international level and the domestic level are *unpacked* and their mutual interaction mapped more systematically. Moreover, we need more research attention on the *causal mechanisms* that link global factors to domestic actors and institutions. In this book I combine both of these tasks by studying the global linkages created by an international trade regime (GATT and WTO) in one country across sectors. I open up the black box of global trade institutions and examine the impact of their specific institutional features on domestic politics, state reform, and business collective action.

---

[47] Lobell (2005) makes a similar argument about Britain's grand strategy. Also see Solingen (1998) for how to combine outside-in and inside-out effects, which is rare in the literature.

[48] Lake (2009, 232).

3   Trade, statecraft, and state capacity in India

On July 25, 2014, the Indian government, on behalf of a group of thirty-three countries, conveyed to the WTO General Council that "the adoption of the TF [trade facilitation] protocol must be postponed till a permanent solution on public stockholding for food security is found."[1] Strangely enough, after years of research and careful preparation, the Indian trade ministry was ready to implement the TF agreement, and India's stance did not represent opposition to the TF agreement per se.[2] While Indian trade negotiators had resisted agreements before, this was a rare strategy of linking two different parts of the WTO agreement, one related to trade facilitation and the other related to the Agreement on Agriculture, when the collapse of the December 2013 Bali Agreement on Trade Facilitation would have been a serious blow to the Doha Round. India's strategic stance was immediately successful. In November 2014, India and the United States arrived at a bilateral agreement that would restore the "peace clause" agreed on in Bali and ensure that India and other developing countries would not be challenged under the WTO's dispute procedure for "stockpiling" 10 percent of their food supplies as long as they were transparent about the food security schemes.[3] What explains the contrast between India's failure in the Uruguay Round (1988–1994) and India's new capability for complex negotiations? We cannot understand this episode without exploring the processes of state transformation and institutional development unleashed by globalization within India.

If war makes states, then trade re-forms states.[4] A more confident state may seek global participation as well as domestic trade reform, using its

---

[1] Statement by Smt. Nirmala Sitharaman, minister of state in the Ministry of Commerce and Industry, in parliament on August 5, 2014, "Regarding India's Stand in the WTO," accessed at: http://commerce.nic.in/trade/CIM_parliamant_statement_WTO _5_8_2014.pdf.

[2] See Section 3.3.1 for an analysis of capacity building on trade facilitation.

[3] USTR, "Transcript of Press Conference Call Remarks by Ambassador Michael Froman," Washington, DC, November 13, 2014, accessed at: http://tinyurl.com/qdz74r6.

[4] Tilly (1985) argued that war makes states and states make war.

external trade commitments to nudge changes in domestic trade politics. How could this process unfold? I argue that a country's participation in a rule-bound global trading system reforms states, changes the direction of their trade policy, and shapes domestic institutional development (Rodrik 2002). Why does this happen? The rule-bound global system creates higher transaction costs and onerous limits on sovereignty. This demands new kinds of expertise, institutional reform, and policy responses. An embedded global trade regime not only necessitates new state capacities but also demands new political strategies of statecraft – tradecraft – to manage trade negotiations and defend them internally. Both functional and political capacities are developed and unleashed through this interaction. This may reorder relationships between state and society in a country, creating the need for varied public–private consultations and partnerships. As a result of these new practices, state actors may negotiate more effectively at the global level, and be more active in global markets, than predicted by their trade share. Policymakers begin to think of themselves as active negotiators rather than rule takers. A country may seek greater global interaction but on its own terms, using protectionist and liberal trade measures selectively and strategically.

This chapter provides evidence for these simple but counterintuitive findings for India. The episode that began this chapter is a small illustration of these institutional transformations in the recent decade. Section 3.1 presents the issue and the argument in brief. Section 3.2 details the complex and layered institutional framework of the WTO. Next, section 3.3 outlines the molecular changes in India's institutions at the national level. I focus on India's trade ministry – the Ministry of Commerce (MOC) – to document changes in size, cognitive capacity enhancements, and new institutional frameworks. Bureaucratic politics is unleashed in a distinct way even as state agencies reach out to nonstate actors such as businesses, lawyers, NGOs, research think tanks, and international agencies like the United Nations Conference on Trade and Development (Section 3.4). These changes have a clear effect, as negotiating outcomes for India in the 2000s are superior to previous decades (Section 3.3.1). All in all, compliance with WTO rules transforms Indian state capacity by increasing state power, expanding the need for different kinds of expertise within the state, and creating institutions to implement the new rules of the game.

3.1   The puzzle, question, and argument in brief

Until the 1990s, trade policies of developing countries were mostly bilateral and episodic. Nation-states defended their sovereign domains both externally and internally; they defended their boundaries as well as their rights to design domestic industrial, trade, and welfare policies. States sought to export goods abroad but also protect their citizens against the rigors of trade competition. In a similar fashion, Indian policymakers resisted opening up their country's markets to the external world for decades. Most countries married their export-enhancing instruments to their domestic industrial strategies, creating a direct link between external and internal agendas. International trade commitments were limited to tariff reductions in commodities, and an elaborate system of exceptions allowed countries to design individually tailored compliance schedules. As an illustration, India could impose restrictions on imports – labeled as quantitative restrictions – on grounds of weak balance of payments. Bargaining and deal making were central to trade negotiations. During this time, India was a closed economy, with a strong self-driven development agenda that emphasized national self-reliance, industrial diversification, and an employment-intensive growth. "Export pessimism"[5] was the order of the day. A former economic adviser to the Prime Minister's Office and a negotiator during the Uruguay Round noted:

Trade and trade policy were not of primary importance and the latter would be determined automatically by whatever was needed to augment and make more favorable conditions under which domestic industry and agriculture had to operate. Over the years, this gave rise to an architecture of permits, permissions, and licenses to provide protection to domestic industry. At the same time, overseas investments, flow of technology and trade [were] strictly controlled by bureaucratic mechanisms, a complicated tariff structure and quantitative restrictions [Narayan 2005].

Then, in the early 1990s, Indian policies began to change. While the 1991 financial crisis and IMF loan created conditions for a homegrown liberalization program, resistance and protectionism continued until the mid-1990s. Then, the next crisis in 1997 was initiated by WTO structures and commitments. In 1997–1998, India lost two cases at the WTO's dispute court in Geneva, followed by a third loss in 2000.[6] The first WTO case, related to quantitative restrictions, directly challenged Indian sovereignty to protect its industries and citizens.[7] The other case related to the protection of intellectual property rights in India.[8]

[5] Bhagwati and Srinivasan (1984) use this phrase.

[6] These cases related to quantitative restrictions, patents, and automobiles. The first two cases were important in terms of "sovereignty costs," a concept that I use to describe the constraints on state autonomy imposed by WTO decisions.

[7] This case challenged the government's ability to impose quantitative restrictions on the import of goods that the government considered sensitive. WTO's Article XVIII allowed developing countries with balance of payments problems to curb imports. It was a measure used by India to protect domestic industry against foreign competition.

[8] In the India-Patents case, the European Union and the United States challenged India's implementation of the TRIPS agreement. The India-QR case is the US challenge of

The transformation of GATT into the WTO in 1995 radically altered the nature of the global trade regime and created new dilemmas and constraints for countries such as India. The rules of the game became multilateral in scope and effect. Agreements and rules now affected all members in a widely encompassing manner. Compliance pressures were intense with few escape routes available.[9] The WTO's expanding reach sought to cover services, investment, and intellectual property rights, all of which were until recently the preserve of national governments. The institutional structure of the WTO requires regular meetings, compliance schedules, and intense procedures. Legal procedures, such as the dispute mechanism and compliance pressures, have created onerous implementation and transaction costs for states and private parties alike (Sinha 2007). In effect, these institutional rules, procedures, agreements, meetings, and practices created new burdens for India and most countries; these burdens demanded new institutional responses.

What did these developments do to the power of states to design new policies and protect their citizens against the vagaries of global competition? Are national states becoming obsolete and their authority undermined as a result of such powerful global institutions?[10] This chapter demonstrates that the answer to these questions, paradoxically, is no. India's defeat at the WTO and its compliance requirements jolted a moribund economy into action and set India on a path that integrated it more closely with the global system. I show that the WTO's demands on the Indian government and its responses to them created the conditions for deeper integration into the international system. Normally, domestic needs and pressures would have dictated a more cautious, slow strategy. Instead, external constraints and opportunities embodied by the new global trading order created the conditions for India to seek greater recognition and power in the international system. In the process,

---

Indian use of quantitative measures on balance of payments grounds. See Appellate Body Report, *India – Patent Protection for Pharmaceuticals and Agricultural Chemical Products*, WT/DS50/R and WT/DS50/AB/R (adopted December 19, 1997); Appellate Body Report, *India – Quantitative Restrictions on Imports of Agricultural, Textile and Industrial Products*, WT/DS/AB/R (adopted January 14, 1999); Appellate Body Report, *India – Measures Relating to Trade and Investment in the Motor Vehicle Sector*, WT/DS175/AB/R (adopted March 19, 2002).

[9] The least developing countries (LDCs) continue to have safety valves and exceptions.

[10] For important works that address this question, see Cerny (1990, 1995), Berger and Dore (1996), Keohane and Milner (1996), Garrett (1998), Vogel (1995), Vogel and Kagan (2004), and Hall and Soskice (2001). The special issue of CPS and the volume that brought together some of the original CPS contributors [Caporaso (1989)] specifically sought to respond to the "wide gap separating the perspectives of those working in comparative and international politics" (1989, 8).

India's negotiating skills became better, and the country achieved better outcomes during key global negotiations.[11] The trends of reversal of liberalization in the early and mid-1990s suggest that, left to itself, India may not have moved toward deeper global integration so soon after initial reforms in 1991. Institutional and state development was the crucial missing variable that ushered in deeper trade integration that started around 1998–1999.

Why did this happen? Global trade organizations created significant implementation costs, with many intended as well as unintended effects. Globalization of trade rules, in fact, creates pressures to strengthen national state agencies and trade policy processes. I show that globalization of trade rules is premised on strong national institutions, which are activated to enhance their cognitive and institutional capacities in order to implement requirements of global agreements.[12] The demand for and incorporation of diverse kinds of expertise – economic, technical, and legal – transform insular and dilapidated state institutions into smarter trading states. In the process, emerging powers, such as Brazil, India, and China, have emerged as better negotiators and more powerful players in the global trade arena.[13] The international and national levels have begun to complement each other as trade liberalization demands both transformed national institutions and new trade politics that favor a more open economy trade regime. This process implies that global trade institutions, such as the WTO, are not static or autonomous, but rather "the WTO legal order is shaped by those who negotiate its terms and who participate in their interpretation, affecting how WTO law is understood and applied" (Shaffer, Nedumpara, and Sinha 2015). Interestingly, similar processes of institutional development are evident across diverse countries, such as India, the United States, Japan, Brazil, China, and even Bangladesh, revealing the common imperative faced by many states. This chapter explores this interesting movement whereby an organization aimed to embed freer markets and trade – the WTO – has catalyzed new state capacities and actually increased the Indian trading state's powers and capabilities. In a similar vein, Olsen and Sinha (2013) argue that the WTO agreements strengthen the ability of some states to seek autonomy within a larger zone of compliance with international

---

[11] Key examples include India's negotiations over the Bali 2013 package, India's participation in the G-20 formation in Cancun in 2003, and India's trade facilitation negotiations in 2006 and services negotiations. See Section 3.3.1 for an analysis of these outcomes.

[12] Mattli (2003) finds similar evidence of complementarity between globalization and nation-states in the field of standardization. Also see Young (2003).

[13] Olsen and Sinha (2013), Narlikar (2010), Shaffer, Sanchez, and Rosenberg (2008), and Sinha (2007).

norms. Next, I document which specific features of the WTO stimulated the Indian state to enhance its institutions, providing a direct causal link between institutional features of the WTO and their accompanying effects on state change in India.

3.2   Institutional design of the global trade organizations (GATT vs. WTO)

In 1995, the trade agreement referred to as General Agreement on Tariffs and Trade (GATT) was transformed into a new global institution with each member country representing one vote. It came to be called the World Trade Organization (WTO) with key enhancements to its institutional structure. This new organization administers agreements and decisions negotiated and accepted by its members. The WTO is a complex, "nested" (Aggarwal 1998) organization constituted by agreements [for example, Trade-Related Aspects of Intellectual Property Rights (TRIPS), General Agreement on Trade in Services (GATS), Agreement on Textiles and Clothing (ATC), Information Technology Agreement (ITA)], rules and procedures, organizations (the WTO's Secretariat housed in Geneva, for example) and forums, and principles [reciprocity, or most favored nation status (MFN)]. The rules are binding, and all members are subject to dispute-settlement procedures administered by a dispute body within the WTO with its own procedures. Each of these elements together establishes a "framework" within which both global trade and the setting of its rules take place (Hoekman and Kostecki 1995, 37). Figure 3.1 outlines the complex structure of the WTO.

Most scholars of international trade acknowledge the radical changes initiated by the formation of the WTO. As noted by John Jackson, "The combination of events and institutional developments of the past few years, with the NAFTA in North America, the European Community (EC) evolution towards deepening and broadening integration, the extraordinary elaborate Uruguay Round results, as well as developments in China and East Europe, probably amount to the most profound change in international economic relations, institutions, and structures since the origin of the Bretton Woods structure itself in the immediate post-war period" (Jackson 2000, 408). This section argues that the institutions of the trade regime – rules, forums, principles, and agreements – and its practices demand numerous policy, legal, and institutional changes by all countries.[14]

---

[14] Many scholars focus on the institutional features and attendant effects of international organizations: Downs, Rocke, and Barsoom (1996), Downs and Rocke (1995), Koremenos, Lipson, and Sindal (2001) and (Koremenos 2005).

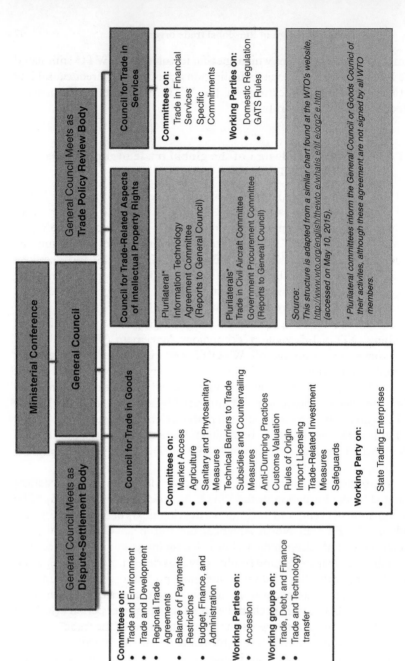

Figure 3.1 WTO structure

International institutions, more than market flows, interact with political institutions, rulers, and state agencies and by so doing *transform* the institutional context of domestic responses. In fact, paradoxically, global institutions, by the virtue of their interaction with domestic state institutions, empower the state as the negotiating actor vis-à-vis its society. These institutional effects are a direct result of high *transaction and implementation costs* imposed by the WTO regime as well as high *sovereignty costs* that are legally binding. The WTO's dispute-settlement procedures add a layer of litigation and transaction costs even as they seek to reduce trade disputes. These features together create the imperative for both legal and institutional changes within countries and enhanced state capacity at the domestic level.

3.2.1   Multiple agreements and the single-undertaking principle

The WTO encompasses numerous global agreements beyond goods and commodities, the traditional preserve of the GATT, governing new areas such as intellectual property, services, and trade procedures. These new issues demand new domestic frameworks that must be created to implement the agreements. WTO agreements seek to regulate a country's trade procedures through transparency in government procurement, and the trade facilitation measures seek to reform customs and entry and exit of goods. Cross-linkage among the agreements demands greater coordination in a country's responses. New capacities are required to prepare a country's industry and civil society to deal with future global challenges. At a meta level, WTO members negotiate both the rules with which they will be governed and the output of trade negotiations (tariff reductions, for example). All in all, WTO agreements and principles seek to harmonize all laws and procedures in keeping with the single overarching principle. A country commits to implementation of all agreements and procedures rather than accept them piecemeal. Each agreement both changes domestic policies and demands new domestic institutions.

A few illustrated examples reveal the broad nature of the agreements. In 1994, the Trade-Related Aspects of Intellectual Property Rights (TRIPS) agreement came into effect, ushering in a comprehensive and enforceable intellectual property regime that "reaches deep into the domestic environment of states" (Sell 2003, 1). The TRIPS agreement harmonized the intellectual property laws of countries and created a new market related to patents and intellectual property. A 1999 estimate assessed global trade in services and intellectual property to be worth USD1.4 trillion (Hoekman and Kostecki 1995, 9–10), which expanded to USD4.5 trillion by 2013 (WTO 2013). India implemented the TRIPS agreement, starting in 1999

Table 3.1 *Date and location of WTO ministerial conferences*

Location	Year
Singapore	1996
Geneva	1998
Seattle	1999
Doha	2001
Cancun	2003
Hong Kong	2005
Geneva	2009
Geneva	2011
Bali	2013

Source: Website of the WTO, www.wto.com.

and finalized in 2005, after it lost a WTO case brought against it by the United States and the European Union in 1997.[15] India started implementing the Agreement on Textiles and Clothing in 2005, as mandated by the negotiations. Simultaneously, the General Agreement on Trade in Services (GATS) was negotiated to regulate legal services, banking, and accounting services, etc. India is in the process of actively negotiating these services. There are other agreements, such as the Information Technology Agreement, which India also accepted in 1996. In addition to legal and formal policy changes, there are many informal policy changes adopted by India, catalyzed by transnational rules, standards, and policies. For example, Indian state agencies and private actors have adopted voluntary standards related to textiles (see Chapter 5 for details) as well as the ISO International Standards. Indian pharmaceutical companies are required to adopt World Health Organization guidelines for the production of medicines and even the organization of their factories and production facilities.

3.2.2   WTO institutions, procedures, and practices

Rules and trade agreements have to be regularly negotiated in diverse WTO forums; this is referred to as "multilateral negotiations." High-level meetings called "ministerial conferences" are held every two years, while regular ongoing negotiations take place in Geneva. Table 3.1 outlines the list of regular ministerial conferences. Since 1996, WTO members have been required to take part in these ministerial conferences and defend their negotiating positions.

[15] Appellate Body Report, *India – Patent Protection for Pharmaceutical and Agricultural Chemical Products*, WT/DS50/R (adopted December 19, 1997).

India's participation in these conferences directed a searchlight on its trade policymaking process. Each ministerial conference was preceded by a number of meetings in India, up to a year ahead, to discuss its negotiating stances at the conference. Such heightened activity and discussions created a remarkable level of scrutiny on the trade policymaking apparatus within India, pushing the state agencies involved in trade policy to enhance their capacities.

The WTO, in contrast to GATT, is a permanent body, constantly making rules, adjudicating trade disputes, and arriving at trade decisions. Three bodies are in permanent attendance: the General Council, the Dispute-Settlement Body, and the Trade Policy Review Body. These bodies are constituted by all members but ruled by different mandates and rules specific to each body. The General Council meets regularly, as do specific thematic bodies such as the Intellectual Property Rights Committee. In addition, there are specific working groups that focus on specific aspects of an issue. Currently, the Trade Negotiations Committee has been formed to discuss the Doha Development Agenda with many subcommittees. Table 3.2 outlines the list of committees discussing various aspects of the Doha Development Agenda. All in all, there are constant meetings any given day (almost ten to fifteen a day), demanding a high degree of attention and participation from the members' missions in Geneva. An official with India's mission at the WTO told me, "We have had to increase our staff strength and preparation levels to deal with the high volume of meetings at the WTO. They are constant and non stop. Everything is in full view and we have to constantly make decisions and arrive at our negotiating positions. There is more at stake too and we have to be vigilant."[16]

Each country undergoes "Trade Policy Reviews" periodically.[17] India undergoes its trade reviews every four years, and the most recent one was in 2015.[18] These reviews are quite intense, accompanied by a secretariat's report, a country report, and questions and answers by members.[19] In effect,

[16] Interview with member of the India mission at Geneva, August 2004.
[17] As the WTO notes: "The four biggest traders – the European Union, the United States, Japan and China (the 'Quad') – are examined approximately once every two years. The next sixteen countries (in terms of their share of world trade) are reviewed every four years. The remaining countries are reviewed every six years, with the possibility of a longer interim period for the least-developed countries." For details about the trade policy reviews, see WTO, "Trade Policy Reviews: Ensuring Transparency," www.wto.org/english/thewto_e/whatis_e/tif_e/agrm11_e.htm.
[18] India's first trade policy review took place in 1993 under the aegis of the GATT, followed by trade policy reviews in 1998, 2002, 2007, 2011, and 2015.
[19] The Trade Policy Review body sends a questionnaire to the relevant country, "writes its reports on the basis of a member's replies to a questionnaire, as well as discussions with

Table 3.2 *Trade Negotiations Committee and its subcommittees*

Trade Negotiations Committee under the Doha Development Agenda
Special Sessions of Services Council
TRIPS Council
Dispute-Settlement Body
Agriculture Committee
Cotton Subcommittee
Trade and Development Committee
Trade and Environment Committee
Negotiating Groups on:
Market Access
Rules
Trade Facilitation

Source: Adapted from WTO's organization chart; the website of WTO, www.wto.org/eng lish/thewto_e/whatis_e/tif_e/org2_e.htm.

all members scrutinize a country's trade policy intensively, and the country has to respond. India, for example, received a number of tough questions during its three reviews in 2002, 2007, and 2011. Many members asked uncomfortable questions and followed it up with a second round of questioning.[20] India was required to provide answers to these written questions. The Indian experience reveals an increased scrutiny of diverse policy arenas, which, until then, were isolated from global view. Hoekman and Kostecki suggest that the frequent reviews increase both transparency and surveillance of members (Hoekman and Kostecki 1995, 43–45). Countries need to review trade policies constantly as a result of these regular procedures. Policies need to be transparent and accessible to outsiders, including nonstate and global actors.

These different dimensions of the WTO structure led to multiple direct and unintended effects. The embedded procedures and regular meetings created higher *transaction and implementation costs*. The diverse agreements combined with a dispute-settlement mechanism levied new *sovereignty costs*, putting new restrictions on countries' internal policies. The numerous negotiations and regular meetings revealed diverse *information* about new international markets to state and private actors. High *transaction costs* and the technical demands of compliance with WTO rules and

officials during mission visits, and information collected from other sources. The entire process usually takes about ten months" (Francois 1999, 4). The reports and minutes of the meetings are large documents of around 300–400 pages.

[20] WTO, *Trade Policy Review: India, Record of the Meeting*, WT/TPR/M/249 (October 14, 2011).

agreements demand institutional reform of national and subnational institutions. Simultaneously, *sovereignty costs* lead some governments not to capitulate to a free-trade agenda of global trade organizations but rather to redefine their role in such international organizations and in the global order more generally. Thus, some governments have been reasserting their authority by deploying innovative instruments of national policy to safeguard their domestic agendas. *Legalization* provides legitimacy to international agreements, making them consistent with domestic obligations. The various WTO agreements also revealed concentrated *information about the creation of future markets*. This created new supply chains, especially in pharmaceuticals and textiles, where new agreements (TRIPS and MFA) provided information about new opportunities to Indian private players. These four mechanisms together – *transaction costs, sovereignty costs, legalization, and information about future markets and new opportunities* – were key in transforming India's protectionist and insular trade politics in favor of greater external integration and a stronger defense of India's trading interests at the global level. The WTO rules and processes unleashed both a functional and a strategic political effect that changed the way domestic actors responded to the agreements over time. In the next section I show how these mechanisms were key to catalyzing Indian state building and capacity enhancements.

3.3   Tradecraft, enhancing institutions, and building state capacity

Despite the competence of specific civil servants, India's capacity to negotiate during the Uruguay Round was inadequate, and the outcomes were poor.[21] As one high-level American trade negotiator said, "During the GATT years and during the Uruguay discussions, India was good at saying no, but given a lack of serious grounding it could also be ignored."[22] A participant in the negotiation process during 1984–1994 expressed a commonly held view: "India has been a pirate: it has made sporadic forays designed to throw negotiations into disarray. . . . However, whether hostile or not, all observers agree that India has not taken any bold initiatives to give a new direction to the proceedings in any of the negotiation groups."[23]

---

[21] Sen (2003).
[22] Interview with Geza Feketekuty, an ex-officer of the USTR, October 2004.
[23] Narayan (2005).

Despite these weaknesses, and despite the claims of "withdrawal of state," India began enhancing its state capacity in response to WTO pressure and institutional imperatives. S. Narayan, Indian ambassador to the WTO in the 1990s, noted that many significant changes have taken in "India's negotiating stances," which have been ignored by most analysts (Narayan 2005). These transformations resulted in many negotiating successes at the WTO level, as elaborated in Section 3.3.1. These successes, in turn, were supported by sustainable capacity enhancements that led to better performance at multilateral and bilateral negotiations (Section 3.3). Together these developments constitute what has been termed "re-forming the state" to refer to rebuilding and recreating institutions of the state.[24]

3.3.1   Global negotiating outcomes for India

During the Uruguay Round (1984–1994), India resisted every proposal by developed countries but was bypassed and rendered irrelevant at key moments.[25] This changed during the Doha Round, when India's negotiating successes were notable. India has come a long way in negotiating in a pragmatic, yet strong way to achieve its perceived trade interests. How did Indian negotiators achieve such advances across the two rounds just a few years apart? Four examples stand out and reveal the effect of better state capacity directly: India's involvement in agriculture negotiations during the Cancun meetings resulting in formation of the G-20; India's ability to negotiate diverse free-trade and preferential agreements; India's participation in the Trade Facilitation negotiations backed by research and relevant consultations, and India's engagement with the GATS service-related negotiations where research from economists played a major role. Later I analyze two of these successful outcomes: the G-20 agriculture proposal and the success around trade facilitation.

India learned to deploy better research and negotiating skills to achieve its goals. Its capacity building (documented in Section 3.4.2) had a definite impact on such outcomes. One of the most successful examples relates to formation of the G-20 and the submission of an alternative agriculture proposal in Cancun (Mexico) on August 20, 2003. This proposal was initially crafted by Brazil, India, and Argentina before the

---

[24] This phrase "re-forming the state" is drawn from in Schamis's book, *Re-Forming the State: The Politics of Privatization in Latin America and Europe* (2002). The book argued that the process of privatization created the need to reorganize state institutions in Chile and the UK.

[25] A parliamentary report analyzed the various failures of India's Commerce ministry extensively (Rajya Sabha 1998).

ministerial meeting and jointly submitted by twenty-two countries.[26] An analysis of this negotiation process reveals how a stronger state was able to shape the WTO negotiations successfully, the role of research in shaping global negotiations, and the emergence of a new coalition that challenged the hegemony of the established powers – the United States and the European Union.

India submitted a thoroughly researched proposal in January 2001 as part of the ongoing negotiations on agriculture.[27] This proposal was the result of multiple consultations within India.[28] This proposal was then revised substantially when a new coalition took shape at the WTO, heralding the rise of G-20 as an emerging power coalition. How did this process unfold? In August 2003, when the European Union and the United States came together to offer a joint proposal on agriculture, Brazil took the initiative in starting a conversation with India. This resulted in a joint proposal drafted by Brazil and India. This submission was a significant departure in a number of ways, with thorough research done by trade officials and excellent negotiating skills on the part of both India and Brazil (author's interviews conducted in 2004; Delgado and Soares 2005; Narlikar and Tussie 2004).

First, the alternative proposal submitted by India and Brazil, which later came to be known as the G-20 proposal, was a serious alternative to the US–EU proposal and was considered as a template for the Cancun discussions. Brazil and India drafted the proposal together. Second, it revealed extensive research and an integration of Brazil's and India's positions in a manner that could not be ignored by the contending parties. Third, the negotiators were well informed about the US and EU positions[29] and came together to craft a solid coalition that has stood the test of time (Narlikar and Tussie 2004). And fourth, the proposal offered a proactive agenda that went beyond the US–EU proposal in significant ways (Narlikar and Tussie 2004, 952).

How did this happen? While many scholars have focused on the coalition formation at the WTO, the domestic-level institutional reforms were an important prerequisite in enhancing the skills of the Indian and Brazilian negotiators. It came as a direct result of enhanced state capacity in India (and Brazil) and the result of the activation of policy-expert

---

[26] For an in-depth analysis of various agriculture proposals and the negotiation process, see Hanrahan and Schnepf (2005).

[27] See Proposals by India to Committee on Agriculture (special session), *Negotiations on WTO Agreement on Agriculture*, WTO, G/AG/NG/W/102 (submitted January 15, 2001).

[28] Priyadarshi (2005). My own research in India, documented later, confirmed some of the findings of Priyadarshi (2005).

[29] Interviews with Indian and Brazilian negotiators, 2003–2004.

linkages that I document later in this chapter. Research input played a major role in building this coalition, indicating that key domestic state enhancements were the necessary building blocks for new global alliances.

Other examples reveal that this behavior was not an isolated event. Research and consultations with the private sector played a major role in changing India's positions in the negotiations on trade facilitation and services.[30] India's positions on trade facilitation were initially defensive and opposed to any negotiations, as Indian policymakers felt that any discussion of trade facilitation would "entail high costs for developing countries."[31] Yet, in keeping with extensive research started by the Ministry of Commerce and documented later in this chapter, the MOC asked the UNCTAD to evaluate the trade facilitation problems encountered by Indian exporters (Das 2007, 7). This research was done between January and June of 2005 and included an exhaustive survey of exporters and two field trips to Europe. Survey-based methods were used in an innovative and systematic manner by the UNCTAD in close consultation with the Ministry of Commerce. Eleven case studies were conducted to document the problems faced by Indian exporters. This study was the basis of Indian proposals made to the Council on Goods and Services at the WTO in 2006 (Das 2007). As a result, the Indian positions evolved, and India was prepared to "see its own trade facilitation proposals as an opportunity for India to consolidate its ongoing domestic reform programme by accepting certain commitments in areas in which it is already undertaking reforms" (Das 2007, 8). That research led to a significant paradigm shift in the way India approached trade facilitation from an "inward-looking" defensive position to a more "proactive position" that defended the interests of its exporters (Das 2007). What factors brought on such successful outcomes? Numerous institutional reforms, state-expert consultations, and interaction with the private sector were the necessary precondition to these changes, and tradecraft capacity has been significantly enhanced as a result.

3.3.2   Building trade negotiating capacity in India

An analysis of Indian trade politics must begin with the policy process and structure that make trade policy but also structure the "authorizing environment" (Baldwin 2006, 928). Trade policy is a central (federal) subject handled mostly by the national Ministry of Commerce, although states have inserted themselves into trade policy in recent times.[32] The

---

[30] Das (2007).
[31] Arun Jaitley's (India's commerce minister at that time) speech in Cancun, 2003, quoted in "India Will Not Compromise on Agriculture," *The Hindu*, September 12, 2003.
[32] Jenkins (2003) and Sinha (2006).

civil service, in accordance with strong British traditions, is the key agenda setter; departmental ministries negotiate treaties largely by "executive fiat."[33] The parliament does not make policy but oversees and evaluates policies framed by bureaucratic officials. This structure gives significant power to the Ministry of Commerce to formulate and shape India's trade policy. This is how the government of India outlines the making of trade policy.

Trade policy is formulated and implemented mainly by the Ministry of Commerce and Industry, along with other concerned ministries and agencies, including the Ministry of Finance, the Ministry of Agriculture, and the Reserve Bank of India. India considers trade policy as an instrument to attain its overall economic policy objectives of growth, industrialization, development, and self-sufficiency. However, India also uses trade policy to attain short-term goals such as containing inflation. The use of trade policy to attain short-term, non-trade related objectives may end up detracting from the stability sought, as constant fine-tuning of policies is required to attain these short-term goals.[34]

Within this larger structure, numerous changes in trade policymaking began to happen around 1998–1999. First, reorganization within the traditionally insular and fragmented bureaucracy led to enhancement of the power of the Ministry of Commerce, which was designated as the nodal ministry to negotiate the GATT and WTO agreements. This led to an enhancement of the power of the Ministry of Commerce vis-à-vis the Ministry of Finance and Ministry of External Affairs (Sinha 2007). In addition, significant capacity building was undertaken within the MOC. The small and powerless Trade Policy Division (TPD) within the MOC was reconstituted in 1997–1998, and its role and power were enhanced. Significantly, the MOC began serious institutional reform by reorganizing various specific state agencies. A new Intellectual Property Rights Administration and a new Tariff Commission were created, while an Office of Anti-dumping – the Director General of Anti-dumping and Allied Duties (DGAD) – was reorganized. Research and expertise began to be incorporated in trade policy discussions, contributing directly to better negotiation outcomes.[35] Coordination and consultation across diverse departments and ministries became common, contributing to more coherent and stronger positions.

---

[33] Rajeev Dhavan, "Treaties and Cancun," *The Hindu*, October 17, 2003.
[34] Government of India, *Statement by India to Trade Policy Review Body*, WT/TPR/G/249 (adopted August 10, 2011).
[35] Traditionally, generalist administrators were dominant within the Indian civil service, but this ratio was reversed in the Ministry of Commerce and agencies associated with negotiating with the WTO.

3.3.3   State capacity

The central agency responsible for negotiating trade and commerce policy at the international level is the Ministry of Commerce. [36] While the WTO expanded to cover new issues, the MOC's workload, power, and status were enhanced. Until then, the Ministry of Commerce was not as powerful as the Ministry of Industry or the Ministry of Finance. In a closed economy, the Ministry of Commerce was considered unimportant; Finance and Industry were more important. [37] In the earlier regime, in addition to the Ministry of Commerce, the Ministry of External Affairs (MEA) and the Ministry of Finance also dealt with foreign actors, including ones related to trade. In the run-up to the Singapore ministerial meetings in December 1996, for example, both the Ministry of Commerce (MOC) and the Ministry of External Affairs (MEA) were responsible for joint preparation of India's position paper. In addition, the Ministry of Finance (MOF) was also involved in achieving a consensus on India's negotiation strategy. [38] By 2004, while ministerial overlap continued to exist, the Ministry of Commerce was allocated primary responsibility for trade negotiations and external economic relations. The MOC won a victory by gaining the responsibility of dealing with multilateral trade agreements, especially against the MEA, which had sought to involve itself in multilateral negotiations in the late 1990s. [39] Similarly, in 1999, the Ministry of Finance and the Ministry of Commerce clashed over administrative responsibility for anti-dumping. Yet, anti-dumping continued to be the responsibility of the MOC. Moreover, the MOC's prestige and status have definitely increased vis-à-vis the Department of Industry, whose regulatory power declined with liberalization in 1991.

This enhancement of power resulted from the greater need for coordination that WTO integration demanded. Nested agreements and

---

[36] This section's evidence is drawn from Sinha (2007) as well as field work that the author conducted in 2003–2004 (India), 2004–2005 (DC and Geneva), and 2009 (India).

[37] Historically, commerce existed as a department of the omnibus Ministry of Industry and was moved around in various different incarnations. In 1955–1956, the Department of Commerce was part of the Ministry of Industry and Commerce. It was made independent in June 1964 when the Ministry of International Trade was renamed Ministry of Commerce. From 1964 until 1978 it existed as a separate department within the Ministry of Industry, when it was joined with the Ministry of Civil Supplies and Cooperation. In the late 1980s, the Ministry of Commerce was again amalgamated with the Ministry of Industry; currently, it exists as a department within the "Ministry of Commerce and Industry"; Ministry of Commerce, *Annual Reports*, various years.

[38] "Stand on WTO Meet after PMO Submits Views," *Business Standard*, November 30, 1996. This article noted that differences between MEA and MOC emerged during the finalization of the draft strategy note.

[39] Interview with a retired MEA official, Washington, DC, August 2005.

cross-sector linkages within the WTO also shaped the domestic power balances and policy jurisdictions within the state. After the Uruguay Round, as a consequence of overlapping demands, the Indian government brought top officials from three to five ministries together to coordinate policies and negotiation stances. The Ministry of Commerce was given the status of the "nodal ministry," and its role was to think of the negotiations in a holistic way: balancing sectoral trade-offs and coordinating trade policy across the various ministries.[40] This enabled the Ministry of Commerce to gain importance even on issues of agricultural liberalization or textile-related negotiations.

In the MOC, the Trade Policy Division (TPD) was a small, unimportant division in the 1970s and 1980s. Its main task was to "keep abreast of the developments in the international organizations like GATT, UNCTAD, ESCAP, etc."[41] – visualized as keeping track of multilateral trade organizations rather than using the forums to enhance India's export potential. Trade policy was not considered an overarching framework within which different aspects of India bilateral and multilateral trade engagement were considered but conceived as a separate department. For example, enhancing exports was the responsibility of another agency rather than an integral part of India's industrial strategy. Clearly, state agencies thought of themselves as receivers and takers of international rules (rule takers) rather than active negotiators. This perception of export promotion and trade negotiations as separate realms seemed reasonable given the limited effect of multilateral agreements but was also reflected in the fragmented way in which global interactions were perceived and organized within the Indian bureaucracy. Julius Sen, in his assessment of Indian negotiation practices in the Uruguay Round, suggests that the international dimension of trade policy was never linked with the intrastate or domestic efforts to enhance export potential (Sen 2003). He notes, "The decision-making procedures of the government of India were incapable of dealing with international treaty making and domestic policy reform at the same time. Government procedures could accommodate either one or the other, but not both" (2003, 2). What happened to this insular and fragmented policy process, which had existed in a stable pattern for decades?

Simply put, the size of the bureaucracy to deal with multilateral issues increased dramatically, as did the prestige of the positions these officials

---

[40] Interview with Ministry of Commerce official, New Delhi, April 16, 2003; Interview with Ministry of Textile official, New Delhi, April 23, 2003; Interview with Ministry of Agriculture official, New Delhi, June 2003; Interview with Retired Ministry of Commerce official, June 2002, Bangalore.

[41] Government of India (1977, 24).

occupy. In the 1960s and 1970s, the majority of officials in the MOC were engaged in export promotion, regulation, and assistance for specific commodities; there was no officer of senior and midlevel rank designated for making trade policy. This reflected domestic and international realities; trade policy was inward looking, and GATT discussions were not as intrusive and important, especially for India.[42] State capacity to deal with global trade negotiations or trade policy was nonexistent. For example, in 1996 at the Indian mission based in Geneva, where most of the deliberations took place, India had only three diplomats, when on any ordinary day there were about ten formal and informal meetings, all with direct bearing on India's interests.[43] A comparison of other similar developing country's staff strengths showed India in a poor light; Argentina had an ambassador plus five officers; Brazil, an ambassador plus six officers; Thailand, an ambassador plus fifteen; Indonesia; an ambassador plus six, and Mexico, an ambassador plus five.[44] India's ratio of officers in Geneva to those supporting them in Delhi was also quite poor, with only four officers in Geneva and five trade policy officers in New Delhi; many other countries had a Geneva-capital ratio of 1:2, that is, two officials in the capital giving and responding to every official in Geneva.[45]

The Ministry of Commerce increased the number of officers, institutions, and staff to deal with the expanding tasks of compliance associated with the WTO. Around 1997–1998, the Trade Policy Division was reconstituted and its role enhanced. By the early 2000s, the number of officials devoted exclusively to trade policy and multilateral trade negotiations had increased significantly. Moreover, officials handling bilateral trade issues were increasingly handling issues emerging from the multilateral trade process. Most crucially, positions in the Trade Policy Division had acquired status, prestige, and importance. Many of the trade policy officials were required to have specialized knowledge about WTO agreements, economic trends, and negotiation strategies. Many officers in the TPD were no longer transferred but kept longer in their positions so that they could build specialized skills. The number of officers in the Geneva mission increased to eight to ten by 2003 and continues to be around eight to ten. In 2010, the mission also had a special dispute-settlement

---

[42] Senior ranks refer to "joint secretary" and above; midlevel ranks are directors. In 1964–1965, for example, the secretariat was headed by one secretary and one additional secretary (textiles) and six joint secretaries concerned with different territorial regions of the world.

[43] Chitra Subramaniam, "Economy of Staff Mars India's Economic Diplomacy at WTO," *Indian Express*, February 14, 1996.

[44] Ibid.   [45] Ibid.

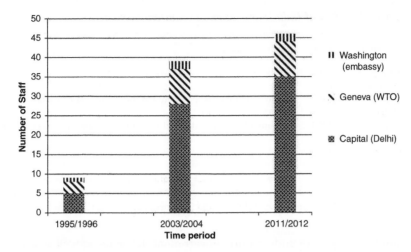

Figure 3.2 Number of state officials dealing with trade policy
Ministry of Commerce's Organizational chart, and Interviews with most
members of the Ministry of Commerce that deal with Trade Policy;
Interviews in Geneva. Author's calculations from Indian Mission;
data at the website of the Indian Ministry of Commerce;
http://commerce.nic.in/dotnet/officer/officer_web.aspx.

specialist.[46] The Geneva-capital ratio became much better (almost 1:4), leading to greater coordination and better policy and research support for Geneva-based negotiators. Currently, the Geneva mission coordinates regularly with the Ministry of Commerce in New Delhi. For example, during the recently concluded ministerial meeting in December 2013, a close minute-by-minute interaction between the Indian ambassador at the WTO and the PMO was possible as a result of new practices of coordination between Geneva and the capital. Figure 3.2 aggregates the total number of officials dealing with WTO issues within the Indian bureaucracy in 1995–1996, in 2003, and then in 2012.

Simultaneously, the government began taking larger delegations to ministerial meetings. In Cancun in 2003, for example, India's delegation was among the largest it had sent to any of the four previous ministerial meetings. That delegation, led by Commerce Minister Arun Jaitley and Commerce Secretary Dipak Chatterjee, consisted of over fifty members from various ministries including Agriculture, Textiles, and the Department of Industrial Policy.[47] In 2013, the Indian delegation was

---

[46] Shaffer, Nedumpara, and Sinha (2015).
[47] "Indian Delegation among the Largest," *Business Standard*, September 8, 2003.

Table 3.3 *Size of India's delegation at ministerial conferences*

Location	Year	India's Delegation Size[*]
Singapore	1996	Three- to five-member delegation
Geneva	1998	NA
Seattle	1999	Five to eight officials that included three business delegates
Doha	2001	NA
Cancun	2003	Sixty-member official delegation includes the business associations
Hong Kong	2005	NA
Geneva	2009	NA
Geneva	2011	NA
Bali	2013	Thirty-member official delegation; a separate business delegation

[*]Gathered by the author during fieldwork and from newspaper reports.

similarly large – including thirty government delegates as well as a separate business delegation. Table 3.3 presents these interesting facts.

I asked a high-level official of the Ministry of Commerce the reasons for the above-demonstrated expansion in the state at a time when a withdrawal of the state was more popular. He said, "The demands on us from WTO had increased manifold; they were watching us and monitoring us. Therefore, this expansion was much needed; in fact it came very late, only in 1999 or so."[48] Thus, the Trade Policy Review mechanism of the WTO, as well as its intrusive monitoring structure, played a role in this transformation as the government was forced to present an elaborate and developed response to the WTO at regular intervals.[49] The size and specialization of state agencies expanded in direct response to the onerous demands placed by the WTO rules and agreements.

Notably, as the next section demonstrates, an expansion of the trade policy community was accompanied by the creation and institutionalization of policy-expert networks. In the space of a few years, the cognitive capacity of the state on international trade and WTO issues was significantly enhanced.

3.3.4   Cognitive capacity of the state: new policy-expert linkages

The WTO regime demanded diverse expertise on the part of member states. The WTO process has economic implications but also has a legal monitoring mechanism – the dispute-settlement mechanism. Thus, the multilateral trade negotiations demand two different kinds of expertise: legal and economic. How did India respond? Surprisingly, given its

[48] Interview with Ministry of Commerce official, New Delhi, December 2003.
[49] Interview with Ministry of Commerce official, New Delhi, February 16, 2003; Interview with retired Ministry of Commerce official, New Delhi, December 23, 2001.

tradition of insular policymaking, the Indian government created new channels of policy-expert communications and input from economists, research think tanks, and legal experts. The government even created a new think tank focusing on the WTO (Centre for WTO Studies) while investing in research expertise on WTO-related matters across Indian universities and other think tanks. In the process, the cognitive capacity of the state in dealing with global trade was distinctly enhanced.

Indian negotiators began to feel the need for economic expertise as the pressure from the WTO increased and the negotiations became more complex and technical. While India has many world-class economists, the civil service was quite insular and relied on "in-house research" through its Indian Economic Service, which was considered to be of poor quality compared to generalist national civil service officials. Research was also not integrated into the policymaking process. This changed after India lost two WTO cases between 1997 and 1999, and the government sought external economic expertise in a more systematic, rigorous, and sustained way.

This shift was evident to me when I visited a civil servant's office in 2003. I noticed that his desk was piled with numerous research reports, books, and working papers rather than government files, which constituted only a small portion of his desk. Another desk in the room was also filled with reading material. He said to me during the interview: "I am having to educate myself in economics, legal issues, and international trade issues. The amount of reading I have to do has gone up immeasurably since I became part of the Trade Policy Division of the government of India. I have to carry heavy books with me and seek help from textbooks! I feel like a student!"[50] The WTO, in contrast to the GATT, is quite complex and technical. Its framework agreements entitled, "The Legal Texts: The Results of the Uruguay Round of Multilateral Trade Negotiations," can be found in a book of 492 pages filled with legal language and technical details.[51] Another civil servant waived the thick book at me and said: "One reading is not enough to understand this text; one has to read it at least twice to understand what it means. To evaluate its long-term implications, that's another level of complexity."[52]

Faced with the technical and complex nature of the agreements, negotiations, and debates, the Indian bureaucracy perceived the need to seek direct, regular, and systematic research help and input from a number of

[50] Interview with MOC official, New Delhi, July, 2003.
[51] In terms of agreements, it comprises twenty-nine individual legal texts and twenty-eight additional ministerial declarations combined with approximately 26,000 pages of computer printouts with each country's schedule of tariff concessions and commitments (Blackhurst 1998, 32).
[52] Interview with MOC official, New Delhi, December 2003.

think tanks, professors, research universities, and research institutions. This ran counter to the bureaucratic tendency to keep negotiations secret and in-house. Research input began to be formally solicited and discussed as a precursor to evolving India's positions and negotiation strategy. As a result, an interaction between the research and expert communities and state officials was started for the first time in the history of India's economic policy and has intensified immeasurably over time.

Starting in 1999, the government began to tap not only the research resources of government think tanks like the Indian Institute of Foreign Trade (IIFT) and Research and Information System for Developing Countries (RIS), which were the designated bodies for research support on WTO issues, but also began to interact with independent, specialized research institutes. For example, institutions like the International Council of International Economic Relations (ICRIER), the Madras Institute of Development Studies (MIDS), and the National Law School in Bangalore were asked to do research and present their findings to the government. The Ministry of Agriculture (MOA) also sought research reports from the Centre for Management in Agriculture (CMA) and the Indian Institute of Management, Ahmedabad. They prepared a report, "Impact of WTO Agreements on Indian Agriculture," for the Ministry of Agriculture. Table 3.4 lists the various independent research institutions and the expanding policy-expert linkages. In a short space of five years, separate government funds began to be allocated for research.[53] In 2002–2003, eleven new studies were commissioned at the cost of around Rs. 80 lakhs (approx. USD160,000). A separate committee, procedures, and budget were created for the purpose of funding research studies amounting to 1 crore (approx. USD200,000) by 2004–2005.[54]

In 2003, the government set up a WTO center (Centre for WTO Studies) within the Indian Institute of Foreign Trade (IIFT) and allocated a significant budget to it for research. This center has become the center for research on WTO-related issues. Its goals are to (a) provide research services for the Ministry of Commerce, (b) connect with industry and civil society to seek their views and input, and (c) assist in the dissemination of information about the WTO to government officials and civil society as well as engage in capacity building. The center had eight staff members as of December 2012, including a lawyer (Shaffer, Nedumpara, and Sinha 2015).

[53] In the late 1990s after Singapore, some studies were initiated: RIS and NCAER were asked to conduct some economic analysis of the impact of the Agreement of Agriculture and industrial tariffs.
[54] Government of India (2004, 29).

Table 3.4 *Research studies on WTO commissioned in 2002–2003*

	Title of Study	Research Institution	Allocated Funds (Rs. Lakhs)	Approx. USD Equivalent* (@ Rs. 50 = 1 USD)
1	Research Proposals on Regional Trade Arrangements	IIFT (Indian Institute of Foreign Trade)	4	8,000
2	Study Pertaining to Trade and Investment	RIS (Research and Information System for Developing Countries)	5	11,000
3	Subsidy Disciplines under GATS, Energy Services Including Oil and Gas, Environmental Services, Road and Rail Services	ICRIER (Indian Council for Research on International Economic Relations)	30	60,000
4	A Study of Trade Facilitation Measures	MIDS (Madras Institute of Development Studies)	6.4	12,800
5	Participation of India in the Working Group on Trade and Competition policy – A Proposal for Analytical Studies and Advisory Inputs	CDE (Culture, Development, Environment)		8,000
6	Technical Review of GATS Provision	M/S Nitish Desai Associates	2	4,000
7	Imbalances in the Current WTO Agreement on Subsidies and Countervailing Measures and Trade	ASCI (Administrative Staff College of India)	7	14,000
8	Trade and Transfer of Technology	ASCI (Administrative Staff College of India)	6	12,000
9	Emergency Safeguard Measures (ESM)	Economic Law Practice	5	10,200
10	A Study on Various Aspects of Subsidization of the Domestic Fisheries Sector in the Context of Possible Sectoral Negotiations at the WTO	ICSF CHENNAI (International Collective in Support of Fishworkers)	5	10,000
11	Study on Various Aspects of Market Access for Non-Agricultural Products in the WTO Round	RIS (Research and Information System for Developing Countries)	10	20,000

Source: Committee on WTO Studies, "List of Studies Approved," 2002–2003.
*The INR/USD exchange rate actually varied from about Rs. 46 to Rs. 49 during the 2002–2003 timeframe.

In response, research institutions enhanced their capacities on international trade and WTO-related issues. In 1999, the Indian Council for Research on International Economic Relations (ICRIER) launched a major project on India's trade in services, sponsored by the Ministry of Commerce, in preparation for the WTO meeting in Seattle, which was held at the end of 1999. The objective of this study was to "spell out the concerns to be addressed during the GATS (General Agreement on Trade and Services) 2000 negotiations" and aimed to "analyze the implications of multilateral trade liberalization in services for India."[55] Specialized skills of different research institutes were considered a significant value addition to the negotiation skills of Indian trade officials. Therefore, the quality of research and independent analysis became the criterion for assigning research. ICRIER, an independent pro-globalization–oriented research institute, was given funds up to Rs. 30 lakhs (approx. USD60,000) to study various aspects of the ongoing services agreement and negotiations.[56] Lawyers were also involved in this process; for the first time, the government sought outside private legal assistance as a background to evolving its negotiating strategy in the WTO.[57] The government partnered with the United Nations Conference on Trade and Development (UNCTAD) in a multiyear "capacity building" project involving numerous state–civil society consultations to improve their ability to comply with the demands of the WTO.[58]

Overall, involvement of experts and research analysis in policymaking became more formal, regular, and important from 1999–2000 onward.[59] An additional secretary in charge of the WTO in the Ministry of Commerce said: "We seek research input *before* we finalize our positions; thus research is indispensable to our negotiating strategy. It's not that we have made up our minds. The WTO process is too complex for that to happen; we need the research input in a crucial way."[60] Currently, the research report or paper prepared by the research institution is submitted to an expert group dealing with the relevant issue, which is constituted of numerous experts, government officials, and industry actors.[61] This

---

[55] Foreword by Isher Ahluwalia, in Chanda (2002, v–vi).
[56] Committee on WTO Studies, Budget (2002–2003), "List of Studies Approved," memo with author.
[57] M/s Nishith Desai Associates; Economic Law Practice and Praveen Anand were consulted by the government of India and funded to provide legal advice on "Technical Review of GATS provision" and "Emergency Safeguard Measures."
[58] This project began in 2003 and lasted until 2010.
[59] The information in this section is drawn from numerous interviews with Minister of Commerce officials, research scholars who were consulted by the MOC, and other members of the expert groups.
[60] Interview with MOC official, New Delhi, July 13, 2004.
[61] Expert groups have been constituted for a number of negotiations: Services, TRIPS, Competition Policy, and Anti-dumping, among others. The agriculture expert group in

expert group uses the research paper to analyze the impact and possible strategic options for India.[62] This paper is also submitted to an interministerial consultation process that brings together different ministries concerned with the issue. For example, for an agreement on agriculture, the Ministry of Commerce, the Ministry of Agriculture, and the Ministry of Finance have overlapping consultations and dialogue.[63] An international observer with whom I spoke, after looking at the services discussions and the research input into the policy process, was clearly impressed. He noted: "India has clearly adopted a state-of-the-art process to incorporate research findings on services negotiations. The sectoral studies conducted by ICRIER are very sophisticated and the role of expert groups process is clearly effective."[64] This activation of knowledge–policy networks and emphasis on research were catalyzed not only at the central level but also across India's provincial states and among local institutions.[65] Across India's regional states, expert and research communities and business actors provided the impetus for WTO-compliant policies and institutions. Currently, India's negotiating positions are based on stronger research and empirical foundations involving a careful consideration of alternatives and cost and benefit analysis.[66]

3.3.5   Bureaucratic politics and interministerial coordination

> Ours is a *cohesive* government and today's meeting [between Minister of Commerce and the Agriculture Minister] was part of our efforts to have a regular dialogue with the agricultural ministry. We want to have a clear understanding with them.[67]

Trade politics in the 1990s unleashed bureaucratic politics in a distinct way, further enhancing the power of the Commerce Ministry as a nodal

---

2004 included M. S. Swaminathan, Abhijit Sen, G. S. Bhalla, R. S. Deshpande, Kirit Parikh, Vaidyanathan, and V. S. Vyas.

[62] The expert group on Services negotiations included B. L. Das, Tarun Das, Dr. Amit Mitra, B. K. Zutshi, Mr. Hoda, S. Narayanan, Dr. Rupa Chanda, Ashoh Haldia, P. R. Mehta, Yogi Mehrotra, Kiran Karnik, I. S. Wahi, R. Mukhariwala, Sunil Mittal, Amit Khanna, Raghu Pillai, and Depak Satwalekar.

[63] These interministerial consultations are both formal, before a formal international meeting, and informal meetings, as the officials finalize their negotiation positions and strategies.

[64] Geza Feketekuty, speaking at the "India–US Cooperation on WTO: Will IT Provide the Bridge," USIBC, NASSCOM, and CSIS, April 4, 2005, US Chamber of Commerce, Washington, DC.

[65] Sinha (2006).

[66] Abhijit Das, head of Center of WTO Centre, said, "Trade policy making became much more participatory and was based on strong empirical foundations." Quoted in an interview to Greg Shaffer, cited in Shaffer, Nedumpara, and Sinha (2015).

[67] Kamal Nath, India's minister of commerce in 2004, told reporters after meeting with the agriculture minister (emphasis added).

body to deal with external economic relations.[68] In a parliamentary system, departments – referred to as "ministries" – have independent power. Ideological predispositions across departments vary, as do the relationships of ministries with their industry and societal constituents.[69] Until recently, the various economic ministries existed in a fragmented back-to-back structure where coordination was nonexistent and turf protection by each ministry was the norm. Compliance pressures of the WTO disturbed this equilibrium in a distinct way. In the pre-WTO days, conflict between departmental ministries did not need to be settled; each ministry could go its separate way (Shourie 2004).[70] However, compliance with the structure of WTO agreements, with its single-undertaking principle, meant that India's negotiators had to come up with a consistent negotiation strategy and position across sectoral agreements as well as balance the needs of different sectors. Deal making across sectors also required discussion and debate over the exact *trade-offs* across sectoral agreements. This disrupted the bureaucratic equilibrium. While the Ministry of Commerce led the WTO/GATT negotiations, as is in keeping with its jurisdiction over international trade, sectoral agreements required a strong participation of other relevant ministries. This participation of different sectoral departments unleashed two somewhat contradictory processes in the post-WTO world. First, greater conflict across ministries ensued as overlap of issues and interests became more intense. Turf protection was no longer possible. Second, this conflict and the necessity of building a combined position at the WTO forums led to greater interaction, consultation, and coordination across ministries.

3.3.6   Interministerial conflict

Two snapshots of conflict, one between the Ministry of Commerce and the Ministry of Finance on quantitative restrictions and the other a conflict between the Ministry of Commerce and the Ministry of Agriculture, reveal some of the emerging patterns. As India's economic situation improved in the early 1990s, its foreign exchange reserves grew. The Ministry of Finance was thrilled to report "a more positive outlook" to the IMF. Yet, the Ministry of Commerce continued to use the argument of the balance of payments crisis to seek to impose quantitative restrictions on many agricultural and consumer goods. In 1997, this

---

[68] For analysis of trade policy that focuses on competing pressures within states and bureaucracies, see I. M. Destler for United States (1995) and L. Schoppa (1997) for Japan.

[69] Julius Sen's conclusions resonate: "the MOC is often accused of isolating itself from other ministries of the government in order to protect its special privileges" (2004, 2).

[70] This norm negatively affected the coherence of government policy.

conflict of interest within the state and across important economic ministries spilled over and affected India's negotiating position at the WTO. In May 1997, India submitted a 'balance-of-payment' argument to justify the continued use of quantitative restrictions to the WTO. Simultaneously, the Ministry of Finance sent a letter to the IMF and the WTO confirming that India did not have a balance of payments crisis.[71] This led a parliamentary Standing Committee on Commerce to note:

> The Committee also took exception to the Ministry of Finance, which has reportedly communicated to the IMF its opinion that the country's balance of payments is excellent; by implication, it has endorsed the view that the country should do away with QRs on farm imports. This has placed the Ministry of Commerce in an "embarrassing position." The Committee has suggested that the Ministry of Commerce approach the Prime Minister's Office so that the Ministry of Finance's communication to the IMF is withdrawn and a fresh representation made to the Dispute-Settlement Body of the WTO with respect to the US complaint against India in the matter.[72]

At that time, India was hauled in front of the WTO Dispute-Settlement Board (DSB) and lost its case. The United States and the DSB cited the letters by the Ministry of Finance and the Reserve Bank of India to make a strong case that India did not have a balance of payments crisis and that its own officials thought so.[73] In its reply, the Ministry of Commerce tried to explain the divergent and optimistic stance of its own Ministry of Finance regarding India's balance of payments situation thus:

> India submitted that a Finance Minister was a steward of his nation's finances and was required to emphasize the positive approach of the new government with respect to foreign inflows and the balance of payments situation. Financial markets would react adversely if a Finance Minister emphasized the negative aspects of the balance of payments situation. *Accordingly the statements of the Finance Minister should be read in the above context and not literally.* Moreover they also related to a situation existing at a particular point of time.[74]

Clearly, the WTO magnified the divergent predispositions toward free trade across these two ministries, with one agency (MOF) using the WTO provisions to nudge the abolition of quantitative restrictions by the

---

[71] This action was deliberate and not accidental as the Ministry of Finance favored import liberalization more than the Ministry of Commerce (confidential interview of a senior Ministry of Finance official with author, January 2002, New Delhi). I confirmed this in numerous interviews.

[72] "Panel Raps Commerce Ministry for Poor Export Show," *Business Line*, April 30, 1999.

[73] Panel Report, *India: Quantitative Restrictions on Imports of Agricultural, Textile and Industrial Products*, WT/DS90/R (April 6, 1999).

[74] Ibid, 86 (emphasis added).

Ministry of Commerce. Such divergence had a negative consequence at the WTO level as India lost the quantitative restrictions case.

In the run-up to Cancun (late 2003), another dispute developed between the agriculture ministry and the Ministry of Commerce. The agriculture ministry's argument was that they should be consulted on proposals readied for the Cancun discussions on tax reductions, standardization, or restructuring of percentage of taxes. Rajnath Singh, the minister of agriculture, was primarily concerned with the political fallout if the government were to succumb to WTO demands on reducing customs duties on certain agriculture products. The WTO demands were to reduce customs duties by half and in some cases to eliminate them entirely. These changes in the tax and duty structure had a huge potential impact on tobacco growers in Andhra Pradesh and Karnataka as well as small onion growers in Maharashtra and groundnut growers in Gujarat.

The focus of the commerce ministry, however, was more on economic and trade issues. What ruffled feathers within the agriculture ministry was the fact that they were not consulted by the commerce ministry before finalizing the list of 842 items that would be subjected to cuts in tariffs. This incident expressed the "need for greater coordination between the Commerce ministry and the administrative ministries handling specific issues related to the WTO."[75] Again in 2004, a dispute arose over India's concessions in the "July framework agreement" between the recently appointed agriculture minister, Sharad Pawar, and the commerce ministry.[76] It seemed that his ministry prepared a note for the prime minister outlining the different interpretation of his ministry. It went as far as to say that "[t]he WTO framework agreement that Commerce Minister Kamal Nath signed in Geneva last month July 31, 2004 was a sell-out." According to the agriculture ministry, "India had conceded much more than it got. While the United States and the European Union made specific gains, "concessions" for India were still to be negotiated. The agreement said the developed countries had agreed to eliminate all forms of export subsidies by an "end date" that was not defined. The agriculture ministry contended that in the absence of any "finality," the developed countries' commitments were meaningless. The so-called flexibility given to India to continue with its export subsidies for a longer period was of no use because Indian exports and export subsidies are negligible. While there was no firm commitment from the developed

[75] "Need for Coordination," *Financial Express*, August 25, 2004.
[76] "India Sold Out to West at WTO: Pawar," *The Hindu*, August 23, 2004, accessed at: www.ifg.org/analysis/wto/IndiaSoldOut.html.

countries on cutting export subsidies, India had agreed to cut its import tariffs. In contrast, the commerce ministry was "happy that India was safe because Indian tariffs were quite high (ibid)." The Ministry of Agriculture later denied that there was a conflict,[77] but, in fact, it was the Ministry of Agriculture that leaked the details of Sharad Pawar's letter to the prime minister.

3.3.7   Interagency coordination and consultations

In partial response to interministerial conflicts documented earlier, in 1999, a formal interministerial group started meeting to discuss WTO-related issues after at the ministerial and bureaucratic levels. On May 14, 1999, the government established a nine-member interdepartmental group on the WTO under the chairmanship of Commerce Secretary P. P. Prabhu. The purpose of the group was better coordination. A government official noted, "The group would ensure effective preparation on WTO issues, devise a communication strategy for wider discussion and building up of a national consensus on India's negotiating position, and deal with all WTO-related aspects of India's interface with foreign countries to optimize India's negotiating leverage and decision-making in the WTO."[78] This group included the secretaries of commerce, agriculture, external affairs (economic relations), finance, industry, law, and textiles, the secretary to the prime minister, and the director general of the Council of Scientific and Industrial Research (CSIR).[79] In addition, formal and informal consultations across sectoral ministries became common, regular, and necessary. The agriculture minister and commerce minister began to meet together before key meetings, preceded by meetings between the secretaries of the two ministries. This was true for Cancun and for the post-Cancun discussions. In June 2004, the two ministers met "to fine-tune the country's strategy for deliberations at the G-20."[80] The two ministers took stock of the ongoing negotiations on agriculture in the WTO, mainly the issue of trade-distorting domestic support and export subsidies in other countries that impeded India's agricultural exports. The meeting underlined the country's livelihood concerns and the importance of safeguarding the interests of farmers in the negotiations.[81]

---

[77] "WTO Pact Not a Sellout to West," *India Abroad*, August 23, 2004, www.rediff.com/money/2004/aug/23wto.htm.

[78] "Secy-level Group Formed to Fine-Tune India's Stand on WTO," *Rediff*, May 14, 1999, www.rediff.com/business/1999/may/14wto.htm.

[79] Ibid.

[80] "India Readies for Farm Talks: Commerce and Agriculture Ministers Hold Talks to Finalize India's Strategy," *Business Standard*, June 8, 2004.

[81] Ibid.

At times, the conflict needed the mediation of the prime minister. For example, in August 2003, as a prelude to the Cancun meetings, the prime minister himself had to step in to mediate the fight between the Ministry of Agriculture and Ministry of Commerce.[82] The conflict between the two departments was over the list of agricultural items to be subjected to taxes and duties. Prime Minister Atal Bihari Vajpayee intervened and "asked Agriculture Minister Rajnath Singh to make peace with Commerce Minister Arun Jaitley." The finance minister, Mr. Jaswant Singh, was asked to mediate and call meetings to break the stalemate.[83]

Thus, international negotiations exacerbated distributional conflict, which then stimulated overlap across fragmented ministries, exposing the need to make government policy consistent across sectors and issue areas. This need also created more frequent disputes across ministries. These conflicts and differences demanded greater interaction, meetings, and joint institutional forums for the mediation of differences. The structure of WTO agreements catalyzed collective mobilization within bureaucratic departments by creating conflict and thus necessitating coordination and consultation. Thus, in addition to enhancement of existing organizations and the creation of new institutions, new practices were instituted in response to compliance imperatives.

3.3.8   Creating new institutions of compliance and protection

Existing institutions were reorganized to deal with WTO compliance. In addition, *different* institutions with *new* capacities were needed. Between 1997 and 1998, three new institutional frameworks were created to deal with the expanding tasks associated with trade negotiations and compliance. These were the Intellectual Property Rights Administration, the Anti-dumping Administration, and a new Tariff Commission. On April 13, 1998, the Directorate General of Anti-Dumping and Allied Duties (DGAD) was constituted within the Ministry of Commerce to "initiate inquiries and give necessary relief and protection to domestic producers against dumping of goods and articles from other parts of the world" (Government of India 1999, 8) to address the concerns of the losing segments of the industrial sector. On September 2, 1997, an independent Tariff Commission was reestablished, "keeping in view the commitments of government in the WTO and complexities in tariff and tariff related matters which may have very vital impact on domestic industry as

---

[82] "Vajpayee Steps in to End Cancun Spat," *Indian Express*, August 14, 2003.   [83] Ibid.

well as on the economy of the country."[84] In 1997, the prime minister and cabinet directed the Ministry of Industry and other ministries to modernize the patent administration and allotted Rs. 65 crores (approx. USD13 million) for that purpose.[85] Thus, WTO compliance pressures and dilemmas stimulated a response toward the reformation of state institutions rather than their withdrawal.

3.3.8.1 Reforming and enhancing the intellectual property rights administration   The demands of compliance with TRIPS created both pressures to reform the intellectual property regime in India and new interest groups in favor of knowledge protection. Many important members of the scientific community, led by Dr. R. A. Mashelkar (director of CSIR), Professor C. N. Rao, and M. S. S. Swaminathan, began to lobby for a stronger system of patent protection.[86] In the mid-1990s, the scientific community argued that compliance with TRIPS will "allow the scientific community to truly capitalize on their intellect."[87] In 1997, the scientific community effectively lobbied the government and especially the prime minister, I. K. Gujral, to reform the governance of science and knowledge so that "technology could be used as an instrument of growth."[88] On June 13, 1997, the government appointed a Science Advisory Committee to the Cabinet (SACC) consisting of thirty-six members from a larger group of scientists, technocrats, and industrialists. This committee's recommendations led the prime minister to "direct the setting up of an all-encompassing patents office to tackle issues relating to intellectual property rights and patents."[89] I. K. Gujaral, then prime minister, headed a committee of parliament during the mid-1990s that argued against India joining the WTO, but in 1998 he initiated India's compliance with the global property rights regime after India's loss at the WTO dispute-settlement court.

[84] Ministry of Industry, *Resolution No. A- 42012 /1/98- EIV- CDN*, Department of Industrial Policy and Promotion, Government of India, 1997.

[85] In 1997 India had only thirty-seven patent examiners, by 2010 it had increased to 257. These are still not enough to handle the increase in patent applications.

[86] S. Chandrasekhar and M. K. Venu, "Scientific Advisory Panel Wants Patent Bill to Be Passed Soon," *Economic Times*, August 2, 1997. Dr. Mashelkar is a noted chemical scientist who had worked both in industry and in government. Dr. C. N. Rao is a material scientist, and Dr. Swaminathan is an agricultural scientist.

[87] Ibid.; also see S. Ganapathy Subramanian, "Need to Amend Patent Act," *Hindustan Times*, August 21, 1997.

[88] R.A. Mashelkar, Director-General of CSIR (Council of Scientific and Industrial Research), at a press conference on June 9, 1997 (Dharamsala, Himachal Pradesh). M. S. Swaminathan, an agricultural scientist, seemed to support stronger legal protection for plant varieties exclusive to India.

[89] "PM Directs Setting Up of Patent Office," *Statesman*, New Delhi, July 6, 1997; "Gujral Directs Setting Up of Patents Office," *Indian Express*, July 8, 1997.

The modernization of the patent offices was aimed to offer services at par with similar organizations in Europe, to computerize the data collection, and to increase the fees charged for the patent applications. These reforms aimed to speed up the processing of patent applications.[90] The SACC plea for modernization received support from the prime minister himself.[91] Again in 1999, the government chalked out plans to hire more patent examiners, and an additional Rs. 70 lakhs (approx. USD140,000) were earmarked for modernizing the patent offices. By the 2007–2012 five-year regular budgetary allocation, up to Rs. 300 crores (approx. USD60 million) were allotted to upgrade the patent offices to keep up with the rising demand of applications.

Four new separate patent offices were built in the four major cities – Delhi, Calcutta, Mumbai, and Chennai – with hundreds of patent examiners. A larger corporate Delhi office was reorganized into a new location at Dwarka, New Delhi, by 2013. The infrastructure in existing patent offices in Delhi, Kolkata, Chennai, and Mumbai was continually modernized. A modernized designs office in Kolkata was made operational in the mid-2000s. Action was underway to set up an integrated patent office in each of the four metro cities so as to house all activities in one building. In addition, an initial level of computerization was completed to generate information about the status of patent applications, and then later comprehensive computerization was undertaken. An Intellectual Property Training Institute (IPTI) was established at Nagpur (Maharashtra) to provide training to newly recruited examiners. Work manuals for IP offices were prepared to ensure uniformity in the operation. The conscious goal of this recruitment drive and reorganization was so that it would be "possible to ensure grant of patent rights within a timeframe *comparable to international levels and consistent with the statutory provisions* [of the new laws]."[92] The problem of the backlog of pending patent applications was also addressed through legislative measures contained in the Patents (Amendment) Act of 2002, which introduced an examination-on-request system in place of examination of all applications. A digital database of over 1 million patent records and 48,000 design records has been prepared so far. Clearly, the patent administration needed a massive enhancement of size, staff, capacity, and expertise. While the changes recorded here have not fully addressed the demand, they are a step in the right direction. At the very least, they reveal how an

---

[90] M. Ahmed, "Indian Patent Offices Set for Major Facelift," *Business Standard*, August 19, 1997.
[91] Ibid.
[92] This is drawn from the website of the patent department: patent department online, www.ipindia.nic.in.

international agreement and its associated rules – TRIPS – requires mobilization of state capacity and a "re-formation of the state" (Schamis 2002) rather than its withdrawal.

3.3.8.2 Tariff Commission India's tariffs have historically been very high, decided by the Tariff Board before 1947 and then by a Tariff Commission set up under the Tariff Commission Act of 1951. The Tariff Commission in the 1960s and 1970s was clearly a protectionist instrument; this is evident from its location in the Ministry of Industry, which was captured by different protectionist lobbies. The Tariff Commission sought to "grant protection for the encouragement of industry in India," adjust duties of customs or other duties in relation to any industry, and monitor dumping of goods and was authorized to take "action in cases where industry has been taking undue advantage of tariff protection."[93] This earlier commission was a quasi-judicial body, and its reports were advisory in character; it submitted reports to the central government, which were then placed in parliament. In 1976, under the Tariff Commission (Repeal) Act of 1976, the Bureau of Industrial Costs (BICP) replaced the Tariff Commission to emerge as its successor. The BICP conducted tariff studies and made tariff recommendations to the government. In 1997, with the demands of tariff reduction stimulated by WTO commitments, the need was felt to revive the Tariff Commission. The new commission's mandate was in keeping with these new realities. No mention is made of "protection of Indian industry"; rather, the language is one of tariff rationalization. It sought to aid the government in recommending the fixation of tariffs and tariff-related issues for goods and services as well as evolve an overall tariff structure and look into the issue of tariff rationalization. In addition, it was asked to "study critically market access offers received from trading partners as part of the WTO framework and advise the government on opportunities and challenges generated by these offers, and to examine the transition period required for selected industries and recommend the gradual phasing-out of tariffs."[94]

In 1999, technical demands on the Tariff Commission grew, so the BICP was merged with the Tariff Commission.[95] The research expertise of the BICP was seen to be necessary for the working of the Tariff Commission. The objective of the merger was defined as follows:

---

[93] These quotes are from the website of the Tariff Commission; Tariff Commission online, http://tc.nic.in.
[94] Ibid.
[95] Interview with a member of the Tariff Commission, New Delhi, August 17, 2003.

The revised TOR [terms of reference] has enlarged the role and responsibilities of the Commission that would now also include the core functions of the Bureau of Industrial Costs and Prices (BICP) as well. In order to discharge its functions as per the revised TORs, the Tariff Commission requires in-house support, continuity and expertise in tariff and tariff-related matters. Over the years, BICP has accumulated extensive data and expertise in the areas of technology, economic analysis, finance and cost accounting.[96]

Initially, the Tariff Commission retained the organizational structure inherited from the BICP. It had a discipline-wise structure with separate costing, technical, and economic divisions, and a secretariat. In the short span of three years, the commission expanded and reorganized its functions. It set up sectoral working groups and sought to bring together experts from diverse competencies in one forum. Three divisions were created: sectoral working groups, an analysis group, and a secretariat. Six sectoral working groups (SWGs) were constituted, based on the International Trade Classification (harmonized series). Specific chapters of the classification have been assigned to each SWG. The groups together cover all products and items contained in the classification. Each SWG was envisioned as a multidisciplinary core team. Consultants can be included in SWGs, if required. The groups are responsible for conducting studies and preparing reports and notes. They are expected to build up an adequate database relating to the assigned products for carrying out (1) impact analysis, (2) cost, price, and resource efficiency studies, (3) studies pertaining to the transition period required for select industries to move to a tariff-based regime, and (4) technical studies on cost of production and competitiveness. These working groups are also expected to build up adequate working knowledge of WTO agreements having a bearing on the items assigned to them. The snalysis group was established for in-depth analysis of not only WTO agreements but also issues concerning multilateral trading. It must maintain a comprehensive database on trade and tariff changes in competing and trade partner countries and an inventory of the tariffs prevalent in relevant countries. Its role was to develop skills and to advise the commission on negotiating strategies while framing trade agreements (WTO and others). It focuses on all matters relating to WTO agreements, their analysis and implications, and strategies appropriate for the country.

The member secretary heads the secretariat of the commission. It is responsible for general administration, accounts, training, etc. In

---

[96] These quotes are from the website of the Tariff Commission; Tariff Commission online, http://tc.nic.in.

2002–2003, the total staff strength of the commission was 108, of which thirty-eight were professionals and experts; some of them were chartered accountants, economists, and even engineers.[97] By 2013, twenty-seven professionals continued to provide research and technical expertise to the organization. Thus, clearly, the establishment of the commission in 1997, its expansion and subsequent reorganization, and the incorporation of a large number of experts were in direct response to the compliance pressures brought on by the WTO.

3.3.8.3 Anti-dumping   Anti-dumping measures are a classic protectionist method used by all countries to protect domestic industry in the face of import competition. From 1995 to 2014, India was the largest user of anti-dumping actions (740 initiations), followed by the United States (527 initiations) and the European Union (468 initiations).[98] This led economists to criticize India's widespread use of anti-dumping measures.[99] Whether one agrees or disagrees with the use of anti-dumping, what is interesting from an institutional perspective is that India's use of anti-dumping has changed over time. Between 1992 and 1997, India was subject to many anti-dumping actions, but its ability to retaliate was quite weak. Between 1993 and 1997, India initiated merely five cases. Instead, India was the target of many anti-dumping cases. In 1999, India faced forty-one cases from other nations. At that time (from 1992 to 1999 or so), India raised its voice against the use of anti-dumping in many forums. For example, at an Indo-European Joint Commission meeting in Brussels, India was quite vocal in criticizing the use of anti-dumping investigations.[100] But slowly, India developed its own ability to initiate anti-dumping actions, and starting in 1998, its anti-dumping actions rose, as outlined in Table 3.5.

In late 1998, a separate office was set up for initiating anti-dumping actions. Between 1998 and 1999, this office handled thirty-two anti-dumping cases, of which twenty-one were finalized.[101] Thus, over time, state capacity to respond to globalization had increased. This specific capability, while a protectionist measure, was learned through interacting with the WTO, specifically by responding to charges against it in anti-dumping cases and by observing how other countries initiated cases. Interestingly, none of India's investigations have been challenged at the WTO level,

---

[97] Government of India (2004, 13).

[98] WTO data on anti-dumping: www.wto.org/english/tratop_e/adp_e/adp_e.htm.

[99] Arvind Panagariya, "Moving Trade Policy Forward," August 26, 2004, www.columbia .edu/~ap2231/ET/et68-Aug26–04.htm.

[100] "India Criticizes Non-Trade Barriers Imposed by Europe," *Asia Pulse*, January 17, 1999, http://global.factiva.com/en/arch/.

[101] Anand Madhavan, "Dangers of the Antidumping Safeguard," *Business Standard*, April 3, 1999.

Table 3.5 *Anti-dumping initiation, by reporting member (India)*

Year	Number of Initiations
1992	2
1993	2
1994	4
1995	6
1996	21
1997	13
1998	28
1999	64
2000	41
2001	79
2002	81
2003	46
2004	21
2005	28
2006	31
2007	47
2008	55
2009	31
2010	41
2011	19
2012	21
2013	29
2014	38
TOTAL	**740**

Source: Author's calculations from WTO's anti-dumping website, www.wto.org/english /tratop_e/adp_e/adp_e.htm.

showing that India was able to learn how to successfully work the system. The use of such techniques symbolized a combination of open-economy and protectionist measures. The Indian state became more adept at using a combination of these measures, using them in a strategic, rather than defensive, way. Overall, the state's imprint and budgets expanded as the task of compliance with global rules demanded new state capacities.

3.4   Changing state–society interactions on trade policy

WTO agreements activated and mobilized societal groups and encouraged greater state–society interactions, especially with business groups. During the Uruguay Round (1986–1994), with the intensification and expansion of global trade talks, India's participation became more active than before but was still essentially state led and bureaucratic. Usually Ministry of Commerce officials and Geneva-based negotiators would brief the minister on India's stance and possible options. This was then placed before the Union Cabinet, which would modify and endorse India's negotiating stance.[102] It was at the level of the Union Cabinet that political aspects of the agreement would be debated, with the cabinet ministers assessing the possible fallouts of India's position. The policy process was secret and insular. This process left no scope for public involvement or public education.[103] The government did not release even basic information about the WTO; in the early 1990s, intellectual activists and a few NGOs performed this task.[104] S. Venkitaramanan, erstwhile Reserve Bank Governor, said in 1997: "The government of India should have been more forthcoming in educating the public about the various details and the implications of the WTO. It is difficult even to lay hands on copies of the final WTO agreements in India."[105] This was the state of affairs until as late as 1998. From August 1995 to December 1996, as a run-up to the Singapore ministerial meetings, the government organized no public meetings or seminars at all; it also participated in very few seminars organized by other actors.[106] Overall, the public presence of the government on WTO issues was minimal. Government officials only made statements in parliament in response to criticism or debate or in Singapore at the site of the ministerial meetings. A few statements were leaked to journalists, but no attempt was made to intervene in any public discussion on the WTO or to provide any information about the government's position and options.

Soon after the Seattle ministerial meeting, it became clear that the government could no longer keep the trade policy process secretive and insular. Given India's loss at the Dispute-Settlement Body on TRIPS

---

[102] "Strategy for Trade Minister's Meet Being Finalized," *Financial Express*, November 27, 1990.

[103] Around 1994, with opposition against the Dunkel proposals very widespread and strong, the ruling Congress Party started a media campaign to counter the opposition. This led the commerce minister to issue a number of statements, explaining that the threat posed by WTO was not as serious as the opposition was making it out to be. See "Media Blitz against Opposition to GATT," *Economic Times*, April 24, 1994.

[104] The National Working Group on Patent Laws played a seminal role in disseminating information and educating the public about the implications of various WTO agreements with a special focus on intellectual property rights.

[105] S. Venkitaramanan, "WTO and Its Implications," *Economic Times*, November 25, 1997.

[106] These conclusions are derived from an analysis of WTO- and GATT-related daily newspaper stories from twenty-five to thirty newspapers. I analyzed about 1,500 thematically arranged newspaper stories. This comprehensive coverage on a daily basis across a large number of newspapers yields a reliable indicator of the government policy process. I also interviewed a number of retired trade negotiators who had been involved with India's trade negotiations in mid-to-late 1990s.

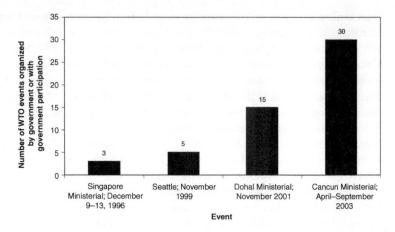

Figure 3.3 Public activities organized by the government on multilateral
trade issues, 1996–2004
Newspaper Database of newspapers constructed by author. I coded and
systemically analyzed all activities related to WTO meetings as well as
the statements of all government officials.
Note: I covered 25 newspapers from March 1995 to December 1996
[Singapore period], and analyzed a total of 1749 news stories exclusively
on GATT, WTO, and International Trade issues; For the Cancun
ministerial I covered January 2003 to December 2003 a total of about
1500 newspaper reports. This wide coverage allows me to be quite
confident that I have not missed any event or activity related to the WTO.
Note 2: I have not included statements made during ministerial meetings
as these were not made with the explicit purpose of sharing and informing
the public and civil society in India, but were more oriented to the
international audience. Also, the minister's statements in the parliament
were not included, as they were required to make these statements.

compliance in 1998, the government started to "educate the public"
about the implications of the WTO agreements. It did so by launching
public seminars to disseminate information about WTO and India's
obligations to states, NGOs, and the broader public, such as farmers,
intellectuals, trade unions, political parties, and other interested groups.
In addition, government officials prominently issued public statements
on WTO-related issues; they began to issue regular briefs, organize press
conferences, and meet with various actors. From April to September
2003, in preparation for the Cancun meeting, the government held at
least thirty seminars, conferences, and meetings to educate the public and
interested parties. Figure 3.3 shows the number of seminars sponsored by
the government around the various ministerial meetings. Clearly, the

number of seminars and statements by government officials has increased dramatically.

The government instituted formal and public processes of information dissemination, which were quite alien to the existing policy process and culture of policymaking in the Indian bureaucracy. In 1999 the government started publishing the "India and WTO Newsletter," which outlined the ongoing developments as well as publicizing ministerial statements and arguments pertaining to the WTO. This newsletter was posted on the Ministry of Commerce website and has become a regular monthly feature from 1999 to the present.[107] The website started posting detailed information on various aspects of WTO as well as India's submissions to the WTO. For example, the booklet on QRs (quantitative restrictions); details of removal of QRs on balance of payments (BOP) grounds; information on TRIPS, the Agreement on Trade-Related Investment Measures (TRIMs), and ITA; information on the work program about electronic commerce; and India's proposals for the ongoing negotiations on "services" are available on the site.[108] An office of the public relations official was assigned the task of interfacing with the public, the press, and other outside groups. This office housed two senior officials and started releasing press releases, interacting with journalists, and recording and keeping track of public reports and press stories on the WTO, the ministry, and the minister.[109] For example, it collates a "Fortnightly Round of News and Views on WTO Issues," which is then circulated to around twenty-four senior officials and ministers. This in-house newsletter brings together news on WTO-related issues from all the prominent newspapers in India and allows the MOC to keep track of public reception of WTO issues and actions by MOC.[110] Thus, the

---

[107] The newsletter can be accessed at the Ministry of Commerce website, http://commerce.nic.in/publications/india_wto_newsletter.asp?id=1.

[108] The Ministry of Commerce website also contains information on India's trade statistics, anti-dumping measures, trade agreements/transit agreements, EOUs/EPZs/SEZs, and the MDA Scheme for promotion of exports. The Exim Policy 1997–2002 is also available on the website. The site also contains information on the organizational set-up of the ministry, including details of India's commercial missions abroad. The latest press releases issued by the ministry have also been put on the website. This information can be found at the MOC website, http://commerce.nic.in

[109] The press releases from November 2000 are made available on the Ministry of Commerce website, and in contrast to many of the business association's press release archives (CII, for example), the web links of the Ministry of Commerce actually work! See the following website: http://commerce.nic.in/PressRelease/pressrelease_year.asp?year1=2000.

[110] Ministry of Commerce, "*Fortnightly Round of News and Views on WTO Issues – Sl. no. 354* (For the Fortnightly ending 25/07/2003)," Ministry of Commerce, 2003, document with author.

public interface of the government increased dramatically between a short period of time from 1998 to 2004.

3.4.1 Consultations with business over multilateral trade policy

In a radical departure, the government began seeking policy input from firms and industry associations during both the formulation and the implementation stages of trade policymaking.[111] The incorporation of business in trade policymaking is one of the few instances of integration of business opinion in policy formulation in India. In other policy domains, business input is sought but rarely as intensively as on issues of international trade. This transformation came as a result of compliance pressures accompanying the WTO and enhanced conflict among those who would lose as a result of the WTO process. The historical evolution of this interaction with business reveals significant change in a very short span of time – from 1999 to 2005. As late as May 27, 1997, the former commerce secretary and India's chief negotiator at the Uruguay Round, A.V. Ganesan, said that apart from some sections of the Indian bureaucracy and politicians, there seemed to be very little awareness of the "dramatic changes" brought about by the WTO.[112] He failed to note that one of the reasons (although not the only one) for this state of affairs was because the government of India never consulted or shared any information about GATT or the WTO with business groups during the Uruguay Round. The policymaking process regarding international negotiations was closed and insular. As noted by an erstwhile joint secretary in the Ministry of Industry: "In the late 1980s – around 1989 – when the discussion on TRIPS had started, I immediately saw that the TRIPs would affect private business. I spoke to my superior officer and suggested that we at least inform the firms about how this will affect them. But I was told that I should do nothing of the kind as the information would leak out and government may be shown in a bad light. I nonetheless went ahead and had a private meeting with some members of the pharmaceutical companies and gave them some hint about what was to come. This was at a considerable personal risk, but I felt it to be necessary."[113] S. Venkataramanan, a senior government official, similarly noted in 1997: "GOI should engage the trade and business community in an intensive dialogue in order to arrive at agreed methods for handling the impending confrontations with WTO. On and off consultations will not

---

[111] Also see Sinha (2010) for details about business–state interactions.

[112] "Call for Awareness Programme on WTO," *The Hindu*, May 28, 1997, Madras edition.

[113] Author's interview with ex-joint secretary, who has since left the service, Geneva, October 2003.

do. We should not face WTO without a proper defense strategy. Such a strategy cannot be devised in isolation at New Delhi or Geneva. It has to involve those who are affected."[114] Another senior government official said, "The Government should be more open with industry and make public details of all trade-related agreements it entered into with the rest of the world. ... The agreements are not supposed to be a secret. If 135 other nations know about it, why [should] not the domestic industry be told about it?"[115]

The insularity of the state apparatus was mirrored in the attitude of the businesspersons and business associations who did not know about or pay attention to the ongoing WTO negotiations until as late as 1999–2000. Indian industry had come to maturity under a closed-economy environment, concerned more with lobbying for firm-specific exceptions than with international trade regimes. Its interest in multilateral trade negotiations was nonexistent.[116] Businesspersons and even business associations did not care to educate themselves about how the WTO would affect them. They hardly did any research on the WTO and GATT. As an illustration, the Confederation of Indian Industry (CII), a business association, thought that the WTO was not at all important in the mid- and late 1990s.[117] In the early 1990s, the three all-industry associations issued "statements" in favor of a globally consistent patent regime without doing any analysis simply because the government asked them to issue supporting statements. As noted by G. V. Ramakrishna: "The fault also lies with industry. There has been a complete lack of initiative on its part. It has never bothered to find out what was happening at the [WTO-related] meetings abroad."[118] One exception to this lack of knowledge was some companies in the pharmaceutical sector, most notably Dr. Parvinder Singh from Ranbaxy, who was one of the few members of the Indian business class to see the "writing on the wall" regarding the upcoming patent regime. A report by the CII acknowledged that Indian industry (during the Uruguay Round) was "not so much concerned with what was happening in the Uruguay Round. It was not even fully aware of the items of agenda that were being negotiated."[119] Rahul Bajaj, a businessman of national repute, said in 2001: "India was a party to the Uruguay

---

[114] S. Venkitaramanan, "WTO and Its Implications," *Economic Times*, November 25, 1997.
[115] "Declare All Trade Pacts: Ramakrishna, The Chairman of the Disinvestment Commission," *Observer*, July 24, 1997.
[116] Author's interview with a member of a business association who has had long interactions with many business leaders, New Delhi, January 2002.
[117] Ibid.   [118] "Declare All Trade Pacts: Ramakrishna," *Observer*, July 24, 1997.
[119] CII, "*WTO: The Reality of the New Trading Order: Proceedings and WTO 2000 Series of Workshops*, 30th March–12 July 1999," Research Department, CII. Available from author.

negotiations from the beginning and it was given an opportunity to participate in these rounds. ... it is unfortunate that neither the Indian government nor Indian business took these discussions very seriously. We did not adequately prepare for these negotiations and we faltered at every point."[120] In 1999, the CII thought about setting up an office in Geneva at the site of the WTO, but nothing came of that proposal till 2004 when Arun Shourie urged the CII to set up an office, and this time it was followed through, but that office was disbanded after a few years.[121] Around 1997–1998, at a seminar organized by the government to discuss the impending ministerial meeting in Singapore, N. Shankar, a prominent businessman, appealed to the government: "Please educate us about how we may prepare for the WTO." The government official replied: "You are too late; the WTO is a done deal now; the negotiations on IPR, on MFA and some other aspects are over; it's over and done with and it may be too late to learn about how to cope with it!"[122] Until as late as 2000, the CII and the Federation of Indian Chambers of Commerce and Industry (FICCI) were not interested in learning about or keeping track of WTO-related issues.[123] In 1999, a CII research report admitted: "However, even today [1999] there is very little awareness about the Uruguay Round of agreements and the developments subsequent to establishment of WTO. One also observes lack of interest about developments in WTO in most segments of the industry."[124] Even in globally oriented industries like software, awareness about GATS, the services negotiation, was minimal. The National Association of Software and Service Companies (NASSCOM) began to be active on GATS-related issues as late as 2002. A senior member of NASSCOM admitted:

[120] Rahul Bajaj, "Foreword," in Sabade (2001).

[121] N. Vasuki Rao (1999). This report confirmed that the Indian government consulted business for the first time as a run-up to the Seattle ministerial meeting. N. Vasuki Rao noted: "The Indian government plans for the first time to involve its domestic industry at the ministerial meeting of the World Trade Organization in late November. Representatives from four major trade and industry organizations will be part of the government delegation to Seattle, where a new round of trade negotiations is expected to start. The Indian government barely consulted domestic industry during the Uruguay Round of trade negotiations that led to the WTO agreements" (ibid.).

[122] Author's confidential interview with a prominent journalist, New Delhi, January 2002. The person was at this seminar and heard the exchange first hand.

[123] They were not willing, for example, to hire a journalist to report on WTO-related activities based in Geneva for a paltry salary of around 200 USD a month. Around 1998–1999 a prominent journalist urged the CII to monitor development at the WTO in Geneva closely but the CII's leadership was not interested (confidential interview, January 2002, New Delhi). In 2004 almost a decade later, the CII set up an office in Geneva, which was closed in the late 2000s.

[124] CII, "WTO: the Reality of the New Trading Order: Proceedings and WTO 2000 Series of Workshops, 30th March–12 July 1999." Research Department, CII. Available with author.

"Industry's time horizon is short run and can't understand all these rules and offers; the software majors were quite unaware of what was going on in the services negotiations."[125]

In 1998–1999, the government made the first overtures to involve business groups in the process of trade policymaking; until then, business associations were asked to comment on the WTO agreements but were not involved in the formulation of policy.[126] In April 1999, the government began organizing workshops on WTO-related issues where "the government called for comprehensive industry involvement in the process of preparation for India's mandate in the World Trade Organization ministerial meeting in November [1999]. The special secretary, Minister of Commerce N. N. Khanna, asked for detailed, specific, but WTO-compatible, demands from the industry that could be included as part of India's mandate for the WTO negotiations."[127]

The government delegation to Seattle's ministerial meeting for the first time included two members apiece from the CII, FICCI, and ASSOCHAM (Associated Chambers of Commerce and Industry of India).[128] As N. Srinivasan,[129] director-general of the CII admitted: "The turning point of this relationship was the Seattle Ministerial Conference, when, for the first time, representatives from industry were formally a part of the Indian delegation."[130] Three members of the CII – Omkar Goswami (economic advisor to the CII), Gopal Krishnan (Tata Group) and T. R. Bhowmick (economist, Research Group) – were in Seattle, two of them part of the official delegation.[131] Seattle, although a failure, brought home to the Indian government the need for much wider consultations and the need to involve industry as a "stakeholder." After the debacle in Seattle, the government created an expert and business group under the aegis of a "Prime Minister's Council on Trade and Industry" to come up with a "strategy paper" on the WTO: "The Group was asked to consider and recommend a strategy for a reconvened

---

[125] Author's interview, Washington DC, April 8, 2004.
[126] In the early 1990s, the CII and FICCI issued statements supporting the Dunkel Draft. These statements were requested by government. Confidential Interviews revealed that at that time, a careful analysis of the Dunkel Draft on Indian industry was not done.
[127] "Government Calls for Industry Involvement in WTO Talks," *Rediff*, April 29, 1999, www.rediff.com/business/1999/apr/29cii.htm.
[128] The CII's then president, Shekhar Datta, was in Singapore in April 1996 for the World Trade Congress meeting; this two-day meeting was a forerunner to the ministerial meetings in December 1996. India was represented by its commerce secretary, Tejender Khanna, and Shekhar Datta; "India Should Push for Global Trade Pact to Avoid Bias," *Observer*, New Delhi, April 25, 1996.
[129] N. Srinivasan, an engineer from Bangalore, is a different person than the industrialist N. Srinivasan, who was the managing director of India Cements, Ltd., in the 1990s.
[130] Priyadarshi (2005).   [131] Author's interview with CII official, January 1, 2002.

WTO Ministerial Conference."[132] This group was led by two industry stalwarts, one from the CII (Rahul Bajaj) and the other from the FICCI (N. Srinivasan, India Cements, Ltd.), and invited a number of experts, government officials, WTO negotiators, and sector-specific representatives to discuss the ongoing WTO negotiations and evolve India's negotiating position.[133] For about three months in 2000, the group met one to two days a week at FICCI's office to discuss both general and sectoral issues and come up with a set of recommendations.[134] One of the recommendations of the group was

the urgent need to strengthen the domestic machinery both at the policymaking level and at the level of regulation and infrastructural support, particularly with respect to the multilateral trade regime. While there has been a considerable increase in the quality and frequency of interaction between government, business and other stakeholders in society in shaping our economic policy in general and trade policy in particular, this interaction must deepen and widen and be sustained on an on-going basis.[135]

This situation changed dramatically by 2000 with regular consultations and input sought from various sections of business. The three national associations – FICCI, CII, and ASSOCHAM – became part of official advisory bodies on trade and were involved in the trade policymaking process. The business associations set up WTO cells, as did some private companies, most notably the Tata Group.[136] These generated important ideas that became useful during the negotiations.[137] Currently, CII and FICCI representatives attend many ministerial meetings. They consult with their member companies regarding compliance with issues and provide regular and careful feedback to the government. The government and business have come closer, faced with global competition and compliance constraints imposed by the WTO (Sinha 2010).

---

[132] N. Srinivasan and Rahul Bajaj, "Strategy for a Reconvened WTO Ministerial Meeting: Report and Recommendations," Prime Minister's Council on Trade and Industry, 2000. Available from author.

[133] A notable feature of the deliberations was the joint collaboration between the CII and FICCI, two competitor business associations, which have usually failed to undertake joint programs.

[134] Author's interviews with a participant of the group.

[135] N. Srinivsan and Rahul Bajaj, "Strategy for a Reconvened WTO Ministerial Meeting: Report and Recommendations," Prime Minister's Council on Trade and Industry, 2000, p. 41. Available from Author.

[136] Author's interview with members of these WTO cells, January 2003.

[137] Author's interview with members of the CII, February 2003.

3.5   Conclusion

The implications of this analysis for the autonomy of the nation-state in the face of globalization pressures are counterintuitive. At a *prima facie* level, India's participation in the WTO subjects it to international discipline, which it did not have to face before. The WTO drives a wedge in a country's trade politics but is also subject to manipulation and shaping. At a deeper level, then, state negotiating strategies with the WTO regime matter. Even more important, the specific rules of the game of the WTO – interlinkage of issues, technical nature of the issues, among others – stimulate reform *of* the state and institutional change. Thus, participation in an international institution established to *implement* globalization might actually enhance a nation-state's capacity to *delay and modify* globalization and to redirect it toward its own ends. Paradoxically, international rules may energize state capacity even when their aim is to embed free markets and encourage free trade. The specific rules of the game of the WTO are not unimportant to this dynamic story; institutional design matters. Certain features of the WTO provide the enabling conditions for the unintended increase in domestic state capacity to take place. Trade has reformed the Indian state, and the new trading state seeks deeper global integration than before. Trade refashions the Indian state, and the emboldened state seeks to create a new *tradecraft* to manage the global order and legitimize its open economic policies internally.

4   Realigning interests toward global reach
Changes in India's pharmaceutical sector

In May 1982, at the 34th World Health Assembly in Geneva, Indira Gandhi, India's prime minister said, "The idea of a better ordered world is one in which medical discoveries will be free of patents and there will be no profiteering from life and death."[1] This sentiment was the dominant consensus of the time, resonating with the general industrial policy and the Patent Act of 1970, which recognized only process patents for medicines. This policy innovation allowed Indian firms to bypass pharmaceutical patents and produce generic versions of medicines.[2] With the transition from GATT to the WTO in the 1990s, the debate over the TRIPS agreement became central to India's international commitments, and a defense of India's autonomy over patents and health policies became contested. In the 1990s, protests against patents animated "mass politics" (parliament, for example) as much as "elite politics," creating huge political costs for compliance to the patents-based regime.[3] Dr. Hamied, CEO of Cipla, one of the largest Indian companies, declared in 1993, "No change is called for in the Indian Patent Act of 1970 and the sooner our government takes a firm and irrevocable stand on this issue, the better, GATT or no GATT, pressure or no pressure."[4]

On the other side, US threats of trade sanctions constrained Indian policymakers. Throughout the 1990s Indian policymakers struggled to

---

[1] Indira Gandhi (1984, 115).

[2] Despite such processing strengths, Indian firms lacked research and development (R&D) abilities. As late as 1993, the R&D expenditure of Indian firms amounted to only 1.5 percent of sales, one of the lowest in the world (Grace 2004, 37; Choudhuri 2007, 3).

[3] A number of street protests followed reports that the WTO would impose intellectual property laws on India. See "Farmers Stage Anti-Dunkel Dharna," *Financial Express,* July 1, 1992; "Protest Against Patenting Organisms," *Times of India,* July 1, 1992; "Government Urged to Reject Demands for Patents on Living Organisms," *Business Standard,* July 1, 1992. The distinction between mass politics and elite politics is from Varshney (1999), who argues that when economic reforms become a matter of debate within the mass politics arena, reforms slow down or reverse. Patents were opposed by both elites and masses – farmers, common people, and middle classes – making their adoption almost impossible.

[4] Hamied (1993, 6).

pass this unpopular law, successfully resisting pressure from the United States and delaying compliance with TRIPS. At this time, domestic politics seemed to triumph global pressures (US pressure) and obligations (WTO). The Indian legislature did not pass any TRIPS-compliant legislation despite repeated attempts by its policymakers. Yet, overturning decades-old consensus in March 2005, India's commerce minister declared, "It suits us to have a modern patent regime in line with what most countries in the world have already adopted, including China and Brazil."[5] Simultaneously, the government declared India as "[t]he world's knowledge hub of the future."[6] By 2005, India was in compliance with a globally recognized product patent regime. Why and how did this policy and ideational shift happen so suddenly, despite intense popular and elite opposition?

A related puzzle about private sector responses demands an answer.[7] It is well known that India's postindependence policy regime germinated a strong domestic pharmaceutical sector (Banerji 2000; Chaudhuri 2004, 2005; Felker et al. 1997; Govindraj and Chellaraj 2002; Long 2000; Redwood 1994). This raises a pertinent question: did pressures *for* globalization originate from within India's industrial sector, which had been strengthened by internal policy support? The evidence suggests otherwise. Despite rapid growth, the pharmaceutical industry's preferences and collective efforts were directed toward modifying the price-control regime and delaying the TRIPS-compatible regime rather than leveraging their domestic dominance into global expansion. In the 1990s, there is no evidence of an emboldened private sector mobilizing for change toward a stronger patent regime or in favor of global markets. Rather, as noted by other scholars: "The Indian pharmaceutical industry opposed the TRIPS agreement tooth and nail, and it lobbied the government to hobble the agreement" (Banerji 2000, 81).[8] In a more colorful way, S. Aiyar, a prominent journalist, noted: "The sad truth is that they [pharma majors in India] were dragged kicking and screaming into new territory, and only then discovered that it was the promised land."[9]

---

[5] Kamal Nath, "Enough Safeguards in Patents Act to Prevent Price Rise – Domestic Pharma Industry Interests Fully Protected," Government of India's Press Information Bureau press release, April 4, 2005.

[6] "Backed by the Patent Amendment Act, 2005, and on the initiative of Prime Minister Manmohan Singh, the government now seeks to promote India as a new global R&D hub to attract pharmaceutical, IT and auto majors to outsource their research work," in "Govt. to Promote India as Global R&D Hub," *Tribune*, July 16, 2005, www.tribuneindia.com/2005/20050716/biz.htm#2.

[7] Ramanna (2005) also raises the puzzle of change in the private sector.

[8] Also see Das (2003) and Jacob (2010).

[9] S. Aiyar, "How Patents Can Produce Cheap Drugs," *Times of India*, February 2, 2000.

The initial resistance by Indian industry lends support to a long-standing consensus in the field of trade policy: in democracies, trade policy is determined by a balancing of the interests of those affected by policy changes. Losers can forestall policy change. Consensus can be difficult to reach and inaction is easier than action, and in a democratic context, this creates status quo bias.[10] The India-specific literature concurs; India's strong distributional coalitions (Bardhan 1998) predict policy stasis and stability.[11] Yet, somewhat unexpectedly, the Indian industry undertook radical technological upgradation after 1998. This poses a puzzle well articulated by Haggard and Webb: "If interest groups determine policy, and interests in the period before reform tend to favor the status-quo, how is reform ever possible?"[12]

The relevant analytical question, then, becomes: what were the sources of these unexpected policy and industrial changes in the pharmaceutical sector? Were they it driven by internal ambitions of a rising power? Were new exporting interests lobbying in favor of a TRIPS-compliant regime? Or were they due to direct US pressure? Or more counterintuitively, were they due to both intended and unintended effects of the TRIPS agreement and WTO's institutional structure? These reasons correspond to four powerful explanations in comparative politics and international relations: (a) external pressure by the United States, (b) domestic trade politics in favor of openness urged by exporters,[13] (c) the effect of international organizations in changing the domestic preferences and structures – the argument articulated in this book – and (d) a realist account that would suggest that India's rising economic profile led the state to accede in favor of greater compliance with international agreements.[14] This chapter attempts to tease out the relative effect of these four powerful explanations about compliance and domestic change with reference to the pharmaceutical sector in India.

Responses by the Indian private sector followed an interesting sequence. While at first the industry resisted global changes, it began changing its market strategies toward internationalization starting around 1999 and then more rapidly from 2000 to 2005. Ajay Piramal, chairman and managing director of Nicholas Piramal, noted in 2000: "And, indeed, the 'threat' of the WTO and IPRs, as perceived by some in

---

[10] Schattschneider (1974). Olson's (1965) argument, further, implies that interest groups tend to be sticky, preventing rather than facilitating policy change.

[11] See Chibber (2003) for an argument about how business influence prevents change. His title is evocative but misplaced given the rapid changes in India's political economy: *Locked in Place* (2003).

[12] Haggard and Webb (1994, 5).   [13] Milner (1988).

[14] Nayar and Paul (2003) and Baru (2006).

India, may well turn into a major opportunity for the country."[15] A sudden switch in their strategies toward supporting intellectual property rights was noticeable after 1999 and more surely after 2005. Indian pharmaceutical firms not only started selling and exporting more but also began investing in markets in advanced countries, a pattern that was at odds with earlier patterns of investment in developing, unregulated markets (Ramamurti and Singh 2009). These unexpected changes in state policy and realignment in domestic private preferences between 2000 and 2005 allow us to explore an understudied topic: the evolution in private sector preferences regarding globalization.

This chapter analyzes the transformations within the pharmaceutical industry at two distinct levels: policy and the industry level, with examples of different firms. Section 4.1 lays out the argument of the chapter. Section 4.2 analyzes the domestic policies and their intended and unintended consequences. This corresponds with the domestic-level argument. Section 4.3 assesses a "second-image reversed" argument, exploring the effect of the US pressure on India and the role played by the WTO's institutional structure in catalyzing change within India. Section 4.4 goes into the transformation at the industry level and presents data about the large Indian firms that have become globally competitive (Section 4.4.4). This analysis should be seen in conjunction with case studies of specific firms, such as Ranbaxy, Dr. Reddy Laboratories, and Wockhardt, to demonstrate the effect of key global mechanisms such as learning, threats, and information on different firms (Chapter 7). Figure 4.1 summarizes the process of shifting interests and strategies at a more macro level, while the rest of the chapter outlines the argument at different levels of analysis.

4.1   The argument

While direct US pressure failed to change India's position, its legal obligations under the aegis of WTO, as well as reputation concerns after the defeat at the WTO dispute panel, led India to start implementing the TRIPS agreement while still seeking to extract as much autonomy as possible within the larger framework of compliance with TRIPS. One can see the effect of *sovereignty costs as well as legal framing* in nudging change within India. India lost two crucial cases at the WTO in 1997–1998, and this loss played a crucial role in India's future policy formation. In the process of resisting and delaying compliance, Indian policymakers were

---

[15] Ajay Piramal, "Drugs Will Enhance India's Performance," *Economic Times*, June 30, 2000, cited in Saket (2001, 222).

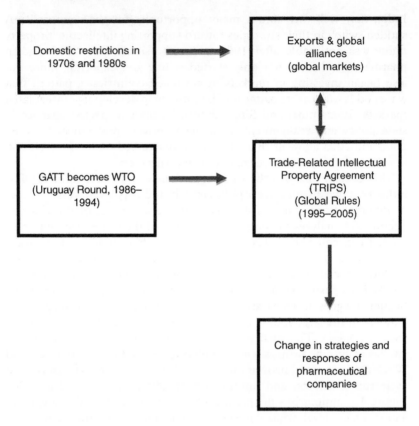

Figure 4.1 Changes in India's pharmaceutical sector

"drawn into the language of TRIPS, seeking to implement its requirements in a manner that met local concerns" (Kapczynski 2009, 1576).
India's attempt to comply as well as extract autonomy within a complying
framework represents a common dilemma faced by Brazil, China, and
other nations and has some similarities with what has been characterized
as "partial compliance" (Mertha and Pahre 2005). The state took initiative in crafting a flexible response to India's compliance dilemma, but the
impetus for such actions originated within the WTO's legal dispute-
settlement mechanism with India's loss at the dispute panel in 1998.
This loss created a different set of incentives for new actors such as
scientists and farmers, with a stake in protecting "indigenous" knowledge, and politicians, who began to see a value in preserving India's
diverse knowledge. The losers from this new system – small-scale

pharmaceutical producers who were not willing to adjust to new rules – resisted, and ultimately some adjusted with state help. Thus, an externally induced change created new internal constituencies in favor of a globally consistent patent regime.

Realignment toward global reach and activation of new interests moved the industry toward newer markets and a different balance of power – toward Indian MNCs that began to defend patents – within India. How did this happen? Most studies argue that large firms with stronger capabilities and technological innovations start exporting and seeking global reach.[16] My evidence leads me to argue the reverse: firms that export and are developing global alliances develop their technological capabilities in newer directions and expand in newer markets. *The causal connection between strength and global expansion is the reverse of what is usually supposed: global expansion and global rules can create incentives to increase capabilities, improve skills, and change focus. In other words, the appearance and recognition of new opportunities may cause an otherwise weak competitor to step up and take advantage of the new playing field.* The information provided by global agreements such as TRIPS is important to this story. Global negotiations yield precious information about the shape of emerging markets (generic and branded generics, for example), which motivates firms to adopt open-economy strategies and positions.

At first sight, the current global power of the Indian pharmaceutical industry is not surprising as India's domestic regulations created a strong pharmaceutical industry. Yet, the same regulations also limited the industry's potential in terms of generics and the nature of their global presence, restricting them primarily to unregulated markets. Most crucially, they created an industry with a strong vested interest in the process patent regulations. The R&D expenditure of Indian companies in 1973 was as low as 1.1 percent of turnover (gross sales), while leading international firms spend close to 10 percent (Narayana 1984, 10). I demonstrate that while the domestic regime provided a certain set of capabilities to Indian industry, global trade and rules of the game – the TRIPS agreement in the case of the pharmaceutical sector – changed not only the calculus but, most strikingly, the ways in which societal actors began to perceive and frame the issues and then organize in favor of global integration. Thus, the effect of the WTO was crucial in changing private sector views and preferences regarding the global patent regime and, thereby, globalization.

---

[16] Studies in business school journals adopt this view. See Aggarwal (2007) and Surie (2008) for an illustration.

The timing of industrial responses offers some clues about plausible causal mechanisms. The transformation of the Indian pharmaceutical industry happened after 1998, when TRIPS-consistent rules became unavoidable due to India's defeat at the WTO Dispute-Settlement Court. Following these larger global changes, the industrial sector initiated multiple changes and technological innovations in order to create, manage, and leverage new strengths in the face of a new global environment. Some pharmaceutical companies started defending the global patent regime in the early 2000s and evolving a multipronged global strategy to deal with the global changes (Kedron and Bagchi-Sen 2011). A marked differentiation among industry responses becomes evident after 2000. An internationalization of a small subset of Indian firms, encompassing upgradation, expansion, joint ventures, and mergers and acquisitions, began in the late 1990s and early 2000s but accelerated around 2004–2005 (Chadha 2009; Chaudhuri 2007; Chittoor and Ray 2007; Export-Import Bank of India 2007; Goldar et al. 2010; Haakonsson 2009; Kedron and Bagchi-Sen 2011; Madanmohan and Krishnan 2003; Rai 2008; Sampath 2006).[17] Many Indian pharmaceutical firms began selling their products in developed countries, an unusual pattern given the propensity of emerging countries to trade and invest in other developing countries (Ramamurti and Singh 2009). Collective action also became more complex and differentiated with the emergence of a new lobbying arm of the "research-based Indian companies": the Indian Pharmaceutical Alliance (see Section 4.4.3). It must also be acknowledged that small firms – losers from the new WTO regulations – continued to see the TRIPS regime as a serious threat well into the 2000s and that their strategies were very different than those of a small number of visible "research-based" firms. These recalcitrant small firms finally began changes after 2005, nudged and supported by the state, which provided crucial subsides for their compliance with global standards and entry into global markets. In the late 1980s and through the 1990s, pharmaceutical firms started to export to regulated markets; this experience transformed their interests, which were further catalyzed by the TRIPS discussions and implementation within India. Both global markets (foray into export markets) and rules (TRIPS) were the intermediate causal levers that transformed interests, strategies, and capabilities. This dynamic argument about *interests in motion* goes beyond a single-year snapshot and allows us to assess how interests and preferences shift over time and whether market or regime characteristics play a role in that

---

[17] For an interesting argument that focuses on traditional medicines, such as Ayurveda, and their move to the market, see Bode (2008).

transformation. No other explanation explains this sudden shift in preferences and interests.

To my mind, the changing external rules of the game were important in this story of preference and interest change, even as domestic actors learned to deploy flexibilities within the global agreement. I show that, initially, India's private sector was strongly opposed to the global changes but that after compliance became necessary, new interests were created and the old views were changed in favor of an internationally consistent TRIPS regime. It may be appropriate to call it a story of *realigning interests* toward global reach. The interaction with the global markets and rules of the game were crucial to these changing interests; without their effects, the shape of Indian actions and strategies would have been very different. This chapter demonstrates that participation in global trade negotiations *changed* the preferences of pharmaceutical producers and *strengthened* the hands of externally oriented domestic producers by bringing them *closer* to the national–state actors and by encouraging collaborative strategies between business and state actors. As noted by a senior journalist in 2000: "When it became clear that strong IPRs were inescapable, the pharma czars suddenly changed their tune. ... Parvinder Singh and others suddenly said that the new IPR regime presented them with opportunities to become world class producers."[18]

4.2 Biography of pharmaceutical policy in India (1947–1990): domestic imperatives and market creation

Did India's domestic ambition and its industries' preferences drive India's compliance and global reach in the 2000s? The early evolution of India's pharmaceutical industry illustrates the growing power of a *dirigiste* state shaping the industrial order as well as orienting business politics toward the domestic economy. Domestic policy drivers crafted in the 1960s and 1970s created a powerful set of market structures, as well as invisible collective action dilemmas, which were to shape India's global adjustment and future policies. Politics and policies created markets, which then shaped India's initial responses and capabilities. Importantly, both the intended and unintended effects on markets and political mobilization deserve careful analysis as they were to shape the domestic responses to the global changes starting in the late 1980s and 1990s.

---

[18] S. Aiyar, "How Patents Can Produce Cheap Drugs," *Times of India*, February 2, 2000.

At independence in 1947, the Indian pharmaceutical industry was small and largely populated by MNCs.[19] Domestic prices were among the highest in the world between 1947 and 1970 (Banerji 2000, 79). While a few well-known firms were set up during the British rule,[20] India's pharmaceutical industry only took off when, in 1972, the government passed the Patents Act of 1970, replacing the colonial Indian Patents and Designs Act of 1911. A number of policies, ranging from price control and tariff policies to technology policies, played a role in creating the conditions for this turnaround (Banerji 2000).

Yet, this change was not easy, and there were delays and resistance.[21] The 1911 Indian Patents and Designs Act was stringent and extended the life of patents from fourteen to sixteen years, which was more generous than international practice, and gave eight to twelve years to the life of patents (Huang and Hogan 2002). From 1948 onward, the government tried repeatedly to change the policy, without success, until the late 1960s and 1970s, when a leftward turn in politics, expressed in the Hathi Committee Report, in favor of an indigenous industry and against the MNCs strengthened and could no longer be resisted.[22] The Indian Patent Act of 1970 reversed the strength of patents and did not recognize product patent protection in drugs and food, thus effectively abolishing patent protection in drugs by allowing only "process patents." The key features of the act reduced the patent cover from ten to sixteen years to seven years in India, restricted patents on drugs, broadened compulsory licensing restrictions, and imposed limits on royalty payments. Indian firms could now produce generic versions of drugs on patent elsewhere as long as the process used in that production was modified. Subsequently, a new policy regime (1978 policy) encouraged the domestic sector to produce essential medicines and dilute the share of MNCs' equity.

---

[19] In 1947, the market size of the Indian pharmaceutical industry was USD28.5 million (Ahmad 1988).

[20] Prafulla Chandra Ray set up Bengal Chemical and Pharmaceutical Works in 1892. Alembic Chemical Works was set up in 1907 and Bengal Immunity in 1919. Other Indian firms at that time included Zandu Pharmaceutical Works, Calcutta Chemical, Standard Pharmaceuticals and CIPLA, UniChem, Chemo Pharma, IndoPharma, etc. (Chaudhuri 2004, 145). Also see Felker, Chaudhuri, and Gyorgy (1997).

[21] Initially the Hathi Committee Report was shelved and its recommendation faced many obstacles (Phadke, 1998, 49). A close reading of the parliamentary (Lok Sabha and Rajya Sabha) debates of the period (1960s and 1970s) confirms this.

[22] As an illustration, the Hathi Committee Report (1975) recommended the takeover of MNCs by the government. The All India Chemical and Pharmaceutical Employees Federation produced publications documenting unethical practices used by MNCs titled, "Multinationals in Drugs and Pharmaceutical Industry in India" (Majumdar 1979). Submissions to the Hathi Committee were in favor of developing the Indian sector and against the MNCs.

A sector like pharmaceuticals has both industrial and health implications, and state policy bore the mark of these twin imperatives. Interestingly, pharmaceutical policy was the responsibility of the Department of Petrochemicals in the central Ministry of Chemicals and Fertilizers rather than the Ministry of Health. The main policy objectives of the government were to ensure the availability of reasonably priced drugs and to promote the growth and development of a nationally oriented, self-reliant domestic industry.[23] The policy framework aimed to encourage an indigenous sector, facilitate the production of bulk drugs,[24] discourage the "monopolies enjoyed by multinationals in India," and "direct the activities of foreign drug companies to serve national objectives and interests."[25] The dominant view at that time was that foreign companies were merely importing drugs and not manufacturing in or transferring technology to India. They were not investing in R&D in India or producing bulk drugs and were making "unduly large profits," keeping prices of drugs high.[26] In addition, the MNCs were using distorted transfer pricing to take profits out of India and not investing back into the country.[27] Thus, the broad objectives of the 1978 policy change included development of self-reliance in drug technology, self-sufficiency in the output of drugs with a view to reducing imports, and a policy to "foster the growth of the Indian Sector" and thus make drugs "available at reasonable prices" (Jain 1987, 43–44). Table 4.1 documents the policy innovations introduced in the 1970s and 1980s when domestic autonomy was paramount.

4.2.1   Expansion, growth, and indigenization

Policy initiatives in the 1970s contributed to growth and diversification of the indigenous sector. The industry grew at 10 percent annually in the 1980s and 1990s, which was well above the average industrial growth rate

[23] Interviews with Vedraman (the architect of the Patent Act of 1970), Bombay, 2003, and B. K. Kyeala (convener of National Working Group of Patents), New Delhi, November 2003.

[24] A bulk drug, also referred to as active pharmaceutical ingredient (API), is the chemical element that gives the drug its medicinal or therapeutic value. A formulation drug is the packaging of a bulk drug into an actual medicine form, which may include inactive elements, color, and other forms in which the chemical molecule may be packaged to be effective for human consumption. It refers to the design of the dosage form.

[25] Policy Statement, 1978, in Jain (1987, 46, 46–47). This was also confirmed in an interview with Vedraman (ibid.).

[26] See "Paper laid on the Table of the Lok Sabha," LT-1196/77 Lok Sabha Secretariat, 1977, cited in Lal (1990, 111).

[27] Lal (1990, 116). Transfer pricing is a technique adopted by MNCs to manipulate the prices of intermediate chemicals received by the subsidiaries from the parent company in order to reduce the total profit shown in the host country.

Table 4.1 *The evolution of pharmaceutical policy, 1947–1986*

Date	Policy	Motivations and Implications of Policies
1947–1970	1911 Patent Act	Minimal regulation of industry; reliance on MNCs[28]
1948–1950	Patents Enquiry Committee (Tek Chand Committee) led to some amendments in the Patents Act of 1911 in 1950 but that lapsed	The grounds for compulsory licensing was broadened, and Section 23C was added, which empowered the Controller of Patents to grant a CL unless there were good reasons for refusing it
1959	Ayyangar Committee Report	Modest changes to the 1911 act modeled on the 1949 US act but were opposed by MNCs[29]
1965	Patent law introduced in parliament but lapsed after opposition from MNCs	Act contained a number of concessions to foreign companies
1972	The Patents and Designs Act of 1911 replaced by the Patents Act of 1970	Encourage local production; ensured local "Working of Patents"; removed the monopoly of MNCs; life of patent reduced to five to seven years from date of filing the application, although the effective time of protection was three years (Banerji 2000, 68)
1975	Hathi Committee Report	Recommended takeover of MNCs and "India-ization" of drug industry; the report was hostile to MNCs and documented their strategies to take profits out of the country and their refusal to invest in indigenous production and technological transfer
1978	New drug policy based on the Hathi Committee Report	Self-reliance in drug technology; reduce imports; encourage self-sufficiency to "foster and encourage the growth of the Indian Sector." "To control, regulate, and rejuvenate this industry as a whole with particular reference to containing and channeling the activity of foreign companies on accord with National objectives and priorities."[30] "To give a flow of technology instead of the flow of foreign equity"[31]

[28] Analysis drawn from Govindaraj and Chellaraj (2002).
[29] Huang and Hogan (2002, 5).   [30] Jain (1987, vii)   [31] Ibid.

Table 4.1 (cont.)

Date	Policy	Motivations and Implications of Policies
1979	Drug Price Control Order, 1979	Four categories of drugs: Lifesaving, Essential, Less Essential, and Non-Essential; price ceilings on the retail prices of the first three; policy measures to ensure production of basic drugs as well as the essential drugs
1986	"Measures for Rationalization, Quality Control, and Growth of Drug and Pharmaceutical Industry in India"	Ensuring abundant availability, at reasonable prices, of essential lifesaving drugs of good quality; strengthening quality control; encouraging new investment; strengthening the indigenous capacity for the production of drugs[32]

Source: Hathi Committee Report (available from Author); 1970 Patent Act; 1978 Policy; Govindaraj and Chellaraj (2002); Jain (1987); author's database on "Policy and Institutional Changes." Also, Gupta (1986) discusses the 1986 policy.

in India. Athreye, Kale, and Ramani argue that the domestic "radical regulatory changes" of the 1970s affected "capability development" and "created new 'winners and losers' " (Athreye, Kale, and Ramani 2009, 1). Until 1950, the Indian industry, dominated largely by multinationals, would refine and package imported formulations. After 1972, the production of bulk drugs (ingredients) as well as formulations (complete, ready-for-sale drugs) proceeded apace. In 1952, the number of manufacturing units producing medicines was around 1752 with a combined capital investment of Rs. 24 crores (approx. USD12 million) (Ahmad 1988, 3; Barnwal 2000, 11). By 1995, there were more than 19,000 such units, employing 3.8 lakhs (380,000) people, and the annual value of formulation production increased from Rs. 10 crores (approx. USD5 million) in 1947 to Rs. 54 crores (approx. USD27 million) in 1958, Rs. 400 crores (approx. USD200 million) in 1974 and Rs. 9125 crores (approx. USD1.825 billion) in 1995–1996 (Chaudhuri 2004, 147).[33] India was no longer reliant on imports for most drugs. By the early 1990s, the Indian sector accounted for 70 percent of formulation

[32] Jain (1987, vii).
[33] 1 lakh = one-hundred thousand, written 100,000; 1 crore = 10 million, written 10,000,000.

and 80 percent of bulk production. From 1970 to 1986, 98 percent of domestic demand was met by local production (Ballance 1992, 76, cited in Eren-Vural 2007).

The small-scale sector benefited from exceptions in price-control provisions, thus creating an easy entry structure. Rapid proliferation of small-scale sector units further increased the number of manufacturing units, encouraged diversification of the production base, and created a competitive industrial structure. Many large Indian companies contracted the production of their bulk drugs to small-scale firms, seeking to escape the clauses of the price control as well as to enjoy the cost advantages of producing in the small-scale sector.[34]

By the 2000s, Indian firms had replaced multinationals, and India was the fourth largest producer of both bulk and formulations by volume and was also a major exporter in the world. Ballance et al. categorized India as a country having innovative capabilities that were below the group with "sophisticated pharmaceutical industry and a research base" (Ballance, Pogany, and Forstner 1992).[35] This understates the growing power of the Indian industry in Africa, Asia, and later the world more generally, where generics produced by Indian companies were used by many governments and NGOs to address health crises. Indian exports were crucial for 175 countries around the globe (Aggarwal 2007, 144). In 2003, India supplied 32 percent of the world's generics (ICRA 2004). Large countries, such as Brazil, South Africa, and Thailand, imported generic medicines from India, while smaller countries relied exclusively on Indian production.

The 1970s policy regime achieved its task of creating an "Indian sector," and Indian firms gained market and production strength at the cost of the multinationals. In 1973, the Foreign Exchange Regulation Act (FERA) restricted the levels of foreign investment in India at 49 percent in pharmaceutical companies, which was later reduced to 26 percent. Extremely restrictive drug price policies and the Patent Act of 1970 encouraged Indian drug manufacturers to develop in an uninhibited fashion and move into the production of formulations and generic drugs production at a scale not even dreamed of in the 1940s and 1950s. Simultaneously, the market power of the Indian companies rose. In 1970, MNCs commanded more than two-thirds of the market share in India, but their market dominance

---

[34] Interview with a small-scale company, Gurgaon, August 2003.

[35] See "Table 1.1. A Typology of the World's Pharmaceutical Industries" in Ballance, Pogany, and Forstner (1992, 8–9). Also see Gereffi (1983, 185), who characterizes India as part of group 5, which "manufactures most of the intermediates required for the pharmaceutical industry and undertakes local research on the development of products and manufacturing processes" (Gereffi 1983, Table 6.5, 185).

Table 4.2 *Market shares of MNCs and Indian companies*

Year	MNCs (%)	Indian Companies (%)
1952	38	62
1970	68	32
1978	60	40
1980	50	50
1991	40	60
1998	32	68
2004	23	77

Source: Cited in Sudip Chaudhuri (2005, 18).

slowly declined and then dwindled to about 60 percent by the late 1970s, 50 percent by the 1980, 40 percent by the early 1990s, about a third by the late 1990s, and less than a quarter by the early 2000s (Chaudhuri 2005, 18). FERA, combined with domestic competition from local companies, forced the MNCs into local sourcing despite the lack of a patent regime (Haakonsson 2009, 276). In 1978, thirty-one FERA companies remained with foreign equity exceeding 40 percent, but by 1984, nineteen had diluted their foreign equity. By 1987, only ten pharmaceutical companies had foreign investment in India (Redwood 1988, 280–281). Table 4.2 illustrates this reversal.

By 2004, of the 298 companies covered by ORG-MARG, 32 companies were controlled by MNCs and accounted for only 23 percent of the retail pharmaceutical market in India. The remaining 266 Indian companies comprised the remaining 77 percent of the market. Many Indian companies – Cipla, Ranbaxy, DRL, Sun Pharma, Torrent Pharma, for example – were transformed into large companies. By 2006, Cipla and Ranbaxy were part of the Fortune Global 500 list of large non-US firms.[36] Of the ten largest companies in India, six are controlled by Indians and four by foreign firms (see Table 4.3).

The pharmaceutical sector is capital intensive, leading to an expectation that it would be constituted by a small number of large firms that internalize various costs. Globally, the industry structure is marked by fewer companies that specialize in the introduction of new products through sophisticated research capabilities and financial power (Ballance et al. 1992, 66). In contrast, in India, a large number of small-scale firms (20,000 units in 2000), as well as a sizable number of large and medium-sized firms, make

[36] Fortune (2006).

Table 4.3 *Top ten pharmaceutical companies in 1970, 1996, and 2003*

Rank	1970	1996	2003
1.	Sarabhai (Indian)	Glaxo-Wellcome (MNC)	Glaxo-SmithKline (MNC)
2.	Glaxo (MNC)	Cipla (Indian)	Cipla (Indian)
3.	Pfizer (MNC)	Ranbaxy (Indian)	Ranbaxy (Indian)
4.	Alembic (Indian)	Hoechst-Roussel (MNC)	Nicholas Piramal (Indian)
5.	Hoechst (MNC)	Knoll Pharma (MNC)	Sun Pharma (Indian)
6.	Lederly (MNC)	Pfizer (MNC)	Pfizer (MNC)
7.	Ciba (MNC)	Alembic (Indian)	Dr. Reddy (Indian)
8.	May and Baker (MNC)	Torrent Pharma (Indian)	Zydus Cadilla (Indian)
9.	Parke Davis (MNC)	Lupin Labs (Indian)	Abbott (MNC)
10.	Abbott (MNC)	Zydus-Cadilla (Indian)	Aventis – w/Hoescht (MNC)

Source: From Athreye, Kale, and Ramani (2009, 733).

India's pharmaceutical sector one of the largest and most fragmented in the world. Four largest firms (Cipla, Glaxo-SmithKline, Ranbaxy, and Nicholas Piramal) controlled 19.68 percent of the retail formulations market in India in 2004, a level of concentration far less than in many other industries (Chaudhuri 2005, 16). In 2000–2001, 20,053 firms or manufacturing units formed the pharmaceutical industry, a rapid increase from 2,257 units in 1969–1970.[37] Among the organized sector there were three kinds of units: government-owned companies (public sector units), wholly owned Indian firms, and foreign companies. Two types of foreign companies – FERA and non-FERA companies – existed.[38] The FERA companies, which had foreign equity of more than 40 percent, included Bayer India, Ltd., Wyeth Laboratories, Johnson and Johnson, Ltd., Roche Products, Ltd., Sandoz India, Ltd., and Alkali and Chemicals, Ltd. There were five public sector units. No single company monopolized the market; in fact, no single firm had a share of more than 10 percent in 1981–1982. The Patent Act of 1970, combined with liberal credit availability and incentives, lowered entry barriers for firms, encouraging many to start production. Intense competition was unleashed both between the MNCs and Indian firms and between large and small-sized Indian firms.

---

[37] OPPI (2002, 37).
[38] The Foreign Exchange Regulation Act of 1973 (FERA) required companies registered in India and having more than 40 percent foreign equity and branches of foreign companies operating in India to register with the government. The companies registered under FERA are known as FERA companies.

4.2.2   And yet, a conflictual relationship

The supportive policy regime did *not* create a smooth relationship between the state and domestic industry. Rather, concurrent with a liberal patent regime, the government instituted an elaborate restrictive price-control regime wherein the Drug Controller would issue periodic notices about the prices of basic products as well as the formulations.[39] In 1979, around 370 drugs were subject to such price ceilings. The government "fixed ceiling prices for formulations by implementing the Maximum Allowable Post-Manufacturing Expense (MAPE) at 75–100 percent of production costs" (Haakonsson 2009, 276). In 1979, the Drug Controller regulated prices of 80 percent of bulk and formulations, besides a ceiling on the profitability of industrial units (Narayana 1984). In 1987, the number of drugs under price control was reduced significantly from 370 to 143, and the overall structure of price control was simplified. Despite this liberalization, 75 percent of the industry remained under price control (Singh 2001a, 89). These notifications were extremely detailed and implemented carefully. Details of material costs were submitted by manufacturers to the Drug Price Control Office (DPCO), which decided on the prices a company could charge consumers.

Further, state policy directly encouraged indigenous bulk drug production and the setting up of small-scale units. This policy required firms to produce bulk drugs at a rate of at least a fraction of their formulation production and to supply at least part of those bulk drugs to other manufacturers for formulation. For instance, the policy demanded a 1:10 bulk drug to formulation ratio for Indian manufactures, with 30 percent supply to other formulators, and allowed formulations to be produced using a ratio of indigenous to imported bulk drugs of 2:1. Foreign manufactures had a more stringent ratio; they had to follow a 1:5 bulk drug to formulation ratio and had to supply 50 percent of their production of bulk drug to other formulators. Foreign companies were required to indigenously manufacture bulk drugs and intermediaries required for their formulations within a stipulated time-frame, and they were required to set up R&D facilities in the country. At least 4 percent of their turnover had to be spent on local R&D facilities.[40]

Paradoxically, this restrictive price policy encouraged a cost-effective industry with low profit margins: A large number of small firms with low

---

[39] The price-control regime came into effect in 1970 and was revised in 1979, 1987, and 1995.

[40] Policy statement 1978; Raizada (n.d,). available from author.

Table 4.4 *Profits in the pharmaceutical sector*

Year	Profit before Tax (Percentage of Sales)
1969–1970	15.5
1974–1975	10.7
1977–1978	11.7
1980–1981	8.8
1982–1983	7.5
1989–1990	3.5
1991–1992	1.0
1992–1993	2.6
1993–1994	4.4

Source: Pharmaceutical Databook 1993, cited in Felker, Chaudhuri, and Gyorgy (1997, 15); after 1991 the data are from OPPI surveys, cited in Das (2003, 9–10).

overheads and costs started producing bulk drugs as well as exporting. The industry, despite its capital-intensive nature, employed about 4.6 million people (in 2001) directly and 24 million indirectly (in the distribution trade).[41] The conflictual nature of the relationship between government and industry is well captured by the declining profits of the industry outlined in Table 4.4. The private sector fought long and hard against the restrictive price controls, in part by seeking judicial intervention in the 1980s and 1990s.[42]

4.2.3   Unintended effects

The relationship between industry and state policy thus was, beneficial and contentious.[43] State policy shaped incentives, industry structure,

---

[41] OPPI (2002, 46); OPPI (2001).

[42] Detailed information on the judicial petitions filed by the industry against the government is available in the author's newspaper database on "Industry Strategies and Responses, 1990–2011." Also, Gaur (1981).

[43] Most scholars note only the positive effects with a couple of exceptions. Similar to my argument, Redwood (1987) argues that "[t]he Indian pharmaceutical scene is one of contrast and paradox: A strong local pharmaceutical industry with more effective backing by its own chemical industry than is to be found anywhere else in the Third World; stifling bureaucratic controls and intervention in the affairs of the pharmaceutical industry in minute details at all levels" (1987, 278). At another place he says, "With one hand, the Indian authorities promoted the industry's growth and investment whilst with the other, they distorted the pattern of growth" (1987, 280).

entry patterns, and patterns of competition in both negative and positive ways (Chaudhuri 2004; Felker et al. 1997; Govindraj and Chellaraj 2002). Private business interests were passive rule-takers but also lobbied heavily to change policies, like price controls, in their favor. The patent regime instituted by the Indian state in 1972 helped the Indian industry, but the price regime pitted the industry against the government. The process patent regime allowed Indian industry to reengineer and develop generic abilities with noninfringing processes. State regulation in this respect not only facilitated the emergence of an indigenous sector from total oblivion but also contributed to its growth. Paradoxically, the restrictive price controls created a cost-effective industry that used export-oriented strategies to escape domestic regulations. Thus, the total policy regime, and not merely the 1970 Patent Act, was responsible for the growth and expansion of the Indian industry (Srinivas 2012).

The policy regime created an industry divided by ownership; patterns of collective mobilization, industry preferences, and political action revolved around the level of domestic versus foreign ownership and equity. Despite common concerns over domestic policy – such as pricing policies, which affected all firms alike – firm preferences and political strategies remained divided into two different tracks. Firms identified themselves as belonging to the "Indian sector" or the "MNC or foreign sector." The Indian Drug Manufacturers Association (IDMA) represented the "Indian sector" and the MNCs formed the "Organization of Pharmaceutical Producers from India" (OPPI) in 1965. Indian firms were invested in a process patent regime. Political access and influence were channeled through these two dominant associations both at the state and national levels. Thus, policy not only shaped the economic and industrial structure but also how firms came to conceptualize their interests and how they framed themselves as representing the Indian or foreign sector.

The regulatory framework created a dualistic structure of firms and shaped the preferences of Indian firms; some were able to acquire definite advantages in securing credit and other facilities from the state. Most lobbying activities were directed to seeking postpolicy exceptions for their specific products, channeling state–business interactions in an individualist "embedded particularism" (Herring 1999) direction. Simultaneously, domestic policy created a set of medium-sized firms that mastered reverse engineering (to skirt the few remnants of patent protection) and began to move from the production of bulk drugs to formulation drugs, creating the precondition for growth in the generic segment of the global market. Athreye, Kale, and Ramani argue that

[m]arket leadership belonged to firms with competence in chemical process technologies necessary for re-engineering targeted drugs and the ability to with-stand technology races in process improvements through pursuing a diversified product portfolio. Some common features of technological capabilities and strategy among all leading firms included low R&D intensity, innovation focus on cost-efficient or quality enhancing processes, direct commercialization of innovation in countries where the product patent regime was not recognized, and technology transactions with Western multinationals in the form of licensing and marketing agreements [Athreye, Kale, and Ramani 2009, 735].

The encouraging policy regime was not conducive to cutting-edge inno-vation as only forty-seven firms out of 23,000 in 1992 registered any R&D expenditures, of which only seven companies spent more than 1.5 percent of their sales revenue on R&D (Athreye, Kale, and Ramani 2009, 735). Interestingly, even the MNCs exhibited low R&D expenditure ratios of 1 to 2 percent (Lal 1990, 111).

Interestingly, the restrictive regulatory framework also encouraged production for export as companies could escape the domestic regulatory controls by producing for export markets. Many companies, such as Ranbaxy, began exporting more aggressively in the late 1980s. They adopted direct sales marketing agreements, as well as joint ventures or subsidiaries in many developing countries, which did not have patent regimes (Rao 2007, 133). During the 1990s, almost 21 percent of phar-maceutical production was directed for export (Aggarwal 2007). Table 4.5 shows the export orientation of the industry starting in late the 1980s and 1990s.

Figures 4.2 and 4.3 show this changing impetus for exports percolating to a larger number of companies. Figure 4.2 shows a dramatic change in total value of pharmaceutical exports in the mid-2000s. By 2013, almost 60 percent of companies were exporting medicines and other products.[44]

While price restrictions nudged companies out of the Indian market into global export markets, their abilities to produce both patented and generic versions of off-patent drugs played a role in their search for

---

[44] Data limitations do not allow me to calculate the percentage of companies engaged in exports on a yearly basis. In the 1990s, the total number of pharmaceutical companies was around 600, but the numbers varied from year to year, and by 2013, the total number of companies had declined to approximately 250 due to mergers, etc. Thus, in 1990, only 10 percent of companies were exporting, while by 2013, it was 60 percent. These are approximate numbers given the paucity of reliable data.

Table 4.5 *Import and export/production ratio,*
1961–2000

Years	Export/Production (Percent)	Import/Production (Percent)
1961–1969	1.5	8.6
1969–1981	4.3	7.5
1981–1986	4.7	8.8
1986–1990	10.1	12.5
1990–1995	21.2	14.4
1995–2000	33.3	19.6
2001–2002	39.5	9.7

Source: Drawn from Aggarwal (2007, 146).

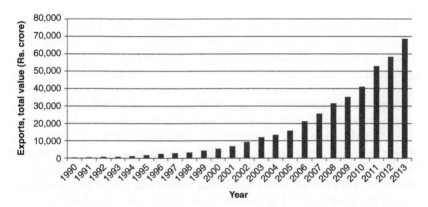

Figure 4.2 Pharma exports, total value (Rs. crore), 1990–2013
Author's Calculations from CMIE Prowess Database, 1990–2014.

markets in the regulated parts of the global marketplace such as the
United States and the European Union. The most impressive exporters
in the 1990s were Cipla, Ranbaxy, Wockhardt, Zydus Cadilla, Lupin
Labs, Torrent Pharma, Sun Pharma, Dr. Reddy's Laboratories, and
Cadilla Pharma. The countries targeted were Nigeria, South Africa,
Egypt, Yemen, Sri Lanka, China, Mexico, Canada, United States, and
Russia. The compound annual growth rate of exports was around
24 percent for 1994–1995 to 1999–2000 (Rao 2007, 134).

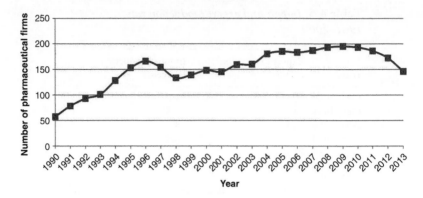

Figure 4.3 Number of pharmaceutical firms reporting exports,
1990–2013
Author's Calculations from CMIE Prowess Database, 1990–2014.

The regulatory environment in the United States also played a reinforcing role. Concerned with the prices of drugs in the United States, policymakers passed the Hatch-Waxman Act in 1984 to encourage generic production. Generic manufactures no longer had to go through a lengthy process of extensive clinical trials. Demonstration of bioequivalence was enough for marketing approval (Ramani and Guennif 2012). Thus, another external factor, specific changes in the policy environment in the United States, was an important demand-driven factor for Indian firms. In essence, the domestic regulatory environment in the 1970s and 1980s provided the impetus for indigenous growth, exports, and diversification. Without this, internally driven Indian companies could not have faced the challenges of globalization in the 1990s. Yet, domestic economic strength and market power did not by itself change the logic of collective action and political mobilization, although it did change the market strategies of some firms.[45] I found no evidence of proactive pressure from the Indian pharmaceutical sector to comply with TRIPS or to leverage its strengths to reorient its global operations *before* TRIPS had become a *fait accompli*. One partial exception is Ranbaxy, as Parvinder Singh was one of the first industry actors to realize the full implications of the TRIPS regime. Yet, he too perceived the TRIPS regime as a "necessary evil" that had to be adjusted to in the early stages. Swaminathan Aiyar, a senior and well-respected journalist, notes that

---

[45] Some firms began exporting but as a way to escape domestic regulatory constraints; interestingly, their growing domestic strength was a direct result of their exporting strategies, which the domestic regulations had, in an unintended way, helped to facilitate.

even Parvinder Singh lobbied against the implementation of TRIPS in the India in the early stages.[46] Yet, by 2005, Indian industry's views were more complex, with some support for global patents. The TRIPS regime played an indispensable, interactive, and catalytic role in changing firm and business interests and perceptions. How exactly did the impending TRIPS regime affect the growth potential of the industry, its structural patterns, and industry preferences?

4.3   The TRIPS agreement and India's compliance: the burden of external sovereignty costs

In the 1990s, the global context for the pharmaceutical sector changed dramatically. The Uruguay Round (1986–1994) resulted in the transformation of the GATT into WTO, which magnified the scope and reach of trade agreements to new issues as well as reducing the scope of exceptions enjoyed by developing countries (except for LDCs). While intellectual property (IP) rights had been governed by the World Intellectual Property Organization (WIPO) since the 1970s, these earlier rules did not require substantive changes in national laws.[47] Under the WTO, the Trade-Related Intellectual Property Rights Agreement (TRIPS) was passed in 1995, and adherence to its principles was not only required but also enforceable through the WTO's Dispute-Settlement mechanisms (DSU) (Wadhera 2005). The governance of IP issues was taken away from management by WIPO and included as part of trade discussions. The inclusion of TRIPS into trade discussions made the WTO and the TRIPS agreement more institutionally powerful. The agreement was specific, substantive, and had enforcement instruments. In comparison to the WIPO and Paris Convention, defection became costlier than before.

TRIPS, once implemented in national laws, would change the patent system in three distinct ways: it banned the production and sale of reverse-engineered goods, it extended product patent protection applied to drugs for twenty years, and it banned discrimination between foreign, imported, and domestic products. Patents were to be made available for any invention whether product or process, as long as they met the criteria of novelty, inventive step, and industrial applicability. This strengthening

---

[46] S. Aiyar, "How Patents Can Produce Cheap Drugs," *Times of India*, February 2, 2000.
[47] Dreyfuss (2010) makes this point. The Berne Convention for the Protection of Literary and Artistic Works (1970) and the Paris Convention (1970) required states to treat other states and their citizens equally, but patent laws were left for national legislatures to decide. Also see Watal (2001).

Table 4.6 *India's failed compliance with TRIPS*

Date and Year	Policy
1980s	India refuses to join the Paris Convention
1989 midterm meeting in Geneva	India agrees to include TRIPS in GATT negotiations
1990s	Preparation for TRIPS but also delay
1990	New drug policy announced but takes four years to take effect
September 15, 1994	New drug policy
April 15, 1994	India signs the GATT charter, including TRIPS
January 1, 1995	WTO comes into effect
1995	Bill to revise domestic laws was introduced in parliament but failed to be passed

Source: Author's database of policy and institutional change, 1990–2011.

of global rules and enforcement mechanisms created harmonization pressures across the world. This was intended to make domestic laws similar and force the creation of new laws to make intellectual property protection stronger. Domestic changes were to be backed by international rules and norms and develop in the shadow of international law. How did India respond to these pressures?

4.3.1 Direct pressure by the United States vs. legal effect of the WTO

By 1989, India was forced to accept negotiations on TRIPS, and on April 15, 1994, India signed the Uruguay Round agreements, accepting membership in the WTO. Significantly, it negotiated a ten-year transition period for the implementation of TRIPS, arguing successfully for the "developing country" transition period. Despite this formal compliance, implementation proved to be contentious and slow. Through the 1990s, the government repeatedly tried to start the process of compliance, without success. At each stage, the minimum possible legislative change was initiated and then reversed. On December 31, 1994, a Presidential Ordinance sought to modify the 1970 Patent Act by providing for exclusive marketing rights and a mechanism for accepting patent applications. Even this diluted version (without product patents) failed to pass in the Indian parliament. In 1995–1996, again, another bill was introduced but failed to pass the lower house of the legislature. Parliamentary opposition and civil society resistance made it impossible to incorporate the TRIPS agreement into domestic laws.[48] Table 4.6 shows the policy stagnation in India during this period.

[48] "Parliamentarians Vow to Oppose Patents Bill," *Business Standard*, January 25, 1996.

4.3.2   US trade pressure against India

Faced with this recalcitrance, the United States deployed direct trade measures against India, aiming to pressure India into compliance. Under the revised "Special 301" provisions of the Omnibus Foreign Trade and Competitiveness Act of 1988, the US government could impose trade sanctions against any trading partner for failure to protect intellectual property.[49] The Special 301 provisions were used repeatedly in an attempt to coerce India into changing its laws but failed to do so. The United States even threatened to stop science and technology joint projects "pending solution of the IPR issue."[50]

I constructed a database of US actions from 1991–1997 and categorized US actions in terms of soft threats (statements and pressure tactics without sanctions undergirding them) and hard threats (when India was categorized as a Priority Watch Country as well as the imposition of actual threats backed with trade penalties). Table 4.7 shows that even as Indian state actors tried to delay US actions, US threats further hardened domestic opposition against implementation of patents. A mobilized civil society, both at elite and mass levels, put increasing pressure on the government opposing India's compliance. Starting from 1990, each day saw increasing opposition to India's acceding to US pressure as well as opposition to India's acceptance of WTO conditions. Headlines like "Don't Modify Patent Laws under US pressure," "Inequity of IPR Demand," "Government Accused of Succumbing to US Pressure on TRIPS"[51] were an everyday occurrence. Such intense scrutiny of the government actions made it very difficult for the state to implement its international commitments under TRIPS or to accede to US pressure. In the 1990s, and even as late as 1998, Indian public opinion and state philosophy were both solidly opposed to modifying Indian patent laws, and US pressure was unable to effect any change. Then, after 1998, when India lost the WTO case, compliance began rapidly. By 2005, India had undergone three different legal enactments ushering in a fully compliant patent system. The changes happened in a very short window, between 1999 and 2005. What led to such a concentrated amount of policy change in that specific short period?

---

[49] Special 301 is an annual review process led by the Office of the US. Trade Representative. US trade law ("Special 301"), as amended by Section 1303 of the 1988 Omnibus Trade Act, requires an annual review of intellectual property protection and market access practices in foreign countries.

[50] "US May Stop Funding Projects Pending Solution to IPR Issue," *Economic Times*, May 27, 1993.

[51] *Financial Express*, June 11, 1993.

Table 4.7 *US pressure on India in the 1990s*

Year	US Threats and Sanctions	Public Reaction	Effect
1989	India threatened with trade sanctions under the Special 301 for the first time	At this stage Indian civil society actors were *not* mobilized against patent laws	**Noncompliance**
1991	India placed on Priority Watch List and then moved to the "Hit List"[52] Negotiations between India and the United States to prevent Special 301 action[53] India seeking IMF and World Bank loans but subject to US support, linked to IPR issues	Medical representatives opposed changes to the Indian patent act describing it as "sell out to the US"[54]	**Noncompliance**
1992	India threatened with US Special 301 after an ongoing "investigation" of the Indian patent regime[55] Bush administration and USTR criticized India's stance on IPRs: India's patent protection regime is "unreasonable, burdens or restricts US commerce"[56] Mexico and China cited as examples that acceded to US pressure[57] Ban on ISRO technology transfer Retaliatory trade sanctions against exports worth USD60 million annually for the failure to implement IP laws	Prominent personalities appealed not to let US pressure affect government policy on patents Editorial pages and media commented on US Special 301 provisions[58]	Despite a deadline imposed by the United States, India did not accept the Dunkel proposals **Noncompliance**

---

[52] "India at the Receiving End," *Business Standard*, December 17, 1992.

[53] "Trip May Head Off Super 301 Action," *Business Standard*, September 23, 1991.

[54] "Sellout to US on Drug Patents Opposed," *Business Standard*, January 8, 1991.

[55] "India's Patent Laws Unreasonable: US," *Financial Express*, February 28, 1992.

[56] Ibid.

[57] "Mexico's Patent laws Should be India's Model," *Observer*, September 28, 1992.

[58] "Suman Sahai, "US Using GATT for Biotech Domination," *Times of India*, March 26, 1992; Kalyan Chatterjee, "West Tightening Grip Over LDC Markets," *Business Standard*, December 18, 1992.

Table 4.7 (cont.)

Year	US Threats and Sanctions	Public Reaction	Effect
1993	Special 301 invoked and India placed on the Special 301 list (May 1993) Science and technology projects to be stopped[59]	Scientists, editors, political parties, judges, and prominent personalities all wrote against the Dunkel draft[60] The civil society across the board was opposed to the passage of the TRIPS bill in India	India threatens retaliatory action State actors accept the necessity of compliance but can't implement it **Noncompliance**
1994	Technology transfer hurdles on account of absence of patent laws Soft threats on patents India to be put on Special 301 watch list Threat of use of Special 301 against India United States threatens to withhold GSP privileges	Public opinion continues to be against India's compliance with IPRs	**Noncompliance**
1995	India placed on Priority Watch List under Special 301[61]	Opposition against US actions in Indian parliament[62] Opposition from the judiciary: former CJ, Rajinder Sachar, said the ordinance to change the patent act was unconstitutional. He further noted that India was showing too much deference to the United States[63]	**Noncompliance**

[59] "Patent Law a Hurdle, says US," *Times of India*, June 26, 1993.
[60] "Scientist Cautions Against Signing Dunkel Draft on TRIPS," *Economic Times*, January 6, 1993; editorial, "Unfair Proposals," *Deccan Herald*, January 18, 1993, Bangalore edition; Kalyan Chatterjee, "IPRs Punishes the Poor," *Business Standard*, January 18, 1993; "Dunkel Draft and Third World Genetic Resources," *Observer*, February 2, 1993; "Patenting of Seeds to Brew Trouble: Experts," *Financial Express*, February 9, 1993; "SP [Samajwadi Party] Stir to Oppose Dunkel from May 10," *Times of India*, April 22, 1993.
[61] "MPs Concern at US Move Over Patents Bill," *Times of India*, May 3, 1995; also see "Government to Face Stiff Opposition on Patents Bill," *Indian Express*, May 10, 1995; "Government Cannot Amend Patents Law: Opposition," *Indian Express*, March 21, 1995.
[62] "Elders Decry US Pressure on India on Patent Law Changes," *Business Standard*, May 3, 1995; "MPs Angry Over US 'Threat' on Patents Bill," *Times of India*, May 3, 1995; "US Earns Elder's Ire Over Patents Law," *Indian Express*, May 3, 1995.
[63] "Patent Law Amendment a Spineless Act, Says Sachar," *Indian Express*, January 3, 1995.

Table 4.7 (*cont.*)

Year	US Threats and Sanctions	Public Reaction	Effect
1996	Statements by US Officials: "India's patent protection is weak and has especially adverse effects on US pharmaceutical and chemical companies. Estimated annual losses to the US pharmaceutical Industry due to piracy amount $450 million"[64] US threatens India with WTO case On July 2, 1996, the United States requested consultations with India concerning the alleged absence of patent protection for pharmaceutical and agricultural chemical products in India. Violations of the TRIPS Agreement, Articles 27, 65, and 70 are claimed.[65] This was the beginning of the United States dispute claim against India In August the US responded to many negative opinions by arguing that "US may retaliate if India does not implement TRIPS compatible regime"	An editorial in a major news daily reported that "US stance was unreasonable"[66] Others argued that India need not implement a TRIPS-compatible law for many years. Rajeev Dhavan noted, "no developing nation needs to amend the general patent laws to conform to TRIPS for five years and bring into effect "product" patents for ten years. The mad rush for change in the area of drugs and fertilizers is America's special baby"[67] Other opinions suggested "calling the American bluff"[68]	**Noncompliance**

[64] "US Criticizes Weak Patent Laws," *Economic Times*, April 3, 1996.
[65] See the WTO document that documents the history of the case: www.wto.org/english/ tratop_e/dispu_e/cases_e/ds50_e.htm. For the final report, see Appellate Body Report, *India – Patent Protection for Pharmaceuticals and Agricultural Chemical Products*, WT/DS50/ R and WT/DS50/AB/R (adopted December 19, 1997).
[66] Editorial, "Unreasonable Stance," *Observer*, May 3, 1996.
[67] Rajeev Dhavan, "Patents and World War II," *The Hindu*, August 2, 1996, Madras edition.
[68] S. H. Venkatramani, "Calling the American Bluff," *Hindustan Times*, August 3, 1996. Also see "Patents Not an Economic Monopoly," *The Hindu*, August 4, 1996, Madras edition.

Table 4.7 (*cont.*)

Year	US Threats and Sanctions	Public Reaction	Effect
1997	**US files WTO case** WTO case against India India appeals in front of the Appellate Body of the WTO	Similar to 1996, there were many negative stories against the US Editors, parties, and NGO activists spoke against US pressure	**Noncompliance**
1998	WTO finds India in default; India loses the case US statement: 'US refused to give a longer time period to implement TRIPS-compatible laws'[69]	Some articles "urge the government to resist WTO pressure"[70] Many articles argue that India needs to take advantage of the new patent system[71] Even I. K. Gujral, India's PM at the time, asked Indian industry to start developing an "intellectual property rights culture"[72]	Cabinet meeting held to discuss India's loss
1999		India implements the first amendment putting a "mailbox facility" into place	**Compliance begins!**

Source: Data in this table are drawn from an original newspaper database collected and constructed by the author. I used almost 800–1,200 stories in each year (total of 10,000 stories) to assess the quantitative and qualitative extent of the US pressure on India.

4.3.3 India loses at the WTO's Dispute-Settlement Court

I argue that it was India's legally binding loss at the WTO's Dispute-Settlement Court in 1997–1998 that left India with no choice except to comply.[73] In 1996, the WTO launched a case of nonimplementation of

[69] "US Rejects India's Claim on IPR at WTO," *Hindustan Times*, February 18, 1998.
[70] "Govt. Urged to Resist WTO Pressure," *Hindustan Times*, March 23, 1998.
[71] Kiyoshi Asamura, "Product Patents Help Industry," *Indian Express*, March 23, 1998; "BJP Moots Legal Cadre to Fight India's Patent Case," *Hindustan Times*, March 13, 1998; editorial, "Off-Patent Sense," *Economic Times*, January 3, 1998; "Patent Bill Causing Gene Drain," *Business Standard*, January 21, 1998.
[72] "Gujaral Calls for Developing Intellectual Property Rights," *Financial Express*, January 4, 1998.
[73] This section draws the details of the WTO dispute case from the WTO website. See Appellate Body Report, *India – Patent Protection for Pharmaceuticals and Agricultural Chemical Products*, WT/DS50/R and WT/DS50/AB/R (date report was issued) (adopted December 19, 1997).

the TRIPS agreement after a complaint by the United States. This case was to reverberate in Indian policy circles, but very few scholars acknowledge its importance.[74] On July 2, 1996, the United States requested consultations with India concerning "the alleged absence of patent protection for pharmaceutical and agricultural chemical products in India." The Dispute-Settlement Board established a panel at its meeting on November 20, 1996, that found that "India has not complied with its obligations under Article 70.8(a) or Article 63(1) and (2) of the TRIPS Agreement by failing to establish a mechanism that adequately preserves novelty and priority in respect of applications for product patents for pharmaceutical and agricultural chemical inventions, and was also not in compliance with Article 70.9 of the TRIPS Agreement by failing to establish a system for the granting of exclusive marketing rights." On October 15, 1997, India notified its intention to appeal certain issues of legal interpretations developed by the panel. The Appellate Body upheld, with modifications, the panel's findings on Articles 70.8 and 70.9 but ruled that Article 63(1) was not within the panel's terms of reference. The Appellate Body report and the panel report, as modified by the Appellate Body, were adopted by the DSB on January 16, 1998. All appeals by India were rejected at that point, and there was no alternative but to implement the agreement by changing Indian laws. At the DSB meeting of April 22, 1998, the parties announced that they had agreed on an implementation period of fifteen months from the date of the adoption of the reports; that is, it expired on April 16, 1999.

The loss of this case was used repeatedly as an argument to implement the letter and spirit of India's commitments signed between 1998 and 2004. The internal record within the civil service revealed by Anil Jacob's doctoral dissertation shows that loss of the two cases of 1997–1998 was considered to be both an immense loss of prestige and a source of shame. Jacob's primary evidence further corroborates my argument that the loss of face represented by the legal defeat of India at the DSB was very important. As an internal file within the Ministry of Commerce noted:

Regardless of the strategy adopted, it is paramount to appreciate that for this set of amendments the time frame is most crucial. Any slippage in meeting the January 1, 2005 deadline will invite retaliatory action under the WTO disputes mechanism because the stakes for different sectors of the pharma industry (especially MNCs of developed countries) are much higher. Having availed of the entire transition period provided under the TRIPS Agreement, India will have no legal leg to defend its default. Its past record of delayed implementation will also not help its case. Further, the "mailbox" applications will hang in balance as there will

---

[74] One exception is Jacob (2010).

be no mechanism to deal with them as on January 1, 2005. ... This would aggravate the situation relating to India's default on its obligations and once again provide an opportunity to the USA and the EC, etc. to raise a dispute against India in the WTO. There will also be an erosion of India's credibility in the international field [Jacob 2010, 192–195].

Many Ministry of Commerce officials drove these points home repeatedly to politicians. In October 2004, a high-level meeting of ministers emphasized that India should not default on its international obligations concerning the implementation of TRIPS agreement as "its credibility would be at stake." The ministers also noted that the stakes were quite high, and other trading partners could raise a "dispute in WTO" in case of a delay in fulfilling India's TRIPS obligations (Jacob 2010, 192–194). This loss led the bureaucrats to take a leadership position in order to implement India's commitments (Jacob 2010). Table 4.8 documents the legal changes that happened quite quickly between 1999 and 2005.

4.4   Changing preferences of Indian industry

The changing global system created uncertainties about the shape of markets and the possible choices faced by firms, making the utility function of a firm hard to determine. Market signals were diffuse and unclear. In addition, the firms needed to navigate complex regulatory environments in other countries and WTO-compliant regimes across the world, requiring new political, legal, and regulatory skills. Moreover, the changes initiated by the TRIPS regime were quite threatening to the Indian industry in that they undercut its ability to produce generic versions of patented drugs. In the late 1980s and early 1990s, all Indian firms saw the impending TRIPS agreement as a threat and felt that they would lose as a result of the TRIPS regime. How did the preferences and strategies of Indian industry *evolve* as Indian policymakers struggled to implement TRIPS?

In this section, I distinguish between *different types of strategies adopted by private firms* over time as the dynamic global environment shifted; these together constituted a significant *realignment of interests* and *creation of new interests*: resistance (1989–1995), differentiation (1995–2000), and leveraging and upgradation (2000–2014). Despite the structure of incentives created by the 1970s' policy regime, the TRIPS regime affected almost all types of firms, although responses were varied.

Initially, the pharmaceutical firms *resisted and were hostile to* global changes and tried every tactic to delay the entry of TRIPS regulations within India. When India lost the WTO case in 1998 and compliance with TRIPS became inevitable, firms began to change their market strategies from late 1990s onward and especially from 2000s onward. As

Table 4.8 *India implements a product patent regime, 1999–2005*

Date	Policy
1997–1998	India loses a WTO case filed by the United States for failure to comply with IPR commitments, and the government commits to passing legislation to comply with TRIPS by April 1999
1998–1999	Mashlekar Committee Report is released; the report recommended development to R&D and development expenditure by the government
1999	1999 Patents Amendment Act came into force from January 1, 1995; introduced a mailbox facility for filing of patents from 1995–2004
2002	Patent Amendment Act of 2002; came into force from January 2003
2002	New pharmaceutical policy announced
December 2004	Patent amendment ordinance
January 2004	Government announces some R&D initiatives. PRDSF set up and DDPB* set up with a corpus of Rs. 150 crores
March 2005	Patent Amendment Act of 2005

*Pharmaceutical Research and Development Support Fund (PRDSF); Drug Development Promotion Board (DDPB).
Source: Author's database of "Policy and Institutional Change," 1990–2011.

noted by many scholars, the large firms adopted a mixture of competitive and collaborative strategies (Athreye, Kale, and Ramani 2009; Sampath 2006). As the compliance process unfolded, industry preferences and market strategies changed in response to the incentives and pressures created by the ongoing implementation of global rules. It is at this stage that the potential stimulated by domestic regulations came to the fore. India's pharmaceutical industry thus sought to *both manage and leverage* the TRIPS agreement, in the process transforming its interests, the perception of its interests, and the industrial structure.

4.4.1   *Resistance, hostility, and opposition during the early years: 1989–1995*

The Indian patent regulations (1970) created a generic industry of great power; the TRIPS Agreement's likely effect would be to *limit* the *future* generic market growth and expansion of Indian firms.[75] At the end of the Uruguay Round of GATT negotiations, India formally accepted that it would implement TRIPS. While the government acceptance was a

[75] By limiting the Indian companies' ability to "reverse engineer" the patented drugs once the agreement came into effect in 2005, the market share and the profit margins of largely generic companies could be affected negatively in the future.

closely guarded secret, one official from the Ministry of Commerce convened a meeting of the top pharmaceutical companies to make them aware of the impending changes.[76] The earliest responses to the TRIPS regime followed expected lines, with the Indian companies opposing the draft and the MNCs supporting it.[77] The Indian Patent Act of 1970 had united Indian companies as all of them benefited directly or indirectly from the process patent system. Thus, from 1970 to the late 1990s, the Indian sector – both large and small, exporting and not exporting – articulated a common, unified position against product patents and sought to delay rather than support the product patent system.

There is clear evidence that industry preferences, and collective action in favor of those preferences, *lagged rather than led* India's compliance process in favor of a TRIPS-compliant regime between 1990 and 1998.[78] No pharmaceutical firm or association proactively sought to push globalization under the aegis of GATT/TRIPS in the late 1980s and early 1990s. Most firms opposed the agreements vigorously, "lobbying the government to hobble the proposed agreement" (Banerji 2000, 81). Even Ranbaxy, India's premier pharmaceutical company, initially thought that the TRIPS agreement needed to be delayed rather than leveraged into global reach. As Swaminathan Aiyar, a prominent editor, wrote, "Parvinder Singh of Ranbaxy, Anji Reddy of Dr. Reddy's Labs and other pharma czars in India claimed that their survival depended upon India's weak patent regime, which allowed them to reverse engineer drugs still on patents abroad. ... These gentlemen were part of the National Working Group of Patens [sic], a left-wing group full of people who wanted India to leave WTO rather than accept the strong IPRs of the Uruguay Round."[79] Thus, all industry actors – individual or collective – *followed rather than mobilized* for change.

Ramanbhai Patel, managing director of Cadila Labs, a prominent pharmaceutical company, said in 1993: "India would be putting the clock back by decades if it signs the Dunkel Draft as it is. India would end up as an importer forever with multinationals getting even microbes

---

[76] Confidential interview with an ex-MOC official, Geneva, November 2003.

[77] "Drug Congress Set to See Battle over Dunkel Draft," *Business Standard*, January 18, 1993.

[78] The government too did not seek to utilize the TRIPS compliance to move toward a global expansion in the knowledge economy in the early 1990s. As an illustration, Parvinder Singh tried to persuade many sections of the government to "meet 50 percent of the indigenous companies' research and development efforts into discovering new drugs in the context of the Uruguay Round of the GATT agreement," "Ranbaxy for Government Funding of R and D," *Times of India*, October 6, 1994.

[79] Swaminathan S. Anklesaria Aiyar, "How Patents Can Produce Cheap Drugs," *Times of India*, February 2, 2000.

and variants of research work in advance. So, India should strive hard to get the draft amended so that it reflects the needs of the Third World."[80] IDMA, the association representing the Indian sector, launched a serious campaign to prevent the acceptance of TRIPS in India.[81] Dinesh Patel, president of IDMA, said, "The government has surrendered to the GATT. Indian drug companies produce 90 percent of the drugs. Now imports will increase. I feel that the monopolistic situation created by the MNCs will get stronger after India goes in for product patents."[82] Thus, the rising economic strength of Indian pharmaceutical companies and changing price signals from the global marketplace were not enough to transform preferences or interests. Most market strategies were directed to protect, consolidate, and, for some, expand the generic market share in the world.

4.4.2   Differentiation within the industry: 1995–2000

While most companies were unaware of the impact of the inclusion of TRIPS in the global trade regime, some companies' top leadership realized that "this would have profound implications, both for the industry and the company."[83] Soon the TRIPS regime drove a new wedge among the various Indian companies, with a few coming out in support of complying with the TRIPS regime. From 1994–1995 onward, the prospect of the TRIPS regime in India divided the industry into three camps: (a) those that felt that TRIPS was a threat that needed to be stopped at any cost, (b) those that realized its significance and threat potential but also the possibility for domestic change, and (c) those that felt that it would not have an impact on the industry and their firms. Yet, most were of the view that it was a necessary evil. D. B. Gupta, chairman of the Lupin Group, noted, "There is really no option. Product patent is not good for us but we have no choice."[84] A prominent official of Ranbaxy noted, "The GATT change made us realize in a concentrated way that we will have to change the way we do business. If it would not have happened in that way – that is, as India accepting an international obligation in a multilateral forum – we may have continued in our old ways for much longer. But now we knew that we could not avoid it."[85] Parvinder Singh, Ranbaxy's CEO, led a strong and somewhat isolated (at that time)

[80] Ibid.
[81] "IDMA Denies Piracy Charge in Note on Dunkel: Accepting the Draft Will Hit Exports, IDMA Claims," *Economic Times*, November 5, 1993.
[82] "A Difficult Agenda for Pharmaceuticals," *Financial Express*, December 29, 1994.
[83] Raizada (n.d., 11).
[84] "The Way Out of the TRIPS Trap," *Business Standard*, November 10, 1993.
[85] Interview with Raizada, 2003.

crusade to persuade the government and other industry actors to change their practices and accept the TRIPS regime.[86] He was one of the first to realize the implications of the TRIPS regime for Indian pharmaceutical industry and sought to explicitly transform his company's market and global strategies in anticipation of a TRIPS-compliant regime. "We realized that you can't afford to isolate yourself if you want to globalize. To sell in the international market, Indian companies have to play according to the host country's rules."[87] He also saw the impending global changes as an *opportunity* for the government and industry to transform the way they do business and leverage their strengths in the changing global regime or be destroyed. He felt that changes were necessary for the survival of the industry. He said, "To set up any kind of decent R&D centre you would need Rs. 50 or 60 crores. If those funds are not made available or they cannot be generated by the industry then the implications will be horrendous."[88] On being asked if the TRIPS rules would sound the "death knell of Indian industry," he said:

I would not like to make such extreme comments. But what will happen is that there are two kinds of industries all over the world, one, which is research based industry, which discovers newer drugs and then you have the generic industry, which makes markets off patent drugs. The latter in essence is what the Indian industry is capable of today. To that extent there will always be a market for off patent drugs and industry will continue to operate in this segment. But, this segment does not give you adequate profits and eventually you have to mature to a research based organization.[89]

In 1993–1994, Parvinder Singh rearticulated Ranbaxy's vision to become a "research based international pharmaceutical company"[90] in direct anticipation of the future challenges presented by the WTO's TRIPS regime. To the question, "Will the enhanced intellectual property protection to multinationals facilitate the transfer of technology to India?" Singh responded, "I believe so. We are in touch with several international companies and many of them are willing to work on a collaborative basis with us [if the regime is accepted in India]."[91] Analogously, a few other companies started investing more on R&D than before. Other companies were more sanguine but did start some preparation for the GATT regime.

---

[86] He repeatedly said, "The government has to understand the urgency of liberalizing and freeing our industry from price and profit controls, which have continued to hurt the growth of our industry. In the light of the GATT decision, the industry must be freed so that those that are efficient are able to function effectively and thereby fund much larger outlays into research, because the *key to survival* will lie in this." "Drug Industry Controls Must Go: Interview with Parvinder Singh," *Telegraph*, January 23, 1994.

[87] "The Way Out of the TRIPS Trap," *Business Standard*, November 10, 1993.

[88] Ibid.   [89] Ibid.   [90] Ranbaxy (1994).

[91] "Drug Industry Controls Must Go," *Telegraph*, January 23, 1994.

Torrent Pharmaceutical stated in 1994, "The effects of the Dunkel Draft will not be seen before 2002 AD and that is a long time. Nevertheless, the draft will affect only about 15 percent area of working of pharmaceutical firms. Keeping in mind the emerging export potential of the country, the Dunkel Draft will not have too much of an impact on our way or any other's pharmaceutical firm's performance."[92] By 2005 or so, companies that were interested in filing for patents developed an interest in a stronger patent system within India. Many of them could get patents abroad but were unable to get them in India. This made them argue for stronger patent implementation within India.[93]

This threat to *future* domestic market share in the generic segment created the pressure to expand in both the unregulated generic markets, such as Eastern Europe and Africa, and the regulated West. Many Indian firms started this expansion and diversification process in the mid-1990s in anticipation of a shrinking domestic market share. The negotiations around TRIPS revealed crucial information about the shape of future markets and the need to expand into northern markets (United States and Europe). As the president of Piramal Enterprises said in 1996:

We feel, worldwide the generic market is growing very fast. To get into that market you must have economic cost of production. . . . we are looking at future growth coming from niche markets where we don't have presence today. And, that's the reason for the joint ventures.[94]

It is clear that one of the most striking effects of the onset of TRIPS was an acceleration of internal differentiation within the "Indian sector," with the emergence of a wide variety of market strategies. This raises an interesting question of whether changing business responses changed the nature of collective action and policy influence sought by pharmaceutical firms and associations.

4.4.3   Collective action, mobilization, and churning within the Indian pharmaceutical sector

Essentially, differences within the united Indian sector were created and magnified as a result of different interests of the various Indian companies

---

[92] "Torrent Pharma Plans Four-Pronged Expansion," *Business and Political Observer*, February 1, 1994.

[93] This point is mentioned in Aggarwal (2007, 181), and it was confirmed during interviews I conducted.

[94] Interview with C. M. Hattangadi, cited in "There Is Room for Growth," *Business Standard*, January 6, 1996.

vis-à-vis the trade regime. Some saw the TRIPS regime only as a threat, while others saw it as an opportunity. Others saw a set of both threats and opportunities. This led some Indian companies into alliances and partnerships with the multinational companies, which would not have been possible under the old policy regime. Thus, a nuanced, intermediate position on the TRIPS regime emerged as different Indian companies sought to seek advantages from it. How did this affect the collective action possibilities?

Indigenous production in the 1970s led to the stark fragmentation of the pharmaceutical sector into the Indian and multinational subsectors. IDMA (Indian Drug Manufactures Association) was formed in 1961 but remained a small, ineffectual organization in its early years. By the end of the 1970s, IDMA had become more active and organized. It began to represent the interests of the "national" Indian sector to the government. Many Indian companies joined the association, including Ranbaxy, Cipla, and other big players. The other industry association was OPPI, the Organization of the Pharmaceutical Producers from India, which represented the foreign and multinational companies, formed in 1965. From 1970s onward, all drug manufacturers in India developed diverse tactics to take advantage of the domestic patent regime, while political mobilization was directed toward reducing the effects of price controls on the profit margins of the companies. Over time, this overwhelming constraint brought the two pharmaceutical associations closer. Both IDMA and OPPI met regularly to evolve a common strategy toward the price-control regime. Price control, not the patent regime, was the dominant issue during this time.[95]

By the late 1990s, new internal changes and collective action patterns became apparent. The Indian sector became internally divided, with some Indian companies moving away from IDMA into OPPI. OPPI members now included both foreign and some Indian companies (Ranbaxy, for example), an impossibility during the prepatent regime days. IDMA continued to represent the small and medium-sized companies that were largely opposed to the patent regime. In 1999, eight large and research-oriented Indian companies, including Cipla, formed a separate coalition to lobby and negotiate with the government, as their interests had diverged from the Indian association, IDMA, and the foreign multinationals, represented by OPPI. This was called the *Indian Pharmaceutical Alliance* and consisted of the eight large Indian companies with a more positive view on

---

[95] The newspaper database (10,000 news events) reveals this clearly.

the patent regime.[96] By 2015, more companies had joined the alliance (nineteen companies), although Cipla had left this group in the early 2000s.[97] Mobilization became internally differentiated. This churning within the pharmaceutical sector and within specific companies, as exemplified by the Ranbaxy story (discussed in the next section), can be directly linked to the patent regime.

Overall, the industry's responses can be divided into the following types: one response can be categorized as a "necessary evil" response, based on the knowledge that TRIPS was a threat that needed to be mitigated. Most Indian companies could be included in this camp. The second response was articulated by Ranbaxy and to some extent DRL. They accelerated a more aggressive plan to use the opportunities that might come their way. These two companies anticipated some of the results of the TRIPS regime when the government, the debate over TRIPS, and their international interactions revealed some important information about the future shape of markets, such as the growth of patented drugs and its effect on generics and branded generics. Without the debate over TRIPS, their adjustment and change in strategy would have been much delayed and slower. Market movements were not enough to give cogent and clear signals to market players without the concentrated debate around TRIPS. Ranbaxy and DRL, as well as other prominent companies, also started a strong lobbying effort to shape the laws and regulations that would emerge. Thus, somewhat counter-intuitively, many pharmaceutical companies came closer to the government and began a lobbying effort to influence future policy through the 1990s. This differentiation can also be witnessed through an interesting power struggle "between generations"[98] that ensued *within* India's most prominent pharmaceutical company, Ranbaxy. This power struggle represented the emerging cleavages created by the global trade regime in intellectual property.

---

[96] In 2008, the following members were part of the new lobbying group: Alembic, Ltd., Cadila Healthcare, Cadila Pharmaceuticals, Dr. Reddy's Laboratories, Emcure, Ltd., Glenmark, Incas, Lupin, Microlabs, Ltd., Ranbaxy, Sun Pharmaceuticals, Torrent, Unichem, USV, and Wockhardt.

[97] Alkem Laboratories, Micro Labs, Cadila Healthcare, Natco Pharma, Cadila Pharmaceuticals, Panacea Biotec, DRL, Ranbaxy Labs, Glenmark Pharmaceuticals, Sun Pharmaceuticals Industries, Intas Pharmaceuticals, Torrent Pharmaceuticals, Ipca Laboratories, Unichem Laboratories, J.B. Chemicals & Pharmaceuticals, USV, Ltd., Lupin, and Wockhardt. D. G. Shah noted, "Together they share 30 percent of the domestic market, account for one-third of exports and contribute 90 percent of R&D spending in the pharmaceutical industry," quoted on D. G. Shah's website: www.vision-india.com/about.htm.

[98] The media characterized it that way.

4.4.4   Ranbaxy: the reorientation in the 1990s

The onset of the TRIPS regime created a divide over company global strategy between Bhai Mohan Singh, founder of Ranbaxy, and his favorite son, Parvinder Singh, in the early to mid-1990s. This family split can be directly traced to differences over the TRIPS regime rather than over more personal questions of control of assets. The split arose as a result of a clash between two different visions for the company in the face of the changing global and domestic environments.

Bhai Mohan Singh and Parvinder Singh were a very close father and son pair; Mohan Singh had the utmost confidence in his son, and the two had hardly any differences (Bhandari 2005, 131).[99] In an earlier division of the family's assets, Bhai Mohan Singh had transferred all his Ranbaxy shares to Parvinder Singh with the implicit understanding that he would be involved in important matters, and the company would take care of his expenses and living costs (Bhandari 2005, 134). Given the close and intimate relationship between father and son, this agreement was completely tacit and informal. Parvinder Singh saw the TRIPS regime as inevitable as well as a set of opportunities. As a result of a misinformed journalist, we have one of the clearest statements in support of the product patent regime in 1994 from Parvinder Singh. A journalist asked him: "Why do you oppose accepting the international patent regime while your father supports it?" He answered: "In the last four years I have been the only one to support the acceptance of the international patent regime. I think you have your facts wrong. I am on record as having supported this. It's very strange that you say this. As far as others are concerned I cannot comment on their views."[100] Again, as early as 1993–1994, he had said:

For the Indian Pharmaceutical Industry, the GATT treaty signaled the emergence of a new era with the acceptance of product patents. Although some in the industry have misgivings on the issue, we at Ranbaxy believe that this can provide new opportunities. With the new intellectual property rights regime that India has agreed upon, focus must now shift to innovation. Industry has not been investing adequately on research and development, as profit margins have remained low on an account of a rigid price control mechanism. The future belongs to those companies who will invest and enhance their research capabilities, initiate change, and avail themselves of the emerging opportunities [Bhandari 2005, 142].

This perception was a minority view at that time and not very popular. Most companies were trying to modify and delay the TRIPS regime rather than seek advantages from it. In fact, this view was unpopular

---

[99] This was confirmed in my interviews with many Ranbaxy officials.
[100] "Drug Industry Controls Must Go," Telegraph, January, 23, 1994.

within Ranbaxy itself. In the mid-1980s, Bhai Mohan Singh had encouraged the formation of an antipatent group within Ranbaxy itself; it was the "National Council for Patent Laws,"[101] and Ranbaxy supported it with money and office space. Led by a Ranbaxy employee, B. K. Kyeala, it organized conferences to discuss the TRIPS issue and build coalitions and networks with NGOs, social activists, intellectuals, and civil servants in opposition to the TRIPS regime. They were encouraged to bring together opposing voices and try to change government policy on patents and TRIPS. In the early 1990s, at the time when Parvinder Singh realized the full import of the TRIPS regime, he told B. K. Kyeala to pack his bags and leave. Thus, Ranbaxy stopped supporting an anti-TRIPS agenda at that time. Parvinder Singh's realization about the changing global environment necessitated significant changes in company strategy, which were alien to Bhai Mohan Singh. The board of directors of Ranbaxy had five family members (of twelve) in 1989; it was restructured to six board members in 1992 with only two family members; the rest were professionals. The board felt it was necessary to pursue investment in R&D in order to respond to the imperatives of innovation. All this required capital infusion into the company, which would have diluted the family's stake in the company. The company also needed to expand its hold over the domestic markets. On February 6, 1993, Bhai Mohan Singh, Air Marshal O. P. Mehra, M. M. Sabharwal, D. S. Bawa, and Manjit Singh, Bhai Mohan Singh's other son, resigned from Ranbaxy's board of directors, and Parvinder Singh took over as the chairman and managing director of the company. This conflict created significant bitterness between father and son, creating a divide that was not sealed until Parvinder Singh's untimely death in 1999. While the story of adjustment within Ranbaxy has some unique elements, all pharmaceutical companies have been faced with major challenge and transformations in the 1990s and 2000s, leading to significant upgradations and reorientations.

4.4.5   Leveraging and upgradation: 2000–2014

The global patent regime transformed Indian firms' interests and strategies. While responses differed across firms based on the size and nature of the firm, almost all pharmaceutical companies were forced to adjust their market strategies after 2000. The large- and medium-sized firms began to change their strategies in the late 1990s in response to the information revealed through public debate as part of the compliance process of the

---

[101] Its name was later changed to: National Working Group on Patent Laws.

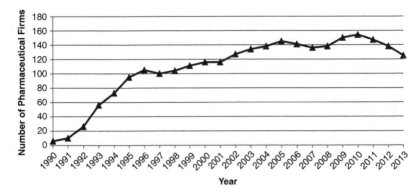

Figure 4.4 Number of pharmaceutical firms investing in R&D
Author's Calculations from CMIE Prowess Database, 1990–2014.

TRIPS agreement, while many smaller companies waited until early 2000 or even after 2005 to change their strategies. Thus, most reorientations in market strategies *followed changes in the global regimes rather than anticipating* them. Indian firms started filing patents at increasing rates and sought approval from the US Food and Drug Administration (USFDA) on a regular basis (Exim Bank 2007). Technological upgradation was also evident despite the inability of Indian firms to discover any new molecules (Athyere, Kale, and Ramani 2009; Basant 2011). A few key firms deployed multiple innovative strategies ranging from legal action to R&D activities to gain the generic market share in the world (Kedron and Bagchi-Sen 2011).[102] I also measured these marked changes in strategies through the creation and analysis of an original database that documents a full range of adjustment strategies adopted by pharmaceutical firms. Smaller firms, while largely unaware of the TRIPS agreement even after 2005, were forced to comply with global standards and WHO norms. They faced a much more restrictive effect of the TRIPS regime, and they also had to comply with many good manufacturing practices dictated by international standards.[103] Two different strategies become salient: protection and resistance versus leveraging and upgradation; paradoxically, some of these were pursued simultaneously.

[102] In 2001, Cipla, Ltd., a Bombay-based pharmaceutical firm, reduced the price of the AIDS cocktail medicines to Africa to about 350USD from 600USD. See "Cipla AIDS-Drugs Offer Changes Outlook," www.thebody.com/content/art21322.html.

[103] In 2001, the Good Manufacturing Practices Guide was notified by the government to accede to the WHO-GMP standards. This was then inserted in the Schedule M of the domestic Drugs and Cosmetics Act, which came into effect only in 2004, as the small-scale industry repeatedly asked for delay in its implementation.

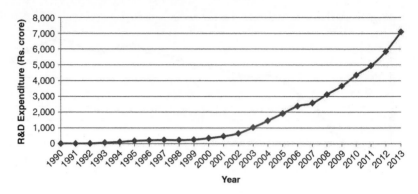

Figure 4.5 Pharma R&D expenditure (Rs. crore), 1990–2013
Author's Calculations from CMIE Prowess Database, 1990–2014.

The 1990s was a time of great transition for Indian companies, and by the end of the decade, most companies evolved their responses to the changed market and regulatory scenario. Fearing that they would lose their ability to reverse engineer patented drugs, many firms increased their plans to capture the generic market share of nonpatented drugs in the regulated markets (Athreye, Kale, and Ramani 2009). Thus, increased activities of Indian firms in the United States and the European Union were more of a protective strategy than an innovative or upgradation strategy. Second, as noted by Athreye, Kale, and Ramani, some firms also focused on participating in contract research and clinical trials for Western MNCs, who were likely to seek Indian partners in India (2009). Nicholas Piramal followed this strategy quite early on. This is reflected in its quite strong pro-TRIPS views: "We are all in favor of intellectual property rights," said Swati Piramal, medical director of Nicholas Piramal, one of a group of companies adapting its strategies to the coming environment. "Not just to protect our discoveries from multi-nationals, but from each other."[104] Very few firms – DRL and Ranbaxy to some extent – followed a much more aggressive strategy of investing in the creation of newer drugs and newer molecules but with limited success.

In order to protect their generic market share, most companies started expanding into newer markets, introducing new products (product upgra-dation), and, most crucially, investing in R&D related to the discovery of new molecules. By 2005, about 109 companies had nonzero R&D expen-ditures. These can be divided into two groups – the top twenty-eight, which spent an average of 8.79 percent of gross sales on R&D, and the

[104] "Interview with Swati Piramal," *Financial Times*, May 24, 2000.

Table 4.9 *Selected companies that changed strategies in the 1990s and 2000s*

Company	Capacity Addition and Vertical Integration	Acquisitions	Brand Acquisitions	Joint Ventures	R&D
Ranbaxy	1. Bought a 30% stake in Vorin Labs, a key supplier of raw materials and intermediates for Ciprofloxacin, one of its key products (backward integration) 2. Subsidiary in Netherlands	1. Acquired Crosslands Research Laboratories in Ireland 2. Rima Pharmaceuticals 3. Ohm Laboratories in United States	1. Acquired Moxa to brand the Amoxicillin drug 2. Picked antibiotic and dermatological brands of Gfic Laboratories	1. Eli Lily in early 1990s 2. Joint venture in China manufacturing and marketing antibiotics	
Cipla	1. 55% stake in Jinhua Economic Development Zone in Zhejiang Province in China			1. Tech licensing arrangements with Novopharm 2. Licensing with Saudi MCPC 3. Licensing with Cipharm Ivory Coast 4. Licensing with Egyptian company Heliopharm 5. Joint Venture with US company, Geneva Pharma	1. Advanced biotechnology center in Pane (Rs 5 crores) 2. R&D facilities in Bangalore for molecular biology cloning

Table 4.9 (*cont.*)

Company	Capacity Addition and Vertical Integration	Acquisitions	Brand Acquisitions	Joint Ventures	R&D
				6. Marketing joint venture with Genpharm of Australia	
Wockhardt	1. Wholly owned subsidiary in US to produce generic drugs 2. Subsidiary in London, Wochradt Europe, Ltd.	1. Took over R.R. Medi Pharma 2. Acquired Merind from TATA, a player in animal vaccines		1. 50% in Saudi firm, Wockhardt Middle East, Ltd. 2. Acquired rights from manufacture Rhein Biotech GmbH (RBH) to license and manufacture insulin technology	1. Started a biotechnology program
Piramal		1. Acquired Boehringer, an MNC 2. Merged Sumitra Pharma 3. Acquired Nicholas Laboratories in 1988 and was renamed as Nicholas Piramal	1. Gained access to Analgib and mlutigesic 2. Added brands such as Supradyn and Valium		

Company	Acquisitions/Brands	Joint Ventures
Sun Pharma	4. Took over Roche products in 1993 5. Acquisition of M.J Pharma 6. Acquired Gujarat Lyka 7. Acquired Tamil Nadu Dadha Pharma, Ltd (TDPL)	
Dr. Reddy Laboratories	1. Acquired the brand Riflux, an antacid extending its range of antiulcer products. 2. Acquired brand Clamp	1. Joint venture with Pharmaceutical Resources, Inc., to supply bulk drugs
SmithKline Beecham Pharmaceuticals	1. Acquired Crocin brand	
Torrent		1. Joint venture with Novo Nordisk of Denmark 2. Joint venture (50:50) with Sanofi Pharma of France
Lupin		1. Merck Generics to market its dosage forms abroad

Table 4.9 (*cont.*)

Company	Capacity Addition and Vertical Integration	Acquisitions	Brand Acquisitions	Joint Ventures	R&D
Max PPIL				1. Geest Brocades 1. Wyckoff (50-50 joint venture	
Cadila Pharmaceuticals				1. Partnership with Murdock Madaus Schwabe (MMS) of Utah	
Shantha Biotechnics Pvt. Ltd.					1. Developed a hepatitis B vaccine
Advanced BioChemical					1. Invested Rs. 24 crore in an R&D center in Maharashtra

Source: Author's compilation from "Industry Strategies and Responses Database," 1990–2011.

Table 4.10 *Worldwide patent filings of leading Indian firms*

Firms	1999	2000	2001	2002	2003	2004	2005
Ranbaxy	14	31	53	69	127	208	259
Cipla	0	5	15	12	21	38	56
Dr. Reddy Laboratories, Ltd.	3	5	5	25	69	77	49
Lupin Ltd.	12	9	8	8	12	25	32
Cadila Healthcare	1	2	3	9	14	19	29
Wockhardt, Ltd.	2	0	3	14	14	18	25
Orchid Chemicals and Pharmaceuticals, Ltd.	0	1	1	7	31	48	25
Nicholas Piramal, Ltd.	0	0	1	7	4	8	11
Sun Pharma Inds., Ltd.	1	0	2	0	2	8	4
Aurobindo Pharma, Ltd.	0	0	0	5	6	9	2
Total	33	53	91	156	300	458	492

Source: B. Dhar and Gopakumar (2009, 121).

bottom eighty-one, which only averaged 1.2 percent. This vividly illustrates a still-remaining divide as to the importance of R&D investment (Chaudhuri 2007). The number of companies investing in R&D increased dramatically after 2000. Figures 4.4 and 4.5 show this rapid change. Taken together, these data point to the reorientation of Indian companies toward technological upgradation starting in the early to mid-2000s.

I argue that the refocus toward R&D was a result of internationalization that had started in the mid- to late 1990s, as well as some anticipation of the shape of future market trends.[105] As Figure 4.5 makes clear, most of this increased focus on R&D started only after 2000. Only three companies – Wockhardt, Zydus Cadilla, and Sun Pharma – spent around 4 percent of turnover on R&D in 1999–2000. The rest (around thirty-six companies) spent only 2.27 of their turnover on R&D in 1999–2000 (Singh 2001b, 138). Smaller firms continued to spend very little on R&D as their main focus was on the drugs that would go off-patent in the future (Pradhan 2007; Athreye, Kale, and Ramani 2009). In the early 2000s, the nature of R&D expenditure also changed, moving into R&D for new drugs and molecules. A few examples of major Indian companies are quite illustrative.

Ranbaxy was one of the few companies to completely reverse direction and reorient its global and market strategy quite early. The first leg of this strategy was an attempt to gain market share in North America, Europe,

[105] Narayanan and Thomas (2010) also make this point and show it through a statistical analysis of Indian firms.

and Asia. On a visit to Thailand in 1996, the CEO of Ranbaxy indicated his commitment to spend USD45 million for setting up a research, development, and manufacturing joint venture in India and a marketing venture in the United States with its US affiliate, Eli Lilly. He is reported to have said: "The interim years of 1996, 1997, and some part of 1998 will be years where we will be transiting from one kind of a model to another. What we are trying to achieve in the next three to four years is a transition from a developing country mix, which is now a major part of our international operations, to a developed country mix. This will increase focus on emerging markets like China, Central Europe, and Russia as well as a thrust into developed countries like Britain, the United States, and Australia."[106] Acquisitions of pharmaceutical firms in other countries also became one of Ranbaxy's strategies, as it was a cash-rich company with large exports.

Torrent Pharma, a newer domestic pharmaceutical company, announced a massive "four-pronged expansion" in 1994. The goal was to raise money, broadly base its bulk drug productions, and expand its formulation product line, as well as invest in R&D. The company noted:

The company also plans to upgrade its marketing infrastructure and modernize its computer-based information processes, *recognizing the changing global scenario* the company is enhancing its research capabilities. Torrent has also established strategic links with R&D institutions worldwide to derive benefits of the expertise of the scientists abroad. In addition, the company has established technology networks with reputed international companies.[107]

Thus, companies started changing their strategies while hoping that the negative effects of the TRIPS regime would be modest and "in the future." Table 4.9 illustrates that many Indian companies responded to the TRIPS agreement in similar ways, by expanding their global reach and upgrading their skills and capabilities into new areas.

These changes in the strategies of firms had a direct impact on the firms' abilities at the global level. Indian companies began to file patents in greater numbers after 1999. Table 4.10 shows that in 1999 Indian pharmaceutical firms filed only thirty-three patents in the world. By 2005, that number had increased to 492.

Clearly, the impending patent regime changed the way industry actors perceived their interests and the shape of global markets. The changing global rules of the game created new incentives and skills as well as changing the way firms framed their interests and capabilities. Strong industry

---

[106] "Ranbaxy to Invest $25 Billion to Widen Market," *Financial Express*, April 9, 1996.
[107] "Torrent Pharmaceutical Plans 126 crore Expansion," *Financial Express*, February 8, 1994.

firms reoriented their domestic and global strategies and began to think of global markets in terms of new opportunities. The domestic discussions around TRIPS revealed information about the shape of future markets and the new possibilities. It also made possible new alliances and joint ventures. The industrial order and trade politics were transformed in the process. In the next section, I analyze how these changes in interests transformed the moral economy of health and the accompanying industrial politics.

4.5   The changing moral discursive economy

Accompanying a change in interests was a fascinating change in the moral economy, a concept that refers to the moral importance attached to health and the role of government in shaping the industrial order of the economy.[108] In the 1970s and 1980s, the moral economy centered on the idea of "public purpose," with a strong consensus that policy should protect the health of the poor population and ensure cheaper medicines. This pitted the Indian drug industry against the government's regulations. From 1977 onward, the government issued drug price-control orders regularly and the industry opposed price controls, lobbying to reduce their effect. The pharmaceutical industry sought to increase prices of drugs as well as reduce its own responsibility in reducing the prices of medicines. In 1996, then commercial director of Pfizer, a multinational company, D. G. Shah said:

Government figures say that only 25 percent of the population use allopathic drugs. We are also told that there is a 200 million strong middle class. Would it be wrong to say that the 200 million are in the 25 percent? Do you feel that people who are not in the position to get two square meals a day are using allopathic drugs? Again, is it the obligation solely of the pharmaceutical industry to ensure availability and cheap prices? The government should buy and subsidize the drugs of mass consumption and lifesaving drugs. The industry is willing to sell such drugs to the government at a concessional rate.[109]

A snapshot of this hostility is well represented in newspaper stories from the 1980s and early 1990s. In 1990, the industry even considered boycotting a meeting with the minister in an effort to "snub him" and thought of organizing a "one-day bandh." Such public criticism is rare in state–business interactions in *dirigiste* contexts where business uses subtle and behind-the-scenes lobbying rather than public confrontation.

---

[108] The idea of moral economy can be found in E. P. Thompson's writings (1971). It was also deployed in Scott (1977) and Polany (1944). Also see Booth (1994).

[109] "Each Company Will Have to Seek its Own Identity," interview with D. G Shah, *Economic Times*, February 26, 1996.

In a newspaper advertisement in a Delhi-based newspaper, three industry associations "held out the specter of drug companies being forced to produce lipstick or toys instead of life saving drugs, if the current trend in drug pricing and costs persists."[110] The issue at stake was the attempt of the government to reregulate prices and to go back on its liberalization orientation initiated in 1987. The government then had brought some twenty-one drugs into the price-control basket.[111] Earlier that year, the industry even planned on issuing an explicit "commitment that they would not invest in the drug industry, if the official attitude on price revisions and other matters continued."[112] Such explicit hostility and confrontation vitiated state–business relations for a long time.[113] A few headlines from the leading newspapers of the early 1990s tell their own story: "Drug Industry Told to Pay Up Arrears"; "Minister Accused of Volte Face"; "Drug Policy Confusion," *Economic Times*, May 31, 1990; "Drug Companies Want Meeting with Government Postponed"; "Drug Units Seek PM's Intervention"; "Drug Companies Told to Pay DPEA Dues"; Drug Companies Likely to Move Courts on DPEA Issue"; "The Drug Industry Misleading People," *Business Standard*, June 21; 1990; "Government Warns Drug Industry." In 1990 alone, stories in which government–pharma hostility was evident occurred numerous times. This explicit confrontation and hostility continued through 1991, 1992, and 1994–1995. In 1996 too, the government issued notices of overdue payments on 150 companies in lieu of "unintended profits made by drug companies in the sale of bulk drug prices."[114] In 1991, for example, confrontational statements were quite common: "Drug Industry Flays Pricing Policy"[115]; "Drug Makers Plan Token Hunger

---

[110] "Drug Industry, Government on Confrontation Course," *Economic Times*, May 24, 1990.

[111] "Drug Policy Review in Offing," *Hindustan Times*, May 28, 1990; "Drug Policy Being Reviewed," *Telegraph*, May 28, 1990; "Tall Drug Order," *Hindustan Times*, May 29, 1990.

[112] Ibid.

[113] "Drug Industry Told to Pay Up Arrears," *Economic Times*, May 30, 1990; "Minister Accused of Volte Face," *Business Standard*, May 31, 1990; "Drug Policy Confusion," *Economic Times*, May 31, 1990; "Government-Drug Industry Meet on June 12," *Business Standard* June 3, 1990; "Drug Companies Want Meet with Government Postponed," *Business Standard*, June 17, 1990; "Drug Units Seek PM's Intervention," *Business Standard*, June 8, 1990; "Drug Companies Told to Pay DPEA Dues," *Financial Express*, June 8, 1990; "Drug Companies Likely to Move Courts on DPEA Issue," *Financial Express*, June 12, 1990; "The Drug Industry Misleading People," *Business Standard*, June 21, 1990; "Government Warns Drug Industry," *Indian Express*, June 21, 1990.

[114] "Ministry Slaps Over 150 Notices on Drug Companies," *Times of India*, February 6, 1990. Also see "Drug Firms Plan to Move to Court Over Hefty Dues to DPEA," *Economic Times*, March 16, 1996.

[115] *Financial Express*, January 22, 1991.

Strike"[116]; "Legal Redress, Not Bandh"[117]; "IDMA Wants Price Controls Dismantled"[118]; "Drug Industry Protests Against Price Supervision"[119]; "Drug Industry Wants Price Controls Removed"[120]; "Drug Companies Cut Output as Government Dithers over Price Revision"[121]; "Drug Industry Gasping for Breath."[122]

It is notable that on the eve of the impending furor over TRIPS, for example, then union petroleum minister, M. S. Gurupadaswamy, set up a review committee to take a fresh look at the drug policy. What is interesting is that in his statement he referred to the grievance that "some of the major companies were exploiting the public and making a lot of money. It was in this context that a committee was set up to ensure adequate supply of quality drugs to the people at reasonable prices. This included procurement of quality drugs at all government hospitals."[123] As late as October 1994, the chemical and fertilizer ministry turned down a proposal by the pharmaceutical industry to exempt a few drugs from price control. The 1994 policy was extremely detailed, with its main aim to provide detailed instructions for price control and exemption.[124]

From 1995 onward, the discourse over policy and the positions of the protagonists in the discussion began to be transformed in a fascinating way. The debate over TRIPS realigned the parties and their positions. From the price of drugs the debate was transformed to one over TRIPS, and the argument about price control and prices of drugs was redeployed by the same actors but in a reverse way. The indigenous industry, which was previously up in arms about the low prices ceilings, began to use the argument about "rising drug prices stimulated by the TRIPS" as a way to fight the onset of TRIPS. They became sudden champions of low drug prices and access of medicines for India's large population. Until the early 1990s, the drug industry had claimed that the increase in the cost of processing drugs was on account of the "cascading impact of overall inflation." Yet, soon the TRIPS agreement started to be identified as the main causal lever for an increase in prices. In many interviews with the author, Indian companies noted that TRIPS would cause an increase in prices, something they had fought for just a year or two ago.

---

[116] *Statesman*, March 7, 1991.   [117] *Financial Express*, April 24, 1991.
[118] *Hindustan Times*, July 30, 1991.   [119] *Economic Times*, July 30, 1991.
[120] *Hindustan Times*, July 31, 1991.   [121] *Business Standard*, August 2, 1991.
[122] *Financial Express*, August 5, 1991.
[123] "Panel to Review Drug Policy," *Hindustan Times*, January 22, 1990.
[124] "Drug Industry Plea Turned Down," *Business and Political Observer*, October 25, 1994.

4.6   Conclusion

The Indian patents story is one of opposition to the global regime (TRIPS) followed by rapid upgradation and adjustment. Realignment of interests was evident as the state sought to extract policy autonomy as well as compliance. What caused this reversal? While conditionality and coercion by the United States were unable to enforce India's compliance on TRIPS, *sovereignty costs*, in the form of a legally binding defeat at the WTO's Dispute-Settlement Court, forced India's hand. India's reputation concerns in the face of a legal defeat at the WTO were very important for Indian politicians as well as policymakers. In this chapter, I have shown that the Indian private sector in the pharmaceutical sector, *despite its many strengths, was more of an enforcer of bargains arrived at the global level than a major proponent of change*. Without external changes in global markets (export markets in the mid-1990s) and global rules of the game (TRIPS Agreement), the domestic industrial order would have stayed the same. External factors are responsible for many of the changes we witness today, even as domestic actors sought to leverage their strengths and modify the juggernaut of externally stimulated processes and institutions.

The global TRIPS Agreement changed India's patent policies not only by tying India's hands but also by creating private sector support in favor of greater compliance. Yet, interestingly, the process of preference change followed a counterintuitive trajectory. Some Indian firms remained opposed to the international agreements until India lost the TRIPS case at the WTO in the late 1990s. Moreover, the pharmaceutical industry's technological capabilities were shaped by the process regime, creating strengths in producing generic medicines but not new drug formulations. Yet, in the postcompliance period (after 2000) industry shifted in its strategies and preferences as well as collective actions. Without the combination of incentives, threats, information revelation, and "framing" that the WTO regime provided, Indian industrial response to global markets would have been slow and fragmented at best and protectionist at worst.

I have shown how these preferences *shifted and changed* in the process of complying (late 1990s). In so doing, the WTO regime affected the interests, strategies, and choices of economic actors. Most important, the collective action dynamic changed in perceptible and intangible ways. This resulted in a shift in the distributional balance of power within sectors and the strategic landscape of state–business relations during this period (Chapter 7). Many scholars have noted the change in firms' business strategies, but very few explore the domestic and global mechanisms that affected Indian strategies. That is an important part of the story and will be analyzed in Chapter 7. I show in Chapter 7 that the role played by global factors worked as much through *nonmarket mechanisms* of threats, information revelation, and collaborative learning as price signals, technological upgradation, or business foresight. Price signals played an insignificant role in this transformation.

5   Mobilizing new interests and tying the state's hands

Decline and revival in the textile sector

Who are the authors and agents of India's global integration? In this chapter and the next, I explicate the process of policy and private sector change in an important sector – textiles and garments – by focusing on the agents who reintegrated India with the global economy. The global Multifibre Arrangement (MFA), a nested agreement within the WTO, which instituted quotas in the 1960s, was to be replaced by the Agreement on Textiles and Clothing (ATC) in 2005, wherein all previously existing quotas were to be eliminated and all countries were free to export and import textile goods. In India, this prospective abolition activated reform elements within the state, who became authors of a fundamental change in policy direction starting in 1999–2000. Globalist notions considered impossible to implement just a few months before became "the idea whose time has come."[1] How did this happen?

The impending global change ruptured the preexisting industrial order in India, creating a window of opportunity for new growth strategies and a favorable inclination toward the global market. In contrast to prevailing views that see state actions to be negative and ineffective, I show that the Indian state became a leader of policy change, revitalized and mobilized by the perceived threat of the onset of global trade rules in the textile sector. Some state agents used India's commitment to abolishing the Multifibre Agreement in 2005 to encourage domestic businesses to transform their decades-old ways of doing business, and tying their hands in favor of reform.[2] In order to do this, they fought many vested interests

---

[1] Manmohan Singh quoted Victor Hugo in his July 24, 1991, speech when he introduced policy reforms. He said at the end of his speech: "I do not minimise the difficulties that lie ahead on the long and arduous journey on which we have embarked. But as Victor Hugo once said, 'no power on earth can stop an idea whose time has come.' I suggest that the emergence of India as a major economic power in the world happens to be one such idea. Let the whole world hear it loud and clear. India is now wide awake. We shall prevail. We shall overcome." See Singh (1991), http://indiabudget.nic.in/bspeech/bs199192.pdf.

[2] The original image can be found in Elster's metaphor of Ulysses and the Sirens (1979), which talks of how Ulysses tied himself to the mast so as not be tempted by the sirens. International relations literature also elaborates on this "hand-tying mechanism." See

within the state and private sector. This precommitment by the state (tying of one's hand) convinced the usually hesitant private actors that state aid for protectionist interests would not be forthcoming. This pushed them to react to markets, seek global reach, and seek state aid for that purpose.[3]

Why textiles? Douglas Haynes notes, "Cloth ... is an invaluable entry point into global economic history."[4] Echoing that sentiment, I start with the assumption that a study of the textile industry offers a glimpse into the embedding of globalization in India's developmental trajectory over time. The industry accounts for 14 percent of India's industrial production, 4 percent of its GDP, and 13 percent of its export earnings. It employs 35 million people directly, the second largest employment sector after agriculture.[5] Moreover, the textile industry is clearly shaped by global rules. In fact, similar to the TRIPS impact on the pharmaceutical industry (Chapter 4), the abolition of the Multifibre Arrangement in 2005 allows us to assess the impact of global trade rules on domestic interests and policies in the textile sector. This chapter builds an analytical timeline of "Policy Reforms" outlining the interests, policy ideas, and policy changes in the textile sector from 1950s to 2000 and onward. In line with the larger focus of the book in bringing international variables into understanding institutional and policy change, this chapter focuses both on the international context and on the domestic priorities in the different phases.

5.1   The puzzle

Historically, Indian cloth manufacturers passed through many trade routes, creating new designs and techniques of cloth processing that were in high demand in different parts of the world.[6] In the mid-nineteenth century, "India clothed the world."[7] The world's first textile factory was set up in India in 1818 and the first spinning factory in 1856.[8]

Goldstein (1996, 1998) and Pevehosue (2002), who focus on this mechanism. Kydland and Prescott (1977) is the classic formulation of the credible commitment argument.

[3] I thank an anonymous reviewer for comments on this point.

[4] Douglas Haynes, "Indian Textiles and the Global Economy," www.h-net.org/reviews/sh owrev.php?id=33001.

[5] These are data for 2013–2014 and come from Ministry of Textiles (2014–2015).

[6] Riello and Roy (2009). Also see Roy (1993, 1996a).   [7] Ibid., 6.

[8] A mill was established by an Englishman near Calcutta called the Fort Gloster Mills and later renamed Bowreach Cotton Mills Company, Ltd. In 1856, a Parsee established the Bombay Spinning and Weaving Company (Wersch 1992, 11; Morris 1965, 25). In 1858, there were four cotton textile mills in India with 300 looms and 108,000 spindles. By 1869, there were seventeen mills with 4,600 looms and 393,000 spindles and by 1880, fifty-eight mills with 13,000 looms and 1,471,000 spindles, (Medhora 1965, 570).

On the eve of independence, despite 200 years of colonialism, India was a leading producer of cotton textiles. Around 1948–1950, India's cotton textiles accounted for approximately 11 percent of the world market, and India was the second largest producer of cotton fabric, after the United States.[9] This preeminence was reflected in the confidence of its producers to not only meet domestic needs but also capture international markets.[10] Yet, soon after, India entered a long period of autarky and decline and "retreated" from world markets.[11] Starting from a disproportionately large share of developing countries' textile and clothing exports – 58 percent in 1953 – India's share of exports by developing nations declined precipitously to 8 percent in 1969 and to 4 percent in 1992.[12] India's share in OECD imports shrank from 11 to 7 percent by 1980.[13] From 1951 to 1979, India's textile exports into the developed world plummeted from 3.93 to 1.95 percent; countries like South Korea increased their exports into those markets from almost nothing to 6.17 percent during the same period.[14] This diminishing world market share cannot be attributed solely to the protectionist attitude of the advanced countries, since other countries, such as Japan and South Korea, increased their world share during this time. By 1969, Japan had tripled its textile exports (Wiemann 1986, 81). In India between 1956 and 1982, the net value added of the textile sector grew at a disappointing 3 percent per annum, compared to 5.5 percent for Indian industry as a whole (Mishra 1993, 16). During this time, India's textile regime became a "high-cost, low-production regime" (Mazumdar 1984, 38) directed to domestic consumption needs. The state policy of encouraging exports was abandoned. Modernization of machinery was never taken up despite its growing obsolescence. No less than India's ex-prime minister, Manmohan Singh, noted, "In 1948, India was the largest exporter of textiles this side of the Suez canal. ... Our rigid domestic laws, complex rules, regulations and excessive controls inhibited the growth of an internationally competitive industry. ... We were therefore overtaken in the world market by other textile exporting economies of Asia."[15] In 1983, 125 factories had been declared "sick," with mounting

---

[9] Bhide (1996, 19).

[10] Speech by Sir Vittal Chandawarkar, president of the Bombay Mill Owners Association, Annual Address, 1944, cited in Bhide (1996, 20).

[11] The term "retreated" is used by Roy (2004, 83). Also see Goswami (1990a, 1990b).

[12] Mellor and Lele (1974), cited in Bhide (1996, 22). Also see Wolf (1982).

[13] Wiemann (1986, 80–81).

[14] Jain (1988, 19). Other countries that gained at India's expense were Pakistan, Taiwan, and Japan.

[15] "Rigid Laws Hamper Textile Units: PM," *National Herald*, January 7, 2006. Also see "Excessive Controls Hampered Textile Industry Growth: PM," *Hindu Business Line*,

losses.[16] The year, 1982, marked Bombay's worst textile strike, lasting twelve to fifteen months, and left many textile workers jobless and the textile mills in ruins.[17] In 1985, a new textile policy heralded some optimism in the industry, but many of the suggested ideas were not implemented, and by 1990, all hope of change had been quashed.

For most analysts, the story of India's textile sector ended with this dark episode of a failed developmental state. Yet, starting in 1999, a new chapter has been written, marking quite a remarkable turnaround. India created an unexpected policy reversal starting in the late 1990s, comprehensively changing the goals and orientation of state and public action. A new textile policy was announced in 2000 that completely transformed the government's priorities in favor of the large industry segment and new kinds of textiles. Rather than pour money into the nationalized, troubled textiles mills, the government heralded a commitment to new investment in areas such as new machinery and technical textiles.[18] The late 1990s saw the beginning of radical policy changes in favor of organized mills, synthetic (man-made cloth with synthetic fibers such as polyester) and technical textiles (textiles used in technical areas such as hospitals or automotive fibers), and greater global engagement and modernization. The government began helping producers that were opposed to these changes – powerloom and handloom producers – but the aim was to help them modernize rather than protect their old ways of doing business. New important initiatives to provide capital, facilitate the technological upgradation of industry, and build new infrastructure were combined with backward linkages, such as increasing cotton production. The goal of generating employment gave way to that of skill development and modernization of the human capital base required by the industry (D'Souza 2003). The government began partnering with the private sector and supporting many complementary activities. For example, the government began exploring new export markets on behalf of textile firms, as exports

---

January 7, 2006 (from author's "Newspaper Textile Sector Database," 1990–2011; available from author).

[16] The Indian government designated loss-making firms as "sick companies" and passed legislation regulating their takeover by the government. The Sick Industrial Companies (Special Provisions) Act (SICA) of 1985 defined a sick industrial unit as one that had existed for at least five years and had incurred accumulated losses equal to or exceeding its entire net worth at the end of any financial year.

[17] In 1983, a massive strike lasting fifteen months took place in Bombay's mills and is considered a turning point in India's textile history, negatively affecting the large-scale mill sector. See Factsheet 1 Collective, *The 10th Month: Bombay's Historic Textile Strike* (Bombay: Rankeen Xerox Service, nd) and Wersch (1992).

[18] Most scholars expected the 1999–2000 policy to continue old patterns, but this was not what happened. See Roy (1998b) for an articulation of skeptical expectation of the 1999 policy shift.

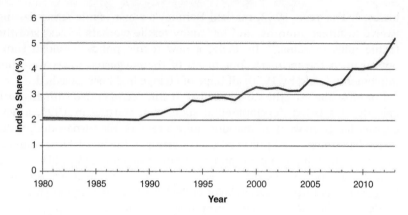

Figure 5.1 India's share of world textiles and clothing exports, 1980–2013
Author's calculations from UN Trade Statistics, 2014.

to the United States came under pressure in 2006–2007.[19] Following these domestic policy changes, the industry began to shift gears and expand investment and production, moving into new areas and new markets, starting around 2003–2005. Indian textile firms reemerged onto the global stage after a long period of decline and ignominy. India was undergoing a surprising "reintegration" with global textile markets and standards.[20] As a result, India's world trade share increased dramatically, as evident in Figure 5.1. How can we explain these changes in a traditional sector? How were embedded ideas, vested political interests, and policies dislodged?

5.2   The argument

Policies must be viewed as a set of congealed interests with the potential to create conflict and contestation as losers fight to keep their benefits. In this view, factors and mechanisms that lead to policy change need careful political economy analysis. The policy changes in favor of global markets initiated in the early 2000s are especially puzzling, as powerful interests had solidified in favor of an internally driven production system that privileged cotton rather than synthetic fibers in the name of national self-reliance. This chapter traces the mechanisms through which international institutions "create an important endogenous dynamic with

[19] "As Exports Dip, Ministry Asks Textile Firms to Eye New Markets," *Indian Express*, April 18, 2007.
[20] The term "reintegration" is from Roy (2010).

important effects on politics" (Lake 2009, 238) in a crucial yet difficult sector such as textile policy. I argue that domestic policies and interests constrained the path of expansion and modernization while opening external markets (exports in the mid-1980s to 1990s), and the dismantling of the Multifibre Arrangement in 2005 disrupted the internal industrial order, setting into motion the radical transitions evident today. Domestic policies and institutions were so much the key to the stasis pervasive in the sector that only external changes and disruptions could shift the stable political equilibrium. In effect, the world markets and, more interestingly, changes in global rules for trade in textiles (WTO's Agreement on Textiles) had a direct effect on the transformations in the textile sector. The mediating effect of domestic state action was also crucial in responding to the need for changes. A reform coalition within the state acted to change the policy order, catalyzed by the impending change in the global regime. An international regime, then, served an important domestic purpose and was deployed by domestic actors "to present a solution to a domestic problem."[21]

This argument and the evidence presented in this chapter resonate with the recent literature on international organizations' effect on domestic purposes through the "tying of hands" of domestic actors.[22] Section 5.3 outlines the emergence of the antecedent regime favoring handlooms, small-scale producers, and cotton. Section 5.3 outlines the tentative attempt at reform in 1985, which was too little, too late and not implemented properly. In Section 5.5, I provide an analysis of the international context as well as the changes unleashed by the abolition of quotas in 2005. Section 5.6 begins with the policy changes initiated by the Indian state, which began in 1998, and describes the struggles around policy reversals from 1998 to 2004. Policy initiatives across a wide range of areas – technology, new investment, human capital, raw material supply, and export-oriented infrastructure development in the form of textile parks – constituted a completely new policy regime. Fiscal reforms, one of the most difficult initiatives, were achieved despite significant opposition between 2002 and 2005 and are explored in Section 5.7. I also explore the politics of such a radical turnaround and the reform elements within the state that made this possible. I combine a unique database from twenty-five to thirty newspapers for twenty-one years (1990–2011) with confidential interviews, economic data analysis, and archival data collection for an important "biography" of the sector. This voluminous database allows a rare peek into *changing policy dilemmas and the struggles around changing policies*, a formidable analytical challenge for comparative

---

[21] Goldstein (1996, 541).   [22] Goldstein (1996, 1998); Pevehouse (2002).

political economy. These rich data also allow me to identify the causal mechanisms underlying the structure of industry as well as the drivers of changes within the government.

5.3   National purpose and agenda after 1947

Theodore Lowi's claim, "Policies determine politics" (Lowi 1972, 299), explains the first puzzle about incremental and ineffective policy change in India's textile sector in the 1950s, 1960s, and 1970s. The textile sector was shaped (and, some would argue, harmed) by the domestic policy regime instituted in the 1960s. Nationalist regulation created new interests, shaping the industrial structure and pattern of production as well as the logic of collective action in the textile sector. Such a policy regime had its own interlocking and feedback effects, making it rigid and resistant to change. It was a system built to survive despite its negative effects on textile output, exports, and technological choices. By the 1980s, India's textile and garment production was fragmented by fiber (jute, silk, cotton, and synthetic fiber), technology (handloom, power loom, organized spinning, and integrated composite mills), size of firms, workers' rights (small and informal vs. large and organized), type of activity (spinning, weaving, etc.), and even type of cloth (yarn vs. cloth). The small-scale sector was privileged over the large modern sector and grew rapidly. The modern organized mill sector atrophied and declined rapidly, but many actors within it benefited from the existing policies. Yet, the state tried to balance the interests of many competing interests and ideas. In the process, the policy system became contradictory, with no levers of change. As the S. S. Verma Committee noted in 1985, "Such distinctions have led to the application of a policy mix which is sector-specific or fiber-specific, resulting in the emergence of special interests on the one hand and fossilization on the other" (Kashyap 1990, 660–661).

A cheap supply of cloth, especially cotton, for the domestic market was the government's priority after independence. In the 1940s, the government brought the textile industry under the Essential Commodities Act, thereby regulating it directly. Cotton was the privileged fiber in India, in contrast to the rest of the world, where man-made fibers showed growth and expansion. The colonial destruction of traditional weavers and artisans by mill-made cloth was foremost in the minds of India's new policymakers. The shortages of cloth during the Second World War stimulated a concern with ensuring the supply of cloth, to which was added the imperative of cheap cloth for a poor population as well as employment generation. Government policy toward textiles supported the small-scale sector handlooms and discriminated against the large and composite mill sector in order to fulfill the goals of employment creation and providing the consumer with cheap, even if low quality, coarse cloth. This was in line with the Mahanaobis Model and the government's attempt to ensure a dual focus on capital and heavy industry combined with labor-intensive industrialization in consumer goods such as textiles (Mazumdar 1984, 14–15; Mishra 1993).

Handloom – the weaving of yarn into cloth via manual looms – was encouraged in a number of ways. The government promoted and prioritized handlooms for increasing employment and did so by constraining the organized mill sector.[23] In 1950, the government reserved many items of common consumer use for exclusive manufacture by handlooms, and mills were prohibited from producing these items. A cess (excise tax) on all mill-made cloth was levied to subsidize handloom and Khadi[24] sectors in 1952. In 1949, the mill sector was charged an excise duty on a gradated scale (fineness of cloth), and the handlooms were exempt from that duty, as were the small power loom operators with four or fewer looms. This excise duty was intended as a consumption tax, with the higher tax imposed on the finer varieties of cotton cloth (Mazumdar 1984, 15). Revenue from the excise duty grew from Rs. 16 crores (approx. USD8 million) to around Rs. 184 crores (approx. USD92 million) by 1975 (Vijayanagar, 1975, 69). This distorted tax structure created different kinds of disincentives as well as a perverse collective action logic. While the organized mill sector had the capacity, technology, and skills to produce high-value-added fine cloth, such finer varieties constituted only 6.5 percent of their total production. This also prevented technical innovation and the movement toward profit-making segments of the garment and textile sector.

The 1956 policy resolution froze the weaving capacity of the organized mill sector to that year's level. The Industries Development Act (1951) further prevented the cotton textile mills from manufacturing noncotton cloth and from using noncotton cloth in blends by requiring a special license. Composite mills were prohibited from using filament yarn so as to ensure easy availability of such yarn to the decentralized sector. High fiscal levies were also imposed on man-made cloth. This was to protect both the cotton farmers and the handloom sector, which, it was thought,

[23] The handloom is the oldest industry in the country. The most common handloom used is the fly-shuttle pit loom. Most such factories are small and exist within the household premises of weavers.

[24] Khadi is a coarse homespun cloth made by handlooms and popularized during India's nationalist movement. See for the historical origins of Khadi, Lisa Trivedi's (2007) excellent study.

were best suited to produce coarse and cheap cotton cloth for the "masses" and people at the lower spectrum of the income scale.[25]

The government subsidized the Khadi and village industries and established a commission that organized the production and sale of hand-spun and hand-woven cloth. Cash subsidies were given to the handlooms, but this created many forms of corruption. Many large cooperatives combining handlooms and powerlooms could claim these subsidies, and many cooperatives only existed on paper in order to claim the subsidies. The government also bought the Khadi cloth for the uniforms of its lower-paid employees, providing some market support. The government banned the installation of new looms by mills in 1956, except for replacement of old looms or for exports, foreclosing capacity expansion in the mill sector. The idea was to let the domestic small-scale and handloom weavers supply the domestic market in order to protect the workers and their manner of production. Only the mills were charged excise duties on yarn and cloth, creating a differential fiscal structure.

Paradoxically, this created a new sector that sprang from the handspun sector; it came to be referred to as the "powerloom sector," as it utilized power-based looms.[26] Over time, and unforeseen by policymakers, the powerloom sector gained at the expense of both the handloom and organized mill segment segments. In 1976, excise duties were charged to powerlooms but at a lesser rate than the mills, keeping alive the discriminatory fiscal structure. Moreover, powerlooms were able to evade duties easily and did so to a considerable extent.

In order to help poor consumers, a hank yarn obligation was imposed on the mills from 1965 to 1978, stipulating that a certain portion of the mill output should consist of coarse cloth (known as hank, with counts of less than ten) and was to be sold below a controlled maximum price.[27] This came to be known as the "controlled cloth scheme" and crowded out

[25] Policymakers differed about the role of handlooms in satisfying cloth demand. One view represented by the Knaungo Committee (1954) believed that handlooms would not be able to satisfy the demand for cloth at the price that was feasible. In contrast, the Karve Committee (1955) recommended the freezing of both mill and powerloom production at existing levels in order to promote the handloom sector. These differences were articulated as contradictory aspects of future policies, but the larger emphasis on the employment-generating goals of the handlooms continued. Powerlooms and handlooms were supported even as the policy rhetoric prioritized handlooms.

[26] The powerloom industry started in the early part of the twentieth century when handloom weavers set up small factories with secondhand, nonautomatic looms sold off by the mills.

[27] Mills were required to produce a very high amount of coarse cloth under this scheme. In 1960 it was 45 percent of their output; it was raised to 50 percent in 1965 and reduced to 25 percent in 1968 as a result of lobbying by the mills; and this obligation was removed in 1978 (Textile Commissioner 1960–2013a).

the organized mills and, counterintuitively, the handloom sector.[28] In addition, certain items of common use and consumption – *dhotis*, *saris*, bedcovers, and towels – were reserved for the handlooms. As more and more mills became "sick," the government took them over – nationalizing them – and used them to manufacture the bulk of the cheap cloth sold to the domestic market. Therefore, the mill owners refused to reinvest their profits into their firms, creating more "sick" firms. In 1968, the National Textile Corporation (NTC) was set up to manage "sick" mills taken over by the government.

5.3.1   *Unintended and intended effects*

Government policy constrained the organized mill sector as a group, discouraging growth and modernization. The mill sector – especially the composite mill sector – shrank significantly from the 1960s to 1990s and exhibited pervasive industry-wide stagnation. In 1951, the mill sector produced 78 percent of total cloth in the country, which declined to 28.4 percent by 1984.[29] In 1992–1993, its share in the total production of fabrics was only 11.5 percent compared to 20 percent in 1989–1990, while 88.5 percent of cloth production was accounted for by the small-scale decentralized sector.[30] The large mills continued to wither and die. Around 123 mills declared losses and were nationalized in the late 1970s and early 1980s. Many policy schemes – such as the controlled cloth scheme – were seen to be responsible for these failures (Bhide 1996, 36).

The rate of technological change in the textile industry from the 1960s to the 1990s was very slow. In 1991–1992, only 2.2 percent of the looms installed in the country were shuttleless, and only 25–30 percent were automatic. Countries like Hong Kong, Taiwan, and even Pakistan had 100 percent automatic looms, but in India, the government did not give permission to install automatic looms unless there was no resulting unemployment. A survey of the machinery in the composite mills sector conducted by the Indian Cotton Mill Federation in 1985 revealed that more than 76 percent of the nonautomatic looms in the mills were more than thirty years old and needed urgent replacement. The study estimated that approximately Rs. 1,000 crores (approx. USD500 million) were needed to replace obsolete machinery at that time.[31]

---

[28] This scheme is seen by many observers to be responsible for sickness in the industry, but it also led to the impetus for diversification among the weaving and composite mills.
[29] Textile Commissioner (1950–2013b).   [30] Ibid.
[31] ICMF Study, cited in Rao (1994, 233).

Two different kinds of fragmentation emerged, one between the handloom and organized mills and the second a tendency for every operator to set up small units, as small units were privileged by policy concessions. Many large powerloom operators broke their units into small mills – less than five powerlooms per firm – to avail themselves of policy concessions. Many organized mill owners set up different kinds of arrangements with small-scale power looms, creating a vested interest in their continuation.

Apart from such obvious consequences, there were other, more complex effects creating a dualistic structure of two types of firms (Uchikawa 1998). Most directly, this policy regime discouraged innovation and exports. The mill owners enjoyed greater profit margins on the domestic market for coarse and medium cloth, while the production of finer cloth was discouraged, except for exports. This created a focus on domestic markets. Many mills did not or could not modernize to automatic looms, which meant that the majority of mills could not produce for international markets. The focus on cotton and the discouragement of synthetic or blended fibers "kept India out of the rapidly expanding world market for such fabrics" (Bhide 1996, 41).

Yet, the various restrictive policies also nudged the new mills, as well as some old mills with an entrepreneurial bent, to look for export markets and introduce innovations to compete with the ascendant powerloom sector. As noted by an industry publication in 1978: "[T]he industry has to concentrate more and more on exports since the bulk of the domestic market is proposed to be reserved for the decentralized sector."[32] Faced with intense competition from powerlooms, some mills started to redirect their attention to producing better-woven fabrics in order to carve out a niche for themselves, creating the conditions for some modernization and technological changes. A small number of mills began producing cloth with better durability, quality, and finish, as well as a finer cloth for export markets. They expanded their capacity by increasing work shifts and productivity. Many of them replaced the older looms with automatic looms, encouraging some amount of modernization in the mill sector (Mazumdar 1984), although the adoption of automatic looms was far below the international norm. Many started their own retail shops and began to integrate marketing and building a brand image (D'Cunha 1982, 100). Many of them integrated more and more of the production process – printing and dyeing, for example – in order to survive in a highly competitive world.[33] Century Textiles and Industries,

---

[32] Kantikumar R. Podar, "Foreword," Kulkarni (1979).

[33] Mills began to compete with hand printers and adopted new rotary screen printing machines, leading to some flexibility into the printing process (D'Cunha 1982, 100).

Bombay Dyeing, Mafatlal, and Piramal were a few prominent business houses in the textile sector that shifted to higher counts in yarn production, incorporated automatic looms, and aimed for product differentiation, as well as building a brand and retail image during the 1980s and, more so, in the 1990s. A few firms, then aimed for exports in order to bypass the restrictive domestic policy regime.

Interestingly, and in contrast to the aforementioned strategies followed by a few firms, some large composite firms and textile business houses also collaborated with the powerlooms to produce cloth and thereby failed to provide any force for change to the larger policy framework. Many entered into subcontractual arrangements with the powerlooms, wherein the cloth was woven in powerlooms but stamped with their brands. In 1964, a government committee assessed that 25 percent of all powerloom units were owned by the large mills. Such circumvention strategies and tactics grew over time and provided a "profitable avenue for the mills to circumvent capacity restrictions" (Mishra 2000, 21). Consequently, a subsection of the mill sector had conflicts of interest and looked the other way when the government subsidized the powerlooms; they did not have any strong incentives to lobby for exports or for expansion and technological modernization.

The political economy consequences of this peculiar mesh of a policy framework were, even more profound. The large mill sector was hampered and constrained but in order to survive it developed three very different, almost contradictory paths of survival and adjustment. Some mill owners moved toward exports and began to introduce different innovations to produce better-quality cloth and increase capacity. A much larger group of mills went sick, diversified out of textiles, and could not survive the policy-induced competition. A third large group established linkages with the powerloom and decentralized sector and tried to work the system so as to benefit from the restrictions imposed on the mill sector as it limited competition within the mill sector. As a result, the mill companies remaining in textiles developed an interest in maintaining the system as such. This group of companies developed different kinds of arrangements with the powerloom sector to bypass capacity restrictions and evade the onerous excise duties, acquiring stakes in the existence of powerlooms and the continuation of the existing policy framework. Thus, even when technological modernization became possible in the mid-1970s or exports were encouraged as an unintended by-product of the policy guidelines,[34] few companies took advantage of the new incentives in the policy framework.

---

[34] Capacity expansion was permitted for the purposes of export, and price freezes did not apply. Paradoxically, the policy framework built incentives toward exports despite claiming to protect the domestic producers.

These political economy interests explain the persistence of the policy since the 1950s and policy stasis until the early 2000s, when during the next episode of possible change – the mid-1980s – despite a major policy initiative and a change in policy goals, the policy did not change. An analysis of the 1985 juncture of policy reforms, which I characterize as a period of policy "nonchange" (no real change despite possibility of change), is provided next.

5.4   Tentative policy change in the 1980s: one step forward and two steps backward

India's textile sector saw many incremental policy changes in the 1960s, 1970s, and early 1980s, with modifications in 1956, 1964, and 1968. Between 1978 and 1985, three major policy statements were issued.[35] Yet, these modifications continued the basic framework outlined in the 1950s, privileging handlooms, cotton, and the small-scale sector despite the emergence of sickness and crisis.[36] Table 5.1 summarizes the slow and incremental nature of policy change in India.

S. Mishra, a joint secretary in the Ministry of Textile in the 1980s, describes the policy process of the 1970s and 1980s as "incrementalism" and notes:

[T]extile policies have shifted only marginally from the existing position over the years. Thus changes have never moved far from the status quo ante. . . . The policies have largely been remedial or reactive, dealing with the problems as they arose instead of anticipating them. The focus inevitably has been on short-term goals without much regard for longer-term consequences. A good example is the controlled cloth scheme making mills sick, which in turn had to be nationalized to keep them operational. Finally, policies have, as a rule, been fragmentary, in that they have viewed the policy arena as being comprised of a number of largely independent segments rather than as an inter-connected whole.[37]

By the early 1970s, the textile industry was in severe crisis, and nationalization and "sickness" were pervasive. The cash losses of the NTC mills had reached a massive Rs. 800 crores (approx. USD400 million) by 1984–1985 (Mishra 1993, 35). Productivity was low and modernization of the industry slow. At that time, even the handloom sector, with slower turnaround times than the powerlooms, faced a shortage of yarn. By the early 1980s, the sense of crisis in the textile sector was systematic and deep.

[35] August 1978, March 1981, and June 1985.
[36] See Mishra (1993) and K. D. Sakesena (2002) for an insider perspective on government's policies.
[37] Mishra (1993, 35).

Table 5.1 *Timeline of textile policy regimes, 1950–2005*

Policy Conjunctures	Policies	Policy Regime
Policy origins (1950s)[38]	Reservation of textile items for handloom sector Imposition of excise duty	Pro-small-scale(new policy regime)
Policy stasis (1960–1985)	Freezing of weaving capacity (1956) Controlled cloth scheme [39] (1964) Nationalization of mills (1968) Sick Textile Undertakings (Nationalization) Ordinance, 1974 Soft loan scheme (1976) Excise duty was increased for superfine cloth The number of looms was capped at the prevailing level[40]	No change Pro-small-scale (policy continuity)
Tentative policy change (1985)	Recognized structural weaknesses with the sector	Need for a structural change recognized
Radical policy regime change (1999–2004)	Discrimination against man-made fiber removed Technological modernization scheme Cotton mission Textile parks Focus on exports Skill development	Complete reversal; a 180-degree change (new policy regime)

Source: Compiled by author from various government documents and newspaper reports. Descriptions of early policies can also be found in Mishra (1993) and Uchikawa (1998) for the 1985 policy.

The long Bombay strike in 1982, lasting fifteen months, added to the general malaise among the workers and mill owners. In the words of S. Mishra, this strike "finally broke the back of the composite mill sector" (Mishra 1993, 21). Almost 29 percent of the country's weaving capacity was shut down for a year and half (Mishra 1993, 21). Policymakers

[38] In the 1950s and 1960s, a number of governmental committees articulated different visions. These committees were Kanundgo Committee (1954), Karve Committee Report of the Village and Small Scale Industries (1955), Joshi Committee (1958), Powerloom Enquiry Committee – Ashok Mehta Committee (1964), Sivaraman Committee (1974), and the Task Force on Textiles (1972).

[39] The private sector disliked this scheme. Some expert committees argued that this scheme was partly responsible for the sickness in the industry.

[40] This was strongly opposed by the mill companies (Kulkarni 1979).

realized that nationalizing mills would not provide a lasting solution to the problem and that the powerloom sector could not be controlled (Mishra 1993, 35). In addition, the demand for noncotton and blended fabrics had grown rapidly, making it apparent that government policies were not meeting the cloth demand by volume or for the kind of cloth (man-made or blended fabric), despite the stated objectives of the policy to satisfy those needs. The public began to perceive that man-made fibers had been discriminated against and that a more balanced approach toward "what came to be called a multi-fiber approach" was necessary.[41] J. Bagchi, a key civil servant in the Ministry of Textiles, noted that "[w]e discovered that other countries were doing very well in textile exports, while India had been declining. China and Thailand had been rising in world exports very dramatically."[42]

This sense of crisis and the long textile strike of 1982 (Wersch 1992) led the government to organsize an Expert Committee (S. S. Verma Committee) in October 1984. Mishra notes that this committee was unique in its autonomous character and inclusion of experts (Mishra 1993, 41–43).[43] According to the Expert Committee, the goals of the textile policy should be "production of cloth of acceptable quality at reasonable prices to meet the clothing requirements of a growing population."[44] The committee found that the industry's problems "are neither cyclical nor temporary" but reveal "structural rigidities."[45] The committee suggested that the problem lay in the fact that the "industry has, so far, been viewed in a compartmentalized manner, either in terms of various sectors, namely organized mills, powerlooms, and handlooms or in terms of fiber use, namely cotton textiles, woolen textiles, manmade textiles and silk textiles."[46] This fragmentation led to poorer technology choices and affected consumer demand. In contrast, the policy suggested that the industry should be viewed in terms of the stages of production – namely, spinning, weaving, and processing – and that the industry shall be provided with greater flexibility in the use and supply of various fibers (Ministry of Textiles 1988; Uchikawa 1998, 150–151). The committee also noted some other serious problems: "Overregulation of industry both in terms of licensing policy and administrative controls as well as inappropriate fiscal policies and fluctuation in the supply and process of raw materials" (Annual Report 1985–1986, 1).

This report and subsequent policy "overturned many basic principles hitherto maintained" (Uchikawa 1998, 150). The new policy lifted the

---

[41] Interview with retired textile ministry official, J. Bagchi, April 16, 2009.   [42] Ibid.
[43] The committee report formed the basis for an announcement of a new policy in June 1985, itself a rare occurrence (Mishra 1993, 41).
[44] "1985 Textile Policy," in Kashyap (1990, 660).   [45] Ibid.   [46] Ibid.

freeze on new looms in the large mill sector. Overall, the committee, and the policy that followed, urged expansion and modernization of the textile firms while also suggesting an easier exit strategy for sick firms and an institutional mechanism to protect workers. A few notable changes envisioned in the policy included removal of the weaving capacity freeze on the mills operative since 1956, a recognition that man-made fibers were to be encouraged, and a freeing of the physical regulations for powerlooms, the last being more a recognition of reality rather than a positive policy change.

The 1985 policy represents a tentative beginning in diagnosing some of the problems that had emerged and sought to change the structure of the policy toward a "multi-fiber approach."[47] It was internally (domestically) driven and a clear recognition by the government that the system was broken and in crisis.[48] Jayanta Bagchi noted in an interview, "We took the external environment – the Textile Quotas – for granted. We were not thinking of the Dunkel Draft or the WTO at that time. At that time, our concerns were largely domestic, to deal with pervasive sickness in the industry, to improve and modernize the industry to the extent possible."[49]

Yet, the modest attempts at policy change in 1985 were confused, inconsistent, and met with resistance. They failed to change the interests and institutions that had been entrenched over many decades. While recognizing the need for a multifiber approach, the handlooms' preeminent role not only remained intact but was also enhanced, thus negating the stated goal of enhancing the organized mills' roles. The committee report did not recommend enhancing the technological basis of the industry and indicated that the export demand could be met without the latest technology. At this time, there was a formal recognition of the need for change without any policy mechanisms to implement it. The institutional mechanisms created, including regional administrative centers to ensure) implementation of the hank yarn obligation, for example,[50] continued the dominance of the small-scale and informal sector rather than supported a truly multifiber approach. Sanjeev Mishra, who played a role in the policymaking process, noted the remarkable character of the policy but also remarked: "Thus, the implementation of the 1985 policy seems to have got bogged down on the potentially

[47] Ministry of Textiles (1985).
[48] Uchikawa (1998, 150); Mishra (1993). Many scholars noted the significant nature of the policy in 1985; all regretted that it was not implemented well. See Bagchi (2004).
[49] J. Bagchi interview to author, April 16, 2009, Delhi. This was confirmed by Sanjeev Mishra, another retired official of the Ministry of Textiles in an interview with the author, February 20, 2009, Delhi.
[50] Ministry of Textiles (1988).

most contentious issues involving a high degree of conflict with entrenched economic interests" (Mishra 1993, 42).

The 1985 policy was, thus a clear departure in terms of its analysis, intentions, and reorientation of goals but also tentative, unsure, and weak in its ability to design a set of instruments and institutions. I argue that the reasons for this stasis were the domestic constellation of interests that had congealed to restrict the sector. The committee itself recognized the political economy problem: "Such distinctions have led to the application of a policy mix which is sector-specific or fiber-specific resulting in the emergence of special interests on the one hand and fossilization on the other" (Kashyap 1990, 660–661). In 1990, five years after the policy was announced, the government set up another committee to evaluate the execution of the 1985 policy. This committee – the Abid Hussain Committee – found crucial failures in implementation of the policy but also reiterated the structural weaknesses of the sector. This diagnosis again gathered dust until 1998, when another committee was set up to evaluate the textile sector. I thus designate the 1985 episode as one of policy change without a corresponding change of institutions, interests, or a shift in the policy regime (see Table 5.1). The stable industrial order, which favored a certain set of interests, remained intact in 1985 despite the perception of crisis and need for change. This industrial order was ruptured only in the late 1990s. Before analyzing the next episode of policy change, I must bring in an analysis of the international context that sustained India's nationalist policy regime.

5.5   Global markets and global rules, 1960s–2005

Between 1973 and 1995, the Multifibre Arrangement shaped the global trade in textiles, allocating specific quotas to developing countries like India. In 1995, when the WTO replaced the GATT, the previous regime of agreements had to be updated. By 2005, all quotas were to be abolished. This radical change was an exogenous one, agreed to by all WTO members in 1995.

For much of its history, the restrictive global trade regime in textiles abrogated the basic principles of the GATT regime: reciprocity and non discrimination. The Multifibre Arrangement, an independent, stand-alone agreement formulated in early 1974, governed international trade in textiles and clothing until its abolition in 2005.[51] The MFA and its

---

[51] The MFA (1974–1994) was a sequel to the Short-term Arrangement on cotton products (1961) and the Long-term Arrangement on cotton textiles (LTA) effective for five years and then transformed into the MFA in 1974. The MFA extended its coverage to wool and man-made fibers in addition to cotton textiles. In 1986, the coverage was further

predecessors are an example of a rule-bound protectionism or, in the words of Friman, "patchwork protectionism,"[52] where the developed countries regulated the import of textiles into their countries.[53] The MFA framework imposed import quotas by developed countries, principally the United States and European Union, on the export of textile products from developing countries. These quotas were negotiated bilaterally under threat of unilateral sanctions by the importer. As an illustration, by 1966, the United States had concluded eighteen bilateral agreements (Aggarwal 1985, 13). Four different MFA agreements were negotiated over the years: MFA I: 1974–1978; MFA II: 1978–1982; MFA III: 1982–1986; and MFA III: 1986–1991.[54] Progressively, the agreements became more extensive, covering cotton, wool, and synthetic fibers, and increasingly one-sided, oriented toward the developed countries' importers and reducing the room to maneuver for exporters in developing countries (Aggarwal 1985). Some protections to prevent abuse were established in the 1973 MFA, but the overall structure was quite restrictive and one-sided. As a result of the Uruguay Round (1986–1994), the MFA was replaced by the Agreement on Textiles and Clothing (ATC), which adopted the same MFA framework but with some liberalization and with a ten-year phasing-out period of all quotas by 2005. Under this agreement, certain products would be removed from the MFA agreement and the quota restrictions were eliminated in a phased manner (16 percent of 1990 import volume on day one, 17 percent at 37 months, then 18 percent in Stage III at 85 months, and finally, 49 percent at 121 months). The integration of products was backloaded, with most (49 percent) of the freeing of trade happening at the end of ten years, around 2005. The ATC gave considerable discretion to the importing countries – the United States and the European Union – in their choice of products and subsectors that were subject to liberal measures. On January 1, 2005, all

expanded to products made of vegetable fibers separate from cotton. See Aggarwal (1985, chapter 1) for a brief history of these arrangements.

[52] According to Friman (1990), the global textile regime instituted by 1974 employed diverse protectionist techniques ranging from global discriminatory quotas governed by the MFA agreement, tariffs, and voluntary restraint (VERs) agreements as well as subsidies.

[53] The MFA was intended to provide the textile and clothing industries in the developed countries temporary protection so that they could adjust the law of comparative advantage, which privileged the production of textiles in labor, rich developing countries. However, this global regime engendered its own protectionist politics as industry actors in the developed countries tried to use this to "re-capture comparative advantage" by investing in capital-intensive production and the development of new synthetic fibers (Bhide 1996, 2).

[54] See Khanna (1991, 21–30) for developments that led to the adoption of MFAs. Also see Bhide (1996).

remaining products were to be integrated.[55] The global rules governing trade in textiles allocated exporting privileges to developing countries and were unilaterally decided by the United States and the European Union.

Did Indian trade benefit or get harmed by the quotas? What are the implications of these rules for the nature of domestic trade politics in India? India initially opposed the MFA on the grounds of its deviation from GATT principles but agreed to it for "pragmatic reasons" as the alternative seemed worse, and India received larger quotas than it had previously.[56] India was also not interested in man-made fibers at that time, although Indian negotiators did ensure that a clause was included to prevent discrimination against entrants in new fibers. India's stated interest continued to be the exclusion of handloom and cottage industry products from the purview of the MFA, which it managed to secure.[57] Despite these concessions, India was not able to fully utilize the quotas in the 1970s given the decline in its productive abilities. Thus, the domestic industry felt that by providing guaranteed access to the developed country markets, the MFA would provide a degree of stability and protection.[58]

This system of global protectionism enhanced the domestic propensity toward rent-seeking behavior. Exporting countries were required to set up their own allocation mechanisms. The domestic political economy unleashed by this system created local interest groups, who saw in the export quotas a stable way to corner market share and therefore lobbied hard for the quotas. Government agencies played a role in the creation of such vested interests as they allocated the quotas to business associations, which were further allocated to exporters.

In India this consolidated an otherwise fragmented mode of interest representation. Various business associations began distributing quotas.[59] In India, quotas were distributed without charge for exporters registered with the Textile Export Promotion Council (TEXPROCIL) or Apparel Export Promotion Council (AEPC) and Synthetic and Rayon Textiles Export Promotion Council (SRTEPC). These business associations enjoyed government patronage and engaged in lobbying activities. AEPC and TEXPROCIL set up numerous offices all across the country

---

[55] Once a product category has been integrated, quotas cannot be reintroduced, but "safeguard mechanisms" under the GATT Article XIX can be invoked in the event of sudden import surges. The European Union and the United States invoked such safeguard mechanisms against China after 2005, which expired in December 2008.

[56] Bhide (1996, 54).   [57] Ibid.

[58] Interview of Kakatkar Rao, who was the secretary-general of the Indian Cotton Mills Federation in the 1970s, cited in Bhide (1996). Also see Kathuria et al. (2001).

[59] TEXRPROCIL was created in 1954, and AEPC was created in 1978 when garment quotas were distinguished from cloth quotas.

for allocation of quotas and charged a subscription fee to exporters.[60] Prior to 1988, quotas were announced annually, creating great uncertainty for exporters. Over time, the government evolved different techniques for quota allocation, and the principles also changed over the years. Initially, three different systems were in force: Past Performance Entitlement (PPE), Contract Reservation System (CRS), and Ready Goods Entitlement (RGE). In 1990, two more allocation modes were introduced, Manufacturers-Exporter's Entitlement (MEE) and Public Sector Entitlement (PSE), and in 1991, Non-Quota Exporter Entitlement (NQE) and Powerloom Exporter Entitlement (PEE).[61] A separate policy was announced for clothing in 1979 when AEPC was authorized to handle the quota distribution. This system of quota management created many inefficiencies, protected current producers and exporters, and discouraged new firms from entering the fray (Kathuria and Bhardwaj 1998, 6; Verma 2002, 26). It also encouraged textile manufacturers to focus exclusively on the local market (Verma 2002, 17).

The quota allocation policies were changed regularly under pressure from competing groups of exporters and also tried to fulfill multiple, contradictory goals (Bhide 1996, 162–164). The government was the main mediator of the quota system and tried to help the large exporting mill companies as well as give quotas to new entrants. As the powerloom exporters lobbied for quotas, the government was forced to open new allocations for them (3 percent in 1991). Clearly, the frequent changes in the quota administration were due to ceaseless lobbying that gave policy-making a piecemeal but stable character. Many exporters foreclosed further capacity by sitting on the quotas or selling them on the black market at a premium. Thus, this system generated many different kinds of problems and pathologies. Although an importer in New York noted that the "Indian quota allocation procedures are more inhibiting to trade than the quotas themselves,"[62] I would argue that the MFA encouraged such classic rent-seeking behavior and perpetuated the combination of export pessimism and configuration of interests that we see in India. In addition, the domestic policy imperatives within India also shaped the nature of the policy regime and the interests it encouraged.

---

[60] "Going with MFA: Clout of Garment Export Councils," *Economic Times*, August 24, 2004.

[61] Over the years, the percentage shares of each of these principles were also changed. PPE allocation increased from 25 percent during 1982 to 40 percent in 1991, while CRS and RGE were brought down to 34 percent in 1991. In 1992, the MEE was allocated 12 percent, and both PEE and PSE 3 percent each. Out of 5 percent reserved for NQE, 3 percent was reserved for nonquota handloom exporters.

[62] Bhide (1996, 165).

5.6   Regime change in 1990s and 2000s

For fifteen years, the stability of the industrial order went undisturbed. The onset of discussions about changing global trade rules began to shift the center of gravity, and in 1998, the Sathyam Committee was set up

[t]o review and evaluate the impact of the existing Textile Policy and identify the changes that are necessary, particularly in terms of the new imperatives of international competition. To suggest policy measures for the textile industry to focus on the changes resulting from overall trade policy reform and specifically the dismantling of the Multi-Fibre Agreement on Textiles and Clothing (MFA) and the associated non-tariff barriers.[63]

In 1999, a new Textile Modernization Scheme was announced, followed by a Cotton Technology Mission (2000). Following this, in 2000, and in contrast to the mid-1980s when policies faltered, the government announced a new textile policy amounting to new directions in policy priorities and goals for the textile sector. The new policy declared its goals to be "export promotion" and "international competiveness."[64] In quick succession, other policies followed, and in 2003, a major initiative to change the fiscal structure was initiated. By 2005, the policy regime in the textile sector had been completely transformed. I call this period (1999–2005) a paradigm-shifting change. Why and how did these changes take place?

5.6.1   The Sathyam Committee Report

The Sathyam Committee Report marked a radical departure in terms of policy thinking and ideology as well the process that created this new paradigm (composition of the committee, for example). [65] In May 1998, the minister of textiles, Kashiram Rana, called S. Sathyam, a retired textile secretary (top civil servant within the textile sector), to his office and asked him questions about how to revive the textile sector. At the end of the meeting, Sathyam was offered the chairmanship of a committee that would reevaluate the policies to revive the sector; the committee was appointed in July 1998. The committee was a small one but included key members of the textile industry – Sanjay Lalbhai (CEO, Arvind Mills) and Ajay Piramal (Chairman, Morajee Goculdas Spinning and

---

[63] "Sathyam Committee: Terms of Reference, Government of India," press release, http://pib.nic.in/infonug/infojan99/i0801991.html.

[64] Union Textile Minister Kashiram Rana announced the policy in the following way: "It is designed to be exporter-friendly and is tailored to prepare the Indian textile industry to face international competition. The emphasis is to encourage exporters to enter the non-quota market." In "New Textile Quota Policy Unveiled," *Colourage*, Vol. 46, issue 11, p. 95.

[65] This section draws upon Ministry of Textiles (1999), *Report of the Expert Committee on Textile Policy*, Government of India; Ministry of Textiles, Udyog Bhavan, August 1999.

Weaving Co., Ltd.) – and such reputable economists as Omkar Goswami (Editor, *Business India*) and Rakesh Mohan (DG, NCAER), as well as key government officials associated with the industry. The two members of the textile industry were known for their radical views and were highly respected. The committee submitted its report in August 1999, a relatively quick turnaround time for such a report.

Its terms of reference were different from those of previous committees. The motivation for the study was the changes arising in the external trade realm and the impending international changes in terms of the MFA. The committee aimed to maintain "international competitiveness," which is mentioned three times in the short terms of reference.[66] The report notes: "The bane of the textile sector has been its inability to move with the times. As technologies trundled along and fashions flourished, the industry stultified and stagnated. . . . Happily for us, *our gait has been galvanized by the globalization process. . . . The WTO calendar casts a heavy time burden on us; and if we have to adhere to difficult datelines, new arrangements have to be devised for installing new systems*" (emphasis added).[67] The vision statement of the report starts with the need to establish a global standing and to energize exports: "Attain and sustain a global standing in manufacture and export of textiles and clothing by entering the top five bracket of competing countries."[68] The report notes that India fares adversely despite great promise: "It is worth noting that among the top six textile exporters, i.e., China, Hong Kong, Italy, Germany, S. Korea, and USA, only the first and last have a raw material base compared to India's while others have built up their competitiveness sheerly on the basis of technology-driven and cost-controlled value addition to a strong import base of input stage textiles."[69] Thus, the WTO and the phasing out of the quotas, as well as the phasing out of the quantitative restrictions and the reduction of tariffs, are the dominant impetuses that shape the report and its recommendations. The report, interestingly enough, does not hide the fact that its main stimulus and pressure come from outside the domestic realm, from the constraints and opportunities presented by changing trade relations and, most crucially, the WTO. In order to address the challenges presented, the committee's aim was to adopt a "holistic" view of the textile sector so as to ensure best productivity from each sector. There was a clear desire to get away from a segmented approach, privileging one sector or ownership type.[70]

[66] Ibid.   [67] Report, vi.   [68] Report, Vision Statement.   [69] Report, 2.
[70] "To evolve a new set of policy guidelines with a view to obtaining the best productivity from each sector and from each segment of the textile industry after taking a holistic view of the textile sector covering: (1) All products (all fibers and value-added products

The committee's recommendation and the analysis of the problems in the textile sector reveal a sobering yet optimistic reading. The report starts by declaring, "One striking feature that must temper our thoughts in anything we seek to do is the fact that it is the most regulated sector of our economy. It will be incongruous to talk about its revival ... without dismantling the regulatory regime. With this realization, our Report is replete with recommendations of deregulation, decontrol, de-reservation, and liberalization."[71] At another place, the report outlines a very different approach regarding the government's role: "To start with, the governmental presence in it must diminish. Even of what will remain must also wear a developmental, facilitation look."[72] Interestingly, it declares that "[m]odernization/mechanization in the textile sector will increasingly be an inevitable proposition. It has to happen. The sheer compulsion of market forces will make it happen. In the overall national interest, it must be the endeavor of everybody to promote such developments. ... appropriate conditions must be established to motivate all concerned not only to accept such changes but adopt them as well."[73] Clearly, then, policy goals were shifting, almost reversing, in response to the impending end of the MFA.

5.6.2   Struggles around policies and domestic mobilization by the state

Around 1998–2000, the textile ministry mobilized to prepare the industry for the end of the MFA with a number of events. Conviction at the ministerial level in favor of changing government policies was a new development. Kashiram Rana, textile minister of the BJP, played a major role in persuading all stakeholders to realize the importance of change. He made a large number of public appearances urging the industry to respond to government initiatives. On April 22, 1998, he first indicated the need for a new policy given "changes in domestic and international markets" at a news conference and announced the constitution of an expert group.[74] He especially noted that the expert group "is being constituted to review the 1985 policy as global trends are changing

resulting therefrom); (ii) All activities (spinning, weaving, processing, finishing and packaging); and (iii) All sectors (organized mills, powerlooms and handlooms)." Ibid.
[71] "Report of the Expert Committee on Textile Policy, Government of India," August 1999, iv.
[72] Ibid., iv, vii.   [73] Ibid.
[74] "Government Will Formulate New Textile Policy," *Times of India*, April 22, 1998; "Expert Group to Review Textile Policy," *Tribune*, April 22, 1998; "Government to Review Textile Policy," *Statesman*, April 22, 1998; "Weaving a New Policy," *Business Line*, March 2, 1998; "Give Attention to Quality in Textile Exports," *National Herald*, May 1, 1998; "Textile Policy to Be Reviewed under Changed Circumstances," *Financial Express*, June 14, 1998; "Government to Soon Finalize New Textile Policy," *Observer*, July 15, 1998.

and the World Trade Organization has come into place."[75] A changed tone is evident in many of his speeches as he combined a warning with encouragement.[76] A newspaper report noted, "Mr. Rana made it clear that the future of the Indian textile industry depended upon quality and productivity improvement. He said that after 2005, the textile sector, including the small-scale industry, would have to compete with others in the field. Therefore it was necessary that the SSI sector strive to improve competiveness to compete even with bigger units."[77] In another context, he warned his key constituents in Surat, nudging them to change direction or be destroyed:

Indian textile industry in general, and the decentralized sector in particular, will have to opt for sophisticated means of production if it has to withstand the fierce competition from countries like Japan, Korea, Singapore and Thailand. The days of traditional manufacturing are past and over.... Decentralized centers like Surat, Bhiwandi, Hyderabad, and Amritsar will have to learn from the mistakes committed by composite textile mills in the once big textile centers of Mumbai and Ahmadabad. The composite mills had lagged behind modernization, which along with other factors led to their ultimate collapse.[78]

Interestingly, he framed the MFA abolition as opening new opportunities rather than embodying threats. He maintained that India and other low-cost producing countries stood to benefit in the post-MFA regime from increased opportunities for exports to developed countries, even though a price war would initially affect the country's interests.[79]

The Government is committed to provide the right environment for the industry to enable it to transform the challenges posed by the MFA phase-out to opportunities. The proposed new textile policy envisaged an action plan that would give a further boost to the textile and clothing exports and enable the sector to achieve a target of $35 billions from the existing $15 billions over a five-year period. This would serve as the ideal launching pad for a self-sustained growth in exports in the post-MFA era.[80]

Kashiram Rana emphasized that manufacturers must consider themselves to be "operating in the global market" and act accordingly.[81] To all

---

[75] Ibid.

[76] "New Textile Policy to Stress on Harmony, High-Growth Path," Observer, August 17, 1998.

[77] "Government Set on Improving Textile Industry: Rana," Business Line, July 20, 1998.

[78] "Duty Relief Likely on High-Tech Textile Machinery, Says Rana," Economic Times, January 27, 1999.

[79] "New Textiles Policy Will Boost Exports Further," Business Line, August 30, 2000.

[80] Kashiram Rana spoke at a seminar on "Implications of the phase out of MFA on export of garments and textiles and the structural adjustments required" organized by the FICCI. "New Textiles Policy Will Boost Exports Further," Business Line, August 30, 2000.

[81] "Textile Industry Must Get Global Edge to Survive: Rana," Colourage, Vol. 48, issue 6, June 2001, pp. 98–99.

audiences, he repeatedly emphasized the opportunities presented by the abolition of quotas in 2005.[82] Importantly, various schemes announced by the government were not with an eye to protect the sick industries and the old protected interests but instead reflected a desire to modernize and nudge new investment. The textile minister noted in 1999 that the Technology Upgradation Fund Scheme (TUFS) was not a scheme for the revival of sick units, nor was it intended to replace old machines with new machines of the same technology. The government wanted companies to upgrade in a serious way.[83] He insisted that the government would no longer invest in the forty nationalized units, "which were perpetually running at a loss."[84] There is no doubt that this politician's views changed when faced with the onset of the quota-free regime in 2005. Since he came from the decentralized textile sector,[85] this transformation of his views, as well as his energy in changing government policy, was credible and had a significant effect on the textile industry.

5.6.3   Policy outputs and institutional changes

Following the acceptance of the Sathyam Committee's recommendations, the government announced a new textile policy in November 2000.[86] This policy started by noting the need to address the population's demand for cloth at cheap prices but also to enhance the export market share of the industry. It specifically refers to the changed global situation, specifically the WTO regime and the anticipated changes, necessitating a new policy. The goal of the policy was "to improve the global competitiveness of the Indian textile and apparel industry and enable the industry to quadruple its exports to USD50 billion by 2010."[87] This time a number of policy initiatives followed in quick succession, and all of them were consistent with the goals and orientations of the Sathyam Committee Report to "help the industry face global competition."[88] Both domestic supply side and external factors – reduction of import tariffs, for example – were the focus of the government. The three initiatives, announced simultaneously, were the Technology

---

[82] Ibid.

[83] "Upgradation Fund Only for New Technology, Declares Textile Minister," *Economic Times*, April 3, 1999.

[84] "New Textile Policy in 6 Months: Kashiram Rana," *Colourage*, Vol. 45, issue 6, June 1998, p. 77.

[85] He had grown up in Surat (Gujarat) and had won many elections with the support of the decentralized textile industry in the area.

[86] See Ministry of Textiles (2000), available from author.   [87] USITC (2001).

[88] "Cotton Technology Mission Launch Within Sight," *Business and Political Observer*, January 28, 1999; "Tech Fund to Give Textiles a Global Edge," *Business Line*, January 29, 1999.

Upgradation Fund Scheme, the Cotton Technology Mission, and a new policy.[89]

An ambitious target of exports of USD50 billion by 2010 with an accelerated focus on garments (to be USD25 billon) was announced. The government articulated a long-term vision, radically different from the existing goals and purposes. The textile minister stated that "India has potential to be a Global Textile Leader"[90]; in order to achieve that target, the government removed the ready-made apparel articles, including knit fabrics and woven garments, from the list of products reserved for the small-scale industries (SSI) sector. Foreign firms could now invest up to 100 percent in the apparel sector through the "automatic route" without any export obligations. The policy declared "full flexibility" between cotton and man-made fibers and the encouragement of consumption in man-made fibers, which reversed decades-old preference for cotton. The government demanded some export commitments in lieu of relaxing import of textile machinery. The textile secretary said presciently:

All the competitive forces across the globe will sharpen their respective focus before the open competition in the global textile markets in 2004, free of all quota restrictions. We hope that the Indian textile industry will be able to take up the challenges and TEXPRCIL will leverage India's advantage in cotton and making top quality cotton available to the exporters. It is important for the textile exporting community to commit enhanced export obligations for import norms of second hand machinery to be relaxed further.[91]

For the spinning sector, modernization was to be encouraged and the hank yarn obligation to be reviewed periodically, indicating flexibility in reducing that obligation. The policy noted that the "organized mill industry" should be restored to its preeminent position through integration of production efforts, technological modernization, and strategic alliances with international companies and by the incorporation of information technology (IT) and better human resource policies. The policy saw the potential of "Technical Textiles" and suggested policy prescriptions (R&D, for example) to prioritize growth and expansion in this new emerging area of textiles. Interestingly, the government foresaw the role of IT in the sector. No less than the Ministry of Textiles instructed: "The efforts to increase the competitive strength of the industry as a whole will depend upon how fast they integrate various IT solutions including ERP solutions, CAD/CAM and other IT-based tools for improving the speed of production, reducing time lag in

[89] Ibid.   [90] *Financial Express*, June 12, 2000.
[91] Sharad Mistry, "India Has Potential to be Global Textile Leader: Rana," *Financial Express*, June 12, 2000.

deliveries."[92] Strikingly, the policy focused attention on human resources and skill training with the setting of a Nodal Center for Upgradation of Textile Education (NCUTE) as well as many National Fashion Design centers to train designers. It also suggested the need to revise the fiscal structure to prevent the various segments of the industry from suffering artificial distortions and fragmentation. Yet, the reform of the fiscal structure remained a weak point, and it was only after 2003 and the setting up of the N. K. Singh Steering Committee that that issue was addressed (see Section 5.6 for analysis).

As for foreign direct investment (FDI), the government began to grant automatic approvals within two weeks of receiving proposals, with foreign equity up to 51 percent, in the manufacture of textile products in the composite mills and in the manufacture of waterproof textile products. Export-oriented units (EOUs) and composite mills that produce yarn for domestic consumption were exempt from the government's hank yarn obligation, which had required each spinning mill to produce 50 percent of its yarn for the domestic market in hank form (80 percent of which was to be in counts of forty and lower) for use in the handloom sector. The hank yarn obligation was abolished in 2002.[93] To boost exports and encourage new industry investment, the government under the quota entitlement policy increased the share of quotas earmarked for units investing in new machinery and plants. To promote modernization of the Indian industry, the government set up the Export Promotion Capital Goods (EPCG) Scheme, which permitted a firm importing new or secondhand capital goods for production of articles for export to import those capital goods at preferential tariffs, provided that the firm exported at least six times the CIF value of the imported capital goods within six years. Overall, exports were to be the priority.

Importantly, the government began addressing the backward and forward linkages of the whole textile commodity chain by initiating policy initiatives for cotton, on the one hand, and for infrastructure development, on the other. To improve the quality and amount of cotton produced, the government started a Technology Mission on Cotton (TMC), which provided better incentives for improved farm practices, quality seeds, improvement in market infrastructure, and modernization of the ginning and pressing sector. The Scheme for Integrated Textile Parks (SITP) was started in 2005, where the government would set up industrial parks for which up to 40 percent of the project cost would be

[92] Kashiram Rana, "India's Textiles: Progress and Challenges," *National Herald*, January 25, 2000.
[93] Karmakar (2007).

Table 5.2 *Government investment in textile reform
initiatives, 2004–2009*

Government Schemes	Expenditure (in Rs. Crores)
Total	**7,519.54**
TUFS (Technology Upgradation Fund Scheme)	5,380
Textile parks	1,636
Cotton Technology Mission	340
National Institute of Fashion Technology	140.99
Government R&D	18.05
Export promotion studies	4.5

Source: Author's calculations from the Annual Textile Budget
Documents, 2004–2009/2010. The Annual Budget documents are
available at www.texmin.nic.in/ budget/annual_plan/.

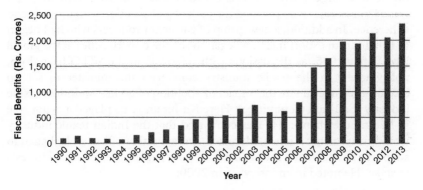

Figure 5.2 Fiscal benefits to the textile industry (Rs. crores),
1990–2013
Author's Calculations from CMIE Prowess Database, 1990–2014.

provided by the government (see Section 5.5.6 for details). Overall, the
government budgetary commitment for these schemes has been quite
substantial, to the tune of Rs. 7,500 crores (approx. USD1.5 billion).
Table 5.2 outlines the budgetary expenditure for various schemes
between 2004 and 2009. In the next section, I present some details of
the operation of three key schemes. All in all, the amount of fiscal benefits
received by the private sector increased dramatically around and after
2005. Figure 5.2 shows this remarkable trend.

5.6.4   The politics of policy change

Who were the actors at the forefront of the change? The previous regime was sustained by policy ideas as well as support of varied interest groups with a vested interest in the status quo. The status quo coalition was comprised of powerloom producers, weavers, and small producers, as well as some large-scale mill owners who had exited out of their main business and started contractual relationships with many small-scale producers. Politicians who gave quotas and policy concessions ensured the continuation of the old policy regimes. The textile ministry was captured by many special interests. An elaborate matrix of policy regulation created a mazelike structure, preventing change.

Yet, some civil servants confronted a deteriorating textile industry and the loss of India's status and market share in the world markets. These policymakers also noticed that the policy regime did not achieve the goals that it set out to achieve, as cotton demand was shrinking and handlooms were hurt by the unplanned growth of the power looms. These civil servants were able to convince Kashiram Rana, India's textile minister, of the need for urgent action. Kashiram Rana was from Surat (Gujarat) and was a key reformer who pursued the path of globalization with urgency and coherence. In addition, a new group of garment producers who had begun to benefit from export markets began to see the opportunities at the global level. After 1995, as discussions with reference to the WTO heated up, policymakers in the textile ministry convinced the minister to set up a committee to evaluate the impact of abolition of quotas on Indian textile industry (Sathyam Committee). Here Kashiram Rana played a major role in leading the change. He was convinced that the Indian textile industry would survive only if it is modernized. On a number of issues, he began to support a paradigmatic change in textile policy against the political interests at stake. He noted in an interview in 2000:

In the past fifteen years no steps have been taken by any government – the Centre or states – to assist and improve the textile industry. Compared to other countries, our costs are high and quality is poor. The Government should and will stem the slide. We have a backlog of neglect to clear. ... The small scale reservation on garment production should go. If we have to compete in the global market, garments cannot be subjected to any investment limits. Several experts have suggested de-reservation of garments. We will take a practical decision on this.[94]

In addition, starting 1998–1999, three different reform elements, some within the state, began to push for a comprehensive review. Key civil

---

[94] Interview of Textile Minister Kashiram Rana with Rohit Saran, "Dressed to Kill," *India Today*, September 2000.

servants, new garment exporters, and organized mill producers – wood work reformers – came together in support of change, but it was steered by key reform elements within the state. Such a massive change that sought to reverse decades of policy was met with intense lobbying in opposition to it. Some changes could not be implemented right away. Yet, government officials continued the pressure and sought intervention at very high levels – the Prime Minister's Office, for example – to implement the changes across many policies affecting the textile industry. Notably, these nascent reform elements within the Ministry of Textiles strengthened themselves by building coalitions in the Ministry of Finance and the PM's Office. This also assured the textile industry that the changes envisioned had the support of a number of agencies. As an illustration, two separate groups organized heavily for domestic change: an official group entitled, "Official Group for Growth in Textiles," was constituted with the finance secretary, the revenue secretary, the director general of foreign trade, and the banking secretary together with the textile secretary. This group was to look into the financial structure affecting the industry as well as address the concerns of exporters.[95]

Civil servants in the Ministry of Textiles took the lead in scaling up their ideas to the PM's Office. In fact, a presentation made to the then Prime Minister Atal Bihari Vajpayee on October 23, 2001, led to the creation of a "High Powered Steering Group" in 2002 to "[r]eview and monitor the implementation of policies and programmes outlined in the National Textile Policy 2000 and devise further measures necessary for attracting requisite investment and growth in the textile sector; review export scenario and identify measures to enhance export competitiveness of Indian textiles in the changing global scenario particularly post 2004; and evolve a growth oriented fiscal policy for integrated development of the textile industry covering all its segments."[96] This group was to monitor the textile ministry's willingness to implement the new policies, forcing it toward reform. The chairman of the steering group was a powerful civil servant in the PMO known for his pro-reform image as well as his powerful connections with the political establishment: N. K. Singh. It is significant that the PM's Office was used as a gateway to set up this steering group. The setting up of this steering group required that members of the textile ministry bypass "even their own Minister" and mobilize a coalition

---

[95] Ministry of Textiles (2002).

[96] See Singh (PMO 2002). Office Memorandum, "Constitution of the Steering Group on Investment and Growth in Textile Industry," Appendix I, Investment and Growth in Textile Industry, Report by the Steering Group, Government of India 2002. Available from author.

of interests that would support such a policy.[97] This indicated both the urgency of the change and the fact that organized and export-oriented mills were getting high-level access to the policy process in a way they had been denied for generations. The differential fiscal structure across different segments of the supply chain prevented change and locked in vested interests at every level. Reforming this fiscal structure took a massive effort at the highest level and was the proverbial straw that could have broken the camel's back. With this change, the man-made-fiber textile sector also gained in political and policy importance, a phenomenon that seemed to reverse centuries-old preference for cotton. These reform coalitions were fragile and fragmentary but were strengthened by the external global crisis. Once the PM's Office became involved, though, the reform elements within the bureaucracy used that wedge to push for a multipronged change. At this stage, the organized mill segment – represented by Indian Cotton Mills' Federation (ICMF) – also deployed all its power in favor of this change.

5.6.5   The N. K. Singh steering group and fiscal reform

Over time, an elaborate set of exceptions and tax preferences allowed different segments of the supply chain to seek and claim various exceptions and concessions. For example, the organized mill owners paid excise duty at 16 percent, while the powerlooms paid 8 percent, which was reduced over time. The fiscal policy framework governing textiles became "moth eaten," wherein policies were announced and then modified or reversed partially as different segments and sectors lobbied on behalf of their particular group interest. The fiscal structure was especially problematic, particularly because excise exceptions and tax evasion occurred with the help of layers of fiscal concessions and policies. This fiscal structure also was consequential because it created formal and transparent, as well as hidden, incentives for investment in certain sectors and encouraged evasions of all kinds. Overall, it kept the textile sector decentralized and fragmented as SSI units were giving many exemptions and concessions based on their size. Even the larger units began sub contracting to smaller firms, creating a network of incentives for a certain kind of industrial structure and growth patterns.

The N. K. Singh steering group set up by the PM analyzed the fiscal structure and made a comprehensive set of recommendations that began to be implemented in the budget of 2002–2003. It is clear that the group was concerned about a back and forth process of policy reform, what

---

[97] Confidential interview with author, Delhi, January 10, 2011.

I have called a "moth eaten" policy framework in the past. Repeatedly, the steering group emphasized that "[t]hese recommendations need to be accepted as a package. Selective applications of the elements of this package will lead to further distortion and hence is not recommended."[98] The steering group noted:

The differential and discriminatory duty structure on processed fabric has impeded the growth, profitability, and competitiveness of the high-tech process houses. With a view to pave the way for attracting large investments in this sector and thereby improving quality, it is imperative that a non-discriminatory CENVAT credit system be put in place. Currently, the dual system for CENVAT credit – document based and deemed credit – creates unfair competition within the sector. The Group strongly recommends that CENVAT credit on deemed basis should be abolished and a single system of CENVAT credit on actual basis (document based) be implemented.[99]

Working together with the Taskforce on Indirect Taxes constituted by the Ministry of Finance, the N. K. Singh Committee endorsed the need to create a unified, consistent, and transparent CENVAT rate of 8 percent by 2005–2006 and to establish a complete CENVAT chain.[100] In 2004–2005 and 2005–2006, further fiscal corrections revamped the fiscal structure, considerably rationalizing various distortions and providing a necessary boost to the man-made-fiber textiles and modern mills sector. Subsequently, the fiscal reforms were continued with regular monitoring of the changes in the budget of 2002–2003. Another task force headed by the textile secretary, S. B. Mohapatra, with a mandate to fulfill the unfinished agenda of the N. K. Singh Committee, was appointed to suggest measures necessary to complete the ongoing tax reforms.[101] Thus, the momentum for the reforms continued, imparting a sense of urgency and energy to the changes proposed in 2000. Policies must be accompanied by institutional change and policy outputs. It is important to assess how their intended beneficiaries received announced policies and whether policies were followed by further action. In the next section, I review implementation of the three main policies – technological modernization, the Cotton Mission, and the policy favoring textile parks – evaluating their success and progress.

5.6.6   Technology upgradation and the state's role

Technological upgradation in the industry had lagged for decades. The debates around technological modernization started in the mid-1980s.

---

[98] N. K. Singh, "Steering Group Report," p. 5.   [99] Ibid., 10.   [100] Ibid., 7.
[101] "Govt. Forms High-level Panel on Textiles Sector," *Financial Express*, August 19, 2002, www.financialexpress.com/news/govt-forms-highlevel-panel-on-textiles-sector /55682/0.

A Textile Modernization Fund Scheme was introduced from August 1986 for a period of five years, with an initial budget of Rs. 750 crores (approximately USD375 million) to provide assistance at concessional rates of interest.[102] Interestingly, at that time, the spinning sector, the strongest sector in the textile commodity chain, was a major beneficiary, with other sectors taking relatively minor shares of this financial assistance. At that time, the scheme, subsequently discontinued, achieved only minimal success due to factors such as the lack of indigenous machinery, the high cost of imported machinery with high import duties, and a lack of interest from industry.

The same idea was revived in the 1990s but in a radically different way. Enacted on March 31, 1999, the Technology Upgradation Fund Scheme (TUFS) was established to ameliorate technological obsolescence and the lack of economies of scale within the textile industry, as well as to modernize weak links in the commodity chain.[103] The government resolution stated, "While the relatively high cost of the state-of-the-art technology and structural anomalies in the industry have been major contributory factors, perhaps the single-most important factor inhibiting technology upgradation has been the relatively high cost of capital."[104] The scheme seeks to provide capital subsidy for weaving, processing, technical textiles, and garmenting segments, all of which have a strong potential for fostering employment opportunities and adding value to goods.[105] It is notable that the non spinning sectors were to be the focus of attention as they were the weak elements of the textile chain.[106] The first TUFS proposal was issued through 2004 and later extended in 2007 through 2012 again.[107]

The original scheme aimed to provide textile companies with a reimbursement of 5 percent of the interest charged by the lending agency on a technology upgradation project.[108] By subsidizing low-interest loans for technology upgradation, the government ensured credit availability for further upgradation at global rates.[109] The eligibility for the scheme required not only that the technology or machinery be at minimum "near state-of-the-art," but restrictions also applied to the acquisition of used machinery.[110]

---

[102] A Jute Modernization Fund Scheme was launched in November 1986 with a corpus of Rs. 150 crores. See Ministry of Textile (1988).

[103] Textile Commissioner (2005, 3).   [104] Ibid.

[105] Indian Textile Ministry, "Technology Upgradation Fund Scheme – FAQ," http://texmin.nic.in/faq/faq_tuf.pdf.

[106] Later on the spinning sector was added in the scheme as a result of lobbying.

[107] Textile Commissioner (2005, 4).   [108] Ibid.

[109] India Brand Equity Foundation (IBEF), "Textiles and Apparel: Market and Opportunities," http://ibef.org/download%5CTextiles_Apparel_220708.pdf, 7.

[110] Textile Commissioner (2005, 5–11). Twelve percent was increased to 15 percent in 2005; the option was 15 percent CLCS-TUFS or 5 percent TUFS. For the powerloom sector, a 20 percent capital subsidy was added in 2003 for adding or replacing old looms.

This basic outline of the scheme has stayed intact since its inception, but there have been some notable modifications to the scheme as well as extensions to the small-scale and powerloom sector, man-made fibers, and technical textiles, thereby creating new winners who benefit from the new policies. In early 2002, an option was provided to the small-scale textile and jute industries to take either a 12 percent Credit Linked Capital Subsidy (CLCS-TUFS) or a 5 percent interest reimbursement under the original TUFS.[111] Only machinery eligible under the original TUFS qualified, and this was subject to a capital ceiling of Rs. 60 lakhs (approx. USD120,000), with a ceiling on the capital subsidy of Rs. 12 lakhs (approx. USD24,000).[112] On January 13, 2005, the capital ceiling on machinery was increased to Rs. 1 crores (approx. USD200,000) and the ceiling on capital subsidy increased to Rs. 20 lakhs (approx. USD40,000). In 2007, spinning machinery reimbursement was reduced to 4 percent in an attempt to reallocate the funds to nonspinning sectors, and powerloom units were allowed make use of a 20 percent margin money subsidy instead of the 5 percent interest reimbursement (at a capital ceiling of Rs. 20 lakhs and margin money subsidy ceiling of Rs. 20 lakhs). The SSI textile and jute sector received the same deal as powerloom units except at a 15 percent margin money subsidy (and margin money subsidy ceiling of Rs. 15 lakhs).[113]

Initially, the scheme did not attract much interest. Of the 1,837 textile mills reported at the end of 1999, only eighty-one total mills applied to TUFS,[114] reflecting a low level of interest in investment and expansion in the sector. The TUFS became more effective over time, attracting more applications and investment. Anil Kumar, the textile secretary, noted in 2007, "The interest in the TUFS scheme increased dramatically after 2003 or so." By 2006–2007, after abolition of the MFA, the scheme became incredibly popular, with 12,336 new applications received and 13,168 completed and disbursed, worth Rs. 26,605 crores (approx. USD5.3 billion), and this pace of implementation persisted.[115] By the mid- to late 2000s, there was a clamor for extension of the scheme by industry actors. Table 5.3 shows this rising trend of new investment aided

[111] Ibid., 4.   [112] Ibid.
[113] Ministry of Textiles Resolution, "Government Resolution on TUFS on Techno-Operational Parameters," November 2007, www.txcindia.com/html/Inside%20page%20Sec-1%20pg%203–112%2022082008%202.pdf.
[114] Dewani, "Technology Upgradation Fund Makes Dismal Progress as Mills Avoid Scheme," *Express India*, July 2000, www.expressindia.com/news/fe/daily/20000703/fc o03034.html.
[115] "Scheme Success Prompts Textile Min to Seek Rs. 1,000 Crore under TUFS," June 1, 2006, www.fibre2fashion.com/news/textiles-policy-news/newsdetails.aspx?news_id= 17871

Table 5.3 *Ratio of disbursal and sanctioned funds for
TUFS*

Year	Amount Sanctioned (Rs. Crores)	Amount Disbursed (Rs. Crores)	Ratio of Disbursed to Sanctioned Funds for TUFS (Percent)
1999–2000	2,421	746	30.81
2000–2001	2,090	1,863	89.14
2001–2002	630	804	127.62
2002–2003	839	931	110.97
2003–2004	1,341	856	63.83
2004–2005	2,990	1,757	58.76
2005–2006	6,776	3,962	58.47
2006–2007	29,073	26,605	91.51
2007–2008	8,058	6,854	85.06
2008–2009	24,007	21,826	90.92
2009–2010	6,612	8,140	123

Source: Author's calculations from data found at Ministry of Textiles
website, Annual Report, 2012–2013.

by the state. Although there was a significant decrease in applications in
2007, this can perhaps be explained by the global slowdown and textile
companies deciding to buy less new technology or even the Indian government creating other support programs in its place.[116]

The government disbursal mechanisms were also slow in the initial
years but improved significantly after 2004–2005. In its first year, 1999,
of the 309 applications approved and sanctioned, only 179 were disbursed. In terms of the money spent in 1999, Rs. 2,421 crores (approx.
USD480 million) were sanctioned, but only Rs. 746 crores (approx.
USD150 million) were actually distributed.[117] Over time, however, the
ratio of disbursal improved, as shown in Table 5.3.

A report by KSA Technopak and the report on the Evaluation of
Technology Upgradation Fund Scheme presented to the Indian government's textile ministry during 2003–2004 demonstrated "clearly and

[116] Srivastava, Mehul, and Nandini Lakshman, "India's Stimulus Package: More Help
Needed," *Bloomberg BusinessWeek*, December 2008, www.businessweek.com/global
biz/content/dec2008/gb2008128_276382.
[117] Author's calculations from the data provided in Ministry of Textiles, Annual Report,
2012–2013. Also see Dewani, "Technology Upgradation Fund Makes Dismal Progress
as Mills Avoid Scheme," *Express India*, July 3, 2000, www.expressindia.com/news/fe/d
aily/20000703/fco03034.html.

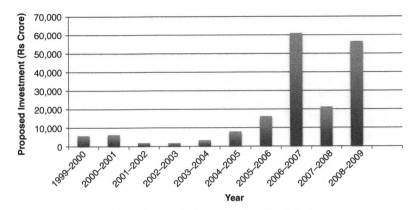

Figure 5.3 Proposed investment in the textile sector over time
Author's calculations from Ministry of Textiles, Annual Reports.

beyond doubt" that investment aimed at modernization has helped to increase productivity and profitability of the textile industry.[118] These economic data are confirmed by interviews with industry actors. Harsh Piramal, CEO of the Piramal group, noted:

> There were two major decisions. One was to reimburse part of the interest on the loans obtained under the TUFS. While this policy was in place, the reimbursements took very long. The government has decided to clear the dues as a result of which companies will have some more inflows. Secondly, the government has increased the moratorium period for repayment of loans by an additional year. These decisions will give the industry a breather going forward.[119]

A related issue is that of the availability of textile machinery for modernization purposes. The indigenous textile machinery industry had operated under a protective environment and did not upgrade to high-quality machines. The growth and expansion of the spinning sector allowed for modernization of the spinning machinery industry, but other sectors suffered. Interestingly, there was an important conflict of interest between the textile machinery producers and their customers, the textile industry. The textile machinery producers wanted the trade walls to be closed so that they could get a larger proportion of the domestic markets, while the textile industry wanted cheaper and better versions of the textile machinery and therefore wanted import tariffs to be lowered. This conflict was magnified by the fact that the textile machinery industry was managed by the Heavy Industries Department and not by the

[118] M. D. Teli (2008).
[119] Interview with Harsh Piramal, www.fibre2fashion.com/face2face/pmp/executive-vice-chairman.asp.

Table 5.4 *Imports of textile machinery, parts, and accessories*

Sector	Increase in Imports, 1997–2001 (Percent)	Increase in Imports, 2000–2004 (Percent)	Increase in Imports, 2003–2005 (Percent)	Increase in Imports, 2004–2006 (Percent)
Weaving	−41.97	304.99	29.77	94.98
Knitting and Garments	26.33	25.41	30.48	139.52
Others	−40.31	55.90	44.93	116.77
Weighted Average	−31.01	75.28	42.58	109.25

*2006–2007 are rough estimates and somewhat provisional
Source: Directorate General of Commercial Intelligence and Statistics (DGCIS), cited in Teli (2008, 6).

textile ministry. TUFS also allowed the import of secondhand weaving and knitting machines, a policy that hurt the interests of local producers and was not welcomed by them.[120] Increasingly, the government tried to hold interministerial consultations between the two ministries on this issue.[121] After 2000, concurrent with the increased modernization and investment in the sector, the import of all kinds of weaving, spinning, and processing machinery had increased dramatically in response to the rising demand by the textile industry and the changes within it. Over a decade – 1997–2007 – the imports of textile machinery increased by 260 percent, and the garment and knitting machine sector imported machinery very rapidly, at a rate of 460 percent per year. In 2003–2004, there was an increase of 73 percent in one year alone, and in 2005–2006, the import of machinery increased by 95 percent from its previous year. By 2011, India was the second largest importer of the world's shuttleless looms, absorbing 5.9 percent of the world's shuttleless looms, second to China.[122] In many other categories of imported machinery, India was also one of the fast-growing markets.[123] Table 5.4 highlights the rapid increase in imports of machinery, especially after 2003–2004. This reflects growing demand for capacity expansion as well as opening up of tariff barriers to aid in modernization of the industry despite opposition from machinery producers. Modernization of the industry's machinery was a significant sign that the industry was undergoing a revival.

[120] Teli (2008).   [121] Ibid.   [122] *Textile Outlook International*, December 2012, 123.
[123] Ibid.

5.6.7   Textile parks and infrastructure, 2005–Present

In July 2005, the government of India approved the Scheme for Integrated Textile Parks (SITP). A hybrid between the previous Scheme for Apparel Parks for Exports (APE) and the Textile Centre Infrastructure Development (TCID) Program, the scheme was to create up to twenty-five textile parks for exports and possibly more in the future.[124] By 2015, seventy parks had been approved, and sixty-one were operational.[125] The scheme was based on a public–private partnership framework leveraging both government grants and private investment. Within such parks the government created facilities, like eco-testing laboratories, that enabled exporters to get garments pretested so as to satisfy the requirements of the importing countries. Existing textile centers like Tiruppur and Coimbatore were to be assisted with the Textile Center Infrastructure Development Scheme (TCIDS). The parks were to house approximately 1,250 state-of-the-art textile units aimed at increasing exports across the weaving, knitting, processing, and finished garment sectors. The initial budget allocation for this was of Rs. 625 crores (approx. USD125 million) for both 2005–2006 and 2006–2007, and the scheme was expected to create 0.5 million new jobs while greatly increasing production output.[126] For the twelfth five-year plan (2012–2017), the investment proposed was a massive Rs. 1,900 crores (approximately USD380 million). These textile parks were to be set up in a Special Economic Zone (SEZ), where the special provisions of the SEZ would apply to them.[127] Benefits would include an income tax exemption of 100 percent for the first five years, 50 percent for the next five years, and 100 percent exemption on profits ploughed back into the business for a corresponding five years. Textile companies in particular would greatly benefit from SEZ status because under those provisions, the textile ministry provided infrastructure facilities (roads, electricity

---

[124] "Cabinet Committee on Economic Affairs Approves Scheme for Integrated Textile Parks to Meet Challenges of Post-MFA Scenario," *Hindustan Times*, July 25, 2005.

[125] BS Reporter, "Textile Parks Will Attract Rs. 300,000 Crore Investment in India," *Business Standard*, April 10, 2015. Accessed at www.business-standard.com/article/econ omy-policy/textile-parks-will-attract-rs-30–000-crore-investment-in-india-115041000 894_1.html.

[126] "Cabinet Committee on Economic Affairs Approves Scheme for Integrated Textile Parks to Meet Challenges of Post-MFA Scenario," *Hindustan Times*, July 25, 2005. Additionally, if a textile park were set up in a non-SEZ zone, then a proposal could be filed to the Ministry of Commerce and Industry to declare the park as an SEZ. The designation, Special Economic Zones, would mean that the textile firms would get tax benefits available under the SEZ act. See Verma, Sunny, and Deepshikja Sikarwar, "SEZ-Like Sops Sought for Textile Industrial Parks," *Economic Times*, October 31, 2006.

[127] Ministry of Textiles (2007).

supply, and telecom lines) to firms willing to set up textile units. The Ministry of Textiles would implement the scheme via Special Purpose Vehicles to keep operational autonomy.[128] The government of India funded the projects at 40 percent of cost, up to a ceiling of Rs. 40 crores (approx. USD8 million). By late 2006, the scheme increased in popularity and utilization, and the textile industry filed applications for fifty more parks in addition to the already approved twenty-six.[129] A total of thirty parks were set up by 2007 under the tenth five-year plan, and an additional twenty-one were planned for the twelfth five-year plan (2012–2017). The government sanctioned a total of seventy textile parks, spread over many states. As of June 2010, the total government cost was Rs. 645 crores (approx. USD129 million), and private investment was Rs. 19,460 crores (approx. USD4 billion).[130] Evaluations of the parks by outside agencies have been very positive. A World Bank study called the SITP one of the best models of industrial parks. It appreciated the fact that the government gave a lot of autonomy to the companies that created these parks, as well as support. Its authors noted:

> The SITP's most prominent innovation is the far greater, and far earlier, role it gives to the *users* of the park. In contrast to almost all other schemes the authors are aware of, the roles of the Centre and State are diminished, consultants are used quite differently than in common practice, and third-party developers are conspicuous by their absence. The former two concentrate on organizing, supporting and monitoring groups of firms, who must then navigate the formal and informal requirements for getting the park built. . . . In more detail, the policy makes the entrepreneurs the drivers and ultimate decision-makers of the entire initiative for the creation and functioning of the park, but with support from the PMC [Project Management Consultant] across the steps of industrial park development [Saleman and Jordon 2014, 10].

It specifically documented the success of these parks in creating infrastructure in a timely manner.[131] Overall, the industrial parks supported by the Ministry of Textiles are far superior to other industrial parks and have been more effective in stimulating new investment and creating the conditions for revival of the textile sector.

---

[128] Srinivasan, G., "Govt. Announces Norms for Textile Parks Scheme," *Hindu Business Line*, August 1, 2005.

[129] "Textile Firms Unwrap Investment Plans; Go Global in 2006," *Press Trust of India Limited*, December 29, 2006.

[130] Ministry of Textiles; *Indian Brand Equity Foundation*, June 2010, www.ibef.org/indus try/textiles.aspx.

[131] Ibid., 18.

5.6.8 Cotton Technology Mission

A rare and politically difficult collaboration between the agriculture and textile ministries, the Cotton Technology Mission, embodied India's changing position as an exporter of textiles as well as cotton and reflected a combination of contradictory interests: both cotton exporters and domestic textile companies with a strong interest in exporting cloth and garments. While cotton exporters wanted to export abroad and seek high prices for their cotton, textiles companies within India wanted cheap cotton and did not want to source those in the global market but from domestic producers. Multiple goals and expectations about the future trajectory coalesced in the design of this mission.

The modernization and new investments in the textile sector that began in the late 1990s would have been impossible without the supply of the raw material, cotton. Given the political interests of cotton growers that were tied to key political parties and governments, the government began a technology mission to increase production of cotton. Since the textile mills were required to compete in a global market, fears arose that they would begin importing better-quality cotton, harming both domestic growers and the local ginning and pressing industry. Therefore, it was also to the benefit of the domestic economy and labor force to keep production in country, which would be made possible by increasing the quality of cotton. In addition to planned or expected domestic demand, strong exports and export-oriented interests had also increased within the cotton growers, further creating the push for a policy to support cotton. The government on its part was also concerned about the quality of cotton produced in India, not merely its quantity. Up to early 2002, Indian cotton had widely been seen as unclean and highly contaminated cotton.[132] With the impending end of the MFA regime and need to compete globally, the government sought to improve its cotton quality and competitiveness.

The government of India launched the Technology Mission on Cotton (TMC) in February 2000. The initiative was originally based on the Intensive Cotton Development Programme, which sought to transfer modern technology from research stations to farmers. The program, which began in 1971, expired in 1999, allowing for creation of the Technology Mission on Cotton (TMC). The TMC was established to act as a crossroads organization where the improvement of cotton, technology, and production would intersect with research, marketing, and processing.[133] The mission itself was divided into four minimissions:

---

[132] "India to Modernize Cotton Industry Technology," *Asia Pulse*, April 19, 2002.
[133] "About Technology Mission on Cotton," http://dcd.dacnet.nic.in/TMC.htm.

Cotton Research and Technology Generation (under the Indian Council on Agriculture), Transfer of Technology and Development (under the Ministry of Agriculture), Improvement of Marketing Infrastructure (under the Ministry of Textiles), and Modernization/Upgradation of Ginning and Pressing Factories (under the Ministry of Textiles).[134] Each mission was in charge of improving yield and quality of cotton through improved seeds and pesticides, increasing the income of cotton growers by reducing costs of cultivation, reducing cotton contamination by providing improved infrastructure, and improving cotton facilities by modernizing the existing ginning and pressing factories, respectively. The mission was originally planned to take up 200 market yards and 450 ginning and pressing units each in the ten plans.[135] The mission was phased out at the end of the tenth five-year plan in March 2007.[136] However, Mini-Missions III and IV were extended through March 2009.

Over the years, the private sector has also played a part in increasing cotton production and in pushing for better-quality cotton while recognizing that the excise duty on superfine cotton was a disincentive to creating demand for high-quality cotton.[137] In April 1964, the Indian Cotton Mills' Federation set up a subcommittee to prepare a scheme where the mill owners' association could participate in the "Grow More Cotton Campaign" started by the government. The committee recommended setting up demonstration and education centers in cotton-growing areas to "interest farmers in modern methods of cultivation" (Kulkarni 1979, 249). A standing committee on cotton was appointed by the ICMF, and in 1970, a new organization called the "ICMF Cotton Development and Research Association" was formed to continue to expand the federation's activities.[138] The ICMF started a number of cotton projects in Tamil Nadu (Coimbatore). The ICMF also interacted with some agricultural universities and state agricultural departments in "undertaking experiments in the evolution of early maturing and uniform

---

[134] Ibid.
[135] "India to Modernize Cotton Industry Technology," *Asia Pulse*, April 10, 2002.
[136] Technology Mission On Cotton, *Ministry of Textiles*, April 2008, www.texmin.nic.in/policy/tmc-introduction.pdf.
[137] An industry study noted: "A heavier duty on fine and superfine varieties of cloth and yarn is a great deterrent to the demand for superior cottons. To illustrate, in the case of cloth of higher medium category up to 40 counts, the duty is 4 percent ad valorem plus 14.9 paisa per square meter of cloth. A mere increase count by one at once puts the cloth in the finer category making it liable to pay an excise of crushing incidence at the rate of 15 percent ad valorem besides 31.9 paisa per square meter. Many of the cottons that come into the market belong to the 40–50 counts. Mills try to spin up to 40 only and stick to the production of higher medium category of cloth in order to avoid paying an exorbitant duty" (Kulkarni 1979, 248).
[138] Ibid.

types of cotton with properties of greater productivity" (Kulkarni 1979, 250).

The Technology Mission on Cotton is considered to be quite successful. Since its inception, market infrastructure has improved significantly – about 250 market yards have been fully developed with financial assistance, and more than 800 ginning and pressing factories have been modernized. Within research and production, there have been increases in both production technology and supply of certified seeds to increase yields and reduce costs to farmers, development of an integrated water management system, decreased contamination, and increased quality of cotton. Other successes include an increased area of production (from 4.4 to 9.2 million hectares), increased production from 13.6 million bales in 2002 to 27 million bales in 2007, increased exports from 0.29 to 4.8 million bales, and decreased imports from 1.08 to 0.6 billion bales as of 2007.[139] In late 2008, the union minister of textiles, Shankersinh Vaghela, announced not only further positive trends for the textile sector but also the fact that India had by this point become the second largest producer (second to China) with a production level of 31.15 million bales and a yield of 550 kg per hectare, crediting much of this success to the TMC and BT cotton.[140]

Success is also shown by domestic companies' continued support for the mission. In 2008, the South India Cotton Association (SICA) appealed to the union government to continue Mini-Mission IV under the plan, stating that many parts of the region (other than just Gujarat) could benefit from the mini-mission being extended for another five years. C. Soundara Raj (of SICA) cited the increased supply of quality genetically modified seeds and improved ginning practices as having helped to strengthen the industry.[141] Clearly, the cotton mission enjoyed the support of diverse groups (cotton farmers and the textile industry) as well as different ministries and many regions of India (north and south), contributing to its success. These policy initiatives were innovative and created a new political economy of reforms going beyond conflicting interests and perceptions.

---

[139] Agarwal, O. P., "Cotton Economy in India," *COTAAP Research Foundation*, September 11, 2007, http://wcrc.confex.com/wcrc/2007/techprogram/P1780.HTM.

[140] "India: Textiles Industry Achieves 16 Percent Growth Rate and Attracts Investment of Rs. 1.21 Lakh Crore," *Tendersinfo*, October 13, 2008. BT Cotton is the genetically modified version of cotton. India's success in BT cotton is interesting as it relies not on corporate seeds from Monsanto but on the dissemination of BT cottonseeds in a more decentralized manner. See Herring (2013).

[141] "Continue Subsidy Scheme for Cotton Units: SICA," *Hindu*, September 29, 2008.

5.7   Conclusion

This chapter has focused on an analysis of the textile policies from the post independence period to the recent transitions (1998 onward) to explore whether textiles can be, once again, at the forefront of a new industrial revolution in India. The story of change in Indian textile policies is puzzling and interesting. From world dominance before colonialism to significant market share until the 1950s, India's textile industry went into a precipitous decline and stagnation after independence. In the textile sector, the domestic policy regime was the clear obstacle to any change. Moreover, the collusion between different segmented interests and political actors cut off all endogenous levers of change. Precisely because policies created interests and market structures, it was very difficult to change it from within. In this chapter, I have shown that the impending abolition of the Multi-Fibre Arrangement unleashed a dormant reform coalition within the state, which opened a window of opportunity to disrupt congealed interests and usher in a radical reversal of policies until then unimaginable. Interestingly, similar to the pharmaceutical sector, textile industry actors were risk averse until the domestic policy environment began to change. State actors used the window of opportunity created by abolition of the global agreement on textiles to scale up, push for change, and design a substantial policy turnaround. It took time and was a struggle, but external institutional crises brought people together in a way that had not been possible before. The MFA and the changing rules of the game on textiles became "an international solution to a domestic problem."[142] The threat of the global agreement blocked the ability of the losers to prevent change, and the international rules paved the way to empowering specific domestic actors to nudge radical change. We must also analyze how the business community reacted to these policy coalitions and state efforts. Chapter 6 documents the textile industry's responses to the momentous global regime changes.

---

[142] Goldstein (1996, 84).

6   Interests in motion
Private sector change in India's textile sector

Mabank Gupta, president of a large textile firm, Raymond Group, noted in 2005: "It is important to realize that we are now moving from an era of subsidies to reality, and the best way forward is to go in for value addition, and move up the value chain."[1] From 2004 onward, Indian textile firms abandoned pessimism and defensive strategies in favor of expansion, acquisitions, and technological modernization. These shifts are extremely significant given historical weakness, fragmentation, and lack of modernization in India's textile industry. Despite such legacies, by 2002, India emerged as one of the top ten exporters of textiles goods (Tewari 2006a, 2006b) and became a sourcing base for many international brands, such as Gap, Walmart, Tommy Hilfiger, Benetton, G-Star, Levi's, and Marks & Spencer.[2] If you are shopping in the United States or Europe for garments, you are much more likely to find the "Made in India" label in medium- to high-end clothing stores and boutiques than ever before. Inserted into buyer-driven networks, Indian garment and textile companies provide a full package of textile goods, with design capabilities, though with less volume and scale (Gereffi 2002; Tewari 2005). India's world market share of textiles and clothing rose from a low of 1.5 percent in the 1970s to reach 4.01 percent by 2010.[3]

These changes were reflected in optimistic business perceptions across the value chain. A small-scale firm owner noted in 2005, "The entire face of the industry has changed from what it was fifteen years back. The factories were very small then with no supporting facilities. Today, the factories are catering to some of the best brands and retailers in the world. ... Today, the industry is geared up to do any kind of order with stringent quality levels."[4] Simultaneously, in 2005, changes in the global regime abolished the mechanism of allocating quotas for developing countries' exports and imports.

[1] "Textile Industry Gearing for Post-Quota Regime," *The Hindu*, January 5, 2005.
[2] Virtus Global Partners (VGP) (2008).   [3] Calculated by author from WTO (2011).
[4] Interview with V. Elangovan, CEO of Tirupur based SNQS International, in "'Garment Units with 1,000 Machines Will Become Common in Tirupur by Next Two Years" *Express Textile* (fortnightly magazine), April 16–30, 2005.

Changes in India's textile sector thus tell a unique story of mutating interests and skills in the context of changing global markets and rules of the game and raise the following question: how did the competing forces of liberalism (export-oriented firms and sectors) and protectionism (import-competing firms and industries) play out as India became more globalized? This framing, though, assumes that the forces of liberalism and of antiliberalism preexisted and struggled over policies and markets. This misses the crucial dimension of *interests in motion*, which raises a more interesting set of questions for dynamic political economy: how do the competing forces of liberalization and protectionism *take shape and change* as the economy becomes global and interdependent?[5] When do business preferences move from protectionism to support for liberalization? How does business respond when the rules of the game are shifting and market signals uncertain? Can changing global configurations – both export markets and new international regimes – create *new* interests in the domestic political economy of a country, unleashing a new logic of collective action? The global transitions underway offer "a fascinating opportunity" to examine businesses' strategic choices in the midst of institutional transitions (Peng 2003, 276), but even more interestingly, they enable a glimpse into how preferences evolve and shift. This is the subject of this chapter.

I provide evidence of the evolution of business preferences in a rigorous way to answer some of these questions. Events data generated by coding of business strategies from a voluminous database of newspapers from 1995–2010 generated the author's "Database of Business Strategies Events."[6] This yielded a detailed set of business strategies from multiple sources. In addition, I used the CMIE's PROWESS database that maps business behavior to generate a timeline of aggregate business behavior in terms of mergers and joint ventures. Government data, interviews, and analysis of business annual reports were used to supplement the two large data sets. Aggregate data at the industry level miss the variable impacts on different subsectors and differently sized firms. I enhance the aggregate data analysis with more micro-level interviews and case histories of specific business actions and strategies. Interviews also provide a finer picture of the dilemmas and challenges faced by firms as they make difficult choices with the opening up of the economy. I let the voices of industry speak at different moments rather than make them invisible. These comments add a real-life picture to larger aggregate changes. I also provide a

---

[5] See J. P. Singh (2006) for a focus on how preferences change in the context of services negotiations.
[6] This generated around 8,152 observations and detailed stories.

glimpse into the changing basis of collective action as well as changes in political lobbying by business associations. With help from the "Policy and Institutional Events Database," I am able to link policies, politics, and institutions to business strategies in a changing global context.

6.1 The argument

Globalization has introduced fundamental changes both in market conditions and in the rules of the game that govern markets. These changes affect not only states and the trade policy process but also business actors. Following David Lake's caution that "[l]ess attention has been paid to how international institutions affect the constellation of domestic interests or institutions" (Lake 2006, 768), this chapter and Chapter 7 integrate the international level of analysis into the analysis of (domestic) interests and institutions in a difficult and resistant sector: textiles. In order to do so, I take the design and structure of the international level seriously after of in terms of the changing incentives and the international bargaining and sifting it unleashed. I pay attention not only to international trade movements and economic variables but also to the rules of the game that shape trade movements and domestic cleavages in countries. Yet, a focus on international levels is not enough as different countries pursue different trade strategies. We must also focus on the "deeper micro-foundations" (Aggarwal and Lee 2011, 18) of how each country's trade strategies are formulated in the domestic arena, suggesting a focus on the domestic institutions and the shifting nature of the domestic political economy.[7] This resonates with a newly emerging approach in management and business studies that focuses on institutions in addition to firm-level strategies (Peng 2003; Peng, Wang, and Jiang 2008). Such an approach points toward the independent effect of the political and institutional environment in shaping market strategies, especially in transitional economies.

Going beyond industry- or firm-level economic variables and bringing in the effect of the institutional and political context in shaping strategy has been the domain of comparative politics and new institutional economics. Comparative political economy can both contribute to and learn from business studies that largely focus on the firm-level strategies. These insights would suggest that Indian business actors' recent outward focus and skill upgradation is not only a function of firm-level factors (size, technology, or resources) but is also shaped by the changing international and domestic contexts in an interactive way. For India, though, prevailing

[7] Also see Aggarwal and Urata (2002).

expectations in comparative political economy and historical sociology are challenged by rapid and paradigmatic shifts in business behavior, even when domestic institutions were stable. Olson's theory (1965), adapted famously by Bardhan for India (1984) and Krueger (1974), suggests the difficulties of successful economic change in the presence of vested interests.[8] Can narrow business interests and distributional coalitions change in response to global economic integration and trade liberalization in long-standing democracies such as India, where the power of vested interest groups has been well established? The lack of answers to such important questions highlights the need to examine the changes in and evolution of private interests over time, and in different contexts.

In contrast to the dominant expectations that predict stasis in India, I argue that in the process of dealing with external economic threats (the impending increase in competition) and opportunities (expanding markets and exports possibilities), the interests of the private sector and its political strategies shifted, in turn altering the political economy of business dynamics in the country. Internationalization transformed well-entrenched interests that influenced policy and held numerous veto points across the economy. Yet, these paradoxical effects were mediated by the domestic policy regime that responded to external changes in a positive way. Internal state-led changes were an important precursor to this shift in business responses, but interestingly, the policy transformations in 1999–2002 were themselves driven by the anticipated changes in the global structure of rules (MFA abolition).[9] As noted by D'Souza (2003) and confirmed by my own analysis and evidence in Chapter 5 of this book, "[a]s trade liberalization proceeds the state is not in retreat but is proactively involved in restructuring to make the industry more competitive."[10] As the abolition of the MFA approached, firms faced a clear alternative either to restructure so as to compete effectively in worldwide markets or go out of business. Yet, firms were extremely risk averse until the domestic policy regime began to change. In the early years of the policy change (1999–2002), business interest in restructuring was very minimal. Yet, starting, 2003 onward, as the internal policy regime shifted, some firms began to take advantage of new investment opportunities and expand their businesses. Existing explanations – both Olson's argument and institutional frameworks – are not able to account for the emergence of new producer groups and new forms of collective mobilization created in the processes of complying with global trade rules and adapting to changing market conditions.

---

[8] Also see Chibber (2003).   [9] This was elaborated in Chapter 5 of this book.
[10] D'Souza (2003, 31).

I examine how the changing structure of global rules – the abolition of the quotas in 2005 – transforms the logic of domestic collective action of industry actors toward a more encompassing and coherent form.

Business reactions need to be understood in the context of the industrial organization of that specific sector. Section 6.2 outlines the basic structure of the industry and the complex and fragmented value chain in textiles. Section 6.3 documents the radical transformations that were unleashed in the early 2000s. Expansion, technological modernization, and joint ventures spread across the supply chain and across large and small sectors. I present both qualitative and quantitative evidence to demonstrate the widespread shift in business strategies and the emergence of more dynamic capabilities. Section 6.4 places the responses within a larger analytical timeline to ask if the private sector took a lead or was a follower to global changes. What were the sources of change given these static structures and predispositions? I identify two different episodes and levers of change. The first source of change began in the mid-1980s, catalyzed by internal restrictions, devaluation of Indian currency, and expanding apparel export markets. External export markets play a major role in the 1980s. However, this change, while important, remained tentative. Real and wide-scale change in business strategies began only around 2004–2005, catalyzed by the global trade rules and supportive domestic policy changes. Section 6.5 analyzes the political economy of business responses focusing on the imperative of consolidation within the textile industry and the struggles around formation of one voice among the textile industry. This section reveals the collective action dilemmas unleashed by the WTO. This led to the creation of a consolidated association to give a single voice and to negotiate at the global level. Table 6.1 summarizes the developmental trajectory of the textile industry's decline followed by resurgence and revival in India's textile sector. The rest of the chapter elaborates on this timeline.

6.2   Structure of Indian textile industry

Production of cloth and garments from cotton can be divided into six stages: the growing and harvesting stage, cotton cleaning and ginning, the spinning of staple fiber into yarn, weaving of yarn into gray fabric, processing of yarn into cloth and then into finished fabrics with design, and finally, the conversion of the finished fabric into garments and apparel, which are sold through retail distribution. Figure 6.1 captures this process.

How are these activities organized in the Indian case? Some unique aspects of India's textile sector are the coexistence of a broad range of technologies (from hand operated to fully automated) and a number of

Table 6.1 *Evolution of the Indian textile sector*

	1950s	1960–1980	1980–2000	2000–2005
Global Trade Environment	Patchwork protectionism quota system	Quota system MFA (1974)	Quota system; bilateral textile agreements	Prospective abolition of quota system - MFA replaced by ATC; WTO rules apply
Domestic Context	New policy regime; small scale, cotton license raj	Previous policy regime; nationalization (of 'sick' mills); pro-handloom	Devaluation of rupee; tentative policy changes (1985)	Radical policy changes; Technology Fund; man-made fiber
Capabilities	Global strength but weak capability	Declining skill set and market share	Exports; no new skills; Technological obsolescence	Investments in modernization; alliances; R&D; export-driven growth
Results	Beginning of decline	Decline	Stagnation	Revival

fibers produced indigenously (cotton, jute, silk, and synthetic), although cotton dominates. The industry is composed of four major types of firms: (1) "organized," or composite, integrated mills that combine spinning, weaving, and processing of yarn into cloth[11] and the spinning mills, both referred simply to as "mills." India also has an extensive decentralized sector constituted by (2) handlooms, (3) power looms, and (4) hosiery (Roy 1998, 2175; Roy 1999). The mills are an example of interaction of the different processes – spinning, weaving, and processing – they use hierarchical organization and were established by mercantile banking communities in the colonial India (Roy 2004, 86). Handloom and power-loom weavers, as well as the composite mills, do the conversion of yarn into cloth. The handloom and powerloom operators procure yarn from other sources and only do weaving, and then they send their woven cloth for further processing. Usually, these are small firms that deploy artisans and new entrepreneurs. Each type of producer caters to a particular segment of the market and has distinct technological elements and products as well as different policy regulations, fiscal obligations, and labor regulations. The uniqueness of the Indian story has produced a peculiar

[11] (Roy 2004, 86).

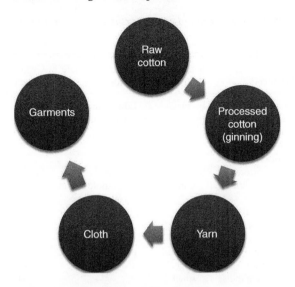

Figure 6.1 The textile supply chain

industrial structure and one of the most complex supply chains in the world (Verma 2002, 20). The supply chain is also fragmented in multiple ways (Desai 1983; Mazumdar 1984; Verma 2002). For example, yarn can be made by three different methods – by hand, in spinning mills, and in composite mills that combine the spinning and weaving of yarn into cloth. Over time, the spinning sector became the strongest as both the composite and handloom sectors lost their competitive edge.

Table 6.2 gives us some sense of the textile commodity chain and India's industrial structure that existed before the quota was abolished in 2005. In Section 6.4, I outline how this structure is changing after the abolition of quotas in 2005.

6.3   Business strategies and responses: expansion, investment, and modernization (1999–2014)

A statement by the CEO of a textile company in early 2004 is reflective of a larger trend. Riju Jhunjunwala, joint managing director of Rajasthan Spinning and Weaving Mills, Ltd., said, "We have now internally restructured ourselves into a more product focused and market oriented company to take advantage of the external changes like elimination of quotas."[12]

---

[12] "Rajasthan Spinning Mulls Foray into Readymade Garments," *Business Line*, April 24, 2004.

Table 6.2 *Industrial organization of cotton textile production in India,*
1960–2000

Value Chain Segment	Producers	Size of Producers	Technology before 2000s	Ownership Structure
Fiber production (cotton)	Until 1966: short staple cotton; 1966–1978: long staple cotton	Farmers	Low technology; recent use of BT cotton	Farms
Cotton preparation and processing (ginning and cleaning)	Small cotton ginning firms in rural and semirural environment	Small-sized units	Outdated technology (saw rollers gins vs. ginning and pressing sectors)	Small enterprise owners
Spinning (strongest sector)	Some hand spinning; spinning mills; composite mills	Small and large, but small dominated until recently	New mills	Cooperatives; nationalized mills; private
Weaving	Handlooms, powerlooms; weaving mills; composite mills	Small dominates; small produce 95% of cloth	Low-level and old technology	Small owners; cooperatives; large private; nationalized sick mills
Processing, dyeing, printing, and finishing (weak sector)	Hand processors and power processors; composite mills	82% hand processors	Low-level (hand) technology	Primarily small shops
Garmenting	Garment firms reserved for small scale until 2003	Small and medium sized	Foot-operated or power-operated fabricators	Subcontracting; no assembly line manufacturing
Retailing	Nonexistent until the 2000s; India not part of buyer-driven networks	Local, small retail shops	Low	Small family shops

Source: Author's assessment drawn from D'Souza (2003), Singh and Kundu (2004), Desai
(1983), and Roy (1999).

Abolition of the quota regime created an impetus for capacity enhancement, expansion, and modernization to deal with the expected increase in demand from the global level. While many firms began to see the need for expansion by 2002–2003,[13] the real expansion began after 2005, when all the quotas were abolished and the domestic policy regime had responded with its own initiatives. Between 1999 and 2010, new investment of USD4.86 billion was initiated for technological modernization and new activities.[14] A survey of fifty composite mills during the 2004–2007 period found that 65 percent of the proposed investment was for capacity building, 25 percent for modernization, and 4 percent for forward integration in the spinning sector.[15] After 2005–2006, the government's Technology Upgradation Fund Scheme (TUFS) contributed in creating higher production capacity as well as accelerating automation.

Initially, the investment scale-up started among the large and integrated firms, followed by small and midsized firms. Together the largest Indian mills (Arvind, Indian Rayon, Vardhman, Raymond, Welspun, Madura, and others) invested USD2.5 billion in new plant, equipment, and technology in 2004–2005 alone.[16] Expansion of manufacturing operations was the common story at that time.[17] "Everybody has been preparing for WTO," noted S. Y. Noorani in 2004, managing director of the shirt maker, Zodiac Clothing Co., who had a full-time executive focusing solely on WTO issues.[18] This was confirmed by Welspun India's executive director: "We had geared up for the post-quota regime a year before the quotas were lifted [2004]."[19] Figure 6.2 shows this dramatic trend in new investment by textile firms after 2002–2003.

This picture contrasts with the state of the industry for almost three decades. In 1958, a doyen of the Indian textile industry described the problems faced by the mills:

---

[13] "Textile Cos Weave Expansion Plans," *Financial Express*, April 4, 2003. The timeline is very clear in the newspaper database. There are very few plans for expansion in the late 1990s, and by 2003 or so, some companies begin to plan ahead. By 2005–2006, expansion is a common imperative.

[14] Ministry of Textiles (2010).

[15] "Textile Sector to See Investment of Rs. 5,951 Crores in 2006–2007: Study," *Financial Express*, May 9, 2006.

[16] Manjeet Kriplani, "India: Speed Up the Sewing Machines," *BusinessWeek*, May 3, 2004. Also see Ema Vasdev, "Textiles Cos Spin Big-Ticket Investment Plans," *Economic Times*, October 13, 2005.

[17] See Amit Jain, "Textile Cos on Major Expansion Drive," *Economic Times*, January 4, 2006.

[18] Manjeet Kriplani, "India: Speed Up the Sewing Machines," *BusinessWeek*, May 3, 2004.

[19] Ema Vasdev, "Textiles Cos Spin Big-Ticket Investment Plans," *Economic Times*, October 13, 2005.

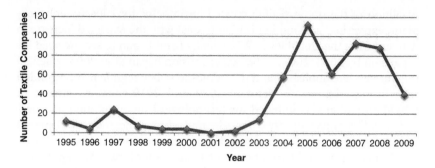

Figure 6.2 Number of textile companies with expansion plans
Calculated by author from the "Author's Database of Business
Strategies Events."

Some mills have taken active steps to renovate their plants, but on the whole the
industry is poorly equipped to meet the competition of the highly modernized
industries of Japan, China, Europe, and America. On average our methods and
equipment are thirty to forty years behind the times, and what we have is not
always operated in the most efficient manner. Modern Mills today in Europe are
employing less than two operatives per 1000 spindles from blow room to spinning
point compared to twelve to fifteen in the average mill in India. ...
     Even more serious is the position in weaving. In Japan, Europe, and America,
and I also believe in China, there is hardly a mill which is not fully equipped with
automatic looms. In India 90 percent of our looms are still of the Lancashire type.
Whereas a weaver looks after sixty to seventy automatic looms in the advanced
countries, we are still discussing whether four looms to a weaver should be uni-
versally adopted. Vast improvements can equally be made in this direction, for there
are mills in India working between thirty to forty automatic looms per operative.[20]

In contrast, in 2006, Mahavir Spinning Mills, Ltd., dominant in the
yarn and sewing thread business, launched a massive Rs. 2000 crores
(approx. USD400 million) capacity expansion and technological upgradation plan, intending to increase its capacity from 5.4 lakh spindles to
7.9 lakh spindles by 2008–2009.[21] DCM Textiles planned a Rs. 70 crores
(approx. USD14 million) expansion noting that in the, "post-Quota
regime there has been an increased demand and hence we need the
capacity expansion."[22] S. P. Oswal, of Vardhaman, enhanced the capacity in his mills to the tune of USD78 million by adding 20,000 spindles
and 200 air jet looms and also increasing his processing capacity to
40 million meters. Vardhaman planned an expansion of Rs. 1,000 crores

[20] Neville N. Wadia, quoted in Kulkarni (1979, 263).
[21] "Winning the Global Sweepstakes," *Outlook Business*, May 20, 2006, p. 67.
[22] "DCP Textiles in for Rs. 70 Crore Expansion," *Business Standard*, October 10, 2005.

Table 6.3 *Number of textile mills in the large organized sector, 2001–2012*

	2001	2007	2011–2012
Spinning Mills	1565	1597	1761
Composite Mills	281	176	196
Total	1846	1773	1957

Source: Ministry of Textiles (2013). Also see Ministry of Textiles (2010).

(approx. USD200 million), a major investment.[23] Rajasthan Spinning and Weaving Mills, of the LNJ Bhilwara Group, invested USD29 million by adding 63,000 spindles. In 2005, Century Textiles planned a significant expansion of its paper and denim units, an investment of Rs. 525 crores (approx. USD125 million).[24] Nahar Industrial Enterprises, Ltd. (NIEL), designed a massive expansion plan of Rs. 800 crores (approx. USD160 million) to be implemented in two phases, ranging from fabric production to expanding its retail presence in men's clothing brands (called Cotton County).[25] Raymond's plan to extend its operations in technical textiles, a new and emerging growth area, also was designated for policy attention by the government.[26] Many new mills were established between 2001 and 2010, especially in the large organized sector, which had been seeing a slow decline in the 1980s and 1990s. The composite sector saw some consolidations and mergers. Table 6.3 shows that new investment intentions were beginning to translate into new factories.

In the early 2000s, small companies expanded their ambitions to the global level, increasing export and modernization plans significantly. Especially in 2005, many smaller companies announced modernization plans. Soma Textiles, Blue Blends, Asarva Mills, Sintex Industries, Chirpal Group, and Aarvee Denim, all smaller companies, began investing around Rs. 500 crores (approx. USD100 million) in diverse expansion plans.[27] Sri Govindaraja Mills, a small unlisted company based in southwestern India (Andhra Pradesh), planned to set up a new plant at Cuddalah (Andhra Pradesh) with 1 lakh (100,000) spindles and also add more spindles to its factory in Tamil Nadu. The company deployed funds from the

[23] "Textile Cos Weave Expansion Plans," *Financial Express*, April 4, 2003.
[24] "Century Textiles to Expand Paper and Denim Units," *Business Line*, January 25, 2005.
[25] Ritu Chhabria, "Textile to Drive Growth," *Financial Express*, February 12, 2006.
[26] "Raymond Plans Foray into Technical Textiles," *Economic Times*, March 4, 2006. Also see "Firms Find a Lucrative Venture in Weaving Technical Textiles," *Indian Express*, April 12, 2006.
[27] "Small Textile Cos Weave Big Plans on Global Demand," *Economic Times*, July 5, 2005.

Table 6.4 *Growth in the small-scale sector, 2001–2012*

	2001	2007	2011–2012
Small Spinning Mills (Number)	996	1,219	1,336
Powerloom Units (Number)	374,000	494,000	520,000

Source: Ministry of Textiles, Annual Reports, various years.

TUFS of about Rs. 350 crores (approx. USD70 million) for that purpose.[28] The expansion of the small-scale sector is surprising given the conventional expectation that it would not survive in the global competition. Aggregate data on the number of factories in the small-scale sector also belie this pessimistic expectation. Table 6.4 shows the rise of spinning mills and powerlooms in the small-scale sector.

Expansion was used to modernize the existing machinery and bring in new machinery. Around 70,000 to 80,000 water jet and rapier looms were installed in textile and weaving companies, improving their productivity. The processing sector saw the installation of dewdrop machines, which emboss cloth. In 2002, only seventy embroidery machines existed in Surat, but in 2007, there were 5,000 deployed with an investment of Rs. 750 crores (approx. USD150 million). Many firms were investing in newer technologies and processes such as blow room and ring frame processes. Much faster air jet looms replaced the old weaving looms.[29] Importantly, India emerged as the largest market for high-end textile machinery; Indian textile firms began to import machinery from Switzerland that they could not have absorbed earlier. At this time, India emerged as one of the largest market for the Swiss machines.[30] Many firms, aided by many textile associations, were employing newer, different kinds of technologies.

The weaving sector, a weaker segment in the textile value chain, saw huge capacity addition as well as improvements in the technology associated with weaving.[31] Raymond Denim planned a capacity expansion of 15 million meters by the end of 2005, in addition to the then current capacity of 20 million meters. This additional plant required an investment of around Rs. 127 crores (approx. USD25 million), primarily for a rope-dyeing technology sourced from the United States. According to

[28] "Textile Companies Gear Up to Ride the Retain Boom," *Business Line*, January 19, 2007.
[29] Melvyn Thomas and Harit Mehta, "Technology a Money-Spinner for Textiles," *Economic Times*, May 21, 2007.
[30] "India Largest Market for Swiss Textile Machines," *International Business Intelligence*, February 7, 2006.
[31] Most of the facts in this paragraph are drawn from *Express Textile*, February 1–15, 2005.

officials, "This expansion was in keeping with our decision to work with bigger clients like VF Corp, who insist on a minimum plant size for doing business. We have already begun supplying to VFC."[32] Nahar Fabrics also planned huge expansions and commissioned a plant of 130 machines in 2006. Others, like Laxmi Mills, were planning to modernize and replace all shuttle looms with modern rapier or shuttleless looms. Diversification was an important component of the strategy of many firms at this time. Shanmugavel Group of Dindigul, Tamil Nadu, along with many other spinners in the region, decided to move into weaving. A newspaper reported, "It is expected that the company would invest to the tune of Rs. 700 crores [approx. USD140 million] in weaving."[33]

Firms started with new investment in capacity building but soon turned to newer activities and value addition. By 2006, value addition had become the dominant goal of most new investment. For example, industry associations began to educate the industry about new technologies, like nonwoven methods, and many firms became interested in such methods.[34] Companies began to adopt "enterprise-wide applications (EWA)" to add in the delivery of orders. Madura planned a virtual digital design library, where swatches could be tried on virtual models with 3D viewing.[35] IT began to be used in the old, traditional industry of textiles. Yet, expansion was soon followed by both backward and forward integration across the supply chain, as mere expansion could not address the underlying structural issues, which necessitated both horizontal and vertical integration.

6.3.1   Forward and backward integration across the textile chain

Historically, the Indian textile value chain was fragmented, with weak links (weaving and processing, for example) in the supply chain. The onset of changes at the global level unleashed a strong integration imperative. Many textile companies initiated horizontal and vertical integration in an attempt to increase scale, counter preexisting fragmentation, and minimize the inefficiencies at each level of the supply chain. Importantly, many companies decided to capture the entire value chain from spinning to garmenting. Significant forward integration into garments by major spinners and weavers is an example of such a trend. Textile companies primarily in spinning or weaving started to move into

[32] *Express Textile*, February 1–15, 2005.   [33] Ibid.

[34] "Industry Told to Adopt Non-Woven Technology," *Press Trust of India*, February 17, 2006. Also, for discussions about the increase in market for nonwoven textile goods within technical textiles, see "Global Non-Woven Textiles Growth Seen at 8 Percent," *Business Line*, August 6, 2006.

[35] "How EWA Helps Textile Manufactures," *Financial Express*, October 3, 2005.

apparel manufacturing in a big way starting 2004 or so. Arvind Mills set up plants to manufacture shirts and knitting garments, as well as a jeans unit in Mauritius; they invested around Rs. 150 crores (approx. USD30 million) for that in 2004. They also set up a cotton trousers unit and a jeans plant at Bangalore around 2004.[36] Raymond, predominantly a cloth producing company, set up a manufacturing facility to produce trousers in Bangalore as well as a denim manufacturing facility. They also set up a Rs. 50 crores (approx. USD10 million) factory in Bangalore to manufacture 5 million suits a year.[37] The Bhilwara Group's Rajasthan Spinning and Weaving Mills shifted focus from exporting yarn and fabrics to manufacturing garments by investing Rs. 150 crores (approx. USD30 million) in 2004. Similarly, Welspun, GTN textiles, S. Kumar's, and Orient Craft also expanded their production capacities and crafted forward expansion plans. Some of the best examples of "full integration" are Alok Industries, Indian Rayon & Industries, Welspun Industries, JCT, Ltd., and Vardhman Industries, which started to straddle the entire range from spinning to branded garments and home textiles (Singh 2008).

Retaining and building of brands became very extensive as many textile companies started to extend their expansion into garments to market high-end brands.[38] S. Kumar's launched the Reid and Taylor brand; Raymond also launched retail brands. Century textile started "Cottons by Century."[39] Alok Industries' CEO Jiwrajika noted, "It's high time that Indian companies went in for front-end acquisitions and got into retailing."[40] Even smaller companies started to expand retail operations.[41] Other companies built a more diversified model by expanding into different countries in an attempt to capture entry points into different markets across the world. "We put our eggs in many baskets, leading to a very scalable model," said Deepak Seth of House of Pearls,[42] which has a chain of manufacturing plants and offices across India, the United Kingdom, Bangladesh, Indonesia, the United States, and China. The firm procures, designs, and processes apparel items though a large network of plants and alliances. It also expanded its warehouses in the United States and the United Kingdom and began supplying to Walmart,

---

[36] "S. J. D. Naik, "Preparing for the Big Leap," *Business Line*, July 24, 2004. Also see "Garment Makers Dressed to Bill," *Economic Times*, July 27, 2005.

[37] "Garment Makers Dressed to Bill," Ibid.

[38] Indian retailing has undergone a significant transformation, and apparel constitutes approx. 39 percent of the Organized Retailing business (KSA Technopak 2005).

[39] Textile Majors Eye Ready-Mades Market," *Hindustan Times*, September 6, 2006.

[40] "No Longer Spinning a Yarn," *Financial Express*, July 16, 2006.

[41] "Vijay Textiles to Invest in Retail Stories," *Financial Express*, February 1, 2005.

[42] "Textile Exporters Opting for Speed to Market Route," *Business Line*, July 3, 2006.

JC Penney, Gap, and Banana Republic, among other major brands. It has also set up an in-house design office in the United States. [43]

Backward integration, more difficult than forward integration, was also evident. Many textile mills in Maharashtra started contract cotton farming in the cotton-rich belt of Vidharba (Maharashtra). [44] Welspun decided to organize corporate cotton farming around its factory locations by procuring large tracts of land. [45] Nahar Industrial Enterprises, Ltd. (NIEL), amalgamated its various companies to emerge as an integrated textile player, with productive capacity in yarn, gray fabric, processed fabric, as well as ready-made garments. As a result, the turnover (gross sales) of the company increased by 58 percent. It expanded its presence across many segments of the textile chain and began supplying to major domestic brands as well as foreign brands such as GAP, Ann Taylor, and Tommy Hilfiger. [46] Tropical Clothing Company, a small company that started with Rs. 10,000 (approx. USD200 million) seed capital in 2001, introduced an interesting innovation in its management of the supply chain. Rather than obtain finished cloth from weavers, it started to source yarn from the weavers and began providing it to five master weavers, who then wove it in innovative ways suggested by the company, such as lycra-blended Khadi (tensel) or work wear using handspun cloth, like Khadi. In 2006, its turnover had increased to Rs. 2 crores (approx. USD400,000). [47]

An interesting development was the integration of cotton and man-made fiber production. Spentex Industries, Ltd., a cotton yarn producer, decided to acquire a majority stake in the Indorama Group in 2006 so as to offer the entire range of yarns from natural to man-made. [48] Many medium-sized fabric producers set up their own garment factories at that time. [49] A significant number of cotton ginners are forward integrating into spinning in the cotton areas of Andhra Pradesh and Punjab. [50] And significant backward integration by small and medium-sized knit-wear exporters in spinning occurred in the Coimbatore-Tirupur region of Tamil Nadu. As an illustration, Gokaldas Exports, a company supplying jackets to GAP and Tommy Hilfiger, started to manufacture its own

---

[43] Ibid.

[44] "Textile Mills Plan to Start Contract Farming in Vidarbha," *Business Standard*, March 16, 2007.

[45] "There Is Need for Consolidation in the Textile Industry," *Financial Express*, January 1, 2006.

[46] Rut Chhabria, "Textiles to Drive Growth," *Financial Express*, February 12, 2006.

[47] Wheels Still in Spin," *Business Standard*, March 8, 2006.

[48] "Spentex Acquires Indorama Textiles," *Financial Express*, February 18, 2006.

[49] One example is Sintex Industries, but many more also set up such dual operations. See "Small Textile Cos Weave Big Plans on Global Demand," *Economic Times*, July 5, 2005.

[50] Singh (2008).

jackets and increased the number of fully integrated factories between 2002 and 2004 for a total investment of Rs. 550 crores (approx. USD110 million) and Rs. 720 crores (approx. USD144 million) in 2003–2004. They also planned on setting up independent manufacturing facilities of reasonable sizes and to identify managers who could manage the business for them.[51]

Interestingly, powerlooms, specializing in small-scale looms for weaving, started their own spinning and composite mills and also established more direct relationships with the mills in order to cut costs. Such consolidation was a direct result of the competition unleashed by abolition of the MFA.[52] Similarly, the Tirupur Cluster, initially set up in 1985, became a leader in exporting garments and knitwear products. In 2005, the entrepreneurs in the Tirupur Cluster Park took an initiative to organize the Nethaji Apparel Park at new Tirupur, which would combine the strengths of diverse skills and forward linkages. The finance minister appreciated "the initiative of the Tirupur knitwear entrepreneurs in a project like the apparel parks even in an era where many in the industry were yet to know which way the winds of fortune would blow in the quota-free regime."[53] Other such integrated parks were planned in Gujarat, aiming to use spatial integration as a way to enhance scale and size.[54]

In addition to adding capacity and enhancing volumes, many firms began to enhance value addition through diverse global strategies. *Takeovers, acquisitions, and global alliances* became an important mode for such a focus on value addition. Figure 6.3 documents the acceleration of mergers, acquisition, and takeovers in the 2000s. Between 2005 and 2009, the rate of such activity had increased dramatically, and acquisitions by Indian companies were a significant part of the global alliances.[55]

Around 2004, there was another wave of new mergers and acquisitions. Big textile companies from India began to look for potential acquisitions, especially in Europe, China, and Taiwan, in order to meet the expansion of demand expected in 2005. Reliance Industries acquired German Trevira, a producer of polyester fabric in Europe. Many other companies, such as Raymond, Grasim Industries, and GTN Textiles, also began looking for possible acquisitions. Some smaller players also ventured outside the country; Sambandam Spinning, for example, set up a wholly

[51] Ibid.   [52] "Cost Cutting and Consolidation for Survival," *Hindu*, August 11, 2005.
[53] "Textile Sector Needs Rs. 27,000 Crore Investments: Chidambaram: Nethaji Park Inaugurated at Tiruper," *Hindu Business Line*, January 11, 2005.
[54] "Adani Is Building Rs. 130 Crore Integrated Textile Park," *Economic Times*, March 29, 2006.
[55] Also see Rakesh Sood, "Textile Sector on a M&A Spree," *Financial Express*, January 17, 2007. Also see "Textile Majors Weave Global Alliances," *Business Standard*, May 25, 2007.

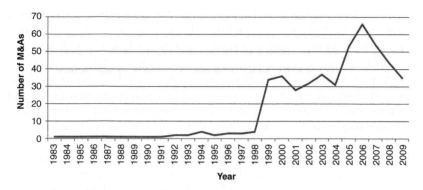

Figure 6.3 Total number of Indian mergers and acquisitions in textile sector
Author's calculation from CMIE PROWESS Database.

owned subsidiary in New York.[56] The desire for global reach as well as the innovation imperative led many companies to start alliances and joint ventures with many non-Indian companies. Arvind Mills started building links with Italian and Japanese designers to differentiate itself from China's scale and volumes. Retail alliances were enhanced significantly as foreign retail chains began to look for alternatives to China. JC Penney, Metro AG, and Walmart began sourcing from India in an attempt to diversify away from China.[57]

In 2006, the need to acquire non-Indian companies accelerated dramatically. As an example, Gujarat Heavy Chemicals, Ltd. (GHCL), acquired an American textile company, Dan Rivers, for USD17.5 million for its marketing network as well as for its manufacturing network in China and Pakistan.[58] Many Indian companies planned new operations in China, such as Sabare International, which planned a Rs. 300 crores (approx. USD60 million) expansion by buying manufacturing units in China. Ambattur Clothing set up a trouser-making facility in Bahrain and began plans to acquire a company in Egypt as many Middle East companies started negotiating with the United States for zero-duty access. The Phagwara-based JCT Company set up a unit in Senegal to take advantage

[56] "Textile Firms Weave Global Ambitions: Companies Eyeing Buyouts in China, Taiwan," *Business Standard*, July 21, 2004.
[57] "Garment Makers Dressed to Bill," *Economic Times*, July 27, 2005.
[58] "Textile Inc. Thinks Global to Solve Machinery Shortage," *Indian Express*, January 27, 2006. Also see "Textile Firms Weave Moves Overseas," *Business Standard*, February 16, 2006.

of the African Growth and Opportunity Act, that allows exports from Senegal to the United States and European Union. JCT also had a unit in Malaysia.[59] Many other companies started to link up with and buy factories in the UAE. South Africa and the Middle East were used as routes to get into the United States and other Western markets. Acquisitions became a route to modernize and acquire new machinery and technology. Grasim Industries set up a joint venture in China for a viscose staple fiber manufacturing unit.[60] Orient Craft acquired Levi's unit in Spain for Rs. 60 crores (approx. USD12 million) in 2006 for its machinery and skilled manpower. Vardhman Polytext, Ltd., acquired two units in Hungary and the Czech Republic, bringing "advanced machinery at competitive rates" to the company.[61] Table 6.5 lists the global acquisitions and alliances completed by Indian companies in just one year: 2006. Many other acquisitions were also under consideration as this database underestimates the extent of such global alliances.

6.3.2   Innovation and R&D

The first priority after the realization of a need for change was the scaling up of volumes. Soon enough, many companies realized the need, in the words of Sanjay Lalbhai of Arvind Mills, "to innovate season after season, to ensure differentiation."[62] Given India's design strengths, many companies started to embark on new design activities. Some companies set up in-house design studios to differentiate themselves. Others formulated their own innovative strategies. Small companies were nimble enough to adapt their operations, especially for smaller orders. A small company based in Calcutta designed Lycra-blended Khadi and Indo-Western style work wear called Indiez.[63] Business associations, like the Confederation of Indian Industry, recommended the adoption of IT in various textile operations so as to streamline the supply chain.[64] By 2007, many companies had adopted different kinds of IT applications to increase efficiency and delivery time. Automation of the factory floor was a rising trend even among garment manufacturers. The managing director of a small Jaipur-based firm noted that "IT components account for almost 10–15% of the total

---

[59] "Textile Firms Weave Moves Overseas," *Business Standard*, February 16, 2006.
[60] "Textile Majors Weave Global Alliances," *Business Standard*, May 25, 2007.
[61] "Textile Inc. Thinks Global to Solve Machinery Shortage," *Indian Express*, January 27, 2006.
[62] "India Looks to Make a Stitch in Time," *Business Standard*, January 7, 2005.
[63] "Wheels Still in Spin," *Business Standard*, March 8, 2006.
[64] "CII Textile Meet to Focus on IT Adoption," *Business Line*, April 4, 2006.

Table 6.5 *Acquisitions and global alliances of Indian textile firms in 2006*

Company Name	Acquiring/Setting Up New Unit	Cost	Year
Gujarat Heavy Chemicals, Ltd. (GHCL)	Dan River (US)	Rs .77 crore/ 17.5 million USD	2005–2006
GHCL	Acquired Rosebys UK's retail chain in home textile (UK)	USD40 million	2006
Orient Craft	Levi plant (Spain)	Rs. 60 crores	2006
Raymond	Regency Textiles (Portugal)	NA	2006
Raymond	United Cotton (Belgium)	NA	2006
Raymond	Joint venture with UCO NV (Belgium)	NA	2006
Banswara Syntex	Carreman Fabrics (French)	Rs. 40 crores	2006
Vardhman Polytex	Acquired two units (EE)	Rs. 17–18 crores	2006
Eskay Knitting	China	NA	2006
Ambattur Clothing	Egypt	NA	2006
JCT	New unit (Senegal)	NA	2006
JCT	Acquired unit (Malaysia)	NA	2006
JBF	Alliance with UAE government for sourcing raw material (UAE)	NA	2006
Welspun	Set up subsidiaries (US/EU)	NA	2006
Trident	Set up subsidiaries (US/EU)	NA	2006
Alok Industries	Set up subsidiaries (US/EU)	NA	2006
Alok Industries	Acquisition of Mileta (Czechoslovakia)	NA	2006
Zodiac Clothing Company Ltd	Acquired shirt-making facility (UAE)	NA	2006
Malwa Industries	Third Dimension Apparels (Jordan)	NA	2006
Malwa	Majority stake (Italy)	NA	2006
Welspun	Acquired 85% stake in CHT Holdings, Ltd., UK's towel brand (UK)	NA	2006
Spentex Industries Ltd[65]	Tashkent Toytepa Tekstil, Ltd. (Uzbekistan)	81 million USD	2006
Winson Yarns	Acquired unit (Italy)	5 million USD	2006
S. Kumars	Acquired America Pacific (US)	USD90 million	2006

Source: Collated from the author's "Database of Business Strategies Events."

investments on textile machinery."[66] Many companies adopted online quality monitoring through IT programs such as Enterprise Resource

[65] Around the same time, Spentex also increased its equity in Indorama to 84.02, expanding its presence in both man-made and cotton fibers.
[66] "Textile Units Get IT Savvy," *Business Standard*, January 19, 2007.

Planning (ERP).[67] Complex product mixes and innovative designs require such IT infrastructure. Companies began to invest large amounts in such technologies. Sutlej Industries invested Rs. 5 crores (approx. USD1 million) to install IT equipment with the help of IBM. Internet connectivity also became more common in an industry used to traditional technologies.[68]

Technical Textiles, anticipated to be a USD4 billion segment in India (global value was expected to be USD107 billion), emerged as a new area of growth, and some companies moved into this nascent area in order to capture the high value-added markets, which was anticipated both by the government and by other experts.[69] The government also sought to provide some support (see Chapter 7). Training of labor to ensure new skills in the changed scenario became important. Many companies began to hire people with skills like logistics, FMCGs, and courier services, as well as top management people from diverse sectors.[70] The government hired foreign consultants to help train labor from South Africa and Sri Lanka.[71] Industry associations, like the Apparel Export Promotion Council, proposed the setting up of R&D centers with the support of the government.[72] Yet, a huge investment shortfall in R&D funds was also apparent. As late as June 2010, a study by the FICCI urged the government to strengthen technology-related aspects of the textile industry by ensuring greater investment in R&D expenditure. The business chamber recommended the creation of a National Textiles Research Council with seed money of Rs. 30 crores (approx. USD6 million) and an annual grant of Rs. 10 crores (approx. USD2 million).[73] Despite this gap, the R&D expenditure of firms increased steadily over this period (2000–2005). Figure 6.4 highlights this trend.

[67] Webopedia defines ERP as "Enterprise resource planning (ERP) is business process management software that allows an organization to use a system of integrated applications to manage the business and automate many back office functions related to technology, services and human resources. ERP software integrates all facets of an operation, including product planning, development, manufacturing, sales and marketing." See the following website, accessed, July 6, 2014, www.webopedia.com/TERM/E/ERP.html.
[68] Ibid.
[69] "Firms Find a Lucrative Venture in Weaving Technical Textiles," *Indian Express*, April 12, 2006. Technical textiles are used in the medical industry (surgical gowns, bandages, and plasters), agriculture (fishing nets, woven and nonwoven covers for crops), automobile sectors, and engineering. The government also introduced new policies to support the growth of the sector. In 2009–2010, a new technology mission for technical textiles was launched. See www.texmin.nic.in/policy/policy_scheme.htm.
[70] "Textile Sector Takes New Spin on Hiring," *Economic Times*, May 23, 2006.
[71] "Ministry to Hire Foreign Consultants to Train Manpower in Textile Sector," *Financial Express*, January 9, 2006. Also see "Textile Sector Takes New Spin on Hiring," *Economic Times*, May 23, 2006.
[72] www.textileintelligence.com/mumbai/1109.html?aid=1109.
[73] "Need to Formulate R&D Policy for Textile Industry: Study," *Business Standard*, June 23, 2010.

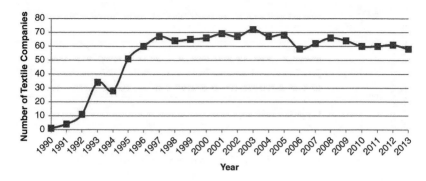

Figure 6.4 Total numbers of Textile Companies investing in R&D
Author's Calculations from CMIE Prowess Database, 1990–2014.

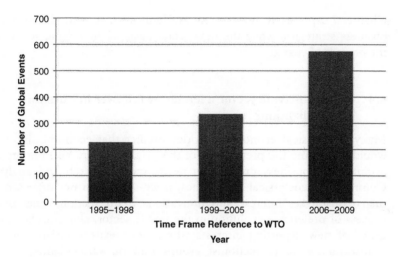

Figure 6.5 Global activities of textile firms
Source: Author's Business Activities and Strategies Database,
1994–2011.
Note: Global Activities includes mergers and acquisitions, joint
ventures, export plans, new investment and R&D investment

Global activities, including mergers and acquisitions, joint ventures,
export-oriented plans, new investment, and R&D investment, increased
after 2003–2004. Figures 6.5 and 6.6 map the move of textile firms to the
global level in terms of their combined business strategies. The regroup-
ing of the data according to the global regime time frame shows the clear
effect of the MFA's abolition on Indian firms' global strategies.

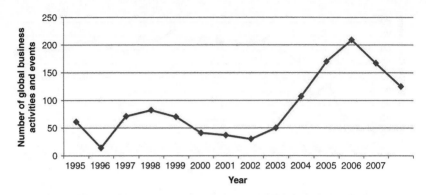

Figure 6.6 Number of global business activities and events
Author's "Business Activities and Strategies Database, 1994–2011."

Chapter 7 explores the reasons and mechanisms that led to the change in business strategies, while the next section asks if the private sector led the process of change.

6.4   Is the private sector a leader or follower in pursuing globalization?

Many neoclassical economic theories predict that economic interests would determine the preferences of the private sector. Yet, the precise evolution of business preferences needs more research and analysis. Contrary to neoclassical approaches, price signals do not offer a clear map of businesses' interests and motivations. In this section, I analyze the process of preference evolution in the textile sector, charting the emergence of new exporting interests where none existed before and the transformation of protectionist groups into outward-oriented actors. Importantly, this process is not a simple translation of economic interests, as political factors play a role in these transformations.

Business actors in the declining textile sector were uncertain and risk averse, even as they faced a different global environment in the 1990s. Their ability to adjust and their willingness to accept the costs of reform depended on the domestic policy regime and the Indian government's ability to reform itself. In the absence of domestic policy change, the industry actors adopted a wait-and-watch attitude. Once they had sufficient stability of expectations, they adjusted radically, and the reform process became more sustainable.[74] The striking conclusion that emerges

[74] For a similar analysis of reform and business in Brazil, see Kingstone (1999).

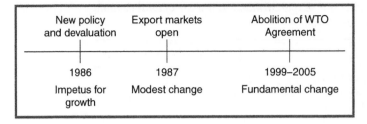

New policy and devaluation	Export markets open	Abolition of WTO Agreement
1986	1987	1999–2005
Impetus for growth	Modest change	Fundamental change

Figure 6.7 Timeline of business shifts

from Section 6.3 is that external factors were the crucial catalyst that changed the priorities of many industry actors. As noted by Nikhil Sen, senior GM of finance and strategy for Gujarat Heavy Chemical, Ltd. (GHCL): "Actually, the foray abroad helps us in expansion of manufacturing capacities, exposure to newer markets, and better design talent."[75]

Business was stimulated to shift its foci and priorities in two distinct periods: 1986–1990 and 1999–2005.[76] In both periods, the textile industry changed its interests in anticipation of international changes, but it did not anticipate or drive the changes. It was led; it did not lead. Change during the second phase was deeper: the dismantling of the final phase of quotas not only changed the calculations of many firms but also created new firms with new interests both in expanding domestic markets and in diversifying into export markets. The process of preference transformation was also mediated by a domestic policy shift, which was driven by external changes. How did private sector preferences evolve over time? Figure 6.7 outlines the evolution in a schematic way, and the rest of the section elaborates on this evolution.

Two different impulses, one originating from the external realm and the other from the onerous domestic policy regime, played roles in shifting business strategies. The first stimulus for change started in the mid tolate 1980s, when large and capable firms began shifting to exports. Both push and pull factors played a role in that shift. In the early 1980s, the textile industry had reached the peak of its crisis, symbolized by pervasive sickness and the infamous strike of 1982–1983 that paralyzed the industry. The restrictive policy regime forced some large firms into exports, which required better technologies. Combined with macroeconomic changes, such as the devaluation of the Indian currency, the expansion of export markets in the 1980s created new demands at home, which fueled further expansion and

---

[75] "Textile Brands Sew Up Global Dreams," *Economic Times*, June 29, 2006.
[76] For a similar argument about the two different historical periods, see Roy (2010) and Bedi (2002).

Table 6.6 *Export demand as a share of total demand for textile goods*

Year	Export Share in Final Demand (%)
1985–1986	11.3
1986–1987	15.1
1987–1988	19.8
1988–1989	17.9
1989–1990	22.1
1990–1991	21.8
1991–1992	26.2
1992–1993	27.1
1993–1994	29.3
1994–1995	32.3
1995–1996	28.1

Source: Drawn from table 3.2 of Roy (2004, 89)

technological innovation, although among a very small number of large-scale firms (Roy 1996b; Bedi and Cororaton 2008). Roy shows how the increase of export markets had definite impacts on the domestic market. He argues, "Briefly, exports created new capacity which in turn induced change of taste" (Roy 1996b, 7).[77] Between 1985 and 1995, exports increased significantly. A few firms began to build "new ties with buyers and suppliers at home and abroad in the late 1980s and early 1990s" (Tewari 2005, 5). Notably, while "new corporate entities have entered textiles in the form of specialized spinners or weavers," the "divisions within the mill sector between obsolete and efficient, profitable and bankrupt, private and public have hardened with the transformation of *a small set of mills into premier fabric exporters*" (Roy 1996b, 8; emphasis added). As recognized by a number of scholars, these changes extend only to a small set of firms and do not yet force massive technological changes and are export led. Table 6.6 maps the increase in export demand from 1985 to 1995.

In the 1980s to 1990s, the story of Century Textiles and Industries, Bombay Dyeing, Mafatlal, and Piramal, a few prominent business houses in the textile sector, is a story of a shift to high-count finer yarn products, the increase in automatic looms, and product differentiation followed by building a brand and retail image and exports.

The story of Morarjee Spinning and Weaving Mills, owned by the Piramal Group, is an interesting example of the emergence of a dualistic pattern in India's textile sector and the creation of a few innovative firms

---

[77] Also see Roy (2010).

within textiles. The Ashok Piramal Group started out in 1934 with a successful textiles venture – the Morarjee Goculdas Spinning and Weaving Co., Ltd. Established in 1871, it is the oldest textile unit in the country and the fifth company to be listed on the stock exchange.[78] After the 1982 Bombay strike and after a few years of serious crisis, in 1995, it changed its strategies to producing very high-end fabrics, investing in new designing skills and limiting itself to a moderate amount of capacity.[79] It invested Rs. 2 crores (approx. USD400,000) in a new studio, which had CAD/CAM facilities, and roped in well-known designers to promote its fabrics.[80] The company decided to shift to products for which there was a world market. In the global market, the company decided to provide customers better value from the same product, for example, by providing shorter delivery times or by changing the fabric construction to reduce cost. It also established key alliances with foreign textile companies. By the 2000s, the group also diversified into other businesses, but the textile arm of this diversified group became a leading player in the premium shirt-producing fabric business and high-fashion printed-fabric business for global markets. Global alliances were key in this transformation. The shirt division was formed as a joint venture with Manifattura di Valle Brembana, a leading Italian textile company, in 1996. Mortared Textiles, Ltd. (MTL), is the first company to have successfully entered a joint venture with an Italian company for yam-dyed shirting fabric. In 2003, MTL bought Brembana's stake of 50 percent and established its own Italian company, a 100 percent subsidiary. This subsidiary – Morarjee International – is the first Indian company to have introduced a seasonal collection.

In the 1980s, Century Textiles and Industries, Ltd., a Birla company, reoriented its strategies and production processes for export and high technology.[81] It fully automated its plants by importing new machinery, a rarity in the Indian context, investing around Rs. 710 million

---

[78] Currently, the group enjoys presence in diversified business areas, viz. engineering and electronics, retail and entertainment, and real estate.

[79] Interview with Harish Piramal, www.fibre2fashion.com/face2face/pmp/mr-harsh-piram .asp. Harish Piramal: "One thing that we did was that we have significantly changed our product portfolio. We have moved to higher-end fabrics. We have got out of the commodity, stand fabrics and moved to higher count business. It is obviously higher margin but also gives a niche in the Indian market and the global market for that matter. We also set up an office for our fabrics company in Milan (Italy). So, today our designing, etc. is driven from there."

[80] Latha Jishnu, "Textiles: The Global Spin," *Business World*, September 20, 1989, pp. 18–24.

[81] I draw on Supriya Roy Chowdhury's excellent study on the textile industry for analysis of Century Textiles and Mafatlalal (1995, 238–239). Her study also documents the emergence of a dualistic pattern in the industry, where some firms restructured but many more industries became sick and closed down.

(approx. USD14 million) for that modernization. During the 1980s, this company began to produce largely for exports, to the tune of 80 percent of its sales, and changed its production profile in order to do so (producing high-quality merchandise at high prices). By producing for exports, the company could avoid capacity and price freezes. In doing so, the company made use of the government regulations to bypass the restrictions imposed on production for domestic firms.

Mafatlala Fine Spinning and Manufacturing Co., Ltd., started modernization in the post-1985 period. In 1984, the export earnings of the company were around Rs. 105 million (approx. USD2 million), but they jumped to 750 million (approx. USD15 million) in 1989. Mafatlal borrowed from the financial institutions' technological upgradation scheme to fund its modernization, which also included labor rationalization and compensation to the laid-off workers.[82]

Yet, the modest advancements in the mid- to late 1980s did not lead to real technological change or new investments. As noted by Jatidner Bedi, "The two reform periods – 1983–1990 and 1990–2005 – have different characteristics. In the first phase, there was an increase in demand due to the opening of yarn to export, which led to better utilization of spindles. However, investment was not sufficient to support the rise in demand. . . . in the second phase, the cut in excise and custom duties on textile products led to a further rise in demand. However, investment in spindles increased substantially during this period." (Bedi and Cororaton 2008, 63–64). Thus, this research shows clearly that while business reoriented to some degree, new investment was slow to materialize in the 1980s. Thus, in the mid- to late 1980s, restrictions (nonreform) led some, though not most, companies to move toward export markets, as exports were free of the domestic policy controls. Yet, most firms were stuck in old molds and not willing or able to innovate or modernize. So, in the mid-1980s, some moderate change started but did not become a trend or a strong momentum spanning all actors and segments.

The second period of reform started in the late 1990s and shows very different characteristics from the first reform period. The scale of change in business strategies was documented in Section 6.3. How did businesspeople *perceive* the impending regime shift in global rules and markets? The changing WTO regime and resulting domestic policy regime created both a sense of crisis and opportunity, directly affecting private sector preferences. At that time, pressures and opportunities presented by

---

[82] In the late 1980s, government polices encouraged exports in terms of a cash credit scheme and import of selected machinery at concessional rates.

abolition of the MFA quotas and the information revealed through various WTO negotiations led to a complex but radical policy regime change initiated by the Indian government (see Chapter 5). Starting in 1999, the government took the lead by conveying a sense of crisis, although the industry was slow to act. The sources of information were not only market based or price mediated but also disseminated by the government. For example, in 2002, the government organized the first of twenty-five educational seminars on "Quality and Compliances: Route to Global Competiveness" for the textile industry.[83]

Despite this, in 2002, the industry's mood was quite pessimistic. A prominent member of the textile industry from the South, the CEO of Lakshmi Mills Co., Ltd., G. K Sundaram, noted in 2002:

The industry has never felt more troubled than it does today. In fact, the consumer is spending less on clothing as a percent of total expenditure than ever before. Imports are surging, sickness is spreading and apprehensions about the future prospects are growing. Inspite of 5 percent interest subsidy, there are no takers for loans under the Technology Upgradation Fund Scheme.[84]

As late as 2005, many in the industry adopted a wait-and-watch attitude. As noted by a government official, "The government has extended all possible support and fiscal incentives to prepare the industry for the post-quota regime. Despite all efforts, domestic companies are not forthcoming. They are still adopting a wait and watch policy. But, we can't miss the opportunities to countries like China, Pakistan and Bangladesh."[85] Others noted in 2005 that "[t]he sector is suffering from a lack of entrepreneurship. People have resources, they have markets, and still they are watching their competitors to make the first move."[86] Explaining the caution on the part of the industry, Dr. Ahluwalia, secretary of the Northern India Textile Mills Association, explained, "Many textile mills became sick in the past, therefore the industry is cautious on the investment front."[87] As noted by a prominent officer of the Alok Industries:

Our share in the world textile trade has remained at 3.5 per cent even after removal of quota. It would be appropriate to say that we have not gained much market share as large expansions started only after December 2004 which was relatively late compared to other countries mainly China. However, now our country is ready with expanded capacities and I am quite confident that the

---

[83] "Textile Panel Seminar on WTO Today," *Times of India*, February 5, 2002.
[84] "Textile Industry Must Pick Up Threads Anew," *Telegraph*, January 29, 2002.
[85] "Booster Dose for Textiles Likely," *Economic Times*, February 25, 2005.   [86] Ibid.
[87] Ibid.

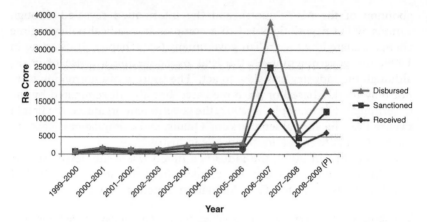

Figure 6.8 Application for investment and modernization by the textile industry, 1999–2009
Author's calculations from Technology Upgradation Scheme data available at the Ministry of Textile website.

share of Indian textile industry in world textile trade is expected to reach to about 6.50 per cent by 2014.[88]

The data of new investment proposed through the Technological Upgradation Fund Scheme in the Figure 6.8 show this delayed trend quite clearly, with new investment picking up only around 2005.

Thus, around 2002–2005, with the abolition of quotas imminent, the private sector began to realize the need for change in its market and global strategies. By 2005–2006, the changes could not be ignored. Many textile segments across the board began to adopt technological changes and capacity additions. Initially, companies were slow to respond to global market shifts, but after 2005, as signals of market-mediated shifts were reinforced by domestic policy and international changes, a positive dynamic was created for change. By 2005–2006, this change became a flood.

By 2006, government and industry had come much closer. In 2006, for example, the government organized a seminar entitled, "Strategies and Preparedness for Trade and Globalization in India in Textiles and Clothing Sector," and signed a memorandum of understanding with many industry associations so as to share information about the implications of the abolition of ATC for the textile sector.[89] Huge investments

[88] Sunil Khandelwal, CFO, Alok Industries, said this in an interview. See http://tinyurl.co m/zuxmqu7 for the interview.
[89] "Textile Panel Inks Pacts with 65 Partners," *Hindu*, May 25, 2006.

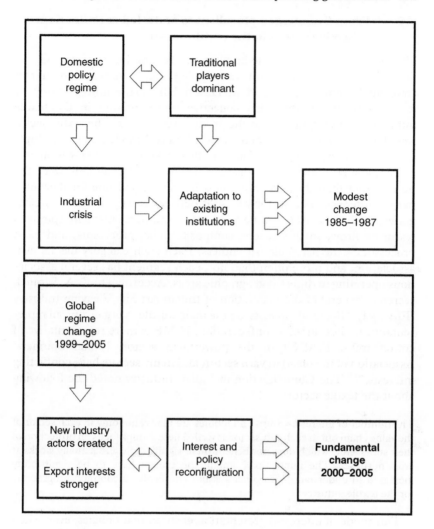

Figure 6.9 Global effects across two time periods

and reorientations happened after 2004–2005, unleashing changes in skills and technological strengths. Figure 6.9 outlines the argument. This raises a pertinent question: did these market strategies have any impact on political representation and the extent of lobbying? The next section explores the changes in the collective action witnessed in the textile industry.

6.5   From fragmented pluralism to state-led coordination: collective action in the textile sector

Until now, this chapter has focused on market and business strategies of firms. Yet, in an environment where policy shapes markets, nonmarket strategies become more important. How did the textile industry represent itself politically? Historically, collective representation in the textile industry was as fragmented as the production process. The textile sector was the archetype of the "fragmented pluralist" model, where multiple groups and interests competed and conflicted with each other without any encompassing associations. Olson's distributional coalitions were the norm rather than the exception, lobbying and mobilizing for their own narrow interests. The sector was split between a large number of categories, such as cotton spinners, blended spinners, filament spinners, texturing firms, small weavers, composite mills, processors, and hand processors – the list is almost endless. Each such category has its own association, and more often than not, each segment has several associations operating in different geographic areas. According to K. A. Samuel, secretary general of the Federation of Indian Art Silk Weaving Industry (FIASWI), "Sectoral interests are the main hurdle in organizing all representative bodies under a confederation. ICMF is more representative of cotton mills, FIASWI of the powerloom sector, Indian Spinners' Association of the blended yarn sector, and many sectors have conflicting interests."[90] The Confederation of Indian Industry noted the following about the textile sector:

The number of interests groups and lobbies are many, not only in each sector of the value chain but in each sub-sector as well. These groups focus on protection of their sub-sector, which does not benefit them significantly and actually works at cross-purposes. The interactions among the groups have to be significantly increased to understand each other's issues and evolve a common programme for the textile industry.[91]

This mode of interest representation ensured that policies, even when announced with fanfare, would be modified in an iterative process of lobbying and constant changes. The textile sector was the embodiment of Olson's (1982) argument that democracy can create a number of distributive coalitions leading to a typical collective-choice dilemma: each group pursued its own group self-interest, in the process hurting the collective interest of the textile sector as a whole. It was this dynamic that prevented the 1985 policy reforms from taking effect and being

---

[90] *Express Textile*, January 16, 2003, www.expresstextile.com/20030116/cover2.shtml.
[91] "Textile Sector Must Develop in Clusters: CII," *Hindu Business Line*, March 2, 2004.

pursued further and ensured the persistence of policies through the 1970s and 1980s. Each attempt at policy change was resisted by some association, creating a "lock-in" effect and preventing significant change.

As the government faced the prospect of quota abolition and possible anti-dumping procedures, the logic of collective action started to change. The impending threat of WTO change forced the associations to try to solve their collective action problems. In the late 1990s, the Indian government began urging the various industry associations to come together in the form of an apex body that could represent the interests of all or most of the industry elements. Clearly, the government took a lead on this.[92] In 1999, the textile secretary, Shyamlal Ghosh, proposed this idea to ICMF and other bodies.[93] The Union Textile Ministry wrote to the Indian Cotton Mills Federation (ICMF) and started nudging all textile and garment associations to come together by forming a body for all segments within the textile industry. In 2001, a couple of years after the initial suggestion, some discussions started within ICMF to form an integrated body. The ICMF began emphasizing the work of strong business associations in Taiwan and the United States – the American Textile Manufacturers Institute (ATMI) and the Taiwan Textile Federation (TTF).[94] At this time, many smaller bodies began recognizing the need for coherent action on the part of all sections of the textile value chain. Mr. Gosai of the Textile Association of India (TAI) noted around 2002–2003 that "[t]here is a definite need for the industry to come together, and the government too has made it amply clear that it is ready to consider all legitimate demands of the industry, provided the industry talks in totality, without trying to outdo each other in getting concessions and exemptions."[95] The Federation of All India Textile Manufacturers Association (FAITMA) was set up for bringing together associations within the textile machinery sector. The president of FAITMA, Arvind Poddar, noted, "FAITMA was established for the synthetic textile sector, and its basic objective was to bring together all the various small bodies representing the synthetic textiles sector. And to a large extent we have been successful."[96] According to him, bringing the entire industry together on a single platform would definitely help in getting better deals from the government, avoid the anomalies that come about in each budget, and project the strengths of the industry globally.[97] By October 2003, a steering committee of many associations

---

[92] I confirmed this from a number of different sources and interviews.

[93] This was mentioned in Paranjit Ahuja, "CII Chalks Out a 21-Point Action Programme," *Financial Express*, December 6, 1999. Also confirmed in interviews.

[94] Cited in D'Souza (2003, 12).   [95] *Express Textile*, January 16, 2003.   [96] Ibid.

[97] Ibid.

was formed to discuss the issue, revealing the coming together of divergent positions.[98] In the context of these discussions, Premal Udani, president of the Clothing Manufacturers' Association of India (CMAI), said:

There has always been a need for such an organization, and if a common minimum agenda can be agreed upon, this would be very beneficial. Today, there are too many lobbies in this industry, working against each other's interests. This needs to stop. There is a need to strengthen the RMG [ready-made garments] sector, which is the driving force for the industry. Every input, starting from the fiber, can find a huge market within the country, if the garment sector is strong. And better the quality and price of the inputs, the more competitive this sector will grow, both in the domestic and export markets.[99]

Many other associations were skeptical, noting that no one association would be able to break the collective action vicious cycle unless the government took some initiative. Some were worried about the big players, like Reliance, dominating any such organization.[100] M. K. Panthaki, director of the Clothing Manufacturers' Association of India (CMAI), observed: "Instead, the office of the textile commissioner could probably set up a separate wing for the purpose. The textile commissioner could hear the views of the industry, hold discussions, and interact with the ministry, on behalf of the industry as a whole."[101]

Global trade rules played a major role in these discussions. C. S. Gokhale of Reliance Industries noted, "The industry has to unite if it wants to survive. International trade barriers – anti-dumping, anti-subsidy, countervailing investigations, etc., are bound to increase in the future, and not many in this industry know how to handle these. A common federation would result in pooling of resources, skills, knowledge, and fighting the cases in a unified manner."[102] The president of the Clothing Manufacturers Association of India (CMAI), Mr. Udani, said, "Even as garments have not been targeted for anti-dumping and such other actions, this could well happen in the future. Moreover, India could become a dumping ground for cheap imported garments, and we have to protect our domestic market too. This is where a common federation

---

[98] Members included Santee Saran, past chairman of the SRTEPC and head of the export panel PDEXCIL; R. L. Toshniwal, president of the Indian Spinners' Association; Arvind Poddar, president of FAITMA; Chintan Parikh, president of ICMF; V. K. Bhartia, chairman of IWMF; Bharat Desai; Rameshbhai Gajjar; Arunbhai Jariwala; V. S. Chalke; and Jain of the Oswal Group.

[99] *Express Textile*, October 1–15, 2003.

[100] Interview with author, January 4, 2011, New Delhi.   [101] Ibid.

[102] *Express Textile*, October 2, 2003; Mr. Gokhale was the president of corporate development at Reliance. See www.expresstextile.com/20031002/coverstory01.shtml.

would be very beneficial."[103] Despite this emerging consensus, the opposition against uniting remained strong, and these debates went on for many years. Internal documents reveal that each organization worried that its viewpoint would be reduced if it included other groups.[104] Finally, on December 28, 2004, faced with the immediate full integration on January 1, 2005, the ICMF transformed itself into the Confederation of Indian Textile Industry (CITI), noting:

The Federation felt the need to convert itself into an umbrella organization representing all the segments of the textile and clothing sector of India including cotton mills, man-made spinning and weaving units, woolen mills, units manufacturing garments, and all such other units which are in production of textile and allied goods. On the basis of extensive consultations within the industry, we changed the name of The Indian Cotton Mills' Federation to "Confederation of Indian Textile Industry (CITI)" in 2005, in order to represent the broad-based membership of the organization. ... The need for an apex body representing the entire textile and clothing sector had been felt by the industry for quite some time and it is after extensive efforts that different segments of the industry could come together and form CITI. Formation of such an apex body will help us to project the textile and clothing sector properly to the domestic and international consumers and to have a coordinated approach to all national and international developments affecting the sector.[105]

CITI includes all the twelve member associations of the erstwhile ICMF as regular members and the Indian Spinners Association (ISA), Tirupur Exporters Association (TEA), Federation of Indian Textile Engineering Industry (FITEI), Indian Woolen Mills Federation (IWMF), Powerloom Development and Export Promotion Council (PDEXCIL), Clothing Manufacturers Association of India (CMAI), and Narrow Elastic Manufacturers Association of India (NEMAI) as associate members.

Global trade rules had a clear impact on the need for such mobilization to take place. A news report noted, "The federation pointed out that while different sub-segments of the industry can afford to represent their own views to the government directly, the WTO doesn't entertain representations unless the concerned trade association represents at least a fourth of the capacity/production of the product in question."[106] The government had urged the associations to come together as a result of the WTO requirement that an anti-dumping duty can only be contested by those associations that represent 25 percent of a particular industry (D'Souza

[103] *Express Textile*, October 2, 2003, www.expresstextile.com/20031002/coverstory01.shtml.
[104] Confidential documents of the associations, available from author.
[105] www.citiindia.com/about_us.asp.
[106] www.allbusiness.com/manufacturing/textile-product-mills/1069389-1.html.

2003, 31). Thus, collective representation became more coherent and encompassing after it was threatened by global competition. The threat was organized in the form of specific procedural requirements of the WTO.

6.6   Conclusion

Most observers of the India's rising global profile focus on its technology industries such as software and pharmaceuticals. Yet, the story of India's textile firms is even more revolutionary, even though a quiet one. The political economy logic in India's textile sector tended toward an inward, domestic-driven structure, increasing protectionism and defensiveness. The global regime in textiles also encouraged "patchwork protectionism" (Friman 1990) within countries, although different countries reacted differently to such predispositions. Yet, in the 2000s, the map of textile firms changed dramatically. Textile firms started investing in massive expansion plans, and technological modernization started across the whole supply chain. Global alliances and mergers became quite common. In this chapter, I have analyzed the evolution of private sector preferences and strategies and the role played by abolition of MFA regime combined with domestic policy changes on those preferences. Export markets in the 1980s provided the first impetus for change, which was magnified by the changes initiated by the domestic state in anticipation of the global regime changes in 1999–2000. The industrial map of the textile sector was completely transformed by 2014.

Were the winners from the changing global regime at the forefront of supporting and lobbying for such policy changes? Most industry actors perceived threats in the global realm. There is no evidence of firms or industries driving or anticipating the policy reform initiated by the government in 1999. Export-oriented firms and garment industries supported the policies once initiated, but none of them anticipated or mobilized for a change of policy. The global trade regime and the changes therein thus played a major role in shifting policy priorities and business preferences as well as changing the logic of collective action. Despite a somewhat delayed response, the textile industry adjusted coherently, revealing the multipronged effort by state as well as business actors across the whole supply chain. State and business came closer and acted in a concerted fashion to face new challenges brought about by the WTO. All in all, these changes were unexpected and quite revolutionary. The next chapter goes deeper into these changes to explore the global and mechanisms that created the impetus for such shifts.

7   Mechanisms of change within global markets

In the 2000s, the Indian private sector turned away from inward-oriented strategies and sought global reach. Firms accustomed to domestic protections and privileges learned to leverage new skills as well as expand into new markets. Insular Indian businesses started exporting new products into new markets, producing in diverse locations, and investing in wider regions of the world. Indian companies diversified beyond exporting traditional goods, such as gems and jewelry, to manufactured goods and new value-added segments of traditional goods such as garments and technical textiles.[1] These diverse strategies demanded new investment, expansion, and technological modernization, as well as new global alliances. Chapters 4, 5, and 6 documented many such strategies and reorientations across Indian pharmaceutical and textile sectors, where Indian companies were inserted into global supply chains in new ways. The evidence presented in these chapters resonates with a larger body of literature that documents diverse types of internationalization strategies across emerging nations.[2] Yet, we lack a deeper understanding of the distinct *mechanisms* that *change* business motivations and strategies. Why and how did internationalization begin among industrial actors that were more acclimated to an environment with domestic protections and privileges? A second, related puzzle is equally compelling: which mechanisms propelled the private sector toward global markets and led it to design strategies of expansion and technological change? Were market-mediated factors (voluntary price-mediated exchange or competition) the primary channels of change in Indian business strategies?

---

[1] Technical textiles are a specialized type of textiles used in medical, automobile, and engineering industries.

[2] Here I provide only a selective sample. For a more comprehensive list of studies, see footnotes in Chapter 4 and 6. Mathews (2006) discusses "accelerated internationalization" across emerging market firms. Studies of the pharmaceutical sector include Kale and Little (2007), Chittoor and Ray (2007), Rai (2008), and Athreye, Kale, and Ramani (2009). For the textile sector, see Tewari (2008) and Roy (2010a and 2010b).

The assertion that globalization strengthens market-mediated behavior is grossly incomplete in that it fails to recognize the pervasive role of nonmarket mechanisms in interaction with market effects. Globalization embodies rules and institutions (constraining elements) that involve legitimate and legal coercion (international standards, for example) as well as the need for public information and learning through cooperative (not merely competitive) means. This effect of global rules in supplementing the power of markets and providing public information to economic actors such as firms and multinationals needs to be analyzed more systematically. This chapter disproves the idea that market-mediated and competition mechanisms alone drove Indian private business forays into the global world. Adopting a microfoundational approach to globalization, I demonstrate the role of distinct nonmarket mechanisms in shaping business responses to a global market. Three such nonmarket mechanisms – public information, learning, and threats – are analyzed with a combination of quantitative and qualitative techniques. I created and constructed an original database that maps business strategies and codes the mechanisms and motivations of such strategies. The study of mechanisms requires detailed research of specific companies and specific sectors as they interact with specific international regimes.[3] Thus, while disaggregating the effect of globalization into its different mechanisms, I also pay attention to differential responses by different types of firms – textile vs. pharmaceutical, small vs. large, proactive globalizers and reluctant globalizers – through case studies, interviews, and quantitative analyses.

7.1   The terrain of the debate and the argument in brief

Can we say something cogent about "the varying logics and degrees of influence" (Bernstein and Cashore 2000, 74) that *different* global mechanisms have on markets and business strategies? Mostly, the outward orientation of business is attributed, in a bundled manner, to globalization. The globalization literature tends to conflate global market mechanisms, rules of the game, and discourse-level effects.[4] Such conflation is misleading for our understanding of sources of business preferences, the dynamics of change, and private sector effects. In the political economy literature, the key mechanism identified is how a change in prices affects the relative power of economic cleavages such as

---

[3] Many international relations scholars recognize the necessity of case study research when analyzing the effect of mechanisms: Cao (2009, 1,101); Bennett (2004, 38); Sprinz and Wolinsky-Nahmias (2004).
[4] Bernstein and Cashore (2000) and Prakash and Hart (2000) also make these distinctions.

classes and sectors (Frieden 2002; Rogowski 1989). Yet, business behavior on the ground also reveals the role of nonprice and regulatory mechanisms, what Baron has termed as the "non-market environment" (Baron 1999). Less well understood, globalization not only changes the market environment but also creates new rules and modifies the regulatory environment for the private sector. Usually, a move toward global markets creates high cost for firms, but what is less well understood is that the nonmarket context of globalization also creates complexity and uncertainty for businesses; they must adopt internationalization strategies in a fast-changing and multidimensional global environment. It is time that our analytical models account for such uncertainty and complexity and we integrate the role of nonmarket mechanisms in our understanding of industrial change and globalization.

While the dominant view is that competition drives companies' and nations' behavior in trade (Simmons, Dobbin, and Garrett 2008, 47), a few management scholars have recognized the role of nonmarket factors in shaping business decisions and argue for more research on the subject (Peng et al. 2008; Ramamurti 2004). Athreye, Kale, and Ramani (2009, 1), for example, argue that "radical regulatory changes can be tantamount to technological revolutions".[5] Issue-specific studies of the patent regime or the textile regime also pay attention to different types of regulatory effects (Shadlen 2007).

What do I mean by nonmarket mechanisms and effects? How important are such nonmarket mechanisms? Let me provide some examples. Threats from anti-dumping actions by the European Union (a threat or coercion mechanism) mobilized Indian industry more than a change in price signals, as it was more concentrated and targeted. The use of dumping procedures demanded new roles for the state and private sector across many countries.[6] Global standards and restrictive rules to enforce such standards did more to change business strategies than purely market incentives. As an illustration, a large number of companies voluntarily subscribe to the Global Organic Textile Standard (GOTS), which encompasses the entire postharvest textile value chain made with organic fiber.[7] India, for example, introduced its own national certification

---

[5] Few scholars in business studies make this argument. The conventional view supports a firm-level "resource-centric" view of business strategies.

[6] The solar panels dispute between a German company and Chinese firms is illustrative. The EU anti-dumping procedures and diplomacy between China and Germany all come into play in this dispute, revealing how nonprice factors have become important. See Kathrin Hille and Joshua Chaffin, "Merkel Urges Diplomacy to Resolve Solar Trade Panels with Beijing," *Financial Times*, August 31, 2012.

[7] See the Web page of Global Organic Textile Standard (GOTS), accessed June 25, 2014, www.global-standard.org/.

standard to converge with international standards but with greater legal authority to nudge its own companies toward those global standards.[8] Such nonmarket mechanisms do change the competitive environment for firms. What must be acknowledged, however, is the fact that they create not only new regulatory costs but also new opportunities for the private sector as compliance with such regulations allows firms to explore new markets that would not have been possible earlier.

How can we identify the effect of such nonprice mechanisms on business action? The fields of political science and international relations should have special advantages in contributing to this recently emerging debate about how the institutional environment, international organizations, and business strategy may "co-evolve."[9] The literature on international organizations and compliance focuses on nonprice global mechanisms, such as conditionality, socialization, and material incentives enjoyed by international organizations. Most arguments in this literature focus on effects on state actors; we need more fine-grained and comparative studies of nonprice mechanisms' effects on the private sector.[10] Three such mechanisms, (1) *public information* about *future* markets and global standards, (2) *threats* from competitors and *coercion* through global standards, and (3) *learning* through joint ventures and new alliances, proved crucial. The changing international environment is complex, variable, and uncertain, thus demanding new ways of collecting information and new learning modes. Information is gained through public discussion and communication, not merely through price signals. Even in the world of decentralized markets and private action, interdependent action and learning from competitors and collaborators (e.g. joint ventures) play a crucial role. Threats are as salient in the world of rational businesspeople as among states in mobilizing and upgrading capacity. In fact, threats and crises do more to focus and change industry's mind than a vague sense of future market opportunities and competition. Comprehensive empirical analysis of these mechanisms is

---

[8] "Organic Textile Exports to Touch Rs. 1,500 Crores in FY13," *Business Standard*, August 19, 2012.

[9] The term "co-evolve" is used by Ramamurti (2004). For a project that focuses on similar questions, see Prakash and Hart (1999; 2000).

[10] A body of literature in international relations examines diffusion but mostly focuses on diffusion and learning by states. See the special issue of the journal *International Organization*, Fall 2006, for four such articles, all of which focus on policy: Swank (2006), Elkins, Guzman, and Simmons (2006), Simmons, Dobbin, and Garrett (2006), and Lee and Strang (2006). Recent research has also begun to focus on other political actors and groups (Kelley 2004). A small body of work looks at private actors and business actors (Haufler 2003; Thacker 2000).

absent in the current literature, even when scholars articulate the logic of some mechanisms.[11] This chapter addresses this lacuna.

7.2   Market-mediated or policy- and rule-mediated effects?

What are the determinants for a turn toward global markets? This chapter makes two main points about the sources of changing business strategies. First, building on Frieden (1999), preferences and business strategies must be kept separate from "characteristics of the strategic setting" (Frieden 1999, 39). This is especially important in tracing the causal effect of the environment on the strategies of firms. As far as I know, no scholar has empirically sought to assess the claim about the differential effects of business strategies versus the environment. In this chapter, I map out that difference empirically for Indian textile and pharmaceutical firms. Second, we need to be explicit about the different sources and mechanisms that may drive business strategies. In my argument, we must be able to identify the mechanisms that cause different strategies within the larger environment. So a clear distinction needs to be made between *strategies of firms* and the motivations *that drive those strategies*. This is so because the same strategy can be driven by different motivations, or viceversa, given the changing institutional context. For example, market share can be increased by efficiency or cost cutting but also greater global integration, which may demand new expansion and increased costs. The same goal – market expansion – can thus be achieved through contradictory strategies of either cost cutting or expansion.

This chapter further argues that it is important to distinguish between market-mediated business strategies and rule-mediated business responses. While market- and non-market-mediated actions are inextricably combined in the real world, analyzing them in a disaggregated way will enable us to analyze the separable effects of market-mediated and rule-mediated mechanisms and assess how they are linked together. In the business strategy literature, less attention is paid to rule-mediated effects, such as those originating from the WTO and the European Union, or to how state and political factors shape the internationalization of firms (Pradhan and Sauvant 2010, 16).[12] This gap is being addressed to some extent in recent scholarship. Pederson analyzes the role of "nonmarket mechanisms, especially those related to home country public

---

[11] Simmons, Dobbin, and Garrett (2008) discuss learning and its potential effects on policies of states but not on markets or private actors. Very few empirical studies of the role of public information or learning on markets and private action exist in the prevailing literature.

[12] Also see the rest of the chapters in Sauvant et al. (2010).

Table 7.1 *Mechanisms driving business strategy*

Level at Which They Operate ⇒ Mechanisms ⇓	Domestic	Global
Market mediated	Domestic market Competition Search for new markets Efficiency seeking	Global economic pressure Currency fluctuations Import surges Search for global markets
Policy or rule mediated	Welfare Compensation for losers Public policy incentive[13] Improve sector competitiveness through public policy	WTO/EU rules Trade disputes Anti-dumping actions Global and EU standards

policies" for outward FDI from India (Pedersen 2010, 58). Thus, we need to assess whether markets (competition) or global rules and policy are the main factor shaping business responses. International regulations, such as those arising from the WTO regarding trade, might remove barriers to trade and exchange, but they also create new markets (for patents, for example) or embed markets in new rules and standards. Broadly, a simple two-by-two table in Table 7.1 captures four mechanisms' impacts on business behavior. This analysis allows me to distinguish between the logic of and influence exercised by different domestic and global forces. I start by providing some evidence about the effect of market-based effects versus policy- or rule-driven mechanisms on firm-level strategy for Indian textile firms. Then I go on to differentiate between domestic versus global sources of both market- and rule-based strategies.

How may we identify market-mediated effects so that we can distinguish them from rule- or policy-mediated effects? I define market-mediated effects in terms of price- or competition-driven effects. If a business responds to competitive pressure and other market conditions, such as currency fluctuations and price changes, then the mechanisms are market mediated. I identified four main market strategies: search for new domestic markets, cost-cutting- or efficiency-driven strategies, new skills and technology-seeking strategies, and search for new global markets

[13] "Public policy incentive" refers to Indian government's policy effort to change the sector. I coded two types of news: (1) new policies, or new intention for policies, announced by the government and (2) public policy needed, which is mostly editorial or opinion articles arguing that a change in textile sector needs policy support.

Table 7.2 *Market-mediated and rule-based business actions in the textile sector*

Year	Market-Mediated Actions (% of Total Events in that Year)	Rule-Mediated Actions (% of Total Events in that Year)	Mixed Action (% of Total Events in that Year [Both Rule and Market Mediated])
1995	36	71.8	1.7
1996	16.6	74.6	3.6
1997	30.5	63.5	3.3
1998	26.2	70.8	1.4
1999	16.4	64.1	19.4
2000	14.8	63.8	21.2
2001	32.2	42.3	25.4
2002	17.6	47.0	33.3
2003	20.2	53.1	27.8
2004	32.5	44.9	22.4
2005	23.0	29.3	47.6
2006	19.6	80.3	0
2007	64.3	27.8	7.8
2008	38.2	56.1	5.6
2009	31.5	66.0	2.3
2010	45.1	52.0	2.7

Source: Author's Database of Business Events and Strategies, 1994–2010.

(global strategies) to gain a market edge. Examples of such strategies in the case of the textile sector are domestic market competition on account of entry of new competitors, import pressure or surges, currency fluctuations, and global market competition with the entry of new players such as China. I code and collect data on these strategies in this section (see Tables 7.2 and 7.3).

While the era of the regulatory state saw many nonprice instruments that shaped and interfered with markets, globalization, it was argued, would be dominated by market considerations, such as competition and efficiency, driven by market competition from aboard. However, as is being recognized by some studies of firms and businesses, "market-based action" hides more than it reveals. Businesses are affected by many other mechanisms, such as coercion, threat, information and learning, that deserve analysis and new empirical data (Thatcher 2007). For example, market strategies must consider decisions about not only what and how much to produce but also which markets to move into. This decision about location brings in questions about political risk and institutions. Globalization, especially global rules, makes such decisions more complex and rule mediated. For example,

Table 7.3 *Share of actions at global vs. domestic levels in the textile sector*

	Global	Domestic	Domestic and Global
1995	29.3	58.6	11.9
1996	46.3	47.1	3.6
1997	75.4	13.5	7.6
1998	81.0	13.8	5.1
1999	86.5	13.4	0.0
2000	87.2	12.7	0.0
2001	77.9	16.9	1.6
2002	96.0	1.6	0.0
2003	55.6	18.9	18.9
2004	88.7	10.1	1.1
2005	89.6	6.3	0.7
2006	81.8	10.9	0.0
2007	80.8	10.4	9.5
2008	83.1	12.3	0.0
2009	77.9	16.2	5.8
2010	79.1	14.5	6.9

Source: Author's Database on Business Strategies and Events, 1994–2010.

businesses from countries that did not want to accept the rules regarding patenting could only sell to unregulated and unpatented markets. Indian pharmaceutical companies that lived under a process patent regime mostly sold to markets in Africa and the Soviet Union rather than the United States. Clearly, market-based motivations – export seeking or skill seeking – are not the only drivers of a change in business strategies and orientations.

What are rule-mediated mechanisms? Almost all actions of firms are with an eye toward increasing market share, but some of those decisions are refracted through the rule-based aspects of global and domestic regulation. As an illustration, in 2004, many firms and textile manufactures sought to change their ways of doing business, and they specifically attributed this change to the anticipation of abolition of textile quotas at the end of 2004. For example, an official noted, "We are looking at integrating the supply chain of fashion. Textiles will be our prime export driver along with IT. Unless we nurture a base of talented designers, *we can't hope to fight in the quota-free regime*" (emphasis added).[14] This suggests

[14] "Textile to Be Main Export Driver: Shahnawaz," *National Herald*, February 4, 2004.

that apart from new market opportunities, the presence or absence of a quota system, a rule-mediated mechanism, does shape business decisions. Such distinctions need to be quantified and analyzed more systematically as the conventional assumption is that globalization is driven by market-mediated mechanisms.

7.2.1   Data coding and creation

A discussion of data creation and codification may be necessary here. I defined and coded market mechanisms in terms of the following reasons and motivations: when a company faces and deals with *competition and new competitors, a proactive search for new markets, cost cutting, and efficiency-reducing measures, seeking new strategies of capital and debt – I coded that as market mediated.* Global market mechanisms need separate assessment and analysis. Most firms are price takers and may be affected by different types of global events such as *import surges, cheap imports, and economic pressures such as currency fluctuations.* Price changes at the global level can lead to market surges. Firms seek global markets and need to adopt different kinds of *export strategies.* Each of these strategies and impulses was categorized as market-mediated strategies in the database. Changes or shifts in business strategies were the focus of attention. Coding was carefully calibrated to assess the underlying business motivations. So I identified the *reason* for a search for new markets, and where information was not available, those events were excluded from the analysis.

What were the observable implications of policy-mediated effects? Policy-mediated and rule-based mechanisms were analyzed in terms of efforts by firms to take advantage of policy incentives or deal with such issues as welfare demands and government regulations and restrictions. Both incentives and restrictions originating from government or public policy at the national level are coded. Rule-mediated effects become much more salient when originating from the external sources as they affected the export potential of firms. During the GATT era, tariff barriers were the policy-mediated constraint faced by firms. After 1995, many WTO agreements directed specific laws and changes in domestic procedures to ensure compliance. I coded such requirements as rule-mediated requirements of the WTO. Any regulations originating from the European Union or other countries (German environment regulations, for example), as well as voluntary standards, which were stated by the firm to be the reason for a change in strategy, were analyzed as rule-driven business responses. Trade disputes about quotas or any other trade matter were categorized as a rule-mediated mechanism.

Global or bilateral standards and anti-dumping actions were also part of the rule-mediated effect originating from the global level.

What is anti-dumping? The WTO states that "[i]f a company exports a product at a price lower than the price it normally charges on its own home market, it is said to be 'dumping' the product."[15] Anti-dumping actions are initiated by governments of the receiving country and target the products of the country where the dumping action is alleged to be coming from. I coded all anti-dumping actions, as well as nontariff barriers initiated by governments, as policy mediated. For example, statements such as the following were coded as rule mediated: "Garment Exporters Association (GEA) has urged the government to consider granting a package of tax benefits for the garment industry to enable it to meet fierce competition from China, Taiwan, and Bangladesh arising out of the complete phase-out of all export quotas by December 2004 under the WTO Agreement on Textiles and Clothing."[16] In this example, the action or strategy is seeking tax benefits, but the mechanism is clearly the onset of the Agreement on Textiles and Clothing (ATC). The extensive "Business Strategies and Events Database" allowed me a rare analysis of how market, as well as nonmarket, mechanisms shaped business motivations. Moreover, detailed information available through the database allows me to distinguish "strategy" (seeking tax benefits) from the contextual environment (mechanisms) that motivates businesses.

What do these data show? Table 7.2 maps the proportion of business actions catalyzed by purely market-based considerations versus rule- or policy-based regulations. The data show a remarkable result. Except for 2007, most actions between 1995 and 2010 were mediated by rules and procedures rather than purely market considerations.[17] Figure 7.1 shows this graphically. The opposition between state-led actions and market-led actions, a conventional way of making distinctions, is not borne out by the evidence. In 2005, when the WTO came into effect, while purely rule-based actions declined, the joint attribution to both rule- and market-based increased dramatically to 47 percent. Market-derived actions are not always easily separable from those based on rules, norms, and procedures. Paradoxically, as globalization proceeds,

---

[15] WTO's Anti-dumping Web page, accessed June 25, 2014, www.wto.org/english/tra top_e/adp_e/adp_e.htm.

[16] "Garment Exporters Want 'Clothing' from Govt. to Meet Competition," *Financial Express*, January 14, 2003

[17] The purpose of the data is not to show change over time but to show that globalization has been accompanied not by market competition but by rule-mediated actions. I computed data from 1995–2005 as the WTO came into effect during that time, and this period can be regarded as the heyday of globalization and trade liberalization.

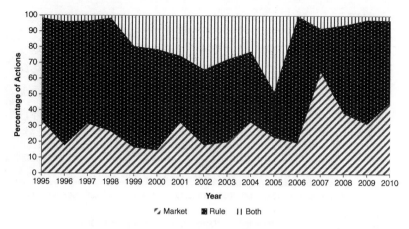

Figure 7.1 Market-based and rule-mediated actions in the textile sector
Author's "Business Activities and Strategies Database, 1994–2011."

more rules and diverse policies become more, not less, necessary. Importantly, the carriers of globalization are both market and state actors. These new data and analysis should change the way we view globalization.

Both market- and rule-mediated effects may start to take place at global or domestic levels. While action takes place in both arenas, it is worthwhile to assess where it starts and how it reverberates across levels. I distinguish global regulation, as well as global market transactions, from domestic-level actions in terms of where the levers of change come from and where regulatory action or market action takes place. Domestic action is defined in terms of the national government's policy actions or the creation of and changes in domestic or local market conditions. I coded and measured this distinction for Indian textile firms. The focus was where the impetus for action started, not where it ended. Table 7.3 and Figure 7.2 show the aggregate results. Clearly, the Indian economy was becoming quite global starting around 1997 and 1998, when global variables such as import surges, or EU regulations and WTO decisions, were as or even more important than domestic levers of change. It must be clarified that global action is not in opposition to domestic action; these data show that global stimulus is shaping different kinds of domestic responses. Making and empirically assessing this distinction allow us to assess how different aspects of globalization interact with each other.

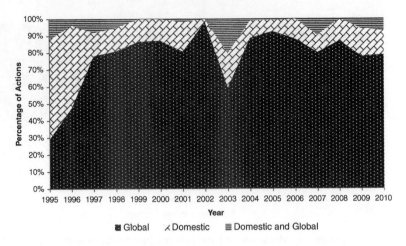

Figure 7.2 Global and domestic effects in the textile sector
Author's "Business Activities and Strategies Database, 1994–2011."

7.3   Case studies of specific mechanisms

Such aggregate analysis masks a number of important distinctions. Which specific global effects were more pronounced? I argue that an analysis of specific mechanisms and levers of change is more fruitful than the explication of such large categories as global or domestic. Business action due to global factors may work through varying micromechanisms. In the rest of this chapter, I tease out the effect of three distinct micromechanisms: *public information about markets, especially new and future markets, as well as about global standards and global regulations, threats from competitors, and the effect of coercive mechanisms such as global standards* and *learning by businesses*. Here I analyze specific cases of firms' evolution and trajectory to tease out the effect of specific mechanisms.

7.3.1   Private and public information about current and future markets

How do businesses get information about changing market trends and regulatory shifts that may affect them? Economic theory suggests that market signals in the form of prices are the main information sources for firms and economic actors. Yet, prices and market signals are decentralized and noisy, not conveying clear and stable information in an organized manner. Moreover, market shifts follow, and therefore lag behind, changes in consumer and client preferences, providing outdated pieces of information to the manager who may want to strategize ahead. As noted by the prominent industrial house Reliance, "The major challenge is about developing business strategies for capturing the expanding markets and to discern the consumer wants and preferences *before* they articulate it."[18] Market signals do not convey information about major shifts in the global market in the future, such as those ushered by the abolition or establishment of the global agreements; the Multifibre Agreement (MFA) and the Trade Related Intellectual Property Rights (TRIPS) agreement are relevant examples. As an illustration, the TRIPS agreement revealed information about the shifting nature of global markets in generics, branded generics, and the need to develop new medicines through research and development. The MFA provided information about new markets in technical textiles, the need to invest in synthetic textiles, and the need for higher volumes of products. Basically, the information about future markets required by companies, which may give them time to plan and react, is quite costly and complex.

I interviewed many businesspeople with this question in mind. I found that they get their information from a diverse set of sources.[19] WTO rules and EU trade actions, such as anti-dumping, reveal much more to business actors than market signals, which are unclear. The pharmaceutical majors revealed some interesting issues in their quest for reliable information that could form the basis of their strategies in a changing and uncertain global environment. In the early 1990s, debates about the transition to the WTO and the Dunkel Draft began to appear. Businesspeople told me repeatedly that rather than market signals, discussions during trade negotiations at the governmental level revealed much more information to industry actors about future trends and policy shifts. At that time (1990s), the Indian market was protected, and the businesspeople did not learn about the changes in pharmaceuticals, biotechnology, or new intellectual property issues through normal market channels. In that sense, the protracted process of compliance offered a lot of information about future market trends to companies. Those companies that had the vision to perceive these trends but, most important, the institutional and financial capacity to change course did so. Most crucially for my argument, it was in the process of negotiating the Dunkel Draft and TRIPS agreements and interacting with global companies that both economic and political information was revealed to many Indian companies. For example, on June 22, 1994, the PHD Chamber of Commerce and Industry published a report pointing out the need for changes in market strategies.[20] It indicated that "[i]n view

---

[18] Mr. Meswani, board member of Reliance Industries, in "Indian Textile Industry to Touch $110 Billion by 2012: Meswani," *National Herald*, January 20, 2007.
[19] Interviews are a useful methodological tool when economic theory is inconsistent with actual business practices (Bewley 1999).
[20] PHD stands for Progress, Harmony, and Development.

of the patent regime, the drug industry would have to invest considerably in R&D. The focus of the R&D would have to be on new molecules that could be used for treatment of diseases prominent in India, due to its tropical climate, like malaria, typhoid, and cholera."[21] Thus, as industry associations and analysts began to think about the future implications of the TRIPS regime, this information was revealed to industry players. Most important in the case of the TRIPS negotiations, government actors revealed some information about the impending regime in the late 1980s. A confidential interview revealed that in the late 1980s, the government had no intention of revealing to the pharmaceutical companies the fact that the government intended to sign the agreement, nor its implications for the private sector. But one official, told her senior officer that it would be good idea to have an informal meeting with the major pharmaceutical players. Although discouraged to do so, she went ahead and called in some of the big pharmaceutical companies for a discussion. They were completely unaware of the impending TRIPS agreement.[22] In the 1990s, however, the government started to reveal information about the intellectual property rights agreement more systematically through seminars and consultations with business.[23] Thus, compliance issues at the global level served the important purpose of revealing information to businesses that formed the basis of their changing strategies.

7.3.2   A product in search of a market: public information in technical textiles

Creating a market is a difficult and complex process requiring new information, incentives, and coordination. How do countries start producing new products when private players are nonexistent, market entry is costly, and information about market structures and future benefits uncertain? In such situations, the role of public information becomes important in creating new markets and conveying knowledge about market size, demand, incentives, or the nature of supply.[24] Moreover, new products demand coordination and the coming together of incentives, information, and governmental action.

Technical textiles, a specialized strand of textiles, was one such product whose market was virtually nonexistent in India. What are technical

---

[21] "Product-Wise Drug Control Not Relevant after GATT," *Economic Times*, June 22, 1994.
[22] Confidential interview with a government official, Geneva 2005.
[23] Author's database, "Policy and Institutions Events Database, 1990–2011."
[24] Morris and Shin (2002) provide a theoretical argument about the conditions under which public information becomes important.

textiles? They are textiles used in medical, automotive, and industrial fields. India met only 1 percent of its domestic demand for technical textiles as late as 2004. The Sathyam Committee Report of 1999 pointed to the potential of technical textiles in India. However, something more substantial was needed, as there was no information or market infrastructure for a whole range of products related to industrial and technical fields. Importantly, the state played a major role in finding and disseminating information, creating demand, and creating a basic framework for this new product, as well as in home textiles (bed sheets, towels, curtains, and upholstery). The government had an ambitious plan: "The implementation of the recommendations of the committee and initiation of the proposed action plan would unleash the investment to the extent of Rs. 10,000 to Rs. 15,000 crore [approx. USD2–3 billion] during the next few years and India will be able to emerge as one of the technical economies to be reckoned with in the international scenario."[25] In 2004, the government set up an "expert committee" to evaluate the prospects for technical textiles in India. This report generated new information about a new product and clearly recognized the challenges in creating new markets:

Entrepreneurship in technical textiles is an essential prerequisite for promotion of technical textiles in India. Entrepreneurship in technical textiles demand simultaneous *development of products and of their markets with proven performance and cost effectiveness*. Entrepreneurship in technical textiles involves challenges in terms of selecting raw materials, machineries, processes and product evaluation and testing to stringent specifications. At the same time, *it demands creating markets through constant interaction with users segment to accept the product*. Simultaneously the entrepreneur is required to move with the emerging textile technologies and exploring ever-increasing application of technical textiles. For the Indian Entrepreneur in particular, he has to gain ground lost in the last two decades. He has to compete with Multi-National Companies having strength of expertise and experience in technical textiles for two decades with full financial muscle strength. With this background, although technical textiles are effective tools for value addition, entrepreneurs in India face an unusual and high degree of risk in the initial phase of five to eight years, depending on the criticality of products and their applications.[26]

In order to create a new market in technical textiles, the government realized the need to define and specify the basic elements of this product line and assess both the current and future (potential) market size. The government defined it in the following manner: "Technical textiles are defined as textile materials and products used primarily for their technical performance and functional properties rather than their aesthetic or

[25] Ministry of Textiles (2004, ii).   [26] Ministry of Textiles (2004, 157), emphasis added.

decorative characteristics. Other terms used for defining technical textiles include industrial textiles, functional textiles, performance textiles, engineering textiles, invisible textiles and hi-tech textiles."[27] Most of the technical textiles use synthetic fibers rather than cotton, an area where India was quite weak. The government report defined the scope of potential demand, new investment required in the future, and started to create new incentives and rules that would be necessary to encourage new investment and new players. The government revealed that the global market for technical textiles would be quite large: USD127 billion by 2010. Raw materials in technical textiles include polyester, citron and viscose fiber in various combinations, nylon, polypropylene, polyethylene, and jute and coir. As for international demand, the government noted:

The trends in the various sectors in the textile industry in many industrialized countries indicate that the use of conventional textiles has reached a static level and its manufacture has become highly competitive, often unviable, and many companies are switching over to value-added technical textiles with capability to meet functional demands for precision applications. As use of technical textiles is dictated by need, its pricing normally offers good margins. There is a steady growth of both consumption and production of technical textiles throughout the world.[28]

It further noted, "A view is gaining ground that technical textile industry in the developed world is maturing in some significant ways and growth of technical textiles in developed economies is expected to be moderate. In contrast, China, India, and other countries in Asia, America and Eastern Europe are expected to experience healthy growth in the near future."[29] The government tried to map the "market size" of each subsector segment, such as Meditech (medical), Mobiletech (automotive industry), Agrotech (agriculture, horticulture, and forestry), Buildtech (building and construction), Geotech (geotextiles and civil engineering), Hometech (home furnishings), and Indutech (industrial applications), by providing detailed information about each segment in terms of market potential, investment required, and raw materials needed. The report recommended modifying the Technological Modernization Fund Scheme (TUFS) with special and enhanced incentives for the technical textiles sector.[30] The task of coordination was recognized explicitly:

Technical textiles have never been a single coherent industry sector and this market segment is also diverse and broad based.... The Committee noted the lack of co-ordination not only amongst the different Ministries but also amongst the institutions coming under the purview of the same Ministry with regard to

[27] Ibid., iii.   [28] Ibid., 4.   [29] Ibid.   [30] Ibid.

application/usage of technical textiles.... Therefore, an Inter-Ministerial Coordination Committee under the Ministry of Textiles needs to be set up for co-coordinating follow-up action by different Ministries and other institutions.

Government initiatives enabled many companies to set up new factories and start investing in this area. Ginni Filaments, a mainstream textile mill, planned a Rs. 125 crores (USD25 million) new factory. Its CEO noted, "We have decided to take a plunge and set up a non-woven factory near Baroda. The product range would comprise hydro-entangled spun lace items, which are meant for consumption in hospitals as disposal fabrics."[31] An American company, Owens Corning World, also sought government permission for a glass reinforcement fabrics factory. Other smaller companies – Kusungar Corporation, Entremond Coater, and Superior Fabrics – planned major expansions.[32] Thus, a massive amount of new information was generated by the government in its desire to create a new market and in order to interest new entrepreneurs. Importantly, the government was concerned with providing information about the global standards that technical textile producers must adhere to. Clearly, the government's role in communicating information about global standards, and in trying to help industry meet those standards, is worth analyzing.

7.3.3   Information about global standards

Markets convey price signals in a disorganized and delayed manner. Moreover, most markets are ineffective in giving information about regulations and standards that companies need to comply with in the future. In such contexts, the role of public information and rule-mediated information acquires greater significance than accounted for in our traditional theories. One such information is about different standards originating from outside the borders. Very few international relations studies assess the impact of international standards on specific industry responses.

Standards originating from Western governments and transnational regimes have proliferated recently and begun to affect the Indian private sector in a big way.[33] International negotiations associated with EU regulations and the WTO provide crucial information about the compliance demands posed by international organizations. In most cases, complying with international standards was nonnegotiable and a significant burden on private firms. Yet, the supposed trade-off between "exports

---

[31] Rajaram Japipura, chairman and managing director of Ginni Filaments in K. Narendra Nath, "Tech Textiles Is the New Driver on High Street of Manufacturing," *Economic Times*, February 11, 2004.
[32] Ibid.   [33] Wiemann (1996) and Mattli (2003).

and compliance did not materialize" (Tewari and Pillai 2005, 246). Wiemann (1996) notes that industry actors went through different stages, finally adjusting to environmental regulations. Most firms saw compliance as a necessary evil to increase exports. Governments and small firms that usually worried about the bottom line found it necessary and advantageous to invest in high-cost testing facilities by attracting into their midst an international firm with reputable testing facilities.[34] In an unintended way, stricter global standards pushed firms to upgrade their production processes, creating new practices more consistent with global standards. Importantly, the state and private firms came together to upgrade the ability of Indian industry to comply with stringent environmental standards, creating "a joint governance" model (Mattli 2003; Pillai 2000; Tewari and Pillai 2005). I suggest that the external international standards together with the state's role solved a crucial collective action dilemma faced by private firms. Market-driven signals would have suggested a narrow efficiency-driven or cost-based approach, which would have proven inferior in the long run. Examples from the Indian leather and textile industries demonstrate the role of public- and rule-mediated information in creating firms with global reach.

7.3.4   Public information about eco-standards in textiles and leather industries

Starting in the 1990s, global regulations began to reshape Indian industry. In 1990, Germany banned PCPs (pentachlorophenols) and azo dyes, two chemicals commonly used in leather goods and relevant for the textile industry.[35] Following the German ban, the European Union banned these compounds in the mid-1990s. Germany followed this by rejecting Indian leather shipments soon thereafter (Wiemann 1996, 183). Thus, external sanctions and standards began to shape domestic business strategies even before the MFA was abolished. This ban affected garments, home textiles, leather clothing, upholstery fabrics, leather components of furniture, seat covers, children's seats, shoes, belts, costume jewelry, and sports equipment (Singh and Phalgumani 1995, 12; Wiemann 1996). Initially, the Indian government resisted the ban, arguing for concessions as a result of its developing-country status (Wiemann 1996, 183). But soon the government acted strongly to ban the chemicals, with different governmental ministries jointly declaring such a ban. It expanded the

[34] See Intertek's website, accessed June 25, 2014, www.intertek.com/news/2012/05–18-in tertek-expands-textile-testing-india/.
[35] Details in this section are drawn from Singh and Phalghumani (1995), Pillai (2000), Wiemann (1996), and Tewari and Pillai (2005).

scope of the ban to all leather production, partly as a way to make the new requirements known to all actors. The Bureau of Standards (BIS), in consultation with the ministries of environment and forests and textiles, introduced a nationally recognized standard called "Eco Mark." Some of these government regulations were supported by industry, but industry actors opposed some regulations, as was the case of strong opposition by the Dye Manufactures Association of India (Pillai 2000). The government began providing incentives to those dye-producing firms that were willing to comply with the regulations, trying to create a wedge between them and dye manufacturers who opposed the regulations. In the language of international relations theory, the government was trying to tie the hands of firms by providing some carrots and in so doing encourage more firms to comply.

A survey of small-scale garment exporters found that awareness about global environmental standards was quite high by 2004.[36] Even more surprisingly, Indian small-scale firms complied and continued to follow these standards even when the monitoring stopped (Pillai 2000, 11). Given the invisibility and small size of the garment producers, how was such information made available or received? Certain surprising facts come to light when we go deeper into the process of information dissemination and compliance. The government and business associations *together* played a major role for textile producers to gain information and ensure compliance. Germany was India's largest market; thus, the Indian government took strong, swift action. The Indian government set up two different committees of experts, industry actors, and involved textile technologists. The committees collected valuable technical information about possible solutions as well as feedback from industry. Four aspects of the issue were evaluated: "dissemination of information to the trade and industry; legal measures to be adopted; research and development work on the identification of substitutes; and creation of reliable testing facilities" (Singh and Phalgumani 1995, 12). Clearly, information distribution was very crucial. All related associations and export associations were specifically asked to share this information with their members. These associations produced pamphlets, leaflets, and other information material in local and national languages. The Silk and Art Silk Mills Research Association and the Apparel Export Promotion Council (AEPC) both started an information distribution program. Detailed information about the banned amines, the list of prohibited dyes, safe substitutes, product-related standards, and other guidance was made available by the government and associations (Singh and Phalgumani

---

[36] Parikh et al. 1995, cited in Narayanan (2005).

1995, 13). The government, through its various agencies, organized twenty seminars and workshops across the country, including the top management of many firms and associations. Clearly, a multipronged effort was launched with the involvement of many groups, and many different agencies of the government, including the Ministry of Textiles and Commerce, played a proactive role in providing and shaping information with the industry actors.

7.3.5   Learning and linkage: upgrading to dynamic capability

New knowledge and expertise are valuable goods in the current global marketplace. The literature on business views the desire and acquisition of new knowledge and expertise as internally generated within a firm and independent of the larger institutional context. The conventional wisdom in business strategy literature is a resource-centric view, which regards the initial resources and firm-level factors, such as innovation, as keys to such upgradation. Yet, the evidence shows that alliances and global networks lead to new knowledge and a shift in strategy (Mathews 2006). I argued in Chapter 6 that firms that export and are developing global alliances are also inclined to develop their technological capabilities. *The causal connection between strength and global expansion is the reverse of what is usually supposed, global expansion as well as rules create incentives and skills for a change of interests and capabilities.* In this section, I use case studies of specific firms to show how linkages and global networks played a role in moving those firms up the value chain and creating a stronger global presence for Indian firms. This analysis shows that learning and linkages and experience with specific alliances shaped future choices of Indian firms. Companies were unsure of what strategies to adopt and what markets to favor until experience and learning gave them the requisite skills and knowledge. This insight resonates again and again with specific business experiences but finds no place in economic theory. Linkage with global markets and global organizations plays a special role in such learning.

Briefly, there are three different kinds of *learning paths* revealed by Indian firms, differentiated by the ways in which the global rules were experienced by firms. One is through *endogenous global learning*, when firms that start exporting and producing abroad acquire new skills and expertise. Two pharmaceutical firms, Ranbaxy and Dr. Reddy's Laboratories, fall into that category; they started exporting in the 1980s and learned through experience with global markets as well as third-party regulatory regimes such as the United States. These firms had to deal with a very crowded and capable incumbent market and learn from other companies, as they lacked resources, technology, and the first-mover advantage (Mathews 2006). As Mathews notes about emerging-market MNCs: "... the firms found new ways to 'complement' the strategies of the incumbents, such as through offering contract services, through licensing new technologies, to forming joint ventures and strategic alliances (Mathews 2006, 14)." Plausibly, through the implementation of these "complementary" strategies, newcomers and latecomers were able to win a place in the emergent global economy, not on the basis of their existing strengths but on the basis of their capacity to leverage resources from the strengths of others by making international connections (Mathews 2006, 14). In this section, I show that the proactive globalizers, such as Ranbaxy and DRL, benefited from an early exposure to the global arena and deployed their learning to move to the next stage of global outreach. While their firm-level strengths and domestically derived capabilities were necessary conditions for their eventual global reach, push and pull factors of the global arena as well as specific learning experiences shaped the manner in which these firms navigated the global arena seeking markets, technology, and expansion.

A second set of firms consists of those that began changing their strategies as a result of varied global agreements such as TRIPS or the prospective abolition of the Multifibre Agreement (MFA). These firms were forced to change their business models after the WTO negotiations revealed the importance of such shifts. They sought new expertise when the global regime changed, necessitating a shift in strategies. In such cases, internationalization took the form of a "gestalt shift" rather than being internally generated. The CEO of Lupin noted in 1994 that the TRIPS agreement was not good for Indian industry but realized that the changes were inevitable.[37] A majority of Indian firms in the textile sector, as well as a significant number of firms in the pharmaceutical sector, falls into that category. Some specific examples include Sun Pharmaceuticals, Neuland Labs, and Dishman.

The third set consists of those smaller domestic firms that learn in partnership with large domestic firms, after having resisted the need for such shifts. The firms that subcontract with global firms, such as Ranbaxy and RDL, fall into this category. This form of learning is more derivative of larger, more globally oriented firms but largely takes place within the domestic arena after 2005. Table 7.4 outlines these three learning modes.

---

[37] "The Way Out of the TRIPS Trap," *Business Standard*, November 10, 1993.

Table 7.4 *Three global learning paths of Indian pharmaceutical firms*

Global Market-Based Endogenous Learning, 1980–1995	Learning Through TRIPS Exogenous Learning, 1995–2005	Derivative or Second-Order Learning, 2005–2012
Export markets 1980–1995	Filing patents	Subcontracting with large firms, learning from business partners
Joint ventures in unregulated markets	USDFA certifications	Adopt WHO standards
Some production experience outside	Deliberations around TRIPS	National regulations
Proactive globalizers: Ranbaxy, DRL, Wockhardt	**Reluctant globalizers:** Sun Pharma, Dishman, Neuland Labs, Cipla	**Passive globalizers:** Small-scale producers

7.3.6   Proactive globalizers: Ranbaxy, Dr. Reddy's Laboratories, and Wochardt, Ltd.

A case history of each of the three categories of firms reveals the role of learning through global experience and alliances. While the global level was important for all firms, the models of global learning paths were different. Ranbaxy's earlier experience in a joint venture with Eli Lilly, in the early 1990s, is an illustrative example of such learning.[38] Eli Lilly had patented an antibiotic named Cefaclor in 1979. Ranbaxy started work on developing a new seven-stage process for the production of Cefaclor in 1989. Ranbaxy emerged as the only other manufacturer of Cefaclor besides the patent holder, Eli Lilly. In 1993, Eli Lilly and Ranbaxy Laboratories agreed to set up two joint ventures in India. One was to conduct research in India and the other to market Eli Lilly's products in the South Asian market. For the purpose of the Indian joint venture, a company named Ranbaxy Lilly was incorporated. Interviews revealed that this joint venture played a crucial role in reorienting Ranbaxy's strategy toward global markets by giving the experience of operating in the United States and in aiming for high payoffs.[39] Even more important, this joint venture changed Parvinder Singh's mind about the upcoming patent regime.[40] He came to realize

---

[38] The facts of this case are drawn from B. Dhar and Rao (2002). Also see Bowonder and Mastakar (2005).

[39] Author's interviews.

[40] Interview of B. K. Raizada, who was the VP of Ranbaxy at the time, by the author. His last assignment with Ranbaxy was as Sr. VP, Allied Businesses, Corporate and Govt. Affairs and Corporate Communications, Ranbaxy, Mumbai.

Table 7.5 *Ranbaxy: history and global activities*

Year	Business Strategies	Global Learning Events
1961	Ranbaxy was registered	
1973	Ranbaxy went public, and a new plant to manufacture APIs was commissioned in India	
1977	Established a joint venture in Nigeria	
1984	Expanded into Malaysia	
1987	Ranbaxy expanded production in India to become the largest manufacture of antibiotics	
1988	Sought USFDA approval for its Toonsa plant	
1990	Ranbaxy sought its first patent in the US market	
1992	Joint venture with Ely Lily	Learning
	Discovered a process for Cefaclor	episode[a]
1994	R&D facility in Gurgaon	
1994	Ranbaxy begins to change its opposition to TRIPS	
1995	Acquired Ohms Labs of United States	
1999	Ranbaxy signed agreement with Bayer Germany for Bayer to market Ciproflaxacin, originally developed by Ranbaxy	Learning event
2000	Acquired Bayers Generics business in Germany	
	Started selling in Brazil	
2003	Alliance with GSK for drug development	Learning event
2004	Ranbaxy became USD1 billion company	
	Ranbaxy filed for a HIV/AIDS drug ARV under the US Pres. ARV emergency fund	
2005	Received USFDA approval for its ARV drug	
	Opened its third R&D faculty in Gurgaon	
2006	Ranbaxy successfully challenged Pfizer's Lipitor patent in the United States	Learning event
	Acquired a company in South Africa and Romania	
	Got USFDA approval for Simvastatin 80 mg	
	Filed a market exclusivity agreement in United States for Simvastatin	
2007	Ranbaxy signed new R&D agreement with GSK	Learning event
2008	Redefined its business model by bringing in Daiichi Sankyo, a Japanese company, as a majority partner	
2012	Ranbaxy launched new drug for malaria, Synraium	

[a] I interviewed five different high-level officials off Ranbaxy. Each of them recollected the role played during this joint venture in convincing the top leadership about the necessity of supporting patents.

Source: Athreye, Kale, and Ramani (2009); Bowonder and Mastakar (2005); Annual Reports and Ranbaxy's company website, accessed June 25, 2014, www.ranbaxy.com/abo utus/history.aspx. The analysis in column three on "Global Learning Events" is my own assessment based on numerous interviews I conducted with officials who worked at these specific companies.

that in order to do business at the international level, Ranbaxy would have to support the implementation of patents at home. Table 7.5 outlines how Ranbaxy progressively moved to become an "Indian MNC" and the role played by key global alliances in its business history.

Dr. Reddy's Laboratories is seen to be an innovative company "which has kept in sync with the changing rules of the game of the knowledge based industry and hence has carved out a niche for itself" (Bowonder et al. 2003, 251). DRL was founded in 1984 and soon thereafter became India's third largest company by establishing a reputation for research-based work, as well as an aggressive strategy of seeking markets in the United States. How did DRL reach these milestones? Table 7.6 documents the important developments in its history. I argue that DRL's early experience in global arenas enabled it to learn capabilities in development to R&D and development and take advantage of new opportunities. DRL's dynamic capabilities were achieved in interaction with these larger global experiences. DRL was involved in numerous joint ventures in the 1980s and 1990s. It established a joint venture in Russia in 1994, in Brazil in 1994, and in China in 2000. While these were in unregulated markets, Dr. Reddy was simultaneously seeking US Federal Drug Administration (USFDA) approval for a few of its manufacturing plants. Experience with the USFDA played a major role in Dr. Reddy's Laboratories' scaling up in the late 1990s and 2000s. DRL filed over 175 product patents in the United States related to cancer and diabetes drugs (Bowonder et al. 2003). DRL moved from a domestic generics company to a global generics company and then to a global research-based company. In 1986, DRL acquired Benzex Laboratories, Pvt. Ltd., a domestic Indian company, to enhance its generics business. DRL's global strategies began in the early to mid-1990s. In 1994, DRL opened a subsidiary in the United States, and in 1995, it filed its first patent for an in-house drug. In 1999, it acquired American Remedies, Ltd. This trajectory indicates a stepped-up learning curve as each phase was used to learn new capabilities. For example, between 1990 and 2000, DRL mastered the art of filing patents and ANDA filings at the USFDA in preparation for the upcoming TRIPS regime. Bowonder (2003) noted, "The increase in the number of patent applications and clinical trials taken up indicate urgency felt in DRL to prepare for the post-2005 scenario when intellectual property rights will be globally harmonized" (Bowonder et al. 2003).

Wockhardt, Ltd., is also a proactive globalizer, despite a slight delay in moving to the global arena. Wockhardt started in 1959 as a small pharmaceutical firm focused on biotechnology. In the mid-1990s, it started to invest strongly in biotech-related R&D. Importantly, its joint venture with a research center in Italy, along with another joint venture with a

Table 7.6 *Dr. Reddy's Laboratories: history and global activities*

Year	Business Strategies	Global Learning Events
1984	Dr. K. Anji Reddy founded Dr. Reddy's Laboratories, based on a bulk actives business he had founded in the 1970s, in order to extend into the production of drug formulations	
1988	The company acquired Benzex Laboratories in order to expand the bulk actives business	Learning opportunity at
	DRL started exporting Methyldopa to the United States	the global level (exports)
1992	Dr. Reddy's Research Foundation is founded as part of the strategy to enter drug development	
1992	Joint venture with Biomed to enter Russian markets	Learning event
1994	The company opened a subsidiary in the United States	Learning event
1995	The company files its first patent for an in-house developed drug	Learning event
1997	Filed first ANDA application with USDFA	Learning event
1998	Licensed DRF 2725 to Novo Nordisk	Learning event
1999	The company acquired American Remedies, Ltd. Submitted first Para IV application for Omeprazole	Learning event
2000	The company acquired Cheminor Drugs, Ltd., and became the third largest Indian drug company	Learning event
	Set up R&D lab in Atlanta, United States	
2001	The company listed shares on the New York Stock Exchange; a new R&D facility opens in Atlanta	
2002	The company acquired BMS Laboratories, Ltd., and its marketing and distribution subsidiary Meridian Healthcare, Ltd., in the United Kingdom.	Learning event
2003	The company gained tentative approval to market generic versions of Serzone, developed by Bristol Myers Squibb	
2004	Acquired Trigeneisis	
2006	Acquired Betapharm	

Source: The history was uncovered from diverse sources and cross-checked in interviews. Bowonder et al. (2003) and Athreye, Kale, and Ramani (2009). The company's history can be found at DRL's website, accessed June 24, 2014, www.fundinguniverse.com/company-histories/dr-reddy-s-laboratories-ltd-history/. The analysis in column three on "Global Learning Events" is my own assessment.

firm manufacturing a hepatitis B drug, were very crucial in learning about new markets. Wockhardt also acquired some firms in the mid-1990s, expanding its scale of operations (Athreye, Kale, and Ramani 2009, 24). In 2000, the company organized a major restructuring to focus its

Table 7.7 *Wockhardt, Ltd.: history and global activities*

Year	Business Strategies	Learning Events
1959	Worli Chemicals was promoted by Khorakiwals family	
1973	Wockhardt, Pvt. Ltd., established	
1984	Merger with two companies	
1990	IPO	
1994	First Indian company to issue a GDR	
1995	Formed a joint venture with German firm for manufacturing hepatitis B drug	Learning opportunity at the global level
1996	Acquired R. R. Medipharma in India and Wallis Laboratories in UK	
1998	Acquired Merind in India	
2003	Indigenously produced insulin Acquired CP Pharmaceuticals (UK)	
2004	Acquired a German firm Esparma GMBH US subsidiary	
2006	Acquired a generic firm in Ireland	

Source: Athreye, Kale, and Ramanai (2009). The analysis in column three on "Learning Events" is my own assessment.

R&D efforts and to enhance its global operations. In 2003, Wockhardt launched its US operations by starting a subsidiary called Wockhardt Americas, Ltd., as well as establishing marketing and regulatory teams there. After 2003, Wockhardt was focused on the US market, filing 17 ANDA applications with the USFDA (Athreye, Kale, and Ramani 2009). Table 7.7 outlines the progressive global strategies of Wockhardt, Ltd. Athreye, Kale, and Ramani also note that the three leading firms learned from each other. They find:

In transitioning to new drug discovery we find that three of the four firms chose different transitioning paths to new drug capabilities – Ranbaxy through improving dosage forms, DRL through specialty chemicals and Wockhardt through pursuing the bio-generics route, yet the strategies that they have used to achieve these transitions have been borrowed from each other. Out licensing, first initiated by DRL was imitated by Ranbaxy and Wockhardt. De-risking drug discovery through de-merger and venture finance of those R&D subsidiaries was initiated by DRL, but is now proving popular among other large drug manufacturers. It seems that inter-organizational learning through observation of other firms' successful strategies has significantly influenced the strategies pursued by the firms and may be as important as own firm learning [Athreye, Kale, and Ramani 2009, 756].

7.3.7   Reluctant globalizers: Sun, Cadila, Dishman, and Neuland Labs

Sun Pharma, Cadila Healthcare, Neuland Labs, and Dishman are a few examples of what I categorize as "reluctant globalizers," who only realized the need for a shift in strategy in the mid- to late 1990s when TRIPS had become inevitable. These firms gained new information about global market and regulatory shifts through the process of the TRIPS negotiations and implementation between 1995 and 2005. They learned from the proactive globalizers, discussions led by the state, and the regulatory debates around TRIPS that were happening in domestic and global arenas. Such *public* information allowed companies to plan for future markets and anticipate market trends. Here again, learning was an important mechanism for a shift in strategy.

The ongoing TRIPS discussions and negotiations had a consequential impact on Sun Pharma's shift in strategies in the early 2000s.[41] Sun Pharma was established in 1983 and initially focused on eastern India. In 1987, it started national sales all over India, and in 1989, it began some exports to neighboring countries. In the 1990s, it started generic research and marketing products to unregulated markets such as Russia, Ukraine, and Belarus. In the 1990s, though most of its expansion strategies were focused on the domestic market, it did start some international acquisitions. It acquired a few companies within India, expanding its scope and scale. In the late 1990s, it began some tentative forays into the American markets. In May 1997, it invested USD7.4 million in an American company as part of a technology transfer agreement. This experience proved very crucial in learning about the changing nature of generic markets in the United States.[42] In 2001, Sun Pharma began to apply for

---

[41] I collected this information from the Sun Pharma website and from pharmaceutical publications.

[42] The Sun Pharma website noted: "Caraco Pharmaceutical Laboratories (CPD: Amex) is a Detroit, US based manufacturer of generic pharmaceuticals with a US FDA approved 70,000 sq. ft. plant. In 1997, Sun Pharma invested an initial $7.5 million and structured a technology transfer agreement with the loss making Caraco that would help it bring new products to market and build sales. A similar agreement was signed in 2002 on completion of the first agreement. Stakes were bought from two large shareholders in 2004, taking the holding to over 60 percent from 44 percent, and now the stake is 75 percent on a diluted basis, which has been reached by technology transfer. Based on the technology transferred out of Sun Pharma, Caraco now markets 34 ANDAs and has witnessed an increase in sales to $223 million in the year ending March 2010. 120 more ANDAs await approval from both the companies. In addition to a well-considered pipeline of generics under development, the US generic opportunity is immense, with products worth over $40 billion likely to go off patent in the next few years. For some key products, Caraco sources API from Sun Pharma's plants and competes as an integrated manufacturer. Such integration offers considerable time and cost advantages in the competitive US generics market." See the website of Sun Pharma, accessed June 24, 2014, www.sun pharma.com/acquisitions.

Table 7.8 *Sun Pharma: history and global activities*

Year	Business Strategies	Learning Events
1983	Incorporated	
1987	National sales	
1989	Exports to neighboring countries	
1991	Set up Sun Pharma Advanced Research Center (SPARC)	
1993	Office in Moscow and started expanding exports to unregulated markets	
1995	Set up offices in Ukraine and Belarus	
1995	Built an API plant in Maharashtra	
1996–1997	Acquired two Indian companies	
1997	Technology transfer agreement: invested USD7.4 million in Caraco Pharmaceutical Laboratories	Crucial learning episode
1998–2000	Acquisitions and mergers	
2000	Caraco received USFDA approval	
2001	Plants in Dadra (India) meet USFDA and UKMHRA approval	
2005–2010	Expanded in Israel, Canada, and United States	

Source: Sun Pharma company website, accessed June 25, 2014, www.sunpharma.com/history. The analysis in column three on "Learning Events" is my own assessment.

USFDA approval for its formulation plant, and in 2002, it began a more focused attempt to target US and EU markets. In 2005, Sun Pharma acquired a firm in Ohio (USA). By 2010, Sun Pharma had doubled the size of its US businesses and had manufacturing facilities in Israel and Canada. Interviews revealed that the TRIPS discussion in the mid- to late 1990s made the company realize the need to scale up its global strategy of acquisitions and reach deeper into the generic business at the international level.[43] Yet, Sun Pharma never moved into researching and discovering new molecules, as did Ranbaxy and DRL, as the company considered those to be high-risk strategies. TRIPS and the changing global environment proved crucial in expanding the ambitions and scope of the company beyond its area of expertise. The technology agreement with Calco in 1997 was an important learning period for the company. Interviews, however, revealed that Sun Pharma gained a lot of information when discussions around TRIPS became frequent in public debates.[44]

---

[43] Interview with the author, December 2009.
[44] Interview with the author, December 2009.

Table 7.9 *Dishman: history and global activities*

Year	Business Strategies	Learning Opportunities
1983	Incorporated Dishman Pharmaceuticals and Chemicals, Limited	
1989	Production of a range of phase transfer catalysts at Naroda facility	
1995	Formation of a joint venture company with Schütz & Co., called Schütz Dishman Biotech, Pvt. Ltd Manufacture of chlorhexidine and derivates for European market	Learning opportunity
1996	Initiation of Bavla facility for bulk intermediates	
1998	Establishment of Dishman Europe and Dishman USA sales subsidiaries	
1997–1999	India loses the WTO patent case and discussions around TRIPS speed up	
2001	First commercial contract manufacturing agreement signed with a major Western pharmaceutical company	Learning event
2004	Dishman IPO on Indian stock exchange	
2005	Acquired IO3S, Swiss-based ozone technology specialists	Global acquisition
2006	Acquired CARBOGEN AMCIS, Swiss-based contract research and manufacturing organization Formed Dishman China	Global acquisition
2007	Formed Dishman Japan; acquired Solvay Vitamins and Chemicals business based in the Netherlands	Learning events
2009	Dishman Shanghai manufacturing facility comes on stream; large-scale high-potency manufacturing facility at Bavla, India, comes on stream	Learning events

Source: See Dishman Group's website, accessed June 25, 2014, www.dishmangroup.com/history.asp.

Dishman, another pharmaceutical company based in western India, demonstrates this learning trajectory well (see Table 7.9). Dishman was an indigenously oriented company in the 1980s and 1990s. It was only in the late 1990s and early 2000s that it began to realize the need for some international alliances. Interviews revealed that Dishman was alerted to the changing regulatory environment in the early 2000s.[45] In 2008–2009, the need for learning and alliances because of the new regulatory challenges of the TRIPS agreement was clearly recognized by the company's

[45] Interview with a journalist who had covered Dishman, Ahmedabad, January 2009.

officials. Theo Uiopoulos, the VP of operations, Polpharma (Starogard Gdański, Poland), in an alliance with Dishman, noted:

> As the development and *manufacturing model changes, and the regulatory requirements become ever stricter,* it is crucial for development and manufacturing to adjust and build partnerships and networks with other groups. The deal will allow us to come up with solutions to meet the market expectations and sustain the increased competition between major pharmas and generic pharmas. Such partnerships are the *future of the pharma industry* [emphasis added].[46]

7.3.6   Is globalization perceived as a threat or as an opportunity?

While economic theory holds that business actors are influenced by material incentives and new opportunities, the real-world experience of business reveals a different story. Global forces create both new threats and stresses and new opportunities; companies must respond to both (Child 1972; Prakash and Hart 2000). The international security literature conceptualizes threats in terms of "balance of power" and "hard power" measures. The international political economy, economics, and policy literature, however, speak the language of incentives and opportunities. Economic theory sees market changes in terms of new opportunities, but real businesspeople notice threats and challenges more than new possibilities. Simultaneously, the planning and strategy of most business owners is short-sighted and crisis driven, constraining their "rational" ability to make informed decisions about their own long-term interests. John Child is one of the few scholars to conceptualize the variable threats embodied by globalization. He makes a distinction between variability, complexity, and stress enjoined by globalization (1972). In this section, I assess whether changes in the global regime and markets were perceived as threats or new opportunities by Indian firms. I find that between 1995 and 2004, globalization was seen to be threatening by most Indian firms. After and around 2004, globalization was seen to generate new opportunities as firms began to view globalization in a more positive light.

The end of the Cold War and the collapse of the Soviet Union had a clear economic effect by creating new economic threats and uncertainties for Indian pharmaceutical players. I found clear evidence that threats of losing generic markets had a direct impact on pharmaceutical firms as they redesigned their global and domestic strategies in the 1990s and 2000s. Interestingly, threats are more important for collective

---

[46] Deepti Ramesh, "Dishamn Signs API Development Deal with Polish Firm," *Chemical Week*, April 13, 2009.

Table 7.10 *Pharmaceutical exports from India*

Year	Share in Total Exports, 1989–1990	Share in Total Exports, 2002–2003
USSR	44.2	4.0
FRG	13.2	1.8
USA	3.9	10.8
UK	2.9	2.1
Hong Kong	2.7	0.6
Singapore	2.0	0.6
Poland	1.9	0.3
Japan	1.7	0.2
China	NA	3.3
Others	27.5	80.3[47]

Source: Aggarwal (2007).

action and industry mobilization than incentives and market opportunities. Two different threats were evident: the loss of the USSR as a market and the loss of generic market share in the regulated markets (United States and European Union) as well as the erstwhile unregulated markets (Africa). Table 7.10 documents the transformation in Indian pharmaceutical export markets. The loss of the USSR had to be made up somehow, which put even greater pressure on the market share of generic companies in the United States and the rest of the world. Indian companies saw the effect of TRIPS not within India but in its indirect threats to their forays into the United States, regulated and unregulated markets, where TRIPS was to be implemented. They felt that their inability to reverse engineer patented drugs in India would hurt their ability to export to a whole range of markets.[48] This explains the attempt by many Indian firms to set up FDA-approved businesses in the United States, their legal fights in US courts, and numerous joint ventures set up after and around 2000.[49] Patent filings in the United States and the European Union increased in an attempt to bypass the Indian regulatory system and capture a first-mover advantage in Western markets.

Similar perceptions were amplified among textile firms. The changes in the global textile regime anticipated since 1995 (abolition of the MFA was planned from January 1, 2005) promised a great opening up of new lucrative (US and EU) markets and diminishing protectionist barriers.

---

[47] This includes African countries.   [48] Interviews with pharmaceutical firms.
[49] Interview, D. G. Shah, Indian Pharmaceutical Alliance, Mumbai, 2003.

For decades, the developing countries had railed against the protectionism enshrined in the quotas on textiles. Mr. Uppal, owner of the exporter Richa and Co., believed in 2004 that the "quota's demise is an opportunity of a lifetime."[50] Yet, removal of the quota system was mostly perceived as a major crisis, not as an opportunity, as the large firms with the potential to compete at the international level had been losing ground for years and felt threatened by the possibility of greater competition.[51] In fact, in the early 2000s, the prospect of removal of quotas was seen to be a "do or die" situation for the industry, galvanizing it to act.[52] A research report issued by the Northern India Textile Mills Association in 2002, entitled, "Wake Up Call for India's Textile Industry," made a strong case for a dire situation that demanded action. As an illustration, garment exporters were quite disappointed by the decision of the European Union in 2000 to release less than the agreed-to quota for garment imports and realized that opening up of external markets would be slow and difficult.[53]

While producers from other countries posed a competitive threat to Indian producers, China, a geopolitical competitor, was viewed with special fear.[54] The comparison with China, as well as such smaller competitors as Pakistan, magnified the doomsday scenario that seemed imminent. A very large number of business actors were worried about the threat from China and feared being swamped by the dragon from the East.[55] This perception was magnified by the framing of China as a threatening competitor by the media, helping to push the industry into changing its market and political strategies, even before market signals

[50] "India Waits to Pounce as Textile Quota Scheme Lapses," *Business Standard*, April 4, 2004.
[51] An important cover story on the textile sector in *Business World* in 1999 suggested that abolition of the MFA was seen as a threat. The article argued: "Although India is part of the global textile elite, its reputation rests on shaky grounds. ... It enjoys a trade surplus owing to the export quota regime guaranteed under the multifibre agreement (MFA) and because its domestic market is protected by high tariff barriers. Yet, under the WTO rules the country will find its crutches jerked away quite soon. While the MFA will be phased out in 2005, imports are already flooding the markets and will become a deluge when the country is forced to lower its barriers in a couple of years" (*Business World*, 1999, p. 19). Numerous such stories were reported across most newspapers. See "It's Now or Never for Struggling Indian Textile Industry," *Financial Express*, January 5, 2002; "Back to 1757," *Financial Express*, January 11, 2002.
[52] A research report issued by the Northern India Textile Mills Association in 2002, entitled, "Wake Up Call for India's Textile Industry," made a strong case for a dire situation that demanded action (NITMA 2001).
[53] "EU Move on Textile Imports Upsets Garment Exporters," *Economic Times*, May 15, 2000, "European Union Allows India to Increase Textile Exports," *Economic Times*, May 13, 2000.
[54] Textile producers faced threats from China, Turkey, Mauritius, Mexico, Pakistan, and Bangladesh.
[55] "It's Now or Never for Struggling Indian Textile Industry," *Financial Express*, June 5, 2002.

had changed. Starting in 2000, 95 percent of newspaper articles expressing views, both by government and by industry, mention China as a threat in addition to Pakistan and Bangladesh, which are mentioned around 3 to 5 percent of the time.[56] Arguably, the removal of textile quotas would usher in global products at cheap prices and force India to compete with other producers rather than being guaranteed a stable quota, which was more beneficial to Indian industries that lacked a competitive edge. Furthermore, given India's industrial structure, the losers from abolition of the MFA were numerous, with the potential to affect the political calculations of the rulers (small-scale producers). Thus, in the initial stages, the transition to globalization was perceived as constituted of danger, threats, challenges, and very few opportunities. The proliferation of global standards was also a constraining effect and deserves discussion.

7.3.7 Global standards for pharmaceuticals

For pharmaceuticals, as exports expanded in the mid- to late 1990s, Indian companies realized the need for adopting international standards. USFDA standards started percolating into India as Indian companies started exporting to the United States. By early 2000s, the WHO-GMP (Good Medical Practices and Standards) were adopted by many firms, and many others sought such certifications despite the high costs. The HIV/AIDS crisis and the debates around TRIPS amplified the attention of Indian companies regarding such global certifications. The Doha Declaration on Public Health (2001) had a direct impact on such WHO certifications. By the mid- to late 2000s, the two important nonmarket standards were the USFDA and WHO certifications. The story of the WHO prequalification program is especially interesting.[57] Around the time of the Doha Declaration, WHO included the fixed-dose formations in its list of "essential drugs." Many organizations, including large NGOs who were using these drugs in their "access to drugs" programs, requested that the WHO certify the quality of these drugs. In 2001, in close consultation with many UN agencies and other drug regulatory authorities, WHO launched a prequalification program for antiretroviral drug manufacturers. WHO invited drug manufacturers to submit dossiers, whereupon WHO would evaluate the drugs for safety and quality. The procedure envisioned by WHO was an elaborate one. First, WHO evaluated the quality and efficacy of the drugs based on the data submitted. If this evaluation was positive, WHO inspected the sites to certify their their conformity with GMP

---

[56] These data are drawn from the author's database of "Business Strategies, 1999–2011."
[57] I draw this information from Coriat (2008).

Table 7.11 *Indian pharmaceutical companies with WHO certification*

Hetero Drugs, Ltd.
Mylan Laboratories, Ltd.
Ranbaxy Laboratories, Ltd.
Cipla, Ltd.
Aurobindo Pharma, Ltd.
Meditab Specialties, Pvt. Ltd.
Strides Arcolab, Ltd.
Emcure Pharmaceuticals, Ltd.
Alkem Laboratories, Ltd.
Macleods Pharmaceuticals, Ltd.

Source: Author's calculation from WHO List of Prequalified Medicinal Products. See WHO's webpage, accessed June 24, 2014, http://apps.who.int/prequal/.

standards. Only the drugs that passed these two tests were included in the list of prequalified drugs published on the WHO website. As noted by Benjamin Coriat, "In practice, inclusion in the list amounted to obtaining a label of quality guarantee awarded by the organization" (Coriat 2008, 11). Interestingly, although the program started as ensuring the quality of generic drugs, which were considered to be of lower quality, the process began to be extended to the patent holders of the drugs, in addition to the generic firms. Moreover, while the certification was initially to cover only the procurement of drugs by UN agencies, it began to be used by other international agencies such as GFTAM (Global Fund to Fight AIDS, Tuberculosis and Malaria) and the World Bank. Thus, a standard inspired by the global campaign for access to HIV/AIDs expanded to include other diseases (malaria and TB) and began affecting the original patent holders as well as other international organizations. This certification process affected the whole market of ARV drugs, with impacts on both generic and nongeneric producers. Interestingly, as noted by Coriat, the price and market for such drugs shrank even as the quality of the drugs rose (Coriat 2008, 12). Many Indian firms have applied for WHO prequalification. In fact, of 294 medicines prequalified under the WHO certification process, 213 were from Indian companies.[58] These 213 medicines are produced by ten Indian companies, which had applied for precertification by 2012 (Table 7.11). Any Indian company that seeks to export drugs to the rest of the world follows and subscribes to the international standard initiated by WHO and UN agencies, despite the high costs.

[58] Author's calculation from WHO (2012).

Thus, international health standards shaped the production and marketing practices of pharmaceutical firms in both the developing world and the developed world.

7.4   Conclusion

Global markets rest on institutions and rules of the game. Even in a globalized era dominated by markets, rules and regimes matter. In fact, markets and new rules of the game have coevolved as the world has become more global. This coevolution was made possible by the dynamic interplay between price-mediated (contract-enforcement) mechanisms and coercion and interdependence mechanisms such as threats, standards, and learning. The state's role in providing and facilitating public information in such a complex and changing global environment has become even more crucial. This chapter has outlined the role of three distinct nonmarket global mechanisms that affect the private sector – information, threats, and learning – and provided empirical assessments of how they work in specific industries and cases within India.

International relations literature outlines different global mechanisms that affect states, such as conditionality, socialization, and learning. But we lack a fine-grained understanding of the different ways in which business strategies are affected by globalization. This chapter has argued that globalization and domestic liberalization can change investment decisions and preferences of industry and state actors by different mechanisms and drivers, which need to be disaggregated. A question about diverse mechanisms is important for understanding how different dimensions of globalization affect how actors think of their preferences and interests (for example, trade protection or liberalization) and how they evolve strategies to achieve their preferences and goals (for example, export subsidies or tariff). This analysis provides a more comprehensive and complete picture of globalization by disaggregating its effects on specific countries and private producers.

8   Conclusion

This book analyzes globalization by unveiling the architecture and agents of globalization. How does globalization actually work? Who are the actors and agencies that implement the various tasks of globalization? Through what exact mechanisms does it affect nations, firms, and individuals? Globalization does not emerge on its own but is created by the activities of individuals and firms as *they interact with states, international organizations, and collective associations*. This interaction is not only mediated by markets and prices but also shaped by rules enforced by international organizations as well as cooperative learning and information sharing among states and firms.[1] This book also challenges the idea that actions originating from either the domestic or the global level are primary or autonomous. The impact of global economic flows and rules depends on the actions and responses of domestic actors, but these actors and institutions are faced with a changed global environment that affects their domestic and external strategies.

What do global forces do? Global forces nudge recalcitrant states to comply not only through coercion or pressure but also through legally framed sovereignty costs. Implementing international agreements is costly and creates onerous transaction and implementation costs, which under some conditions can lead to a building of state capacity, new tradecraft, and new state–society mechanisms of consultation. This may contribute to better negotiation outcomes and the combined use of free-trade and protectionist measures. Contrary to conventional wisdom, globalization rests not only on competition or price signals but also on involuntary nonmarket mechanisms. Three such mechanisms – *public information* revealed by state and international organizations, *learning abilities* of states and firms to manage global challenges in an interdependent as well as a competitive context, and economic *threats* that originate

---

[1] This idea is similar to the idea that firms and states make markets. See Anderson and Gatignon (2008) for the claim that firms make markets.

outside the national boundaries of states – played a major role in nudging Indian capital to become global.

Where do these nonmarket mechanisms of globalization come from? This book finds that global rules of the game, and agreements enshrined in international organizations such as the WTO, have created new non market mechanisms that are as important as global markets and economic flows in shaping domestic politics of nations around the world. The effects of such mechanisms and the strategies by domestic actors can be understood with the help of the Global Design-in-Motion framework articulated in this book. This Global Design-in-Motion framework opens up the black box of international rules of the game and examines the recursive effect of how specific institutional features of the global order – legal framing, for example – affect and transform interests within states and the private sector. Global organizations, thus work with and through states. States have proven to be indispensable in managing the threats and opportunities presented both by global markets and by the involuntary rules of such global organizations. State actors facilitate sectoral adaptation and industrial upgradation in diverse ways. Where state action fails to act in positive ways or actually hinders the changes needed, adjustment to global markets is slower, and vested interests continue to seek protectionist advantages. Essentially, states mediate the effects of globalization in specific contexts but may also be transformed in the process. This complex argument about the unintended effects of globalization challenges the idea that economic globalization only changes market incentives (costs and benefits) or prices. Rather, globalization may also change the structure of cost and benefits and the institutional basis of calculating those costs and benefits, which slowly, but surely, may create Indian consent for globalization.

This book, in line with a large literature on international relations, has disaggregated the complex microfoundations of global trade structures and analyzed their effects on diverse agents, sectors, and organizations in a large country, India, revealing many counterintuitive insights about a puzzling country. The transition from India's insular protectionism of the 1980s and 1990s to its current trade strategy that combines liberal and protectionist measures is the empirical focus of this book. I elaborated an open-economy politics framework (Lake 2009) for India by disaggregating the way we analyze the global level, enhancing and modifying the framework. In doing so, this book teases out different dimensions and agents of globalization as adapted by Indians and Indian institutions.

This book makes three central points about India. First, the changes toward global markets and global alliances that picked up pace after 1999 were more dramatic and sudden than most people and scholars realize. Continuity in India's political institutions and lack of a complete break with the *dirigiste* past have led most observers to underestimate the impact of global forces on India. India has initiated significant economic policy changes in trade and other arenas related to global integration despite the rhetoric of nationalist autonomy that pervades the surface-level discourse. The second-generation reforms were much more rapid and widespread, diffusing across the Indian economy surely and suddenly, creating winners and supporters, some losers, but also reluctant reformers. Reformers emerged from the woodwork, whom I call *woodwork reformers*. These findings about post-1990s reform run counter to the dominant argument about incrementalism in India and suggest that Indian reforms have become wider, broader, and were sustained. As a result, trade in goods and services constituted half the Indian economy in 2013 (53.2 percent of GDP).[2] Yet, Indian actors and institutions have also made globalization their own, modifying, adapting, and changing the terms of globalization. Economic reforms have been successful in India because Indian actors and institutions have both resisted and adopted globalization. The political struggle to redefine and implement globalization has also enmeshed global forces within India through the activities of governments, firms, and collective associations.

Second, the Indian state has facilitated deeper integration than expected and has been at the forefront of change in trade policy and economic institutions as well as markets. The state has led the process of global integration, seeking diverse public (other state agencies, think tanks), expert (economists and lawyers, for example), and private partners in the process. Somewhat counterintuitively, it has played a major but largely unrecognized role in shaping India's outside orientation. The trading state has reformed itself and transformed itself across many policy domains even as other dimensions of state institutions remain ineffective. In fact, the trading state has used globalization to serve India's commercial interests. It has done so by strengthening the position of specific sectors (not only IT but also pharmaceuticals and textiles and garments) and introduced many new initiatives, such as the textile investment funds, R&D funds and subsidies, and fiscal reform, thereby playing "a direct role in guiding" globalization (Cortell 2006, 5). As I argued elsewhere, "internationalization, under some conditions, leads to domestic institutional change as it affects the domestic *supply* of responses and the domestic re-regulation of global forces" (Sinha 2007, 3). These micro foundations of state change, as well as economic strength, explain the

---

[2] The data are from the World Development Indicators (World Bank 2013).

growing assertiveness of India's actions at the global level and India's rising power in global arenas. India not only acts more assertively at the WTO but has also become an active member of the BRICS group as well as the G-20 coalition. Its actions go beyond resisting globalization to negotiating for better terms in a more pragmatic and more capable manner.

This argument, though, must also recognize the many imperfections of state action across policy areas. The trading state has shown both public purpose and many pathologies. Its enhanced capacity has coexisted with a movement toward private and business power that undermines the power of citizens. Some sectors, such as hardware, have been ignored by the state despite their potential. Some industry actors have sought privileged access and benefits from the state. Until now, only the patho-logic elements in the Janus-faced state has been recognized (Gupta 2012). In contrast to a one-dimensional view of the Indian state, I find that the Indian state and key state agencies are flawed but powerful facilitators of the globalization process.

Third, globalization may have increased the power of business, but the business sector in India does not work autonomously in its search for new markets or new strategies. Business has realized the need to work with state actors and international rules, even as its power has increased. Private actors both resisted and delayed globalization in the 1990s but slowly adjusted to become new partners of the Indian state and agents of globalization in the 2000s. How did this transformation in business engagement with the global world happen? While the business press focuses on success stories, of which there are many, a more complex story emerges beneath such apparent successes. Many businesses in India have moved from opposing globalization to embracing it. Business evolution from opposition to embrace of globalization offers an interest-ing account of how domestic interests shift in interaction with domestic reform agents as well as within the crucible of global forces. This book started with the premise that you can't assume that globalization leads to a closer relationship between state and business but that you must scru-tinize the transformations in the business–state relationships carefully and empirically.

A new partnership has emerged between the state and the private sector, shaped by the challenges presented by global forces and the proactive pro-business actions of the Indian state. New competitive sec-tors and export-oriented segments within sectors have emerged as distinct from protective sectors. Many protective sectors are under pressure to reform and adapt. Chapters 4 to 7 analyzed two important sectors – pharmaceuticals and textiles – and how they adjusted to the new global order. I find that the Indian private sector deployed an unexpected model of global growth, one of linkage, incremental innovation, and collaboration with state actors, to expand beyond India's borders and to deal with the opportunities and challenges of globalization.[3]

This book provides empirical validation but also greater empirical specification to Kohli's idea of a state–business alliance that has consolidated power across many industrial sectors while modifying the timeline offered by Kohli for the emergence of this alliance (2004, 2012). My analysis also offers a theory about the sources of this state–business alliance. My analysis shows that this business–state alliance was fractured and weak in the 1980s and 1990s, and it only came together in the early 2000s when the combined force of global markets and global rules became urgent. Global forces played a major role in consolidating this alliance. While I provide new evidence for how the state–business alliance was crafted, I also challenge the idea that business was at the forefront of globalization in the 1980s or 1990s. In the 1980s and until the late 1990s, most business actors were fighting to protect their privileges acquired under the *dirigiste* system. Business support for globalization only changed in the 2000s, when business was faced with the inevitability of globalization as well as crucial state aid for their globalization. While I agree with the broad strokes of Kohli's argument, I suggest that he gives too much credit to business classes in the 1980s and 1990s. Businesses were not strong proponents of policy reforms in the early to mid-1990s and failed to steer India toward globalization until nudged by global forces and state aid to do so.

The findings of this book also challenge the claim that a "narrow ruling coalition" rules India. The evidence presented in this book reveals that a new set of interests has been created that supports India's engagement with the outside world, and the actors have defeated many nonperforming protectionist elements. The state–business coalition in favor of economic reform has become broader and wider even as new *woodwork reformers* and fragmentary but crucial elements within the state have supported India's rise in the world. While inequalities have arisen, new winners have been created across India's economy and society, broadening the ruling coalition. A broad ruling coalition consisting of woodwork reformers, export-oriented sectors, small sectors that have adjusted to seek global reach, the middle class, and members of the intelligentsia, including the Indian diaspora, has been created and consolidated in the crucible of global arenas and domestic ambitions. We see less political contestation around

---

[3] Mathews also finds that developing-country multinationals use "linkage and leverage" to seek global markets (2002).

trade liberalization because losers, such as handloom sectors, weavers, and those businesses that were unable or unwilling to modify their business practices, have lost crucial state support that made them politically viable.

This book does not seek to generalize across all industries but stresses the need to carefully analyze other sectors to understand the interaction between global and domestic imperatives. I do not argue that all of India's private sector has been changed in the manner outlined in this book. But we can no longer ignore the effect of global factors as they interact with domestic industry's weaknesses, strengths, and capabilities across India. A careful analysis of other industrial and agricultural sectors, which pays attention to the diversity of actors within each sector and how they were affected differently by global and domestic reform episodes, will tell us more about the changing balance of power emerging in India's political economy.

In sum, by now, India is deeply embedded in global markets and institutions, even as its domestic institutions both resist and modify such interactions. These developments within India resonate with a larger insight: the structural and institutional transformations that characterize the world's largest economies are not the product of domestic imperatives and designs alone, although domestic priorities and institutions shape the nature of that engagement. Rather, most countries are linked to global rules and markets in ways that were not possible earlier. These developments lead me to argue that we must not perceive the national goals and international engagement of countries as mutually exclusive. India must be viewed in an open-economy framework. This open politicaleconomy framework must incorporate attention to global markets, as well as rules of the game, to understand India and other emerging powers. Global forces are also in motion and can be understood with the help of the Global Design-in-Motion framework presented in Chapter 2. In this concluding chapter, I outline my findings in general terms and their implications for our understanding of four important themes: trajectory of India, globalization, international organizations, and developmental states.

8.1   How do international trade and global institutions affect India

For India watchers, the implicit story of "India's turn"[4] is rooted in internal expansion and growth of the economy.[5] This view suggests that

---

[4] The term is from Subramanian (2008).

[5] In 1985,. limited and short-lived liberalization started, which was followed by a more comprehensive and systematic liberalization in 1991. These policy reforms unleashed

internal growth unleashed in the 1980s and 1990s induced external integration: a growth-induced globalization story. This book recasts this conventional narrative about India, arguing that while the 1991 policy changes and the expansion of GDP during the 1980s were necessary conditions, they were not *sufficient* to sustain a high growth path or to *re orient* India toward global markets. This book suggests a different, nuanced account of transformation in India, arguing that global markets and global trade rules catalyzed a change in domestic interests and preferences as well as a transformation in domestic institutions. This book starts with a "second-image reversed" argument that focuses on how international variables affect domestic politics (Gourevitch 1978) but goes on to examine which specific aspects of globalization (rules or markets) *shape and change* Indian preferences and interests toward global integration. This generates a Global Design-in-Motion framework that takes the interaction between global and domestic actors seriously. This argument refuses to treat domestic and international affairs as separate or disconnected, thereby altering how we view India's changing place in the world.[6]

The Indian economy was undergoing structural changes in the 1980s, accelerated by the 1990s' reforms, but the global changes that I document in this book precipitated and accelerated these tendencies toward a deeper global integration that would not have been possible without the cumulative global effects. This argument makes it "necessary to rearrange the geography"[7] and place India's growth trajectory within a broader global context. How do national and global forces interact with respect to India? In order to explicate how the domestic and international levels interact in shaping India's rise to power, I relax the assumption of national political economies as closed systems, even for an insular country like India, which has resisted global interaction in the past. This book deploys this insight to analyze India's trade policy and institutions in the 1990s and beyond. An analysis of trade policy within India finds that international forces and institutions have not only shaped India's relations and trade with other nations but also redefined the internal policy process, domestic preferences, and domestic institutions and designs. While the 1991 reform originated in crisis, the WTO

---

a higher growth rate (4–5 percent between 1991 and 1995 and 6 percent from 1995 to 2003, and it accelerated to 9 percent between 2003 and 2007). Liberalization of industrial and trade policies in the early 1990s increased the competitiveness of much of India's industry and service sectors, sparking robust growth in output and consumer demand (Government of India, *Economic Survey*, various years).

[6] Katznelson (2013, 9) in a similar way analyzes America's New Deal.

[7] This phrase is used by Katznelson (2013).

structure enjoined a sense of purpose to the domestic state, which saw itself as an agent of global integration even as it sought to protect its own industry. This reorientation in our analytical lens, of viewing India as an open political economy, offers clues about why compliance with global norms occurs despite initial resistance and despite the loss of sovereignty that it entails. It also reveals how Indian actors renegotiate the terms of national autonomy even as they comply with international norms and rules (Olsen and Sinha 2013). This calls for a renewed emphasis on the international level, but the global level should not be seen as opposed to notions of domestic autonomy and variation across national systems. This analytical lens of viewing India as an *open economy* must simultaneously pay attention to the national and international processes through which governments and private actors seek to shape global institutions and markets (Fioretos 2011, 9). This book has, thus analyzed the effects of domestic and international politics *in jointly shaping* economic reforms in India and in transforming India into a rising power in the world.

8.2   Economic effects of globalization on India

This book argues that global trade and global trade agreements have changed India's domestic institutions, transforming the state's trading capacity as well as private interests around trade.[8] India, one of the most restrictive economies in the world, has become a relatively open and globally integrated economy despite the remainder of some barriers. Trade has become a driver of structural change in India. In 1991, trade in goods was at 15.7 percent of GDP, and it has risen to 42 percent in 2013. If services are added to data, then trade in 2013 is around 52 percent of GDP. More than half the Indian economy is linked to the global trading network, a trend not anticipated in 1991 when India initiated its paradigm-shifting reforms.

Trade barriers have come down in terms of both import tariffs and tariff and nontariff barriers. Quantitative restrictions were abolished in 2001. Williamson and Zagha note, "Trade barriers have declined further than anyone thought possible when reforms started in 1991, both on exports and imports." (Williamson and Zagha 2002, 8). Trade policies have been fundamentally transformed. Trade in services was liberalized, and India began negotiating a much more aggressive agenda in global trade. India has signed numerous trade agreements with its neighbors and with other

---

[8] For an argument about how trade increases the growth rate, see Bhagwati and Panagariya (2012). Also, the debates about whether trade increases or decreases poverty can be found in Topalova (2007, 2013), Hasan, Mitra, and Beyza Ural (2006–2007), and Cain, Hasan, and Mitra (2011).

Asian countries such as Singapore, Japan, and MERCOSUER, Malaysia, and ASEAN.

Essentially, trade has become a driver of economic change in India, creating structural change in India's economy. This refers to a number of developments. The trade to GDP ratio has tripled since 1991, and trade constitutes almost a half the Indian economy. The export intensity of many sectors has increased dramatically. Other structural changes are also evident. India began exporting nontraditional goods, such as electrical, chemicals (especially pharmaceuticals, plastics, paints, and toiletries), automobiles and automotive components, engineering goods, cigarettes, domestic appliances, and food-processing industries after 1990 (Banga 2006).[9] The story of India's pharmaceutical growth in external markets is well known (see Chapter 4 of this book), but India's revival in textiles and garments after decades of crisis and decline is especially noteworthy and cannot be explained by domestic arguments alone (see Chapters 6 and 7 of this book). Some of this would not have been possible without the opportunities created by changes in global agreements such as the Multifibre Arrangement (MFA) and the Agreement on Trade-Related Aspects of Intellectual Property Rights (TRIPS). Tradable sectors and industries have grown faster. For the service sector, for example, tradable services have seen a much faster growth rate than the nontradable service sector.

8.3   India's new political economy in an open global age

Globalization in the 1990s redrew the boundaries of India's political economy and transformed the structure of class dominance. First, the composition and nature of different classes that constitute the Indian capitalist class became broader, more diverse, and more fragmented with the emergence of new entrepreneurs, the creation of new business groups, and the consolidation of regional capitalists in regional, national, and global spaces (Baru 2000; Chatterjee 2011; Damodaran 2008; Sinha 2005b). While the hegemony of traditional monopoly businesses was challenged, they also adjusted to become better global and national players, as is evident in this book. Yet, the transformations did not stop there. Second, globalization generally and multilateral trade negotiations more specifically provided the stimulus and the site for changing state–business relations in India. As the

---

[9] India's traditional export industries were tea, leather and leather manufactures, gems and jewelry, garments, iron ore and metal ferrous ores, and medicinal and pharmaceutical products.

Uruguay Round was completed and the WTO came into existence, increased global dependence and integration urged business actors to seek new relationships, partnerships, and interactions with domestic state actors. State actors, in turn, sought to legitimize their international negotiations with increased interactions with industry leaders. Trade policy, then, provided the push and the context for transforming state–business relations in India. Regular consultations between business and the state became the norm.

Globalization had two related but distinct effects. It brought the national bourgeoisie closer to the state, which saw the national government as crucial to its global engagement. Yet, Indian businesses also began moving outside the national arena for capital and technological modernization (Chapters 4, 6, and 7 of this book). It made foreign capital and Indian capital in foreign markets more central to the policy debate and the policy formulation process. These transformations comprised a number of related changes: formal and public consultations between policymakers and business actors during policymaking and active input from industry and civil society groups. In turn, these changes enhanced the power of the Indian state in an open economy and global world as the Indian state sought greater power on behalf of its reinvigorated business classes and services sectors across a number of global arenas and domains. These findings challenge the usually negative assessments of the Indian state common among business press and much of academic scholarship on India.

This book has elaborated on an open political economy framework to understand the new India. India's model of development has moved from a rent-seeking "particularistic" system (Herring 1999) to a "new developmental state" (Trubek et al. 2013). However, the new developmental state in India is distinctive in that it combines statism with multiple plural interests, which can be captured by the phrase "statist pluralism." Statist pluralism is characterized by the dominance of the Indian state that facilitates and is shaped by a multiple set of plural interests, the equilibrium of class elements that Bardhan analyzed in 1984 and is referenced by Rudolph and Rudolph as "involuted pluralism" (1987). Over time, both the Indian state and Indian businesses have become more diverse and fragmented even as they face outward. The creation of new capitalists in the crucible of the developmental state as well as in interaction with global forces must also be analyzed as part of the Indian story. As an illustration, even some elements of salaried professionals (software entrepreneurs) have become global entrepreneurs (for example, Infosys, Ltd., from Karnataka).

In sum, three different trends are important. First, new winners have been created that seek greater global integration than ever before. A diverse coalition of varied interests supports greater economic reforms and global reach. Second, the capitalist or the industrial sector has become broader, diversified, and fragmented. While there are signs of the emergence of coordination and encompassing associations, especially in the textile and pharmaceutical sectors, Indian business remains quite divided. The divided state faces a divided capitalist class even as the power of producer classes has increased. The Indian capitalist class is a more indigenous and diversified class than ever before. For example, the Indian pharmaceutical sector is divided into three distinct segments: the MNCs, the large Indian players, and the large number of small-scale players. It seeks different relationships with different kinds of state agencies both domestically and across issue areas. Third, different elements of capital have established new linkages with global capital and global locations. The global linkages of Indian businesses as well as the salaried classes need to be inserted into our models of the changing political economy of India.

These findings challenge our conventional framework of India's political economy, which argued that relatively narrow groups and classes – rich farmers, industrial capitalists, and the salaried professionals or the dominant property classes – were served by the state in a rent-seeking relationship (Bardhan 1984). Each of these groups received special favors and subsidies from the state. The combination of balance of power gave the state some autonomy, as it acted as a referee among the three groups (Bardhan 1984). In a similar vein, Anne Krueger characterized India as a rent-seeking state (1974). Many scholars confirmed this view (Kaviraj 1988; Rudolph and Rudolph 1987; Vanaik 1990), while some others challenged it (Dhar 1987). Bardhan recently admitted that this view of the balance of power among the classes no longer holds. So what has replaced the old equilibrium of class dynamics? Bardhan argues that the balance may have "tilted in favor of capitalist business" (2010, 135), but he does not provide any direct evidence for that shift. Akhil Gupta also notes, "Liberalization signaled the breakup of this precarious balance between dominant classes and also signaled the decisive movement of the state machinery in favor of industrial capitalists" (2012, 280). Yet, in terms of direct subsidies and state expenditure, industrial capitalists have received less from the state in the last two decades. Between 1985 and 1990, industry received 13.4 percent of state budgetary funds, but that declined to 4.2 percent between 2007 and 2012.[10] These numbers

---

[10] Government of India, *Economic Survey*, various years.

indicate that the power of the industrial capitalists may be overestimated in the current literature.

This book has attempted to provide solid empirical evidence for the shifts in business power (see Chapters 4–7). Industrial capitalists may have power under the current regime, but externally oriented businesses do much better than domestically oriented capital. In fact, a differentiation between competitive (export-oriented) and protected sectors has emerged, with greater pressure on the protective sectors to become more export oriented. This has created a wider and broader coalition supporting economic reforms, especially global integration. This finding led me to go beyond the current approaches that see India as a closed economy and analyze the role of trade and external interdependence on India's changing class balance. The existing reformulations fail to do justice to these significant changes in India's political economy.

8.4   States and entrepreneurs in a global world of rules and markets

This book offers a new triangular perspective on the nature of globalization, the evolution of the developmental state in India, and the emerging nature of capitalism. First, I suggest that globalization must be seen in its multifarious forms and as creating both new opportunities and new pressures (Weiss 2005). Research on global organizations has moved toward delineating just *how* international institutions matter in *altering* preferences or politics within a country.[11] Many of these studies outline the role of key mechanisms such as conditionality, normative pressure, socialization, learning, rational adaptation, and diffusion. This book also outlines the role of mechanisms such as sovereignty and transaction costs, legal framing, and public information discovery about global markets. Very few studies unpack the architecture of global regimes and systematically analyze how these mechanisms work in specific cases and the processes through which global rules impact domestic politics in specific countries.

We need to go deeper into the domestic realm of many countries to test the various mechanisms outlined by the international relations literature. How exactly does the domestic trade politics *shift* as a result of the intervening role of international rules, incentives, and opportunities *even when* an international agreement may be contested within the domestic politics, as was the case with India? This builds on the idea that not all

---

[11] Pevehouse (2002); Hafner-Burton (2009); Goldstein (1998); Johnston (2001); Kelley (2004), Acharya (2004); Greenhill (2010); Zangl (2008).

international institutions or regimes are equally facilitative for global integration; specific aspects of the institution change the likelihood that actors will comply with the rules. Thus, why some international negotiations succeed while others run fail becomes crucial?[12] We need to know what specific dimensions of a global governance regime affect domestic priorities, reframe global ambitions of erstwhile recalcitrant nations, and change perceptions of interests.

To assess whether an international institution actually affected domestic policy and interests is extremely difficult as some change might be consistent with internal rational incentives or domestic actors may make superficial compliance noises to international organizations but do something very different in actual practice. Similarly, it is important to distinguish between the effect of purely market forces and the role played by international rules-mediated effects. Thus, the key challenge is to isolate the effect of markets versus institutions and domestic versus international factors. Domestic actors and institutions certainly mediate and alter the processes of globalization, as suggested by domestic politics approaches, but static concepts of domestic effects fail to capture the revelation of and *change* in trade preferences and the changing modes of collective action within a country.

8.5   The developmental state and globalization

How have the global system of markets and the rules affected the goals and capacities of the Indian state? It is commonly believed that global trade interdependence undermines the Westphalian sovereignty, a basic premise of the nation – state system (Rodrik 1997; Sobel 1999). Similarly, many argue that India has moved closer to "Washington consensus" (Williamson 1990) and neoliberalism since 1991 (Kohli 2007, 1). There is no doubt that multilateral trade institutions, like the World Trade Organization, altered the nature of markets within India as well as what a government could do to design its own agendas. More specifically, the Indian government had to accept global legal constraints on its powers, operationalized through the WTO dispute-settlement procedures. This global structure carries the potential of quietly eroding national sovereignty. Autonomy within compliance is also possible, but expertise in negotiations – rather than political slogans, headlines, and photo ops – counts. Governments that can make trans-national agreements work favorably gain an upper hand in the bargain.

---

[12] Davis (2004) also raises this question for agricultural liberalization in Japan and the European Union.

Thus, overgeneralized conclusions about state sovereignty or the loss of sovereignty need to assess the specific actions of the state across varied policy areas and sectors. As the saying goes, the devil is in the details.

This book shows that rather than moving toward a neoliberal order where the state has been weakened, new state capacities have been strengthened through incorporating expertise and explicit consultation with private actors in India. In so doing, this book contributes to the theoretical debates around the ongoing trajectory of developmental states and their transformation into new developmental states (O'Riain 2004; Stubbs 2011; Trubek et al. 2013). While India was seen as a failed developmental state (Herring 1999; Sinha 2005a) in the postwar period, this book's findings challenge a dominant consensus that the economic reforms of 1991 mark a return to market-oriented reforms. In keeping with the arguments of the reregulation literature, which argues that free markets require more rules (Hsueh 2012; Schamis 2002; Thelen 2014; Vogel 1995; Vogel and Kagan 2004), this book shows how global markets also require rules and nonmarket mechanisms to reinforce global flows and trade. This book builds on, but also goes beyond, conclusions of the new developmental state literature, which suggests that after the recognition of government failures in the 1980s and 1990s, some states have evolved into new developmental states that work with public–private models and feature greater interaction between private and state actors in shaping economic policy. In the new developmental state model, states play a steering not regulative role (Jacobs 2010; Nedumpara, Shaffer, and Sinha 2015; Sinha 2007). This book has built a theoretical framework to outline how global mechanisms and effects work in and through molecular transformations in India's state capacity. Thus, the state transformations revealed by the reregulation and new developmental state literature are a joint product of changing domestic interests, unleashing of new capacities, and global institutional structures. Without a theory of how domestic changes are unleashed by a global order that is legally framed, we are unable to assess and predict changes across states, markets, and the private sector. The Global Design-in-Motion framework developed in this book offers us a way to analyze such interactions in a systematic way as well as builds a theory of causal mechanisms.

Simultaneously, the Indian experience of dealing with global responsibilities has shown a fascinating transformation in the way state actors view what the state does and should do or how it defines sovereignty. In the earlier era, the state's task was to protect its borders and protect its self-reliant autonomy. At the global level, the Indian state sought to defend the rights of all developing countries and resist US hegemony. In the current era, an additional goal has come to the fore. Governments now compete economically in an open world and seek global status. The aspiration toward self-reliance has given way to economic growth and expansion at the global level. Seeking export markets and competitive strength and defending the ability of its economic organizations to compete in an open-world economy are seen as important goals.

State facilitation of trade reforms has happened in molecular and inconsistent ways. It has not been perfect and has had had many collateral effects. Yet, it has been consequential. An analysis of trade liberalization reveals a different, more positive view of the Indian state. The trading state has pursued global integration and increased its own capacity – tradecraft – significantly. Yet, the other side of the coin has been its closeness with capital of diverse shades including foreign capital.

8.6   Changing private preferences in a global age

Modern economic theory has ignored and neglected an analysis of the origin of and change in preferences of the private sector. To be sure, it is very difficult to measure preferences and the changes therein. Yet changes in the large economic context such as globalization can be useful and important conjunctures to make visible such preferences and strategies as they are "revealed" in a direct way. I adopted this research strategy in this book to assess private sector strategies and the contextual mechanism that may drive those strategies. An analysis of interests in motion related to textiles and the pharmaceutical sector was one of this study's contributions.

Economists outline the following mechanisms through which liberalization may affect firms: competition, prices, and market structures. This book finds that globalization also rests on institutions and constraining mechanisms such as the international agreements required by the WTO. The development of global exchange relies on both voluntary, price-mediated exchange and constraining mechanisms, such as economic threats and new globally defended compliance costs, generated by global organizations such as WTO, IMF, and the World Bank. Importantly, public information provided by the state and learning and linkage rather than independent market behavior hold the key to global growth and expansion. Both state and private sector actors must learn these secrets of globalization to navigate the complex environment framed by rules, states, and markets.

What does this research find? New global firms from countries like India do not emerge fully formed on the global stage. Private sector firms used to domestic protections do not adjust to a new global age by themselves. They are coerced, nudged, and catalyzed by activities of global organizations, even as new markets and supply chains in the global arena create new threats and new opportunities, and states nudge domestic firms to export. While scholars have begun to recognize the changing activities of latecomer firms from countries like India (Mathews 2002), this book challenged the assumption that their rise is driven by firm-level considerations alone.

In order to study the impact of global rules of the game, we need a dynamic political economy approach to international organizations that examines the multiple and diverse changes unleashed in domestic institutions and private interests over time. Most studies of international institutions focus on state actors, while the impact of international organizations on private sector and nonstate actors may be even more important.[13] Such changes, in turn, affect the way countries design policies and respond to international agreements in the future.[14] We thus need more studies that link mechanisms with actual domestic changes across specific cases. This book enhances the theoretical arguments found in recent scholarship on global organizations by exploring the impact of global trade rules on domestic structures and political economy of an important and globally crucial country: India.

---

[13] See Dai (2007), who also makes a case for looking at nonstate actors. Other scholars have also begun to emphasize the role of private actors. An early study was Cutler, Hauffler, and Porter (1999). See Mattli (2003), who analyzed the role of private interests and international standards, Mosley and Singer (2008) for a role of private actors in financial regulation, and Sell (2003) for an analysis of the effect of private firms on the intellectual property rights regime (TRIPS).

[14] In a similar vein, Shalden (2009) notes: "[W]e need to reorient our attention from the legal to the political economy aspects of international agreements – that is, not the rules per se but how such agreements unleash economic and social changes than in turn affect policy choices" (2009, 43).

Appendix: Field trips, list of interviews, and libraries visited

I conducted this research over many visits to India (Delhi, Mumbai), Geneva, and Washington, DC. Research trips were conducted to India during (1) December 2002, (2) July 1, 2003–August 2004, (3) July 15, 2006–August 20, 2006, and (4) January 2009–June 2009. I visited Geneva in November of 2002. Interviews at Washington, DC, were conducted during 2004–2005. Many respondents requested anonymity, and their identities have not been revealed.

Government interviews, New Delhi

Minister of State for Commerce, Jairam Ramesh, 2009
Secretary, Ministry of Commerce, Government of India, 2004
Secretary, Ministry of Commerce, Government of India, 2009
Additional Secretary, Ministry of Commerce, Government of India, 2004
Joint Secretary 1, Trade Policy Division, Ministry of Commerce, Government of India, 2003
Joint Secretary 2, Trade Policy Division, Ministry of Commerce, Government of India, 2003
Joint Secretary 3, Ministry of Commerce, Government of India, 2003
Joint Secretary 4, Ministry of Commerce, Government of India, 2003
Advisor, Ministry of Commerce, Economic Division, Government of India, 2003
Director 1, Trade Policy Division, Ministry of Commerce, Government of India, 2003
Director 2, Trade Policy Division, Ministry of Commerce, Government of India, 2003
Director 3, Trade Policy Division, Ministry of Commerce, Government of India, 2003

Director 4, Trade Policy Division, Ministry of Commerce, Government of India, 2003
Director 5, Trade Policy Division, Ministry of Commerce, Government of India, 2003
Official, Director General of Anti-Dumping, Government of India, 2003
Joint Secretary, DGAD, Government of India, 2003
Official, Tariff Commission, Government of India, 2004
Director, Ministry of Industrial policy and Promotion, Government of India, 2003
Joint Secretary, Ministry of Industry Policy and Promotion, Government of India, 2003
Joint Secretary, Ministry of Textiles, Government of India, 2003
Joint Secretary, Ministry of Textiles, Government of India, 2003
Additional Secretary, Ministry of Textiles, Government of India, 2003
Additional Secretary, Ministry of Rural Development, Government of India, 2004

Retired civil servants

Jayantro Bagchi, Retired Civil Servant, Ministry of Textiles, Government of India, 2004, 2009
Prabir Sengupta, Retired Secretary, Ministry of Commerce, 2002; interview was conducted when he was with IIFT, in 2003
B. K. Zutshi, Former Ambassador of India to the WTO, 2004
M. Dubey, Former Foreign Secretary, Government of India, 2003
P. P Prabhu, Former Commerce Secretary, Government of India, Bangalore, 2004
Ex-Ambassador Kishan Rana, Delhi, 2004, 2009
S. P. Shukla, Retired Secretary from Ministry of Commerce, Government of India, 2004
Sanjeev Mishra, 13th Finance Commission, was part of Textile Ministry in the 1980s, New Delhi, 2006

Industry, pharmaceuticals and textiles

Senior Officer, Pfizer, Mumbai 2003
Mr. Shahani, Novartis, India, Ltd., Mumbai, 2003
Manager 1, Ranbaxy, New Delhi, 2004

Manager 2, Ranbaxy, New Delhi, 2004
Manger 3, Ranbaxy, New Delhi, 2004
Consultant, Ranbaxy, New Delhi, 2004
Manager, small-sector pharmaceutical firm, Gurgaon
Manager, small-sized pharmaceutical firm, Delhi
Major industry CEO, pharmaceutical sector, Mumbai
CEO of a large-sized company, pharmaceutical sector, Mumbai
TATA, WTO cell, Officer, Mumbai, 2004
TATA Office Director, 2009, Washington, DC, 2005
Sun Pharmaceutical, Interview, Ahmedabad, 2004
Official, Dishman, Ahmedabad, 2004
Consultant Pharmaceutical Industry, Ahmedabad, 2004
Cipla, Senior Officer, Mumbai, 2004
Shahi Export House, Textile large-scale company, New Delhi,
2009
Li Fung, Textile distributor, New Delhi, 2009
Textile company, medium-sized, New Delhi, 2003
Garment company, Mumbai, 2004
Garment company, Mumbai, 2004
Large-sized textile company, Ahmedabad, 2004
Garment Company, medium-sized, Ahmedabad, 2004

Business associations

CII, Head of WTO Cell, T. K. Bhaumik, New Delhi, 2004
CII, Officer, WTO Cell, New Delhi, 2004
Officer 2, CII WTO Cell, New Delhi, 2004
CII, Consultant who served at the CII Geneva Office in 2003,
New Delhi, 2004
Officer 3, CII International programs, New Delhi, 2004
Secretary-General of CII, N. Srinivasan, New Delhi, 2004
Tarun Das, Mentor, CII
Secretary-General, IDMA, Mumbai, 2004
Officer IDMA, Mumbai, 2004
Officer IDMA, Mumbai, 2004
Secretary-General, OPPI, Mumbai, 2004
Officer at OPPI, Mumbai, 2004
Officer at OPPI, Mumbai, 2004
N. B. Zaveri, Lawyer specializing in WTO, Mumbai, 2004
D. G. Shah, Director-General, Indian Pharmaceutical Alliance,
Mumbai, 2004

Secretary-General, Confederation of Indian Textile Industry, D. K. Nair, New Delhi, 2003, 2004, 2009
Officer, CITI, New Delhi, 2004

Interviews at WTO, Geneva (November 2002)

Jayashree Watal, Counselor to the Intellectual Property Rights Division, WTO, Geneva
Officer at the Information and External Relations Division, WTO, Geneva
Officer, Capacity Building Department, Institute for Training and Technical Cooperation, WTO, Geneva
Permanent Mission, Pakistan at WTO
Permanent Mission, Brazil at WTO

Indian Mission at Geneva

Ambassador to the WTO, Indian Mission, November 2002
Deputy Permanent Representative to the WTO, November 2002
Counselor, WTO, Indian Mission, November 2002
First Secretary, WTO, November 2002
First Secretary, Legal, November 2002
First Secretary, WTO, November 2002
Atul Kaushik, Consultant, Legal
Hardeep Puri, India's Ambassador to UN, Geneva
Ravi Kanth, Journalist in Geneva

Washington, DC, 2004–2005

Frank Wisner, US Ambassador to India in the early 1990s, 2005
Teresita Schaffer, Washington, DC
Robert Hathaway, September 2004, Washington, DC
Dennis Kux, October 2004, Washington, DC
Official at Indian Embassy, Washington, DC
Official at Brazil Embassy
Official at Chinese Embassy
Head of CII in DC, Kiran Pasricha
Official at CII, Washington, DC
Secretary-General, NASSCOM, June 2005, Washington, DC
Geza Feketekuty, Consultant, Washington, DC

Research think tanks, academicians, and professors

Director-General, Dr. Nagesh Kumar, Research and Information System for Developing Countries (RIS)

Dr. Prabir De, Researcher, RIS, Research and Information System for Developing Countries (RIS)

Director, Isher Ahluwalia, ICRIER

Dr. Arpita Mukherjee, Researcher, ICRIER

Professor, IIFT, B. Dhar

IIFT, Director, Dhar, 2009

Professor Rupa Chanda, IIM, Bangalore, Interview in Delhi, 2004

Errol D'Souza, IIM, Ahmedabad

Rakesh Basant, IIM, Ahmedabad

Subhashish Gangopadhyaya, Director, India Development Foundation, 2003

Amir Ullah Khan, Associate Fellow, India Development Foundation, 2003

Pradeep Mehta, CUTS (Consumer Unity and Trust Society, International), New Delhi, 2004

Member, CUTS (Consumer Unity and Trust Society, International), New Delhi, 2004

Dr. Uttam Gupta, Chief Economist, Fertilizer Association of India, New Delhi, August 2006

Journalists

Dr. Sanjaya Baru, Chief Editor, *Financial Express*, New Delhi, August 2003, 2006

Dr. Chandra Mohan, Senior Editor, *Financial Express*, New Delhi, 2003

Reporter 1, *Financial Express*

Senior Editor, *Outlook*

T.N. Ninan, Chief Editor, *Business Standard*, August 2006

AK. Bhattacharya, Senior Editor, *Business Standard*, New Delhi, August 2006

Rohit Saran, Senior Editor, *Business Today*

Editor, *Business Today*

Editor, *Business Standard*

Journalist, *ExpressTextile*, Mumbai

Reporter, *ExpressPharma*, Mumbai

Reporter, Mumbai

Paranjoy Guha Thakurta, Editor and Journalist, New Delhi, August 2006

NGOs

B. K. Keayla, National Working Group on Patent Law
Suman Sahai, Convener, Gene Campaign, New Delhi
Member, Gene Campaign
Member, Gene Campaign
Amit Sengupta, Delhi Science Forum
Member, Indian Peoples Campaign Against the WTO (IPCAWTO)
Member, Indian Peoples Campaign Against the WTO (IPCAWTO)

Libraries visited and consulted

Parliament library, New Delhi
Indian Institute of Industrial Development Library (ISID), New Delhi
Research and Information System for Developing Countries (RIS) library
Indian Council on International Economic Relations library (ICRIER)
Indian Institute of Foreign Trade library, New Delhi
World Affairs, Sapru House library
World Bank library, New Delhi
Ministry of Commerce, Government of India, library
CII library, Gurgaon
OPPI library, Mumbai
IDMA library, Mumbai
CITI library, New Delhi
PHD Chambers library, New Delhi
FICCI library, New Delhi

References

Abbott, Kenneth, and Duncan Snidal. 1998. "Why States Act through Formal International Agreements." *Journal of Conflict Resolution* 42 (1): 3–32.

Abbott, Kenneth, and Duncan Snidal. 2000a. "Hard and Soft Law in International Governance." *International Organization* 54 (3): 421–456.

Abbott, Kenneth W., Robert Keohane, Andrew Moravcsik, Anne-Marie Slaughter, and Duncan Snidal. 2000b. "The Concept of Legalization." *International Organization* 54 (3): 17–35.

Acharya, Amitav. 2004. "How Ideas Spread: Whose Norms Matter? Norm Localization and Institutional Change in Asian Regionalism." *International Organization* 58 (2): 239–275.

Aggarwal, Aradhna. 2007. "Pharmaceutical Industry." In *International Competitiveness and Knowledge Based Industries in India,* edited by Nagesh Kumar and K. J. Joseph, 143–184. New Delhi: Oxford University Press and RIS.

Aggarwal, Vinod K., 1985. *Liberal Protectionism: The International Politics of Organized Textile Trade.* Berkeley: University of California Press.

Aggarwal, Vinod K., ed. 1998. *Institutional Designs for a Complex World: Bargaining, Linkages, and Nesting.* Ithaca, NY: Cornell University Press.

Aggarwal, Vinod K., and Rahul Mukherji. 2008. "India's Shifting Trade Policy: South Asia and Beyond." In *Asia's New Architecture: Evolving Structures for Managing Trade and Security Relations,* edited by Vinod Aggarwal and Min Gyo Koo, 215–258. Heidelberg: Springer Verlag.

Aggarwal, Vinod K., and Seungjoo Lee. 2011. "The Domestic Political Economy of Preferential Trade Agreements in the Asia Pacific." In *Trade Policy in the Asia Pacific,* edited by Vinod K. Aggarwal and Seungjoo Lee, 1–28. New York: Springer.

Aggarwal, Vinod K., and Shjiro Urata, eds. 2002. *Winning in Asia, Japanese Style: Market and Non-Market Strategies for Success.* New York: Palgrave Macmillian.

Ahluwalia, Montek S. 1995. "India's Economic Reforms in India: The Future of Economic Reform." Unpublished working paper.

Ahluwalia, Montek S. 2002. "Economic Reforms in India Since 1991: Has Gradualism Worked?" *Journal of Economic Perspectives* 16(3): 67–88.

Ahluwalia, Montek S. 2006. "India's Experience with Globalization." *Australian Economic Review* 39 (1): 1–13.

Ahmad, Husain. 1988. *Technological Development in Drugs and Pharmaceutical Industry in India.* New Delhi: Navrang.

Alamgir, Jalal. 2009. *India's Open-Economy Policy: Globalism, Rivalry, Continuity.* London: Routledge.

Allen, Douglas W. 1991. "What Are Transaction Costs?" *Research in Law and Economics* 14:1–18.

Amsden, Alice. 1989. *Asia's Next Giant: South Korea and Late Industrialization.* Oxford: Oxford University Press.

Anderson, Erin, and Hubert Gatignon. 2008. "Firms and the Creation of New Markets." In *Handbook of New Institutional Economics,* edited by Claude Menard and Mary M. Shirley, 401–431. The Netherlands: Springer.

Athreye, Suma, Dinar Kale, and Shama Ramani. 2009. "Experimentation with Strategy and the Evolution of Dynamic Capability in the Indian Pharmaceutical Sector." *Industrial and Corporate Change* 18 (4): 729–759.

Bagchi, Jayanta. 2004. *Indian Textile Industry: Liberalization and World Market.* New Delhi: Samskriti.

Bailey, Michael A., Judith Goldstein, and Barry R. Weingast. 1997. "The Institutional Roots of American Trade Policy: Politics, Coalitions, and International Trade." *World Politics* 49 (3): 309–338.

Baldwin, David A., ed. 1976. *America in an Interdependent World: Problems of United States Foreign Policy.* Hanover, NH: University Press of New England.

Baldwin, Matthew. 2006. "EU Trade Politics–Heaven or Hell?" *Journal of European Public Policy* 13 (6): 926–942.

Ballance, Robert, Janos Pogany, and Helmut Forstner. 1992. *The World's Pharmaceutical Industries: An International Perspective on Innovation, Competition, and Policy.* England: Edward Elgar.

Banerji, Shondeep. 2000. "The Indian Intellectual Property Rights Regime and the TRIPs Agreement." In *Intellectual Property Rights in Emerging Markets,* edited by Clarisa Long, 47–95. Washington, DC: American Enterprise Institute for Public Policy Research.

Banga, Rashmi. 2006. "The Export-Diversifying Impact of Japanese and US Foreign Direct Investments in the Indian Manufacturing Sector." *Journal of International Business Studies* 37 (4): 558–568.

Banga, Rashmi, and Abhijit Das. 2012. *Role of Trade Policies in Growth of Indian Manufacturing Sector.* In *Twenty Years of India's Liberalization: Experience and Lessons,* edited by Rashmi Banga and A. Das. Geneva: Centre for WTO Studies and UNCTAD.

Bardhan, Pranab. 1984. *The Political Economy of Development in India.* New Delhi: Oxford University Press.

Bardhan, Pranab. 1998 [1984]. *The Political Economy of Development in India.* Expanded Edition. New Delhi: Oxford University Press.

Bardhan, Pranab. 2010. *Awakening Giants, Feet of Clay: Assessing the Economic Rise of China and India.* Princeton: Princeton University Press.

Barnett, Michael N., and Martha Finnemore. 1999. "The Politics, Power, and Pathologies of International Organizations." *International Organization* 53 (4): 699–732.

Barnwal, Bijay Kumar. 2000. *Economic Reforms and Policy Change: A Case Study of Indian Drug Industry.* New Delhi: Classical Publishing Company.

Baron, David P. 1999. "Integrated Market and Nonmarket Strategies in Client and Interest Group Politics." *Business and Politics* 1 (1): 7–34.

Barton, John H., Judith Goldstein, Timothy E. Josling, and Richard Steinberg. 2006. *The Evolution of the Trade Regime: Politics, Law and Economics of the GATT and WTO*. Princeton: Princeton University Press.

Baru, Sanjaya. 2000. "Economic Policy and the Development of Capitalism in India: The Role of International Capitalists and Political Parties." In *Transforming India: Social and Political Dynamics of Democracy*, edited by Francine Frankel, 207–230. New Delhi: Oxford University Press.

Baru, Sanjaya. 2006. *The Strategic Consequences of India's Economic Performance*. New Delhi: Academic Foundation.

Barzel, Yoram. 1997. *Economic Analysis of Property Rights*. Cambridge: Cambridge University Press.

Basant, Rakesh. 2011. "Intellectual Property Protection, Regulation and Innovation in Developing Economies: The Case of Indian Pharmaceutical Industry." *Innovation and Development* 1 (1): 115–133.

Basheer, Shamnad. 2007. *The "Glivec" Patent Saga: A 3-D Perspective on Indian Patent Policy and Trips Compliance*. ATRIP, www.atrip.org/Content/Essays/Sh amnad%2520Basheer%2520Glivec%2520Patent%2520Saga.doc +&cd=1&hl=en&ct=clnk&gl=us.

Bates, Robert H. 1997. *Open-Economy Politics: The Political Economy of the World Coffee Trade*. Princeton, NJ: Princeton University Press.

Bedi, Jatinder S., and Caesar B. Cororaton. 2008. *Cotton-Textile-Apparel Sectors of India: Situations and Challenges Faced, IFPRI Discussion Paper, 00801*. Washington, DC: International Food Policy Research Institute (IFPRI).

Bennett, Andrew 2004. "Case Study Methods: Design, Use and Comparative Advantages." In *Models, Numbers and Cases: Methods for Studying International Relations*, edited by Debra Sprinz and Yael Wolinsky-Nahmias, 19–55. Ann Arbor: University of Michigan Press.

Berger, Suzanne, and Ronald Dore. 1996. *National Diversity and Global Capitalism*. Ithaca, NY: Cornell University Press.

Bernstein, Steven, and Benjamin Cashore. 2000. "Four Paths of Internationalization and Domestic Policy Change: The Case of Ecoforestry in British Columbia, Canada." *Canadian Journal of Political Science* 33 (1): 67–99.

Bewley, Truman F. 1999. *Why Wages Don't Fall during a Recession*. Boston: Harvard University Press.

Bhagwati, Jagdish, and Arvind Panagariya. 2012. "Introduction: Trade, Poverty, Inequality, and Democracy." In *India's Reforms: How they Produced Inclusive Growth*, edited by Jagdish Bhagwati and Arvind Panagariya, 3–17. Oxford: Oxford University Press.

Bhagwati, J. N., and T.N. Srinivasan. 1984. "Indian Development Strategy: Some Comments." *Economic and Political Weekly* 19 (47): 2006–2007.

Bhandari, Bhupesh. 2005. *The Ranbaxy Story*. New Delhi: Penguin Global.

Bhide, Sheela Thakar. 1996. "India's Textile and Clothing Exports to the USA and EEC: The Multi-Fibre Arrangement and Beyond." Ph.D Dissertation, University of Geneva.

Blackhurst, Richard. 1998. "The Capacity of the WTO to Fulfill its Mandate." In *The WTO as an International Organization*, edited by Anne O. Krueger, 31–58. Oxford: Oxford University Press.

Bode, Maarten. 2008. *Taking Traditional Knowledge to the Market: The Modern Image of the Ayurvedic and Unani Industry, 1980–2000*. Hyderabad: Orient Longman Private Limited.

Booth, William. 1994. "On the Idea of the Moral Economy." *American Political Science Review* 88 (3): 653–667.

Botcheva, Liliana, and Lisa L. Martin. 2001. "Institutional Effects on State Behavior: Convergence and Divergence." *International Studies Quarterly* 45 (1): 1–26.

Bowonder, B., and Nrupesh Mastakar. 2005. "Strategic Business Leadership Through Innovation and Globalization: A Case Study of Ranbaxy Limited." *International Journal of Technology and Management* 32 (1/2): 176–198.

Bowonder, B., Manoj Thomas, Vamshi Mohan Rokkam, and Artie Rokkam. 2003. "Managing Strategic Innovation: An Analysis of Dr. Reddy's Laboratories." *International Journal of Technology Management* 25 (3/4): 247–267.

Burley, Ann-Marie, and Walter Mattli. 1993. "Europe Before the Court: A Political Theory of Legal Integration." *International Organization* 47 (1): 41–76.

Busch, Marc, and Edward D. Mansfield. 1995. "The Political Economy of Nontariff Barriers: A Cross-National Analysis." *International Organization* 49 (4): 723–749.

Busch, Marc, and Eric Reinhardt. 2002. "Testing International Trade Law: Empirical Studies of GATT/WTO Dispute Settlement." In *The Political Economy of International Trade Law: Essays in Honor of Robert E. Hudec*, edited by Daniel L. M. Kennedy and James D. Southwick, 457–481. New York: Cambridge University Press.

Buthe, Tim, and Walter Mattli. 2011. *The New Global Rulers: The Privatization of Regulation in the World Economy*. Princeton, NJ: Princeton University Press.

Cain, Jewel, R. Hasan, and D. Mitra. 2011. "Trade Liberalization and Poverty Reduction: New Evidence from Indian States." In *India's Reforms: How They Produced Inclusive Growth*, edited by J. Bhagwati and Arvind Panagariya, 91–185. Oxford University Press.

Callaghan Helen. 2010. "Beyond Methodological Nationalism: How Multilevel Governance Affects Clash of Capitalisms." *Journal of European Public Policy* 17: 564–80.

Cao, Xun. 2009. "Networks of Intergovernmental Organizations and Convergence in Domestic Economic Policies." *International Studies Quarterly* 53 (4): 1095–1130.

Caporaso, J. A. 1989. *The Elusive State: International and Comparative Perspective*. Newbury Park, CA: Sage.

Cerny, P. G. 1990. *The Changing Architecture of Politics*. London: Sage.

Cerny, P. G. 1995. "Globalization and the Changing Logic of Collective Action." *International Organization* 49 (4): 595–625.

Chadha, Alka. 2009. "Product Cycles, Innovation and Exports: A Study of Indian Pharmaceuticals." *World Development* 37 (9): 1478–1483.

Chanda, Rupa. 2002. *Globalization of Services: India's Opportunities and Constraints*. New Delhi: Oxford University Press.

Chanda, Rupa, and G. Sasidaran. 2007. "GATS and Developments in India's Services Sector." In *India's Liberalization Experience: Hostage to the WTO?*, edited by Suparna Karmakar, Rajiv Kumar, and Bibek Debroy, 169–212. New Delhi: Sage.

Chatterjee, Partha. 2011. "Democracy and Economic Transformation in India." In *Understanding India's New Political Economy: A Great Transformation*, edited by Sanjay Reddy Sanjay Ruparelia, John Harriss, and Stuart Corbridge, 17–34. London: Routledge.

Chaudhuri, Sudip. 2004. "The Pharmaceutical Industry." In *The Structure of Indian Industry*, edited by Subir Gokarn, Anindya Sen, and Rajendra R. Vaidya, 144–179. New Delhi: Oxford University Press.

Chaudhuri, Sudip. 2005. *The WTO and India's Pharmaceutical Industry: Patent Protection, TRIPS, and Developing Countries*. New Delhi: Oxford University Press.

Chaudhuri, Sudip. 2007. "Is Product Patent Protection Necessary in Developing Countries for Innovation?: R and D by Indian Pharmaceutical Companies After TRIPS." In *IIM, Calcutta Working Paper Series*. Calcutta: Indian Institute of Management, Calcutta.

Chayes, Abram, and Antonia Chayes. 1995. *The New Sovereignty: Compliance with International Regulatory Agreements*. Cambridge: Harvard University Press.

Chibber, Vivek. 2003. *Locked in Place: State-Building and Late Industrialization in India*. Princeton, NJ: Princeton University Press.

Child, John. 1972. "Organizational Structure. Environment, and Performance: The Role of Strategic Choice." *Sociology* 6 (1): 1–22.

Chittoor, Raveendra, and Sougata Ray. 2007. "Internationalization Paths of Indian Pharmaceutical Firms–A Strategic Group Analysis." *Journal of International Management* 13 (3): 338–355.

CII. 1999. "*WTO: The Reality of the New Trading Order*." Proceedings and WTO 2000 Series of Workshops, New Delhi.

CMIE. Various. *PROWESS Database*. Edited by CMIE. New Delhi: CMIE.

Coase, R.H. 1937. "The Nature of the Firm." *Economica* 4 (16): 386–405.

Coase, R.H. 1960. "The Problem of Social Cost." *Journal of Law and Economics* 3: 1–44.

Collective, Factsheet 1. ND. *The 10th Month: Bombay's Historic Textile Strike*. Bombay: Rankeen Xerox Service.

Commerce, Ministry of. 2003. *Fortnightly News and Views on WTO Issues*. Edited by Trade Policy Department. New Delhi: Ministry of Commerce.

Corbridge, Stuart, John Harriss, Sanjay Ruparelia and Sanjay Reddy. 2011. "Introduction: India's Transforming Political Economy." In *Understanding India's New Political Economy: A Great Transformation?*, edited by Sanjay Reddy Sanjay Ruparelia, John Harriss, and Stuart Corbridge, 1–16. London: Routledge.

Corbridge, Stuart, and John Harriss. 2003. *Reinventing India: Liberalization, Hindu Nationalism and Popular Democracy*. New Delhi: Oxford University Press.

Coriat, Benjamin. 2008. "Introduction: A New Stage in the Fight Against HIV/AIDS Pandemic-An Economic Perspective." In *The Political Economy of HIV/AIDs in Developing Countries: TRIPS, Public Health Systems and Free Access*, edited by Benjamin Coriat, 1–19. Cheltenham, UK: Edward Elgar.

Cortell, Andrew P. 2006. *Mediating Globalization: Domestic Institutions and Industrial Policies in the United States and Britain*. Albany: State University of New York Press.

Croome, John. 1995. *Reshaping the World Trade System: A History of the Uruguay Round*. Geneva: World Trade Organization.

Cutler, Claire A., Virginia Hauffler, and Tony Porter, eds. 1999. *Private Authority and International Affairs*. Albany: State University of New York Press.

D'Costa, Anthony P. 2009. "Economic Nationalism in Motion: Steel, Auto, and Software Industries in India." *Review of International Political Economy* 16: 618 –46.

D'Costa, Anthony P., ed. 2012. *Globalization and Economic Nationalism in Asia*. Oxford: Oxford University Press.

D'Cunha, Jean. 1982. The Evolution of the Textile Industry. Edited by FactSheet 1 Collective, *The 10th Month: Bombay's Historic Textile Strike*. Bombay: Collective.

D'Souza, Errol. 2003. The WTO and the Politics of Reform in India's Textile Sector: From Inefficient Re-Distribution to Industrial Upgradation, Working Paper for the Research Project on "Linking the WTO to the Poverty-Reduction Agenda," DFID-Funded Globalization and Poverty Research Programme, Indian Institute of Management, Ahmedabad, India.

Dahlman, Carl J. 1980. *The Open Field System and Beyond: A Property Rights Analysis of an Economic Institution*. Cambridge: Cambridge University Press.

Dai, Xinyuan. 2007. *International Institutions and National Policies*. Cambridge: Cambridge University Press.

Dam, Kenneth W. 1970. *The GATT: Law and International Economic Organization*. Chicago: University of Chicago Press.

Damodaran, Harish. 2008. *India's New Capitalists: Caste, Business and Industry in a Modern Nation*. New Delhi: Permanent Black.

Das, Abhijit. 2007. *The Role of Research on Trade Policy Changes in India: Experience of UNCTAD India Programme*. New Delhi: UNCTAD.

Das, Kesab. 2003. *The Domestic Politics of TRIPs: Pharmaceutical Interests, Public Health and NGO Influence in India*. Ahmedabad: Gujarat Institute of Development Research.

Das, Kusum Deb. 2003. Quantifying Trade Barriers: Has Protection Declined Substantially in Indian Manufacturing. In *Working Paper No. 105*. New Delhi: ICRIER.

Davis, Christina L. 2004. *Food Fights Over Free Trade: How International Institutions Promote Agricultural Liberalization*. Princeton, NJ: Princeton University Press.

Delgado, Nelson, and A.C. Soares. 2005. *The G-20: Its Origin, Evolution, Meaning and Prospects*. Berlin: Heinrich Boll Stiftung.

Desai, Ashok V. 1983. "Technology and Market Structure Under Government Regulation: A Case Study of Indian Textile Industry." *Economic and Political Weekly* 18 (5): 150–159.

Destler, I. M. 1995. *American Trade Politics*. Washington, DC: Institute for International Economics.

Dhar, Biswajit, and K. M. Gopakumar. 2009. "The Case of the Generic Industry in India." In *Intellectual Property and Sustainable Development: Development Agendas in a Changing World*, edited by Ricardo Melendez-Ortiz and Pedro Roffe. Cheltenham, UK: Edward Elgar.

Dhar, B., and Niranjan Rao. 2002. *Transfer of Technology for Successful Integration into the Global Economy: A Case Study of the Pharmaceutical Industry*. New Delhi: UNCTAD.

Dhar, P.N. 1987. "The Political Economy of Development in India." *Indian Economic Review* 22 (1): 1–18.

Dijck, Pitou van, and K. S. Chalapati Rao. 1994. *India's Trade Policy and the Export Performance of Industry*. New Delhi; Thousand Oaks, CA: Sage.

Downs, G. W., and D. M. Rocke. 1995. *Optimal Imperfection?: Domestic Uncertainty and Institutions in International Relations*. Princeton, NJ: Princeton University Press.

Downs, G. W., D. M. Rocke, and P. N. Barsoom. 1996. "Is Good News About Compliance Good News About Cooperation." *International Organization* 50 (3): 379–406.

Draper, Peter, Philip Alves, and Razeen Sally, eds. 2009. *The Political Economy of Trade Reform in Emerging Markets*. Cheltenham, UK: Edward Elgar.

Dreyfuss, Rochelle C. 2010. "TRIPS and Essential Medicines: Must One Size Fit All? Making the WTO Responsive to the Global Health Crisis." In *Incentives for Global Public Health*, edited by Thomas Pogge, Matthew Rimmer, and Kim Rubenstein, 35–55. Cambridge: Cambridge University Press.

Drezner, Daniel W., ed. 2003. *Locating the Proper Authorities: The Interaction of Domestic and International Institutions*. Ann Arbor: University of Michigan Press.

Elkins, Zachary, Andrew Guzman, and Beth A. Simmons. 2006. "Competing for Capital: The Diffusion of Bilateral Investment Treaties, 1960–2000." *International Organization* 60: 811–846.

Elster, Jon 1979. *Ulysses and the Sirens: Studies in Rationality and Irrationality*. Cambridge: Cambridge University Press.

Eren-Vural, Ipek. 2007. "Domestic Contours of Global Regulation: Understanding the Policy Changes on Pharmaceutical Patents in India and Turkey." *Review of International Political Economy* 14 (1): 105–142.

Evans, Peter B. 1993. "Building an Integrative Approach to International and Domestic Politics: Reflections and Projections." In *Double-Edged Diplomacy*, edited by Peter B. Evans, Harold Jacobson, and Robert D. Putnam, 397–430. Berkeley: University of California Press.

Export-Import Bank of India (EXIM). 2007. "*Indian Pharmaceutical Industry: Surging Globally*." Occasional Paper No. 119, Mumbai: Quest Publications.

Farrell, Henry, and Andrew L. Newman. 2014. "Domestic Institutions Beyond the Nation-State: Charting the New Interdependence Approach." *World Politics* 66: 331–63

Federation, (AICPEF) All India Chemical and Pharmaceutical Employee. 1979. *Multinationals in Drug and Pharmaceutical Industry in India*. Second Edition. Patna: Roy Printing Works.

Felker, Greg, Shekhar Chaudhuri, and Katalin Gyorgy. 1997. *The Pharmaceutical Industry in India and Hungary: Policies, Institutions and Technological Development*. Geneva: World Bank.

Finlayson, Jock A, Mark W. Zacher, and Stephen D Krasner. 1983. "The GATT and the Regulation of Trade Barriers: Regime Dynamics and Functions." In *International Regimes*, edited by Stephen D. Krasner, 273–314. Ithaca, NY: Cornell University Press.

Fioretos, Orfeo. 2011. *Creative Reconstructions: Multilateralism and European Varieties of Capitalism after 1950*. Ithaca, NY: Cornell University Press.

Fortune. 2006. Fortune's Global 500 List. http://money.cnn.com/magazines/fortune/global500/2006/full-list/: Forune.

Francois, Joseph F. 1999. *Trade Policy Transparency and Investor Confidence–The Implications of an Effective Trade Policy Review Mechanism*. Adelaide, Australia: Centre for International Economic Studies, University of Adelaide.

Freeman, Jo. 1975. *The Politics of Women's Liberation: A Case Study of an Emerging Social Movement and Its Relation to the Policy Process*. New York: Longman.

Frieden, Jeffry. 1991a. *Debt, Development and Democracy: Modern Political Economy and Latin America, 1965–1985*. Princeton, NJ: Princeton University Press.

Frieden, Jeffry. 1991b. "Invested Interests: The Politics of National Economic Policies in a World of Global Finance." *International Organization* 45 (4): 425–51.

Frieden, Jeffry. 1999. "Actors and Preferences in International Relations." In *Strategic Choice and International Relations*, edited by Robert David A Lake and Powell, 39–76. Prindeton, NJ: Princeton University Press.

Frieden, Jeffry. 2002. "Real Sources of European Currency Policy: Sectoral Interests and European Monetary Integration." *International Organization* 56 (4): 831–860.

Frieden, Jeffrey, and Lisa Martin. 2002. "International Political Economy: Global and Domestic Interactions." In *Political Science: The State of the Discipline*, edited by Katznelson Ira and Helen Milner, 118–146. New York: W.W. Norton.

Frieden, Jeffrey, and Ronald Rogowski. 1996. "The Impact of the International Economy on National Policies: An Analytical Overview." In *Internationalization and Domestic Politics*, edited by Robert Keohane and Helen Milner, 25–47. Cambridge: Cambridge University Press.

Friedman, Thomas. 2005. *The World is Flat: A Brief History of the 21st Century*. New York: Farr, Straus and Giroux.

Friman, Richard H. 1990. *Patchwork Protectionism: Textile Trade Policy in the United States, Japan, and West Germany*. Ithaca, NY: Cornell University Press.

Gandhi, Indira. 1984. "PM's Speech." *IDMA Bulletin* 15 (8): 115–124.

Gang, Ira, N., and Mihir Pandey. 1998. "What Was Protected? Measuring India's Tariff Barriers 1968–1992." *Indian Economic Review* 33 (2): 119–152.

Gangopadhyay, Shubhashis. 1998. "Trade Prospects for India." In *Economic Reforms; the Next Step*, edited by Tirthankar Roy. New Delhi: Frank Bros. & Co.

Garrett, Geoffrey. 1998. *Partisan Politics in the Global Economy*. Cambridge: Cambridge University Press.

Garrett, G., and P. Lange. 1996. "Internationalization, Institutions, and Political Change." In *Internationalization and Domestic Politics*, edited by R. O. Keohane and Helen Milner, 48–78. Cambridge: Cambridge University Press.

Gaur, Madan. 1981. *Medicine for the Masses: A Window on the Pharmaceutical Industry*. Bombay: Press and P.R. Services.

Gereffi, Gary. 1983. *The Pharmaceutical Industry and Dependency in the Third World*. Princeton, NJ: Princeton University Press.

Gereffi, Gary 2002. *Competitiveness of Asian Economies in the Apparel Commodity Chain*. Asian Development Bank.

Gilligan, Michael J. 1997. *Empowering Exporters: Reciprocity, Delegation, and Collective Action in American Trade Policy*. Ann Arbor: University of Michigan Press.

Goldar, Biswanath, and Indrani Gupta. 2010. *Effects of New Patents Regime on Consumers and Producers of Drugs/Medicines in India*. Edited by Research Team. New Delhi: UNCTAD.

Goldstein, Judith. 1993. *Ideas, Interests, and American Trade Policy*. Ithaca, NY: Cornell University Press.

Goldstein, Judith. 1996. "International Law and Domestic Institutions: Reconciling North American "Unfair" Trade Laws." *International Organization* 50 (4): 541–64.

Goldstein, Judith. 1998. "International Institutions and Domestic Politics: GATT, WTO, and the Liberalization of International Trade." In *The WTO as an International Organization*, edited by Ann O. Krueger, 133–152. New Delhi: Oxford University Press.

Goldstein, Judith. 1998. "International Institutions and Domestic Politics: GATT, WTO, and the Liberalization of International Trade." In *The WTO as an International Organization*, edited by Anne O. Krueger, 133–152. New Delhi: Oxford University Press.

Goldstein, Judith, Miles Kahler, Robert O. Keohane, and Ann-Marie Slaughter, eds. 2001. *Legalization and World Politics*. Cambridge, MA: MIT Press.

Goldstein, Judith L., and Lisa L. Martin. 2000. "Legalization, Trade Liberalization and Domestic Politics: A Cautionary Note." *International Organization* 54 (3): 219–248.

Goldstein, Judith L., and Lisa L. Martin. 2001. "Legalization, Trade Liberalization and Domestic Politics: A Cautionary Note." In *Legalization and World Politics*, edited by Judith L. Goldstein, Miles Kahler, Robert O. Keohane and Anne-Marie Slaughter, 219–248. Cambridge, MA: MIT Press.

Goldstein, Judith L., and Richard L. Steinberg. 2009. "Regulatory Shift: The Rise of Judicial Liberalization at the WTO." In *The Politics of Global*

Regulation, edited by Walter Mattli and Ngaire Woods, 211–241. Princeton, NJ: Princeton University Press.

Goswami, Omkar. 1990a. "Sickness and Growth of India's Textile Industry, Part I." *Economic and Political Weekly* 25 (44): 2429–2439.

Goswami, Omkar. 1990b. "Sickness and Growth of India's Textile Industry, Part II." *Economic and Political Weekly* 25 (45): 2496–2506.

Goswami, Omkar. 1998. "Twenty Questions for Every Answer: The Tragedy of Industrial, Financial and Corporate Reforms." In *Economic Reforms: The Next Step, Vol. 1*, edited by Ashok V. Desai. New Delhi: Frank Bros. and Co.

Gourevitch, Peter A. 1978. "The Second Image" Reversed: The International Sources of Domestic Politics." *International Organization* 32 (4): 881–911.

Gourevitch, Peter Alexis. 1986. *Politics in Hard Times: Comparative Responses to International Economic Crises*. Ithaca, NY: Cornell University Press.

Govindaraj, Ramesh, and Gnanaraj Chellaraj. 2002. *The Indian Pharmaceutical Sector: Issues and Options for Health Sector Reform*. Washington, DC: World Bank.

Government of India. 1977. *Annual Report. Edited by Ministry of Commerce*. New Delhi: Government of India.

Government of India. 1999. *Annual Report. Edited by Ministry of Commerce*. New Delhi: Government of India.

Government of India. 2002. *Annual Report, 2001–2002*. Edited by Ministry of Commerce and Industry.

Government of India. 2004. *Annual Report. Edited by Ministry of Commerce*. New Delhi: Government of India.

Government of India. Various Years. *Economic Survey*. Edited by Ministry of Finance: Government of India.

Grace, Cheri. 2004. The Effect of Changing Intellectual Property on Pharmaceutical Industry Prospects in India and China: Considerations for Access to Medicines. In *DFID Health Systems Resource Center Issues Paper*. London: DFID.

Greenhill, Brian. 2010. "The Company You Keep: International Socialization and the Diffusion of Human Rights Norms." *International Studies Quarterly* 54 (1): 127–145.

Greif, Avner. 2008. "Commitment, Coercion and Markets: The Nature and Dynamics of Institutions Supporting Exchange." In *Handbook of New Institutional Economics*, edited by Claude Menard and Mary M. Shirley, 727–786. Heidelberg, Germany: Springer.

Grieco, Joseph M. 1984. *Between Dependency and Autonomy: India's Experience with the International Computer Industry*. Berkeley: University of California Press.

Grossman, Gene M. and Elhanan Helpman. 2001. *Special Interest Politics*. Cambridge, MA: MIT Press.

Guennif, S., and Shyama V. Ramani. 2012. "Catching Up in the Pharmaceutical Sector: Lessons from Case Studies of India and Brazil." In *Economic Development as a Learning Process: Variation Across Sectoral Systems*, edited by Franco Malerba and Richard R. Nelson. Cheltenham, UK: Edward Elgar.

Gupta, Akhil. 2012. *Red Tape: Bureaucracy, Structural Violence and Poverty in India*. Durham, NC: Duke University Press.

Gupta, Amit Sen, ed. 1986. *Drug Industry and the Indian People*. New Delhi: Delhi Science Forum and FMRAI.

Haakonsson, Stine Jessen. 2009. "How does 'Linking up with Global Buyers' Impact the Prospects for Upgrading in Pharmaceuticals? The Case of India." In *Transnational Corporations and Development Policy: Critical Perspectives*, edited by Eric Rugraff, Diego Sancez-Ancochea and Andy Sumner, 274–301. Hampshire: Palgrave Macmillan.

Hafner-Burton, Emilie M. 2009. *Forced to be Good: Why Trade Agreements Boost Human Rights*. Ithaca, NY: Cornell University Press.

Haggard, Stephan, and Robert Kaufman. 1995. *The Political Economy of Democratic Transitions*. Princeton, NJ: Princeton University Press.

Haggard, Stephan, and Steven B. Webb. 1994. "Introduction." In *Voting for Reform: Democracy, Political Liberalization and Economic Adjustment*, edited by Stephan Haggard and Steven B. Webb, 1–36. Oxford: Oxford University Press.

Hall, P. A., and D Soskice. 2001. *Varieties of Capitalism: The Institutional Foundations of Comparative Advantage*. Oxford: Oxford University Press.

Halliday, Terence, and Greg Shaffer. 2015. *Transnational Legal Orders*. Cambridge: Cambridge University Press.

Hamied, Y.K., 1993. *Patents and the Pharmaceutical Industry: A Review*. New Delhi: International Conference on Patent Regime Proposed in the Uruguay Round.

Hanrahan, Charles, and Randy Schnepf. 2005. *WTO Doha Round: Agricultural Negotiating Proposals*. Washington, DC: Congressional Research Service, Library of Congress.

Harriss, John. 1987. "The State in Retreat? Why has India Experienced Such Half-Hearted Liberalization in the 1980s?" *IDS Bulletin* 18: 31–8.

Hart, Oliver. 1995. *Firms, Contracts and Financial Structure*. Oxford: Oxford University Press.

Hasan, Rana, Devashish Mitra, and Beyza P. Ural. 2006–2007. "Trade Liberalization, Labor Market Institutions and Poverty Reduction: Evidence from Indian States." *The Brookings Institution: India Policy Forum* 3: 70–135.

Haufler, Virginia. 2003. "Globalization and Industry Self-Regulation." In *Governance in the Global Economy: Political Authority in Transition*, edited by and David A. Lake and Miles Kahler, 226–252. Princeton, NJ: Princeton University Press.

Herring, Ron. 2013. "Reconstructing Facts in BT Cotton: Why Skepticism Fails." *Economic and Political Weekly* XLVIII (33): 63–66.

Herring, Ron H. 1999. "Embedded Particularism: India's Failed Developmental State." In *The Developmental State*, edited by Meredith Woo-Cumings, 306–344. Ithaca, NY: Cornell University Press.

Hoekman, Bernard M., and Michel M. Kostecki. 1995. *The Political Economy of the World Trading System: From GATT to WTO*. Oxford: Oxford University Press.

Hsueh Roselyn. 2012. "China and India in the Age of Globalization: Sectoral Variation in Postliberalization Reregulation." *Comparative Political Studies* 45: 32–61.

Huang, Yasheng, and Harold Hogan. 2002. *India's Intellectual Property Rights Regime and the Pharmaceutical Industry.* HBS Case, 9-702-039, March 25, 2002, Boston: Harvard Business School.

Hudec, Robert E. 1993. *Enforcing International Trade Law: The Evolution of the Modern GATT Legal System.* Salem, NH: Butterworth Legal Publishers.

Hurrell, Andrew, and Amrita Narlikar. 2006. "A New Politics of Confrontation?: Brazil and India in Multilateral Trade Negotiations." *Global Society* 20 (4): 415–433.

ICRA. 2004. *Drugs and Pharmaceuticals: International Pharmaceutical Industry: A Snapshot.* New Delhi: ICRA.

Industry, Ministry of. 1997. *Resolution No. A-42012/1/98-EIV-CDN.* Edited by Department of Industrial Policy and Promotion. New Delhi: Government of India.

Jackson, John. 2000. *The Jurisprudence of GATT and the WTO: Insights on Treaty Law and Economic Relations.* Cambridge: Cambridge University Press.

Jackson, John H. 1969. *World Trade and the Law of GATT: A Legal Analysis of the General Agreement on Tariffs and Trade.* Indianapolis: Bobbs-Merrill.

Jackson, John H. 2000. *The Jurisprudence of GATT and the WTO: Insights on Treaty Law and Economic Relations.* Cambridge: Cambridge University Press

Jacob, Anil G. 2010. "Steering The State: The Politics of Institutional Change In The Pharmaceutical and Telecommunications Sectors In Post-Reform India." Ph.D. Dissertation, Political Science, Rutgers University.

Jaffrelot, Christophe. 2009. "India, An Emerging Power, but How Far?" In *Emerging States: The Wellspring of a New World Order,* edited by Christophe Jaffrelot, 76–89. New York: Columbia University Press.

Jain, S.K. 1987. *The Drug Policy.* Delhi: India Investment Publication; SS Books Associates.

Jain, Sanjay K. 1988. *Export Performance and Export Marketing Strategies (A Study of Indian Textiles).* 2 vols. Vol. 1. Delhi: Commonwealth Publishers.

Jenkins, Rob. 1999. *Democratic Politics and Economic Reform in India.* New York: Cambridge University Press.

Jenkins, Rob. 2003. "How Federalism Influences India's Domestic Policies of WTO Engagement (and Is Itself Affected in the Process)." *Asian Survey* 43 (4): 598–515.

Johnson, C. 1982. *MITI and the Japanese Miracle: The Growth of Industrial Policy, 1925–1975.* Stanford, CA: Stanford University Press.

Johnston, Alastair Iain. 2001. "Treating International Institutions as Social Environments." *International Organization* 45 (4): 487–515.

Kale, Dinar, and Steve Little. 2007. "From Imitation to Innovation: The Evolution of R&D Capabilities and Learning Processes in the Indian Pharmaceutical Industry." *Technology Analysis and Strategic Management* 19 (5): 589–609.

Kale, Sunila. 2014. *Electrifying India: Regional Political Economies of Development.* Stanford, CA: Stanford University Press.

Kambhampati, Uma S., and Ashokh Parikh. 2007. "Disciplining Firms: The Impact of Trade Reforms on Profit Margins in Indian Industry." In *Trade Liberalization: Impact on Growth and Trade in Developing Countries*, edited by Ashok Parikh, 27–45. New Jersey: World Scientific.

Kapczynski, Amy. 2009. "Harmonization and Its Discontents: A Case Study of TRIPs Implementation in India's Pharmaceutical Sector." *California Law Review* 97 (6): 1571–1649.

Kapur, Devesh. 2010. *Diaspora, Development, and Democracy: The Domestic Impact of International Migration from India*. Princeton, NJ: Princeton University Press.

Kapur, Devesh, John P. Lewis, and Richard Webb. 1997. *The World Bank: Its First Half-Century*. Washington, DC: Brookings Institution.

Karmakar, Suparna. 2007. "From Uruguay to Doha: India at the Negotiating Table." In *India's Liberalization Experience: Hostage to the WTO?*, edited by Suparna Karmakar, Rajiv Kumar and Bibek Debroy, 56–77. New Delhi: Sage.

Kashyap, Subhash C., ed. 1990. *National Policy Studies*. New Delhi: TATA McGraw-Hill Publishing Company Limited.

Kathuria, Sanjay, Will Martin, and Anjali Bhardwaj. 2001. *Implications for South Asian Countries for Abolishing the Multifibre Arrangement*. Washington, DC: World Bank.

Kathuria, Sanjay, and Anjali Bhardwaj. 1998. *Export Quotas and Policy Constraints in the Indian Textile and Garment Industries*. Washington, DC: World Bank.

Katznelson, Ira. 2013. *Fear Itself: The New Deal and the Origins of Our Time*. New York: Liveright Publishing Corporation.

Katznelson, Ira, and Martin Shefter, eds. 2002. *Shaped by War and Trade: International Influences on American Political Development*. Princeton, NJ: Princeton University Press.

Kaviraj, Sudipta. 1988. "A Critique of the Passive Revolution." *Economic and Political Weekly* 23 (45–7): 2429–44.

Kedron, Peter, and Sharmistha Bagchi-Sen. 2011. "US Market Entry Processes of Emerging Multinationals: A Case of Indian Pharmaceuticals." *Applied Geography* 31 (2): 721–730.

Kelley, Judith. 2004. "International Actors on the Domestic Scene: Membership Conditionality and Socialization by International Institutions." *International Organization* 58 (3): 425–457.

Keohane, Robert O. 1984. *After Hegemony: Cooperation and Discord in the World Political Economy*. Princeton, NJ: Princeton University Press.

Keohane, R. O., and Helen Milner. 1996. *Internationalization and Domestic Politics*. Cambridge: Cambridge University Press.

Khanna, Sri Ram. 1991. *International Trade in Textiles: MFA Quotas and a Developing Exporting Country*. New Delhi: Sage.

Kim, Moonhawk. 2008. "Costly Procedures: Divergent Effects of Legalization in the GATT/WTO Dispute Settlement Procedures." *International Studies Quarterly* 52 (3): 657–686.

Kindleberger, C. P. 1951. "Group Behavior and International Trade." *Journal of Political Economy* LIX (1): 30–46.

Kingstone, Peter R. 1999. *Crafting Coalitions for Reform: Business Preferences, Political Institutions, and Neoliberal Reform in Brazil.* University Park, PA: Pennsylvania State University Press.

Kohli, Atul. 2004. *State-Directed Development: Political Power and Industrialization in the Global Periphery.* Cambridge: Cambridge University Press.

Kohli, Atul. 2007. "State, Business, and Economic Growth in India." *Studies in Comparative International Development* 42 (1–2): 87–114.

Kohli, Atul. 2012. *Poverty and Plenty in the New India.* Cambridge: Cambridge University Press.

Koremenos, Barbara. 2005. "Contracting Around International Uncertainty." *American Political Science Review* 99 (4):549–565.

Koremenos, B., C. Lipson, and D. Snidal. 2001. "The Rational Design of International Institutions." *International Organization* 55 (4): 761–799.

Krasner, Stephen D. 1983. *International Regimes.* Ithaca, NY: Cornell University Press.

Krueger, Anne. 1974. "The Political Economy of the Rent Seeking Society." *American Economic Review* 64 (3): 291–303.

KSA-Technopak. 2005. *India Retail Report, 2005.* Delhi: Images Multimedia Pvt. Ltd.

Kulkarni, V.B. 1979. *History of the Indian Cotton Textile Industry.* Bombay: Millowner's Association, Bombay.

Kumar, Rajiv. 1993. "The Walk Away from Leadership: India." In *The Developing Countries in World Trade: Policies and Bargaining Strategies,* edited by Diana Tussie and David Glover, 155–169. Boulder, CO: Lynne Rienner.

Kumar, Satish, ed. 2011. *India's National Security: Annual Review 2010.* New Delhi: Routledge.

Kydland, Finn E. and Edward C. Prescott. 1977. "Rules Rather than Discretion: The Inconsistency of Optimal Plans." *Journal of Political Economy* 85 (3): 473–492.

Lake, David. 2009. "Open Economy Politics: A Critical Review." *Review of International Organizations* 4 (3): 219–244.

Lake, David A. 1988. *Power, Protection, and Free Trade: International Sources of US Commercial Strategy, 1887–1939.* Ithaca, NY: Cornell University Press.

Lake, David A. 2006. "International Political Economy: A Maturing Interdiscipline." In *The Oxford Handbook of Political Economy,* edited by Barry R. Weingast and Donald A. Wittman, 757–777. Oxford: Oxford University Press.

Lake, David A. 2009. "Open Economy Politics: A Critical Review." *Review of International Organizations* 4 (3): 219–244.

Lal, Deepak. 1999. *Unfinished Business: India in the World Economy.* New Delhi: Oxford University Press.

Lal, Harivansh. 1990. *Drug Industry, Social Responsibility, and the Multinationals.* New Delhi: Commonwealth Publishers.

Lee, Chang Kil, and David Strang. 2006. "The International Diffusion of Private Sector Downsizing: Network Emulation and Theory-Driven Learning." *International Organization* 60 (4): 883–909.

Lipson, Charles, and Stephen D. Krasner. 1983. "The Transformation of Trade: The Sources and Effects of Regime Change." In *International Regimes*, edited by Stephen Krasner, 233–271. Ithaca, NY: Cornell University Press.

Lobell, Steven E. 2005. *The Challenge of Hegemony: Grand Strategy, Trade and Domestic Politics*. Ann Arbor: University of Michigan Press.

Lohmann, Susanne, and Sharyn O'Halloran. 1994. "Divided Government and U.S. Trade Policy: Theory and Evidence." *International Organization* 48 (4): 595–632.

Long, Clarisa, ed. 2000. *Intellectual Property Rights in Emerging Markets*. Washington, DC: AEI Press.

Lowi, Theodore. 1972. "Four Systems of Policy, Politics, and Choice." *Public Administration Review* 32 (4): 298–310.

Madanmohan, T.R., and R. T. Krishnan. 2003. "Adaptive Strategies in the Indian Pharmaceutical Industry." *International Journal of Technology Management* 25 (3/4): 227–246.

Mahbubani, Kishore. 2008. *The New Asian Hemisphere: The Irresistible Shift of Global Power to the East*. New York: Public Affairs.

Majumdar, J.S. (AICPEF). 1979. *Multinationals in Drug and Pharmaceutical Industry in India*. Patna: All India Chemical and Pharmaceutical Employees Federation.

Mansfield, Edward D., and Jon Pevehouse. 2008. "Democratization and the Varieties of International Organizations." *Journal of Conflict Resolution* 52 (2): 269–294.

March, James G., and Johan P. Olsen. 1998. "The Institutional Dynamics of International Political Orders." *International Organization* 52 (4): 943–969.

Martin, Lisa. 1992. *Coercive Cooperation: Explaining Multilateral Economic Sanctions*. Princeton, NJ: Princeton University Press.

Martin, Lisa. 1999. "An Institutionalist View: International Institutions and State Strategies." In *International Order and the Future of World Politics*, edited by T.V. Paul and John A. Hall, 78–98. Cambridge: Cambridge University Press.

Martin, Lisa. 2013. "Against Compliance." In *International Law and International Relations: Synthesizing Insights from Interdisciplinary Scholarship*, ed. Jeffrey L. Dunoff and Mark Pollack, pp. 591–610. New York: Cambridge University Press.

Marx, Karl. 1852. *The 18th Brumaire of Louis Bonaparte*. 2008 Edition. New York: Wildside Press.

Mathews, John A. 2002. *Dragon Multinational: A New Model for Global Growth*. Oxford: Oxford University Press.

Mathews, John A. 2006. "Dragon Multinationals: New Players in 21st Century Globalization." *Asia Pacific Journal of Management* 23 (1): 5–27.

Mattli, Walter. 2003. "Public and Private Governance in Setting International Standards." In *Governance in a Global Economy: Political Authority in Transition*, edited by Miles Kahler and David Lake, 199–225. Princeton, NJ: Princeton University Press.

Mazumdar, Dipak. 1984. *The Issue of Small versus Large in the Indian Textile Industry: An Analytical and Historical Survey*. Washington, DC: World Bank.

McGillivray, Fiona. 2004. *Privileging Industry: The Comparative Politics of Trade and Industrial Policy*. Princeton, NJ: Princeton University Press.

Medhora, Phiroze B. 1965. "Entrepreneurship in India." *Political Science Quarterly* 80 (4): 558–580.

Mertha, Andrew C., and Robert Pahre. 2005. "'Patently Misleading': Partial Implementation and Bargaining Leverage in Sino-American Negotiations on Intellectual Property Rights." *International Organization* 59 (3): 695–729.

Milner, Helen, and Peter B. Rosendorff. 1996. "Trade Negotiations, Information, and Domestic Politics." *Economics and Politics* 8 (2): 145–189.

Milner, Helen V. 1988. *Resisting Protectionism: Global Industries and the Politics of International Trade*. Princeton, NJ: Princeton University Press.

Milner, Helen V. 1997. *Interests, Institutions and Information: Domestic Politics and International Relations*. Princeton, NJ: Princeton University Press.

Milner, Helen V. 2002. "International Trade." In *Handbook of International Relations*, edited by Walter Carlsnaes, Thomas Risse and Beth A. Simmons, 448–461. London: Sage.

Mishra, Sanjiv. 1993. *India's Textile Sector: A Policy Analysis*. New Delhi: Sage.

Mishra, Sanjiv. 2000. "India's Textile Policy and the Informal Sectors." In *India's Development and Public Policy*, edited by Stuart Nagel. Aldershot: Ashgate.

Mohan, C. Raja. 2003. *Crossing the Rubicon: The Shaping of India's New Foreign Policy*. Delhi: Penguin Viking.

Moore, Barrington. 1966. *Social Origins of Dictatorship and Democracy: Lord and Peasant in the Making of the Modern World*. Boston: Beacon Press.

Moore, Thomas G. 2002. *China in the World Market: Chinese Industry and International Sources of Reform in the Most-Mao Era*. Cambridge: Cambridge University Press.

Moravcsik, Andrew. 1998. *The Choice for Europe: Social Purpose and State Power from Messina to Maastricht*. Ithaca, NY: Cornell University Press.

Morris, Morris David. 1965. *The Emergence of an Industrial Labour Force in India; A Study of the Bombay Cotton Mills, 1854–1947*. Berkeley: University of California Press.

Morris, Stephen, and Hyun Song Shin. 2002. "Social Value of Public Information." *American Economic Review* 92 (5): 1521–1535.

Mosley, Layna, and David Singer. 2008. "Taking Stock Seriously: Equity Market Performance, Government Policy, and Financial Globalization." *International Studies Quarterly* 52 (2): 405–425.

Mukherji, Rahul. 2014. *Globalization and Deregulation: Ideas, Interests, and Institutional Change in India*. New Delhi: Oxford University Press.

Narayan, S. 2005. "Trade Policy Making in India." Paper Presented at the Workshop on Trade Policy Making in Developing Countries, London School Economics.

Narayan, S. 2009. "India." In *The Political Economy of Trade Reform in Emerging Markets: Crisis or Opportunity?*, edited by Philip Alves and Rajeen Sally Peter Draper, 170–199. Cheltenham, UK: Edward Elgar.

Narayana, N. S. S., ed. 2001. *Economic Policy and State Intervention: Selected Papers of T. N. Srinivasan*. Oxford: Oxford University Press.

Narayana, P.L. 1984. *The Indian Pharmaceutical Industry: Problems and Prospects.* New Delhi: NCAER.

Narayanan, Badri G. 2005. "Questions on Textile Industry Competitiveness." *Economic and Political Weekly* 40 (9): 905–907.

Narayanan, K., and Ronny Thomas. 2010. "R&D and Internationalization in the Pharmaceutical Sector in India." In *Indian and Chinese Enterprises: Global Trade, Technology and Investment Regimes,* edited by N. S. Siddharthan and K. Narayanan, 211–238. London: Routledge.

Narlikar, Amrita., 2006. "Peculiar Chauvinism or Strategic Calculation? Explaining the Negotiating Strategy of a Rising India." *International Affairs* 82 (1): 59–76.

Narlikar, Amrita. 2010. "New Powers in the Club: The Challenge of Global Trade Governance." *International Affairs* 86 (3): 717–728.

Narlikar, Amrita, and Diana Tussie. 2004. "The G20 at the Cancun Ministerial: Developing Countries and Their Evolving Coalitions in the WTO." *World Economy* 27 (7): 947–966.

Narlikar, Amrita. 2013. "India Rising: Responsible to Whom?" *International Affairs* 89 (3): 595–614.

Naseemullah, Adnan. 2016. *Development After Statism: Industrial Firms and the Political Economy of South Asia.* Cambridge: Cambridge University Press.

Nayar, Baldev. 1999. "India as a Limited Challenger?" In *International Order and the Future of World Politics,* edited by T.V. Paul and John A. Hall, 213–233. Cambridge: Cambridge University Press.

Nayar, Baldev. 2001. "Opening Up and Openness of Indian Economy." *Economic and Political Weekly* 36 (37): 3529–3537.

Nayar, Baldev, and Paul, T.V. 2003. *India in the World Order: Searching for Major Power Status.* Cambridge: Cambridge University Press.

NITMA. 2001. *Wake Up Call for India's Textile Industry.* New Delhi: Northern India Textile Mills Association.

Nooruddin, Irfan. 2011. *Coalition Politics and Economic Development: Credibility and the Strength of Weak Governments.* Cambridge: Cambridge University Press.

Nooruddin, Irfan, and Joel W. Simmons. 2009. "Openness, Uncertainty, and Social Spending: Implications for the Globalization-Welfare State Debate." *International Studies Quarterly* 53 (3): 841–866.

Nooyi, Indra. 2008. Interview. *India Abroad* 37 (38): 1.

O'Halloran, Sharyn 1994. *Politics, Process, and American Trade Policy.* Ann Arbor: University of Michigan Press.

O'Riain, Sean. 2004. *The Politics of High-Tech Growth: Developmental Network States in the Global Economy.* Cambridge: Cambridge University Press.

Oatley, Thomas. 2011. "The Reductionist Gamble: Open Economy politics in a Global Economy." *International Organization,* 65 (2): 311–341.

Olsen, Tricia, and Aseema Sinha. 2013. "Linkage Politics and the Persistence of National Policy Autonomy in Emerging Powers: Patents, Profits, and Patients in the Context of TRIPS Compliance." *Business and Politics* 15 (3): 323–356.

Olson, Mancur. 1982. *The Rise and Decline of Nations: Economic Growth, Stagflation and Social Rigidities.* New Haven, CT: Yale University Press.

OPPI. 2001. *Pharmaceutical Compendium.* Bombay: OPPI.

OPPI. 2002. *Pharmaceutical Compendium*. Bombay: OPPI.

Organizations, Yearbook of International. 2012–2013. *The Yearbook of International Organizations*. Edited by Union of International Associations. The Netherlands: Brill.

Paemen, Hugo, and Alexandra Bensch. 1995. *From the GATT to the WTO: The European Community in the Uruguay Round*. Leuven, Belgium: Leuven University Press.

Panagariya, Arvind. 2004. "India's Trade Reform." *India Policy Forum* 1 (NCAER, New Delhi): 1–57.

Panagariya, Arvind. 2008. *India: The Emerging Giant*. New York: Oxford University Press.

Parikh, Ashok. 2007. "Introduction." In *Trade Liberalization: Impact on Growth and Trade in Developing Countries*, edited by Ashok Parikh, 1–25. New Jersey: World Scientific.

Parikh, Jyoti Sharma, V.K Ghosh, Upal and Manoj Panda. 1995. *Trade and Environmental Linkages: A Case Study of India*. UNCTAD.

Parthasarathi, Ashok, and K.J. Joseph. 2004. "Innovation Under Export Orientation." In *India in the Global Software Industry: Innovation, Firm Strategies and Development*, edited by Anthony P. D'Costa and E. Sridharan. New York: Palgrave Macmillan.

Paul, T.V. 2005. "Soft Balancing in the Age of U.S. Primacy." *International Security* 30 (1): 46–71.

Paul, T.V. 2007. "The US-Indian Nuclear Accord: Implications for the Non-Proliferation Regime." *International Journal* 62 (4): 845–861.

Pedersen, Joergen Dige. 2010. "Political Factors Behind the Rise of Indian Multinational Enterprises: An Essay in Political Economy." In *The Rise of Indian Multinationals: Perspectives on Indian Outward Foreign Direct Investment*, edited by Karl P. Sauvant and Jaya Pradhan, 57–77. New York: Palgrave Macmillan.

Peng, Mike W. 2003. "Institutional Transitions and Strategic Choices." *Academy of Management Review* 28 (2): 275–296.

Peng, Mike W., Denis Y. L. Wang, and Yi Jiang. 2008. "An Institution-Based View of International Business Strategy: A Focus on Emerging Economies." *Journal of International Business Studies* 39 (5): 920–936.

Pevehouse, Jon C. 2002. "Democracy from Outside-In? International Organizations and Democratization." *International Organization* 56 (3): 515–549.

Phadke, Anant. 1998. *Drug Supply and Use: Towards a Rational Policy in India*. New Delhi: Sage.

Pillai, Poonam. 2000. "The State and Collective Action: Successful Adjustment by the Tamil Nadu Leather Clusters to German Environmental Standards." M.A, Urban Studies and Planning, MIT.

Polanyi, Karl. 1944. *The Great Transformation: The Political and Economic Origins of Our Time*. Second edition New York: Beacon Press.

Pollack, Mark A. 2003. *The Engines of European Integration: Delegation, Agency and Agenda Setting in the EU*. Oxford: Oxford University Press.

Pradhan, Jaya Prakash. 2007. *New Policy Regime and Small Pharmaceutical Firms in India*. New Delhi: Indian Institute of Industrial Development.

Pradhan, Jaya Prakash, and Karl. P. Sauvant. 2010. "Introduction: The Rise of Indian Multinational Enterprises: Revisiting Key Issues." In *The Rise of Indian Multinationals: Perspectives on Indian Outward Foreign Direct Investment*, edited by Karl P. Sauvant and Jaya P. Pradhan, 1–24. New York: Palgrave Macmillan.

Prakash, Aseem, and Jeffrey A. Hart, eds. 1999. *Globalization and Governance*. London: Routledge.

Prakash, Aseem, and Jeffrey Hart. 2000. "Coping with Globalization: An Introduction." In *Coping with Globalization*, edited by Aseem Prakash and Jeffrey Hart, 1–26. London: Routledge.

Prestowitz, Clyde. 2005. *Three Billion Capitalists: The Great Shift of Wealth and Power to the East*. New York: Basic Books.

Priyadarshi, Shishir. 2005. Decision-Making Processes in India: The Case of Agriculture Negotiations in India. www.wto.org/english/res_e/booksp_e/case studies_e/case15_e.htm: WTO.

Purfield, Catriona, and Jerals Schiff, eds. 2006. *India Goes Global: Its Expanding Role in the World Economy*. Washington, DC: IMF.

Putnam, Robert. 1988. "Diplomacy and Domestic Politics: The Logic of Two-Level Games." *International Organization* 42 (3):427–460.

Rai, Rajnish Kumar. 2008. "Battling with TRIPS: Emerging Firm Strategies of Indian Pharmaceutical Industry Post-TRIPS." *Journal of Intellectual Property Rights* 13 (4): 301–317.

Raizada, B.K. n.d. *Note on Indian Pharmaceutical Industry*. New Delhi.

Rajya Sabha. 1998. *Thirty-Fifth Report on India and the WTO*. Edited by Parliament of India. New Delhi: Parliament of India.

Ramamurti, R. 2004. "Developing Countries and MNEs: Extending and Enriching the Research Agenda." *Journal of International Business Studies* 35 (4): 277–283.

Ramamurti, Ravi, and Jitendra V. Singh, eds. 2009. *Emerging Multinationals in Emerging Markets*. Cambridge: Cambridge University Press.

Ramanna, Anitha. 2005. "Shifts in India's Policy on Intellectual Property: The Role of Ideas, Coercion, and Changing Interests." In *Death of Patents*, edited by Peter Drahos, 150–174. London: Lawtext Publishing Limited.

Ranbaxy. 1994. *Annual Report*. New Delhi: Ranbaxy.

Rao, Manohar 2007. *Globalization, Technology and Competition: IPRs, Indian Pharmaceutical Industry and WTO*. New Delhi: Serials Publications.

Rao, Narasimha. 1994. *Financing of Cotton Textile Industry in India*. New Delhi: Ashish Publishing House.

Rao, N. Vasuki 1999. "India Enlists Industry to Boost WTO Role." *Journal of Commerce*, March, n.p.

Redwood, Heinz. 1987. *International Handbook of Pharmaceutical Trends*. London: Macmillan.

Redwood, Heinz. 1988. *The Pharmaceutical Industry: Trends, Problems and Achievements*. Suffolk, England: Oldwicks Press.

Redwood, Heinz. 1994. *New Horizons in India: The Consequences of Pharmaceutical Patent Protection*. Suffolk, England: Oldwicks Press.

Riello, Giorgio, and Tirthankar Roy, eds. 2009. *How India Clothed the World: The World of South Asian Textiles, 1500–1850*. Leiden: Brill.

Rodrik, Dani. 1997. *Has Globalization Gone Too Far?* Washington, DC: Institute of International Economics.

Rodrik, Dani. 2002. "Trade Reform as Institutional Reform." In *Development, Trade, and the WTO: A Handbook*, edited by B. A. Mattoo and P. E. Hoekman, 3–10. Washington, DC: World Bank.

Rogowski, Ronald. 1987. "Trade and the Variety of Democratic Institutions." *International Organization* 41 (2): 203–223.

Rogowski, Ronald. 1989. *Commerce and Coalitions.* Princeton, NJ: Princeton University Press.

Rogowski, Ronald. 1999. "Institutions as Constraints on Strategic Choice." In *Strategic Choice and International Relations*, edited by A. Lake David and Robert Powell, 115–136. Princeton, NJ: Princeton University Press.

Rosenstein-Rodan, P. N. 1943. "Problems of Industrialization of Eastern and South-Eastern Europe." *Economic Journal* 53: 202–2011.

Roy Chowdhury, Supriya. 1995. "Political Economy of India's Textile Industry: The Case of Maharashtra, 1984–1989." *Pacific Affairs* 68 (2): 231–250.

Roy, Tirthankar. 1993. *Artisans and Industrialization: Indian Weaving in the 20th Century.* Delhi: Oxford University Press.

Roy, Tirthankar, ed. 1996a. *Cloth and Commerce: Textiles in Colonial India.* New Delhi: Sage.

Roy, Tirthankar. 1996b. *Market Resurgence, Deregulation and Industrial Response: Indian Cotton Textiles in the 1990s.* Bombay: Institute of Social Studies.

Roy, Tirthankar. 1998. "Economic Reforms and Textile Industry in India." *Economic and Political Weekly* 33 (32): 2173–2182.

Roy, Tirthankar. 1998b. "A New Textile Policy: Do We Need One?" *Economic and Political Weekly* 33 (40): 2563–2565.

Roy, Tirthankar. 1999. *Outline of a History of Labour in Traditional Small-Scale Industry in India.* Noida: V.V. Giri National Labour Institute.

Roy, Tirthankar. 2004. "The Textile Industry." In *The Structure of Indian Industry*, edited by Subir Gokarn, Anindya Sen, and Rajendra R. Vaidya, 82–111. New Delhi: Oxford University Press.

Roy, Tirthankar. 2010. "The Long Globalization and Textile Producers in India." In *The Ashgate Companion to the History of Textile Workers*, edited by Lex Herma van Voss et al., 253–274. Aldershot, UK: Ashgate.

Roy, Tirthankar. 2010a. "The Long Globalization and Textile Producers in India." In *The Ashgate Companion to the History of Textile Workers*, edited by Lex Herma van Voss et al, 253–274. Aldershot, UK: Ashgate.

Roy, Tirthankar. 2010b. "Technological Change in Indian Textile Industry, 1991–2006." *International Journal of Technology and Globalization* 5 (1/2): 124–131.

Rudolph, Susanne, and Lloyd Rudolph. 1987. *In the Pursuit of Lakshmi: The Political Economy of the Indian State.* Chicago: University of Chicago Press.

Ruggie, John G. 1983. "International Regimes, Transactions and Change: Embedded Liberalism in the Postwar Economic Order." In *International*

Regimes, edited by Stephen D Krasner, 195–231. Ithaca, NY: Cornell University Press.

Ruggie, John G., ed. 1993. *Multilateralism Matters: The Theory and Praxis of an Institutional Form.* New York: Columbia University Press.

Ruparelia, Sanjay, Sanjay Reddy, John Harriss, and Stuart Corbridge, eds. 2011. *Understanding India's New Political Economy: A Great Transformation?* New York: Routledge.

Sabade, B.R. 2001. *WTO: A Threat or an Opportunity.* Pune, India: Center for Business and Industry.

Saez, Lawrence, and Chrystal Chang. 2009. "The Political Economy of Global Firms from India and China." *Contemporary Politics* 15 (3): 265–286.

Sakesena, K.D. 2002. *Dynamics of India's Textile Economy: Towards a Pragmatic Textile Policy.* Delhi: Shilpa.

Saket, ed. 2001. *Indian Pharma Industry-Issues and Options.* Ahmedabad: Saket Projects Ltd.

Saleman, Yanick, and Luke Jordan. 2014. *The Implementation of Industrial Parks: Some Lessons Learned in India.* Washington, DC: World Bank.

Sampath, P.G. 2006. *Indian Pharma within Global Reach.* The Netherlands: United Nations University.

Santos Alvaro. 2012. "Carving out Policy Autonomy for Developing Countries in the World Trade Organization: The Experience of Brazil and Mexico." *Virginia Journal of International Law* 52: 551–632.

Sauvant, Karl P., and J.P. Pradhan, eds. 2010. *The Rise of Indian Multinationals: Perspectives on Indian Outward Foreign Direct Investment.* New York: Palgrave Macmillan.

Schamis, Hector. 2002. *Re-Forming the State: The Politics of Privatization in Latin America and Europe.* Ann Arbor: University of Michigan Press.

Schattschneider, E.E. 1935. *Politics, Pressures and the Tariff: A Study of Free Private Enterprise in Pressure Politics, as Shown in the 1929–1930 Revision of the Tariff.* New York: Prentice Hall.

Schattschneider, E.E. 1974. *Politics, Pressure and the Tariff.* New York: Arno Press.

Schelling, Thomas. 1981. *The Strategy of Conflict.* Boston, MA: Harvard University Press.

Schoppa, Leonard J. 1997. *Bargaining with Japan: What American Pressure Can and Cannot Do.* New York: Columbia University Press.

Scott, James C. 1977. *The Moral Economy of the Peasant: Rebellion and Subsistence in Southeast Asia.* New Haven, CT: Yale University Press.

Sell, Susan K. 2003. *Private Power, Public Law: The Globalization of Intellectual Property Rights.* Cambridge: Cambridge University Press.

Sen, Julius. 2003. Lessons Not Learned: India's Trade Policymaking Process from Uruguay to Doha. Unpublished paper.

Sen, Julius. 2004. *Negotiating Trade Agreements with India: The Reality Below the Water Line.* South Africa: South Africa Institute of International Affairs.

Sengupta, Mitu. 2009. "Making the State Change its Mind–the IMF, World Bank and the Politics of India's Market Reforms." *New Political Economy* 14 (2): 181–207.

Shadlen, Kenneth C. 2007. "The Political Economy of AIDS Treatment: Intellectual Property and the Transformation of Generic Supply." *International Studies Quarterly* 51 (3): 559–581.

Shaffer, Gregory, Michelle Ratton Sanchez, and Barbara Rosenberg. 2008. "The Trials of Winning at the WTO: What Lies Behind Brazil's Success." *Cornell International Law Journal* 41: 383–501.

Shaffer, Gregory, ed. 2013. *Transnational Legal Ordering and State Change*. Cambridge: Cambridge University Press.

Shaffer, Gregory C. 2003. *Defending Interests: Public-Private Partnerships in WTO Litigation*. Washington, DC: Brookings Institution Press.

Shaffer, Gregory C. 2005. "Can WTO Technical Assistance and Capacity Building Serve Developing Countries?" *Wisconsin International Law Journal* 23: 643–686.

Shaffer, Gregory C. 2006. "The Challenges of WTO Law: Strategies for Developing Country Adaptation." *World Trade Review* 5 (2): 177–198.

Shaffer, Gregory C. 2009. "Developing Country Use of the WTO Dispute Settlement System: Why it Matters, the Barriers Posed." In *Trade Disputes and the Dispute Settlement Understanding of the WTO: An Interdisciplinary Assessment*, edited by James Hartigan. London: Emerald Group Publishing Limited.

Shaffer, Gregory C., Michele Sanchez, and Barbara Rosenberg. 2008. "The Trials of Winning at the WTO: What Lies Behind Brazil's Success." *Cornell International Law Journal* 41 (2): 383–404.

Shaffer, Gregory C., James J. Nedumpara, and Aseema Sinha. 2015. "Indian Trade Lawyers and the Building of State Trade-Related Legal Capacity." *Law and Society Review* 49 (3): 595–629.

Shalden, Kenneth C. 2009. "The Politics of Patents and Drugs in Brazil and Mexico: The Industrial Bases of Health Policies." *Comparative Politics* 42 (1): 41–58.

Sharan, Vyuptakesh, and Indra Nath Mukherji. 2001. *India's External Sector Reforms*. New Delhi: Oxford University Press.

Shastri, Vanita. 1997. "The Politics of Economic Liberalization in India." *Contemporary South Asia* 6 (1): 27–56.

Shourie, A. 2004. *Governance and the Sclerosis That Has Set In*. New Delhi: Rupa.

Simmons, Beth, Frank Dobbin, and Geoffrey Garrett. 2006. "Introduction: The International Diffusion of Liberalism." *International Organization* 60: 781–810.

Simmons, Beth, Frank Dobbin, and Geoffrey Garrett. 2008. "Introduction: The Diffusion of Liberalism." In *The Global Diffusion of Markets and Democracy*, edited by Beth Simmons, Frank Dobbin, and Geoffrey Garrett. New York: Cambridge University Press.

Simmons, B. A. 1998. "Compliance with International Agreements." *Annual Review of Political Science* I (1): 75–93.

Simmons, B. A. 2000. "International Law and State Behavior: Commitment and Compliance in International Monetary Affairs." *American Political Science Review* 94 (4): 819–835.

Singh, J.N. 2008. "Indian Textile and Clothing Sector: Poised for a Leap." In *Unveiling Protectionism: Regional Responses to Remaining Barriers in the Textiles and Clothing Trade*, edited by UN ESCAP. New York: US.

Singh, J.P. 2006. "The Evolution of National Interests: New Issues, and North-South Negotiations During the Uruguay Round." In *Negotiating Trade: Developing Countries in the WTO and NAFTA*, edited by John S. Odell, 41–84. New York: Cambridge University Press.

Singh, Karma Pal, and Surinder Kundu. 2004. "Indian Cotton Textile Industry: The Feat of Fairy Tale in WTO Regime." *Delhi Business Review* 5 (2): 93–109.

Singh, Manmohan. 1991. *Budget, 1991–1992, Speech of Shri Manmohan Singh, Minister of Finance*. Edited by Finance. New Delhi: Government of India.

Singh, Manmohan. 2005. "Open Democracy and Open Economy." *Indian Express* 6 (12): 8.

Singh, N.K. (PMO). 2002. *Office Memorandum: Constitution of the Steering Group on Investment and Growth in Textile Industry*. Edited by PMO. New Delhi: Government of India.

Singh, Pradeep K. 2001a. "Introduction to the Policies, Regulations and their Implications on the Industry." In *Indian Pharma Industry: Issues and Options*, edited by Saket, 87–101. Ahmedabad: Saket Projects, Ltd.

Singh, Pradeep K. 2001b. "Introduction to Research and Development in Pharmaceutical Industry." In *Indian Pharma Industry: Issues and Options*, edited by Saket, 135–157. Ahmedabad: Saket Publishing Ltd.

Singh, Y.P., and G.R. Phalgumani. 1995. "Meeting Eco-Requirements for Export: Examples of Indian Textiles." *International Trade Forum* 3: 12–15.

Sinha, Aseema. 2005a. *Regional Roots of Developmental Politics in India: A Divided Leviathan*. Indianapolis: Indiana University Press.

Sinha, Aseema. 2005b. "Understanding the Rise and Transformation of Business Collective Action in India." *Business and Politics* 7 (2): 1–35.

Sinha, Aseema. 2006. "Federalism and Global Governance: World Trade Organization and Decentralization In India." Annual Meeting of the American Political Science Association, Philadelphia, September 2006.

Sinha, Aseema. 2007. "Global Linkages and Domestic Politics: Trade Reform and Institutional Building in India in Comparative Perspective." *Comparative Political Studies* 40 (10): 1183–1201.

Sinha, Aseema. 2010. "Business and Politics." In *Oxford Companion to Politics in India*, edited by Niraja Gopal-Jayal and Pratap Bhanu Mehta, 459–476. New Delhi: Oxford University Press.

Sobel, Andrew C. 1999. *State Institutions, Private Incentives, Global Capital*. Ann Arbor: University of Michigan Press.

Solingen, Etel. 1998. *Regional Orders at Century's Dawn: Global and Domestic Influences on Grand Strategy*. Princeton, NJ: Princeton University Press.

Sprinz, Debra F., and Yael Wolinsky-Nahmias. 2004. *Models, Numbers and Cases: Methods for Studying International Relations*. Ann Arbor: University of Michigan Press.

Srinivas, Smita. 2012. *Market Menagerie: Health and Development in late Industrial States*. Stanford, CA: Stanford University Press.

Srinivasan, T.N. 2000. *Eight Lecturers on India's Economic Reforms.* New Delhi: Oxford University Press.

Srinivasan, T.N. 2002. "Developing Countries and the Multilateral Trading System After Doha", New Haven, CT: Economic Growth Center, Yale University, Working Paper Series, pp. 1–37.

Srinivasan, T.N., and Suresh Tendulkar. 2003. *Reintegrating India with the World Economy.* Washington DC: Peterson Institute of International Economics.

Srinivasan, T.N., and Rahul Bajaj. 2000. *Strategy for a Reconvened WTO Ministerial Meeting: Report and Recommendations.* New Delhi: Prime Minister's Council on Trade and Industry.

Steinberg, Richard H. 2002. "In the Shadow of Law or Power?: Consensus-based Bargaining and Outcomes in the GATT/WTO." *International Organization* 56 (2): 339–374.

Stubbs, Richard. 2011. "The East Asian Developmental State and the Great Recession." *Contemporary Politics* 17:151–66.

Subramanian, Arvind. 2008. *India's Turn: Understanding the Economic Transformation.* New Delhi: Oxford University Press.

Surie, Gita, and De Sud. 2008. *Knowledge, Organizational Evolution and Market Creation: The Globalization of Indian Firms from Steel to Software.* UK: Edward Elgar.

Swank, Duane. 2006. "Tax Policy in an Era of Internationalization: The Spread of Neoliberalism." *International Organization* 60 (4): 847–882.

Tarrow, Sidney. 2010. "The Strategy of Paired Comparison: Toward a Theory of Practice." *Comparative Political Studies* 43: 230–59.

Teli, M.D. 2008. "Textile Coloration Industry in India." *Coloration Technology* 124 (1): 1–13.

Tewari, Meenu. 2005. *Post-MFA Adjustments in India's Textile and Apparel Industry: Emerging Issues and Trends.* New Delhi: ICRIER.

Tewari, Meenu. 2006a. "Adjustment in India's Textile and Apparel Industry: Reworking Historical Legacies in the Post-MFA World." *Environment and Planning* 38 (12): 2325–2344.

Tewari, Meenu. 2006b. "Is Price Competitiveness Enough for Apparel Firms to Gain Market Share in the World After Quotas." *Global Economy Journal* 6 (4): 1–46.

Tewari, Meenu. 2008. "Varieties of Global Integration: Navigating Institutional Legacies and Global Networks in India's Garment Industry." *Competition and Change* 12 (1): 49–67.

Tewari, Meenu, and Poonam Pillai. 2005. "Global Standards and the Dynamics of Environmental Compliance in India's Leather Industry." *Oxford Development Studies* 33 (2): 245–267.

Textile Commissioner. 2005. *Technology Upgradation Fund Scheme for Textiles and Jute Industries.* Mumbai: Government of India.

Textile Commissioner. 1960–2013a. *Indian Textile Bulletin.* Bombay: Office of the Textiles Commissioner, Government of India.

Textile Commissioner. 1950–2013b. *Compendium of Textile Statistics.* Bombay: Office of the Textiles Commissioner, Government of India.

Textiles, Ministry of. 1985. *National Textile Policy.* Edited by Lok Sabha Secretariat. New Delhi: Lok Sabha Secretariat.

Textiles, Ministry of. 1988. *Annual Report, 1987–1988*. Edited by Textiles. New Delhi: Government of India.

Textiles, Ministry of. 1999. *Report of the Expert Committee on Textile Policy*. Edited by Textiles. New Delhi: Government of India.

Textiles, Ministry of. 2000. *New Textile Policy*. Edited by Textiles. New Delhi: Government of India.

Textiles, Ministry of. 2002. *Annual Report, 2001–2002*. Edited by Textiles. New Delhi: Government of India.

Textiles, Ministry of. 2004. *Report of the Expert Group on Technical Textiles*. New Delhi: Government of India.

Textiles, Ministry of. 2007. *Guidelines of the Scheme for Integrated Textile Parks During the 11th Five Year*. Edited by Textiles. New Delhi: Government of India.

Textiles, Ministry of. 2010. *Textiles Resurgence: Milestones*. Edited by Ministry of Textiles. New Delhi: Government of India.

Textiles, Ministry of. 2011. *Annual Report, 2010–2011*. Edited by Textiles. New Delhi: Government of India.

Textiles, Ministry of. 2013. *Annual Report, 2012–2013*. Edited by Textiles. New Delhi: Government of India.

Textiles, Ministry of. Various Years. Annual Report. Edited by Textiles. New Delhi: Government of India.

Thacker, Strom C. 2000. "Private Sector Trade Politics in Mexico." *Business and Politics* 2 (2): 161–187.

Thatcher, Mark 2007. *Internationalization and Economic Institutions: Comparing European Experiences*. Oxford: Oxford University Press.

Thelen, Kathleen. 2014. *Varieties of Liberalization and the New Politics of Social Solidarity*. Cambridge: Cambridge University Press.

Thompson, E.P. 1971. "The Moral Economy of the English Crowd in the Eighteenth Century." *Past and Present* 50 (1): 76–136.

Tilly, Charles. 1985. "War Making and State Making as Organized Crime." In *Bringing the State Back In*, edited by Peter Evans, Dietrich Rueschemeyer and Theda Skocpol, 169–186. Cambridge: Cambridge University Press.

Topalova, Petia. 2007. "Trade Liberalization, Poverty and Inequality: Evidence from Indian Districts." In *Globalization and Poverty*, edited by Ann Harrison, 291–335. Chicago: University of Chicago Press.

Topalova, Petia. 2013. *How are the Poor Affected by International Trade in India: An Empirical Approach*. New York: United Nations.

Trivedi, Lisa. 2007. *Clothing Gandhi's Nation: Homespun and Modern India*. Bloomington: Indiana University Press.

Trubek Dave, Helena Alviar Garcia, Diogo Coutinho and Alvaro Santos, eds. 2013. *Law and the New Developmental State: The Brazilian Experience in Latin American Context*. New York: Cambridge University Press.

Tsebelis, George. 1990. *Nested Games: Rational Choice in Comparative Politics*. Berkeley: University of California Press.

Uchikawa, Shuji. 1998. *Indian Textile Industry: State Policy, Liberalization and Growth*. New Delhi: Manohar.

USITC. 2001. *India's Textile and Apparel Industry: Growth Potential and Trade and Investment Opportunities*. Office of Industries, USITC.

Vanaik, Achin. 1990. *The Painful Transition: Bourgeois Democracy in India.* London: Verso.

Vanaik, Achin. 2011. "Indian Foreign Policy Since the Cold War: Domestic Determinants." In *Understanding India's New Political Economy: A Great Transformation?*, edited by Sanjay Reddy Sanjay Ruparelia, John Harriss, and Stuart Corbridge, 221–236. London: Routledge.

Varshney, Ashutosh. 1999. "Mass Politics or Elite Politics? India's Economic Reforms in Comparative Politics." In *India in the Era of Economic Reform*, edited by Jeffrey Sachs, Ashutosh Varshney, and Nirupam Bajpai, 222–260. New Delhi: Oxford University Press.

(VGP), Virtus Global Partners. 2008. *Investment Opportunities in the Indian Textile and Garments Industry.* New York: Virtus Global

Verdier, Daniel. 1994. *Democracy and International Trade: Britain, France, and the United States, 1860–1990.* Princeton, NJ: Princeton University Press.

Verma, Samar. 2002. "Export Competitiveness of the Indian Textile and Garment Industry." pp. 1–46. New Delhi: ICRIER.

Vijayanagar, R. L. N. 1975. "Landmarks". Edited by Bombay Millowner's Association, *Proceedings of the Centenary Celebrations of the Millowner's Association, Bombay.* Bombay: Millowners's Association.

Vogel, D. 1995. *Trading Up: Consumer and Environmental Regulation in a Global Economy.* Cambridge, MA: Harvard University Press.

Vogel, D., and R. A. Kagan. 2004. *Dynamics of Regulatory Change: How Globalization Affects National Regulatory Policies.* Berkeley: University of California Press.

Vreeland, James Raymond. 2003. *The IMF and Economic Development.* New York: Cambridge University Press.

Wade, Robert. 1985. "The Market for Public Office: Why the Indian State is Not Better at Development." *World Development* 13 (4): 467–497.

Wade, Robert. 2003. *Governing the Market: Economic Theory and the Role of Government in East Asian Industrilization.* Princeton, NJ: Princeton University Press.

Wadehra, B.L. 2005. *Patents, Trade Marks, Copyright, Designs, and Geographical Indications.* Delhi: Universal Law Publishing Co. Pvt. Ltd.

Watal, Jayashree. 2001. *Intellectual Property Rights in the WTO and Developing Countries.* New Delhi: Oxford University Press.

Weiss, Linda, ed. 2003. *States in the Global Economy: Bringing Domestic Institutions Back In.* Cambridge: Cambridge University Press.

Weiss, Linda. 2005. "The State-Augmenting Effects of Globalization." *New Political Economy* 10 (3): 345–353.

Wersch, H. Van. 1992. *The Bombay Textile Strike, 1982–1983.* Bombay: Oxford University Press.

WHO. 2012. *WHO List of Prequalified Medicinal Products.* Geneva: World Health Organization.

Wiemann, Jurgen. 1986. *India in Transition: Industrialization, Industrial Policy and Economic Cooperation.* Translated by Anjuli Gupta. New Delhi: Allied Publishers Private Limited.

Wiemann, Jurgen. 1996. "Exports of Environmental Standards Through International Trade: The Case of Indian Leather Exports Adjusting to German Eco-Standards." *Geograpische Zeitschrift* 84 (3/4): 179–186.

Williamson, John, ed. 1990. *Latin American Adjustment: How Much Has Happened?* Washington, DC: Institute for International Economics.

Williamson, John, and Roberto Zagha. 2002. *From the Hindu Rate of Growth to the Hindu Rate of Reform.* Stanford, CA: Center for Research on Economic Development and Policy Reform.

Williamson, Oliver E. 1975. *Markets and Hierarchies: Analysis and Antitrust Implications.* New York: Free Press.

Williamson, Oliver E. 1985. *The Economic Institutions of Capitalism: Firms, Markets, Relational Contracting.* New York: Free Press.

Williamson, Oliver E. 1996. *The Mechanisms of Governance.* New York: Oxford University Press.

Winters, L. Alan, and Shahid Yusuf, eds. 2007. *Dancing with Giants: China, India and the Global Economy.* Washington, DC: World Bank.

Wolf, Martin. 1982. *India's Exports.* New York: World Bank and Oxford University Press.

Woll, Cornelia. 2008. *Firm Interests: How Governments Shape Business Lobbying on Global Trade.* Ithaca, NY: Cornell University Press.

World Bank. 2013. *World Development Indicators.* Washington, DC: World Bank.

World Bank. 2015. *World Development Indicators.* Washington, DC: World Bank.

WTO. 2002. *The Legal Texts: The Results of the Uruguay Round of Multilateral Trade Negotiations.* World Trade Organization.

WTO. 2015. *International Trade Statistics.* Geneva: World Trade Organization.

Ye, Min. 2014. *Embedded States: India and China.* Cambridge: Cambridge University Press.

Young, A. R. 2003. "Political Transfer and "Trading Up?" Transatlantic Trade in Genetically Modified Food and US Politics." *World Politics* 55 (4): 457–484.

Young, Oran R., and Marc Levy. 1999. "The Effectiveness of International Environmental Regimes." In *The Effectiveness of International Environmental Regimes: Causal Connections MA and Behavioral Mechanisms,* edited by Oran R. Young, 1–32. Cambridge, Mass: MIT Press.

Zangl, Bernhard. 2008. "Judicialization Matters!: A Comparison of Dispute Settlement Under GATT and the WTO." *International Studies Quarterly* 52 (4): 825–854.

Index